East Asia and the Modern International Order

This crucial interdisciplinary work brings together historians and international relations specialists to reexamine fourteen events in twentieth-century East Asia that shaped world and regional politics. In a series of case studies framed by conceptual essays, the authors examine key moments and their wider significance, including the Chinese Exclusion Acts in the United States; the Japanese racial equality proposal at the Versailles conference of 1919; anticolonial movements in Southeast Asia before 1945; and the changing nature of sovereignty in the Pacific Islands. The authors decenter the Cold War in Asia away from American and European perspectives and examine how countries in the region positioned themselves given distinctive domestic coalitions. These historical examples demonstrate the unique East Asian experience of war, empire, and political independence, shedding valuable light on contemporary international relations and the challenges faced in Asia-Pacific today.

STEPHAN HAGGARD is Distinguished Research Professor at the School of Global Policy and Strategy, University of California San Diego and Research Director for Democracy and Global Governance at the Institute on Global Conflict and Cooperation. His recent work on East Asia includes *Developmental States* and (with Marcus Noland) *Hard Target: Sanctions, Inducements and the Case of North Korea*.

DAVID C. KANG is Maria Crutcher Professor of International Relations at the University of Southern California and director of the USC Korean Studies Institute. He is the author of *East Asia before the West* and coauthor, with Xinru Ma, of *Beyond Power Transitions*. He is the coeditor with Stephan Haggard of *East Asia in the World: Twelve Events that Shaped the Modern International Order*.

East Asia and the Modern International Order

From Imperialism to the Cold War

Edited by

Stephan Haggard
University of California San Diego

David C. Kang
University of Southern California

Shaftesbury Road, Cambridge CB2 8EA, United Kingdom

One Liberty Plaza, 20th Floor, New York, NY 10006, USA

477 Williamstown Road, Port Melbourne, VIC 3207, Australia

314–321, 3rd Floor, Plot 3, Splendor Forum, Jasola District Centre, New Delhi – 110025, India

103 Penang Road, #05–06/07, Visioncrest Commercial, Singapore 238467

Cambridge University Press is part of Cambridge University Press & Assessment, a department of the University of Cambridge.

We share the University's mission to contribute to society through the pursuit of education, learning and research at the highest international levels of excellence.

www.cambridge.org
Information on this title: www.cambridge.org/9781009545204

DOI: 10.1017/9781009545198

© Cambridge University Press & Assessment 2026

This publication is in copyright. Subject to statutory exception and to the provisions of relevant collective licensing agreements, no reproduction of any part may take place without the written permission of Cambridge University Press & Assessment.

When citing this work, please include a reference to the DOI 10.1017/9781009545198

First published 2026

Cover image: Fireshot / Universal Images Group / Getty Images

A catalogue record for this publication is available from the British Library

A Cataloging-in-Publication data record for this book is available from the Library of Congress

ISBN 978-1-009-54520-4 Hardback
ISBN 978-1-009-54517-4 Paperback

Cambridge University Press & Assessment has no responsibility for the persistence or accuracy of URLs for external or third-party internet websites referred to in this publication and does not guarantee that any content on such websites is, or will remain, accurate or appropriate.

For EU product safety concerns, contact us at Calle de José Abascal, 56, 1°, 28003 Madrid, Spain, or email eugpsr@cambridge.org

Contents

List of Figures and Tables	*page* vii
List of Contributors	viii
Acknowledgments	xi

Part I Introduction

1 East Asia in the World: From Imperialism to the Cold War   3
   STEPHAN HAGGARD AND DAVID C. KANG

2 The Myth of the San Francisco Settlement: Understanding Post-World War II East Asian Order   29
   EVELYN GOH

Part II The Imperial Era

3 Survival through Reforms: Siam and Its Escape from Colonialism   55
   PONGKWAN SAWASDIPAKDI

4 The Russo-Japanese War, 1904–1905   76
   SCOTT WOLFORD

5 The Chinese Exclusion Act   90
   ENZE HAN AND D. G. KIM

6 Race and Great Power Politics: The Japanese Racial Equality Proposal of 1919   109
   EREZ MANELA

Part III To the Pacific War

7 Reform, Revolution, and State Failure in Early Twentieth-Century China   133
   RICHARD S. HOROWITZ

8   The Second Sino-Japanese War and Its Aftermath, 1931–1965   148
    AMY KING

9   Japan and New Orders in East Asia, 1914–1945   166
    JEREMY A. YELLEN

Part IV   The High Cold War in Asia

10 The Division of Korea   187
    DAVID FIELDS

11 The Taiwan Straits Crises Revisited   207
    HSIAO-TING LIN

12 Alliances, State-Building, and Development in Asia   225
    JAMES LEE

13 Credibility and the US Intervention in Vietnam in the Era
    of Incomplete US Hegemony   242
    YUEN FOONG KHONG

14 Nationalism and Anglo-American Neo-colonialism in Southeast
    Asia, 1945–1965   260
    WEN-QING NGOEI

15 Mandates, Trusteeship, and Decolonization in the North Pacific:
    Balancing Self-Determination, Development, and Security   278
    JOANNE WALLIS AND JACK CORBETT

Part V   Conclusion

16 Conclusion: A Newly Dynamic East Asian International Order   299
    ANDREW J. COE AND SCOTT WOLFORD

Bibliography   321
Index   360

Figures and Tables

Figures

5.1	US immigration flows from China and Japan by timeline	*page* 93
6.1	The seating chart for the plenary session of the Paris Peace Conference in 1919	113
6.2	The Japanese delegates to the Paris Peace Conference	114
8.1	Japanese trade with mainland China, Manchuria, and the Guandong leased territory, 1934–1944	157
8.2	Japanese trade with free and occupied China, 1931–1945	159

Tables

8.1	China–Japan trade, 1880–1980	149
14.1	Southeast Asia decolonization timeline, 1946–1965	261
14.2	Selected left-wing movements of Southeast Asia, 1945–1965	262
14.3	Cold War alignments of Southeast Asian states, 1940s–1960s (selected)	263
15.1	Transitions between colonization and sovereignty in the North Pacific	284

Contributors

ANDREW J. COE is Associate Professor of Political Science at Vanderbilt University. His work is devoted to understanding the causes and consequences of violent conflict in human civilization.

JACK CORBETT is Professor and Head of the School of Social Sciences at Monash University, Australia. His latest book is *Statehood à la Carte in the Caribbean and the Pacific: Secession, Regionalism, and Postcolonial Politics* (2023).

DAVID P. FIELDS is Associate Director of the Center for East Asian Studies at the University of Wisconsin–Madison. He is the author/editor of *Foreign Friends: Syngman Rhee, American Exceptionalism, and the Division of Korea* (2019), *The Diary of Syngman Rhee* (2015), and *Divided America, Divided Korea* (2024 with Mitchell B. Lerner).

EVELYN GOH FBA, FASSA is the Shedden Professor of Strategic Policy Studies and the Director of the Southeast Asia Institute at the Australian National University. She specializes in the international relations, security, and history of East Asia and the Asia-Pacific, and her latest book is *Rethinking Sino-Japanese Alienation* (2020 with Barry Buzan).

STEPHAN HAGGARD is Distinguished Research Professor, School of Global Policy and Strategy and Research Director for Democracy and Global Governance at the Institute on Global Conflict and Cooperation. He is the editor, with David Kang, of *East Asia in the World: Twelve Events that Shaped the Modern International Order* (2020).

ENZE HAN is Associate Professor at the Department of Politics and Public Administration, the University of Hong Kong. His latest book is *The Ripple Effect: China's Complex Presence in Southeast Asia* (2024).

RICHARD HOROWITZ is Professor of History at CSU Northridge. His scholarship explores China's foreign relations, and foreign involvements in China during the nineteenth and early twentieth centuries.

List of Contributors ix

DAVID KANG is Maria Crutcher Professor of International Relations at the University of Southern California, where he also directs the USC Korean Studies Institute. His latest book is *Beyond Power Transitions: The Lessons of East Asian History and the Future of US-China Relations* (2024 with Xinru Ma).

AMY KING is Associate Professor in the Strategic and Defence Studies Centre at the Australian National University, where she is also Deputy Director (Research) of the Coral Bell School of Asia Pacific Affairs. She is the author of *China–Japan Relations After World War II: Empire, Industry and War, 1949–1971* (2016).

YUEN FOONG KHONG is Li Ka Shing Professor of Political Science and Co-director of the Center for Asia and Globalization at the Lee Kuan Yew School of Public Policy, National University of Singapore. He is the Principal Investigator of *The Anatomy of Choice: Southeast Asia between the Superpowers*, a multiyear project supported by a Singapore Social Science Research Thematic Grant.

D. G. KIM received his PhD in Political Science at the University of California San Diego in 2022 and was most recently an Inequality in America Postdoctoral Fellow at Harvard University.

JAMES LEE is Assistant Research Fellow/Professor at the Institute of European and American Studies at Academia Sinica, and an affiliated researcher of the University of California's Institute on Global Conflict and Cooperation. His research in strategic studies is at the intersection of political science and diplomatic history, with a focus on US foreign policy and the security of Taiwan.

HSIAO-TING LIN is a research fellow and curator of modern China and Taiwan collection at the Hoover Institution, Stanford University. His research interests include US-Taiwan relations during the Cold War and political history of Taiwan from authoritarian period to democratization.

WEN-QING NGOEI is Associate Professor of History at the Singapore Management University and studies US foreign relations with Southeast Asia. His book *Arc of Containment: Britain, the United States, and Anticommunism in Southeast Asia* (2019).

EREZ MANELA is the Francis Lee Higginson Professor of History at Harvard University. His latest book (coedited with Heather Streets-Salter) is *The Anticolonial Transnational: Imaginaries, Mobilities, and Networks in the Struggle against Empire*.

PONGKWAN SAWASDIPAKDI is Lecturer in International Relations at the Faculty of Political Science, Thammasat University in Bangkok, Thailand. Her research focuses on political psychology and emotions in international relations and Southeast Asia's interactions with major powers. She earned her PhD from the University of Southern California.

JOANNE WALLIS is Professor of International Security in the Department of Politics and International Relations at the University of Adelaide. Her latest book is *Girt by Sea: Re-imagining Australia's Security* (2024 with Rebecca Strating).

SCOTT WOLFORD is Professor of Government at the University of Texas at Austin and Co-director of the Correlates of War Project. His latest book is *The Politics of the First World War: A Course in Game Theory and International Security* (2019).

JEREMY A. YELLEN is a historian of modern Japan and Associate Professor at the Chinese University of Hong Kong. His latest book is *The Greater East Asia Co-Prosperity Sphere: When Total Empire Met Total War* (2023).

Acknowledgments

In *East Asia and the World: Twelve Events that Shaped the Modern International Order* (Cambridge University Press, 2020), we assembled a group of prominent historians and political scientists to consider some classic episodes in the international relations of Asia viewed over the *longue durée* (c. 643–1900). The purpose was threefold: to decenter the history of IR from the dominant Westphalian narrative; to consider a set of historical experiences that comported only partially with those centered on Europe; and to reflect on how those experiences might enrich IR scholarship. Following two introductory chapters on the long cycles of more- and less-concentrated Chinese leadership and the early political economy of the region, the book divided roughly in half. One revisited a number of debates about the nature of the hierarchical China-centered tribute system; the second discussed the politics of contact with the West, from the fall of Dutch Formosa to the rise of the Philippine nationalist movement. These two sections, in turn, addressed core theoretical issues in contemporary IR, including the logic and empirical consequences of hierarchical regional systems; and the complicated normative and ideational as well as material effects of Western imperialism. The book concluded with a theoretical overview by two IR theorists: Andrew Coe and Scott Wolford.

This second volume picks up the story roughly where the first volume left off. Beginning with the end of the nineteenth century, we explore key events in East Asian international relations up to the early Cold War. This makes a natural stopping point, and keeps us from attempting too much current history. Similarly to the first volume, this volume reconsiders and critically appraises some of the conventional viewpoints in the English-language literature on this important time and place. We rethink questions of periodization and detail why conventional markers, such as the American perception of 1941–45 as constituting World War II, are not entirely accurate. The traditional Sinitic order was not instantly replaced by a Westphalian one, in part because of the extended life of imperialism and colonialism. The Pacific War began at least as far back as 1931 if not earlier; and postwar US hegemony was not nearly as complete as is often thought. These new perspectives promise to deepen and enrich our understanding of the region, and also speak directly to key theoretical and conceptual issues in the study of international relations.

The generous support of the Korea Foundation was central to publishing this second volume, and we are deeply grateful for their support. Kang also received funding from the USC Center for International Studies and the USC Korean Studies Institute. The Korea–Pacific Program at the School of Global Policy and Strategy at the University of California San Diego contributed to the effort, if more modestly. Stephan Haggard appreciates the support of the Lawrence and Sallye Krause Chair and the Pacific Century Institute and the advice of Jesse Driscoll on the organization of the lead chapter. We thank all of our funders effusively for their support of this type of scholarship, which is unusually interdisciplinary and cross-national.

In addition to the authors and attendants at two workshops, we want to extend a particular thanks to Alexis Dudden. She was involved from the very beginning and brought her usual warmth, insights, and scholarship to the two meetings we held. Lucy Rhymer at Cambridge University Press was a dedicated and supportive editor, always enthusiastic about moving the project to conclusion. We are grateful to two referees for their careful comments and for helping to make the overall arc and substance of the book much sharper. Zoe Wallace provided wonderful RA support in putting all the files together.

Part I

Introduction

1 East Asia in the World: From Imperialism to the Cold War

Stephan Haggard and David C. Kang

The first volume of the *East Asia in the World* project (Haggard and Kang 2020) sought to bring Asia more squarely into the canon of international relations, and that remains our purpose in this second volume. We did not attempt a history of the region, which would have been impossible given our consideration of the *longue durée* running from the foundations of the Sinitic order to its gradual unwinding over the course of the nineteenth century (Kang and Swope 2020). Rather, we solicited contributions from historians of Asia influenced by a dynamic new international history movement that situated national developments in their larger global context (Manela 2020). We brought them together with political scientists pursuing a complementary project: to decenter the history of international relations from a dominant, and often triumphalist, European narrative (see, for example, Hobson 2004, 2012; Acharya and Buzan 2007; Kang 2010, 2013; Goh 2013a, 2013b; Kang and Ma 2018; Kang and Lin 2019; Buzan and Goh 2020). The objective was to stimulate a fresh look at how international relations theory fared in the face of new historical material on – and from – the region.

The project was also motivated by disagreements we had with structural or systemic international relations theories. These largely grew out of Western experience, initially multipolar during the nineteenth and early twentieth centuries and bipolar during the Cold War. We considered the Sinitic order and its imperialist aftermath as alternative international systems that could be used for broader comparative effect.

The first volume devoted roughly half of its contributions to the Sino-centered political order. We advanced a number of descriptive as well as causal propositions, particularly in the conclusion by Andrew Coe and Scott Wolford (2020). First, the hierarchical structure of what Coe and Wolford called "historical East Asia" was quite different than the European one of competing great powers of roughly equal military and economic heft. Second, the normative foundations of the tribute system were quite different than the European state

3

system as well, later characterized – controversially as we will see – as the Westphalian model of equal sovereign states. These differences could be traced back to processes of state formation. Early East Asian states were formed less by war than by emulation of the Chinese model (Huang and Kang 2022). Partly as a result, international relations were explicitly hierarchical and embedded in complex normative and even performative structures that sustained legitimacy (see Ji-Young Lee's 2020 contribution on the Chosun dynasty in particular).

The final difference was the existence of long periods of relative peace, at least among a cluster of the system's constitutive states (Kang 2010; Rosenthal and Wong 2011; Zhang 2015; Lee 2016; Kang, Shaw and Fu 2016; Park 2017; Dincecco and Wang 2018). We drew attention to several important – even systemic – wars, looking at both their causes and consequences (Kanagawa 2020; Swope 2020). But the finding with respect to the incidence of war in a hierarchical system was of theoretical significance. Until recently, little empirical attention has been given to the distinctive properties of hierarchies (Lake 2009, 2024; Zarakol 2017). This lacuna arose in part because balance of power theory would suggest that hierarchies were unlikely to arise in the first place, in part because of the failure to exploit examples outside of Europe, such as historical East Asia.

The treatment of the Sinitic order was by no means limited to the logic of the state system and conflict; contributions also reflected a new revisionism with respect to the political economy of the region prior to the nineteenth century (von Glahn 2020). It is often assumed that the tributary system subjected commercial relations to the rigidities of ritualized diplomatic process, and that early commercial relations with Europe played an important role in dissolving these ties and "opening" the region. Yet despite some periods of commercial closure, a dense network of trading ties extended from the Indian Ocean through Southeast Asia to the Chinese coast and Japan well before the arrival of European powers on the scene. Moreover, it rested on a quite distinctive "port polity" political model that has echoes to this day in small trading states. Yet another important network extending to China centered on Manila and the Spanish galleon trade in silver with the new world.

Europe's role in Asian trade was not dominant, however. In an essay on early Dutch contact, Tonio Andrade (2020) showed how the Dutch East India Company operated as only one among many players in the regional political economy, which included prominent Chinese and Japanese groups. The broader lesson – developed by J. P. Sharman (2019) in particular – is that early European imperialism reflected the strategies of states and trading companies that were much weaker than the standard imperial narrative suggests. That changed dramatically over the course of the nineteenth century when force was increasingly deployed by the imperial powers to advance their commercial interests; this theme returns with a vengeance in the current volume.

Our interest in the Sino-centered order was not only theoretical. The idea of such an order has proven an enduring trope in China's self-conception (Allan et al. 2018). It constitutes a crucial backdrop to the relative decline associated with imperialism and the "one hundred years of humiliation" that typically dates to the Opium Wars (1839–42 and 1856–60) and ends with the founding of the People's Republic in 1949. It is highly unlikely that China could reconstruct such an order today given the ongoing role of the United States in the region, the stakes of other extra-regional actors and the preferences of the countries on China's extensive periphery. Yet China's "neighborhood diplomacy" and projects such as the Belt and Road Initiative have made the idea of a China-centered regional order an issue of serious debate. Realists as well as analysts of Chinese foreign policy without their theoretical priors have pondered what a hierarchical regional order centered on Beijing might look like (Allan et al. 2018; Yan 2020).

The second half of the first volume of the project took up the gradual unwinding of the Sino-centered order over the course of the nineteenth century, the legacies of which persist to this day (Buzan and Goh 2020; Chapter 2, this volume). The root causes of this systemic transition included both external and internal factors. On the one hand was imperialism: the willingness and capacity of the European powers to seize colonies directly, use coercive diplomacy for achieving strategic and commercial objectives, and to impose various forms of indirect rule. With important exceptions such as the Spanish assertion of control over the Philippines and the Portuguese concession on Macao, the majority of direct and indirect imperial claims in East and Southeast Asia occurred in the nineteenth century.

On the other hand, the shifting balance of power reflected the complex of domestic weaknesses – political and institutional as well as economic – that prevented countries in the region from countering external pressures by mounting an effective defense of traditional forms of rule. Despite the persistent focus of the PRC leadership on the role of external actors, revisionist Chinese scholarship has plumbed these institutional factors in great depth (e.g., Mao Haijian 2016 on the collapse of the Qing dynasty) and they figure in discussions of the vulnerability of Korea and the pre-European Southeast Asian political systems as well. Of all the many states and other political formations in the region, only Japan and Thailand managed to evade these external pressures, in Japan's case only gradually and in Thailand's case by bringing domestic policy in line with British and French preferences.

We dealt with a number of important episodes in this new imperial phase of the region's history in the first volume of the project. We started with the political economy of the Opium Wars (1839–60; Horowitz 2020), which set in train the system of treaty ports and extraterritoriality which were at the heart of China's "one hundred years of humiliation." In addition to the European scramble, we placed particular emphasis on the entry of new imperial powers onto the scene. America's presence was considered via Matthew Perry's foray into Japan (1852–54; Dudden 2020) and the brutal American response to the Philippine nationalist movement and insurgency (Yeo 2020). Two essays detailed Japan's increasingly imperial interactions with China and Korea from the 1870s (Saeyoung Park 2020) to the Sino-Japanese War 1894–95 (S.-H. Park 2020) and the important role Russian expansionism played in those episodes. We conceived the decline of the Sinitic order and nineteenth-century imperialism as two sides of the same coin. As Saeyoung Park (2020) showed in her fine-grained dissection of Japanese–Korean diplomatic relations, the new imperialism marked "the death of Eastphalia."

The focus on imperialism also raised issues about how to theorize the most fundamental characteristics of international relations, and we return to those themes in this volume as well. Over the long run, it was certainly true that the idea of nominally equal sovereign states was a European export to the world, and got seized by nationalist movements and newly independent governments in subversive ways. Yet the emergence of this long-run political equilibrium worked through a very long period of imperial domination that extended well into the postwar world. Nor can it be considered Westphalian, at least as that term has come to be used. No less than the Sinitic order, the new imperialism was a hierarchical system, albeit generated in part by pressures stemming from intra-imperialist rivalry. The imperial "system," such as it was, rested on constant threats of the use of force, indirect as well as direct rule, and the complex use of law and diplomacy to advance commercial interests, including in the system of extraterritoriality imposed on both Japan and China.

1.1 An Outline

This second volume of the project builds on the first, and we invite readers to consider them in tandem. With no self-evident historical cut points, we concluded *East Asia in the World I* around 1900. We pick up from that point here and extend our analysis into the first fifteen years or so of the Cold War era.

Following two introductory chapters, Part II extends the discussion of imperialism, the breakdown of the Sinitic order, and the roles that two new-comers – Japan and the United States – played in the emerging regional order. We start with the case of Thailand, which proves an instructive introduction to the fundamental issues. Even though it managed to avoid formal colonial rule, it did so only by adjusting its domestic political economy in ways that conformed with British and French interests (Chapter 3). We then extend the consideration of Japanese imperialism in the nineteenth century into the twentieth, looking at the causes and consequences of the Russo-Japanese war (Chapter 4). We close Part II by considering the complicated role of race in the imperial order, with essays on America's Chinese Exclusion Acts (Chapter 5) and the politics of Japan's racial equality proposal at the Versailles conference (Chapter 6).

Part III takes up the interwar period. It may seem strange in a book of this sort to sidestep the proximate causes of World War II or the Pacific War in Asia. But we think it is appropriate. The events leading up to Pearl Harbor, the conduct of the war itself and its endgame in the entry of the Soviets, and the bombing of Hiroshima and Nagasaki have been treated in extraordinary detail elsewhere. Rather, we focus primary attention on Japan–China relations over a somewhat longer time frame. The liberal project outlined by Wilson held out the promise of a new order "after imperialism" to draw on the title of Akira Iriye's (1965) influential overview of the 1920s. Components of this initiative – although pursued inconsistently – included resistance to the continued carve-up of China, commitment to principles of nondiscrimination and the effort to manage changes in the balance of power through multilateral agreements such as the Washington Naval Treaty of 1922 and its ill-fated successors. Yet this liberal project proved unable to forestall Soviet intervention in Chinese politics and the more fateful imperial ambitions of Japan (Iriye 1965; Beasley 1987; Paine 2017 for useful overviews of Japanese imperialism), to which the League had no answers.

We draw particular attention, however, to the perverse effects of imperialism on Chinese politics, manifest in its fateful descent into warlordism and the implications of these domestic political developments for regional order (Horowitz, Chapter 7). In Chapter 8, Jeremy Yellen underlines the irony of Japanese grand strategy: that the new type of thinking about empire – what he calls "total war thought" – emerged in the Japanese army through observation of the demands placed on the great power combatants in World War I. In Chapter 8, Amy King takes up the political economy of the empire in more detail and considers how – contrary to liberal theories – war did not necessarily derail the growing economic integration between the two countries, in part precisely because of the growth of imperial ties.

In Part IV, we contribute to the literature – now vast – on the emergence of the Cold War order in Asia. We know from that literature, syllabi, and personal experience that contemporary research and teaching on the international relations of East Asia typically starts with the relations among the great powers, victorious and defeated. In this telling, the foundational events leading to the Cold War order in Asia include the strategic bargains implicit in the fateful disposition of military forces in the region and the trifecta of shocks in 1949–50: the first Soviet nuclear test, the Chinese revolution, and particularly the Korean War. As in Europe, if following a somewhat different timeline, great power rivalry was interpreted through the lens of a new red scare and

McCarthyism in the United States, with distinct Asian components centered on the question of who "lost" China and the shock of the Korean War.

The postwar settlement in Asia has been dubbed "the San Francisco system," with its origin story in the conference that produced both the peace agreement and security treaty with Japan in 1951. The wider system of which those agreements were a part included the hub-and-spokes alliances, naval dominance, and the gradual integration of allies into the US market and with one another (Schaller 1985).

A second introductory chapter by Evelyn Goh, Chapter 2 challenges this orthodoxy. For starters, several important players did not even attend the San Francisco conference – most notably China and Korea – and the Soviet Union did not ultimately sign the peace treaty. Far from resolving key issues – including territorial ones – Goh and others argue that the postwar settlement locked them in place (Hara 2001, 2006, 2007; Lee 2002; Lee and Van Dyke 2010; Dower 2015). The issues that went unresolved in San Francisco constitute a proverbial laundry list of every outstanding territorial dispute that the region is grappling with this to this day: the Dokdo/Takeshima and Senkakus/Diaoyus disputes between Japan and Korea and China, respectively; the disposition of the Kuriles and the ongoing failure of Japan and Russia to reach a legal conclusion to the war; the contested legal and political status of Taiwan; and the competing claims that continue to roil the South China Sea.

Part IV takes up the early Cold War period. There can be little doubt that the Cold War in Asia was driven by the strategic interactions among the United States, the Soviet Union, and China. Again, we do not have comparative advantage in addressing the missed opportunities in US-China relations and their consequences, a topic that has received extensive treatment not only from historians but from prominent political scientists as well (e.g., Foot 1995; Christensen 1996).

Rather, the contributions in Part IV all refocus on how American ambitions in the region were shaped by political coalitions in both allies and adversaries. Whether the American presence is conceived in terms of a new hegemony or as a defensive balancing coalition, its foundations ultimately rested on choices made not only in Washington, Beijing, and Moscow but in other Asian capitals as well. David Fields in Chapter 10 shows how the division of Korea, often attributed to Soviet and American designs, had much more to do with political pressures from South Korean actors and the personal political ambitions of Syngman Rhee in particular. Hsiao-ting Lin's reinterpretation in Chapter 11 of the Taiwan Strait crises of the 1950s shows, drawing on newly retrieved documents, how the moderation of conflict hinged on negotiations between the PRC and the KMT as much as Washington's role. In Chapter 12, James Lee's political economy of the alliance system in Asia emphasizes how states in the region exploited US strategic interests to pursue quite independent economic policies, including those associated with the so-called developmental state (Haggard 2018).

Perhaps no other event in postwar Asia has received as much thoughtful treatment from American historians and political scientists as Vietnam, and even research on the origins of American involvement in the 1940s – the relevant literature for our purposes – would constitute a small library (starting with Schaller 1985 and Rotter 1987). Two contributions take up the fateful question of American commitments in Southeast Asia. Yueng Foong Khong in Chapter 13 develops the argument that reputational concerns played a crucial role in American engagement, but precisely because the United States was fearful about its capacity to effectively project force. Ngoei Wen-Qing in Chapter 14 by contrast believes that while this dynamic might have operated with respect to Vietnam, that case was the anomaly rather than the rule in the region. He shows that domestic political coalitions favorable to a continuing American and European presence – for example, in Malaysia and the Philippines – had already formed prior to independence, providing the domestic political foundations not only for the alliance system but also for American hegemony more broadly conceived. These domestic political configurations also help explain later developments in the region such as the formation of the Association of Southeast Asian Nations in 1967.

The empirical chapters conclude with a fascinating chapter on the Pacific Islands by Joanne Wallis and Jack Corbett (Chapter 15) that returns to the exact same questions raised by the Thai case with which we begin. From World War I to the present, the islands cycled through a variety of different institutional arrangements: as mandates, under trusteeship and through hybrid sovereignties such as "free association" and formal independence. Yet, precisely because of their extreme dependency, these cases raise deep theoretical issues about empire, hegemony and hierarchy, and the real significance of Westphalian norms where asymmetries in power are large.

1.2   Using This Book: Some Themes

This second volume in the project covers a more limited time span, less than a hundred years. As a result, it is more amenable to being read as an historical introduction of the period. How did we get from a post-Sinitic imperial order to the Cold War? Yet we do not pretend to cover every development of significance and as noted have purposefully omitted crucial events – Pearl Harbor and the onset and termination of the Pacific War; the causes of the Korean War – which have been addressed extensively elsewhere. Rather, in choosing cases we thought in terms of recurrent questions in international politics. In the remainder of this Introduction, we briefly prime several of these overarching themes. We close with a preview of the conclusion to the book by Coe and

Wolford, which as in the first volume returns to some central theoretical debates in the study of both comparative politics and international relations.

We start in the remainder of the Introduction by revisiting the concept of imperialism, which until recently has gone fallow in international relations. We touch on the relative weight of economic as opposed to strategic causes, the central role of war, coercion and violence in colonial rule, and the variety of institutional forms the empire took. We do this not solely out of historical interest but to engage an important strand of work on hierarchies as a distinctive type of international or regional system and how political orders structured by the European imperial powers – Japan, the United States, and ultimately China – might vary.

We then turn to competing views of how historical time is broken up and the narratives behind apparently innocuous efforts at periodization. These choices are not neutral analytic ones; they often reflect national mythologies and in turn affect the construction of collective memories. Third, we bring out the role that domestic factors played in structuring the Cold War order in the region. We close with our enduring interest in ideational factors in international politics by revisiting the role of race in Asia's relationship with the advanced industrial states, another topic that is sadly enduring. Across all these issues, we reference new scholarship on the region that is chipping away at similar problems, whether from the new international history or from political science.

Coe and Wolford add to this list of themes by drawing out a number of broader implications of the project for debates in political science. As the project seeks to trace a long arc from the Sinitic order, through the European colonial presence to the rise of Japan and the United States, it is not surprising that power transition approaches get attention. However, Coe and Wolford seek to ground such theories in a political economy of growth: why some countries were able to modernize while others – particularly China – were not. We close this Introduction with a summary of several themes they introduce that are relevant for the current conjuncture, including shifting economic strategies and the nature of ideological competition.

1.3 Theme I: Imperialism Revisited

Our focus on imperialism is not simply the result of the period covered by the two volumes of this project nor the weight that historical issues play in the international relations of the region. We also want to revive a theoretical conversation that has – with a limited number of recent exceptions (Blanken 2012; Sharman 2019; Kohli 2019; McNamee 2023; Lake 2024) – gone nearly dead in academic political science and international relations. In the 1970s and 1980s, classic theories of imperialism would appear regularly on graduate international relations syllabi, including not only the classics such as Hobson,

Lenin, and Schumpeter but also Marxist, dependency, and world-systems approaches that emerged in the postwar period. Yet the last attempts to provide broad theoretical treatment of imperialism for mainstream IR audiences date to the 1980s, for example, in Tony Smith's *The Pattern of Imperialism* (1981) and Michael Doyle's *Empires* (1986). Ironically, this silence descended just as the imperial, colonial, and postcolonial turns were completely transforming the humanities (inter alia, Said 1979; Spivak 1988; Chakrabarty 2000; Bhabha 2012) and reviving – and reinventing – a hidebound study of colonial history (for reviews, see, for example, Kennedy 2013 and Manela 2020; on the link to IR theory and postcolonialism, see Seth 2012; on Asia see Farrell 2018). While much of this work centered on the European colonial powers, revisionist historians had long offered economic interpretations of American foreign policy over the long run and the Japanese empire now has a dense literature (see Beasley 1987 and Paine 2017 for overviews from different periods).

This turn away from imperialism may have to do with concerns about the term's normative baggage, although this is hardly unique to that concept; most important concepts in political science – including war, peace, and democracy – are also normatively laden and contested. Moreover, conceptual alternatives to the imperial lens have consequences too, such as subsuming the study of empire and colonialism under more generic covering concepts such as "hierarchy." Particularly in its social-contractarian form, the concept of hierarchy can elide important components of imperialism, from its complex political economy to the central role of power and violence to the international legal agreements reflected in the exercise of a kind of ideational power: rule by – rather than of – law. At worst, the concept of hierarchy can drift into a kind of academic euphemism, a problem some of its proponents have recognized and sought to remedy (compare, for example, Lake 2009 and Lake 2024).

In short, the study of imperialism is relevant because it is not clear that it completely went away (see, for example, Chapter 14, this volume). Imperialism was never coterminous with outright colonial rule, but encompassed a variety of informal as well as formal arrangements that students of hierarchy are continuing to mine.

We adopt a relatively expansive approach to the concept of imperialism, but with an important disciplinary caveat. We see it not simply as a set of economic processes – as some structural Marxist approaches do – but requiring *political* control over another state or people. As Gallagher and Robinson (1953) outlined in their famous essay on the imperialism of free trade, however, such control may be formal (involving the creation of colonies or other truncated state forms such as protectorates and mandates) or informal. In the latter, the metropole exercises veto power over policies that infringe on the metropole's interests, often through client political forces, but always under the threat of outright coercion. This last component of the definition would fit with some conceptions of American hegemony, particularly those emphasizing the long history of American interventions in the developing world. But in our view, the shadow of violence is important in differentiating imperialism from more routine efforts at influence (Kohli 2019, 7).

It is far beyond the scope of this Introduction to review the vast historical literature on imperialism in Asia. But we can touch on three issues around which the history and political science literatures join forces in this volume: the question of the causes of empire, including strategic ones; a reminder of the role of force and coercion in initiating and sustaining imperial rule; and the variety of institutional forms imperialism took in Asia. Over these more discrete questions hangs the much larger one of whether the American postwar order in the region should be seen as a kind of neo-imperial project, as Ngoei does most explicitly in this volume.

1.3.1 Causes: Economic and Strategic Factors

Any discussion of imperialism must take up the question of the causal factors at work, with economic interests clearly playing an enduring role; Kohli's (2019) recent account is an important exemplar. However, we are skeptical of macroeconomic explanations of empire, such as Marxist and neo-Marxist ones that emphasize how secular or cyclical trends – overproduction or underconsumption – map neatly onto imperial moves. Rather, it makes more sense to see economic interests as one component of imperial coalitions that include entrepreneurial politicians and other political forces in addition to economic ones. These other allies of imperial projects can range from the atavistic militaries emphasized by theorists such as Schumpeter – and clearly in play with respect to Japan's empire (Chapter 9, this volume) – to those grounded in religion and missionary ambitions, which played a well-researched role in American expansion in Asia (see, for example, Green's 2017 synthetic account, which weaves together a variety of social forces that played a role in the expanding US presence in the region).

This conception of imperialism and colonialism fits with typologies of the way that different economic endowments might generate different forms of imperial control (Frieden 1994), with Asia providing examples of each type:

- There is nothing quite like the large-scale mining and plantation extractive social orders of the new world, even under the Spanish in the Philippines. Nonetheless, Southeast Asia provides examples that also involved resource extraction and associated issues of labor supply and control: oil in Indonesia; rubber and tin in Malaysia; sugar in Taiwan; rice in Korea; and plantation agriculture in the Pacific islands.

- Asia is not typically considered a region of the world in which settler colonialism played a significant role, as it did both in the Anglophone "lands of recent settlement" and a number of African cases such as Kenya and Rhodesia. But that view is clearly being revised as we learn more about the role played by Japanese settlers in Korea, Manchuria, and Taiwan (Young 1998, Chapter 8 on Manchuria; Uchida 2011 on Korea; Shirane 2022 on Taiwan).
- One of the most distinctive features of imperialism in Asia was the focus on ports, with their corresponding role as hubs or nodes for trading companies. These companies were initially granted state monopolies but gradually came to encompass a wider array of private interests, including financial ones. Nor should we see such a focus on core trading centers as a relic of the era of extraterritoriality; consider the pervasive role that export-processing zones played in the take-off both of the newly industrializing countries and of China during the reform era.

Clearly, each of these transnational factors – extractive investments, diasporas, and trade centers – continue to play causal roles in the international relations of the region well after the end of formal and informal colonial rule.

In addition to actual economic pressures to expand – whether structural or instrumental – there is interesting historical work on how prevalent economic *theories* played a role in imperial expansionism. Thomas McCormick's *China Market* (1967) is a classic work in the early revisionist mold that made this case with respect to American interests in Asia. He showed how even the private sector became preoccupied with overproductionist analysis of the economic headwinds the country faced in the decades of economic crisis between 1873 and the Spanish American War. In somewhat different ways, the contributions by both Yellen and King on the interwar period focus on how theories of the relationship between economics and security were animating factors in the empire Japan sought to construct on the Asian mainland.

Closer to the hearts of political scientists is a second important theoretical thread about empire that has also run cold: how strategic considerations and inter-imperial rivalry can generate pressures to expand even if economic interests are indirect. This hypothesis was also advanced in Gallagher and Robinson's famous article (1953) on the imperialism of free trade and in their *Africa and the Victorians* (1978). They hypothesized that the annexation of East Africa was undertaken to control the sources of the Nile and its hold over Egypt, which in turn was little more than a "giant footnote" to defending the route to the jewel in the imperial crown, India. These themes come up in the chapters in this volume dealing with both Thailand and the Russo-Japanese war and are revisited in the conclusion chapter by Coe and Wolford.

To this day, the first volume of D. J. M.'s *The Making of Modern Southeast Asia* (1971) contains one of the most complete compendiums of the moves and countermoves of the British, Dutch, and French conquest of the region. Once Great Britain and the Dutch had reached a broad division of their competing interests in Southeast Asia in 1824, the subsequent expansion of their holdings – which extended up to the eve of the twentieth century – typically occurred as a result of political or military challenges on the peripheries of their initial stakes. Similar processes drove France's expansion in Indochina. Pongkwan Sawasdipakdi's analysis in Chapter 3 of the anomalous case of Thailand is the exception that proved the rule. Siamese relations with both the British and the French sometimes escalated into armed conflict and its own tributary relations with neighboring states gradually contracted. Yet Britain and France were able to reach a modus vivendi because Siam constituted a reasonable buffer between the two European imperial powers and embraced Western concepts of government and law.

Because of the tremendous asymmetries between the colonial powers and the traditional governments they conquered in Southeast Asia, the theoretical apparatus for understanding war among major powers was not always germane. For example, displays of force were often – although by no means always – adequate to resolve information asymmetries and secure capitulation.

But bargaining failures did play out quite clearly in other confrontations among imperial powers, most notably in Japan's contest with first China and then Russia over influence in Northeast China and Korea. Both wars provide clear examples of imperialism driven by strategic calculations. Wolford's reinterpretation of that conflict in this volume emphasizes how Russian uncertainty over Japan's willingness to fight was responsible both for the onset of the war and Russia's effort to strengthen its hand in Manchuria in the first place; only fighting could make commitments credible. But underneath Wolford's analysis are assumptions about imperial preferences: that both parties not only sought to advance their interests but did so with the purpose of denying imperial control to their adversary.

1.3.2 War, Violence, and Repression

Our consideration of the economic and strategic causes of imperialism rests on an even more basic starting point: that imperialism not only involved the use of force for the purpose of conquest or securing capitulation but became an enduring feature of colonial rule itself, whether direct or indirect.

When and where the European powers did not have the capacity to project force at a distance, they were of necessity forced to accommodate and negotiate with local rulers. But once they did have that capacity, coercive diplomacy, war, and subsequent repression became integral components of the imperial enterprise. According to Caroline Elkins, there were over 250 armed conflicts in the British empire in the nineteenth century, with at least one in any given year (Elkins 2023, 9). China's century of humiliation was by no means limited to the First Opium War (1839–1942) and the Second Opium War (1856–60), but included Japan's Formosa Expedition or the so-called Mudan incident on Taiwan in 1874; the Sino-French War (1884–85); the First Sino-Japanese War (discussed in the first volume of this project, Park 2020); and the Eight-Nation intervention to suppress the Boxer Rebellion (1899–1901), each of which was followed by demands not only for concessions but also for reparations.

Needless to say, these depredations were hardly limited to the Europeans. In the first volume of this project, Andrew Yeo (2020) considered the origins and aftermath of the Philippine independence movement, and the brutal tactics the United States employed to squash it. That conflict has now produced a small library of work detailing the violent nature of the American occupation (e.g., Miller 1982). In addition to the larger wars in which they were embedded, Japanese war crimes have now been catalogued at length, with numerous massacres of not only prisoners of war but also civilians: Nanjing, Manila, the Sook Ching incident in Singapore, Kalagon in Burma, and the Pontianik incidents in the Dutch East Indies among many others.

Yet the role of violence does not stop at the stage of victory or even formal conquest. Elkins' (2023, 9) description is a reminder of the sheer scale of British imperial reach:

Among [the wars identified] were revolts in Barbados, Demerara (British Guiana), Ceylon, St. Vincent and Jamaica. They also included sustained efforts to conquer and dominate – or "pacify" as Britain termed it – the Ashante in the Gold Coast, Mahdists in Sudan; the Xhosa, Zulu, and Afrikaners in South Africa; the Afghans in Central Asia; the Burmese in South Asia. Rudyard Kipling called these conflicts the "savage wars of peace"; some were short, others protracted and recurring. They became part of imperial life, consuming British manpower, lives, and taxpayer funds while devasting local populations.

As Jeremy Yellen argues in his contribution to the volume, Japan continually struggled with the contradictions of its Greater East Asian Co-Prosperity Sphere. Tokyo sought willing Asian followers in an anti-Western project but the new order was ultimately sustained by absolutist political means. The cycles of imperial violence extended to bloody showdowns with nationalist forces. As Thomas and Asselin show with respect to Algeria and Vietnam, the final violent stages of French decolonization in the postwar period quickly devolved into "cycles of internecine killing, massacre and counter-massacre, normalized summary killing, maltreatment of detainees, and loss of distinction between civilians, seditionists, and 'traitors'" (Thomas and Asselin 2022).

Colonial rule should thus be considered in the wider context of our understanding not only of war but also of authoritarian systems, including their use of repression for the purpose of maintaining power. Indeed, it is surprising to us that this link has not been made in the political science community given the theoretical apparatus that could be brought to bear on how different imperial systems functioned to maintain support and suppress dissent. Elkins again is a worthwhile starting point, noting how even "ordinary" legal codes and regulations were not adequate to maintain order in the colonies; rather, colonial governments resorted to legal exceptionalism in the form of martial law and states of emergency, and again well into the postwar period.

This consideration of imperialism as a regime type raises a series of interesting counterfactuals as well as puzzling normative questions. For example, should we judge foreign colonial rule by different standards than indigenous autocracies? Why? Why have international norms developed that effectively outlaw old-fashioned imperialism but permit autocratic behavior that is equally if not more abusive? Would major players – most notably China – necessarily have been better off under local than imperial rule? The question is typically posed by colonial apologists, but it is clearly one that requires more serious consideration than that.

1.3.3 Institutional Forms

A final theme to come out of the project has to do with very ambiguity in our understanding of sovereignty as articulated in the Westphalian vocabulary of international relations. The idea of equal sovereign states was suited for a theatre of great power competition in which the key players were the major countries of Europe and the outcomes of interest were their interactions with one another: whether peace could be kept or whether war transpired. But this vocabulary is not of much use when thinking about the relationship between political entities of vastly different capabilities. A reconsideration of imperialism not only allows us to think about hybrid political forms of various sorts. It raises the question of the very meaning of sovereignty and independence in the context of power asymmetries and dependencies that reduce the range of choice.

The Asian stage provides a virtual museum of the institutional forms that imperial rule could take. At one extreme was the outright annexation of colonies that then fell under direct metropolitan control, even if those colonial governments negotiated explicitly or tacitly with local political forces: Hong Kong and Singapore, Macau, the Philippines, and Indonesia.

However, no foreign actor had the appetite for swallowing China whole, and the political arrangements that governed China's relations with the imperial powers were rooted in extraterritoriality. Southeast Asia had its own hybrid forms: protectorates and protected states. Here we focus on these two dominant hybrid institutional forms, but also note the succession of multilateral arrangements that also made an appearance on the regional stage, particularly mandates and trusteeships. As Wallace and Corbett outline in their chapter, these forms had surprising longevity in the Western Pacific.

The treaty port model is a good starting point because it sets a baseline for the shifting balance of power between the colonizing states – from Europe, but later Japan and the United States as well – and China. Moreover, it shows clearly what the unraveling of the Sino-centered order meant in practice. Prior to the Opium Wars, China managed trade through the so-called Canton system, which did not fully integrate Europeans into the tribute system but nonetheless provided for trade while allowing substantial controls on the pace of integration (Carroll 2010). At the core of the Canton system were two monopolies: one held by the British East India Company, and the other by the thirteen licensed *hong* merchants or *cohong*. These houses facilitated trade as guarantors, collected customs and taxes, but also kept foreigners at a distance from the court. The British complained about the restrictiveness of these arrangements, but the Canton system worked more effectively than has been thought. Nonetheless, as Horowitz (2020) shows clearly in the first volume of this project, the breakdown of the monopoly on the British side in 1833 and the entry of independent opium traders placed renewed political pressure on the Canton system that ultimately led to war.

The objectives of the British were by no means limited to the economic issues of changing the terms of trade and opening new opportunities outside Canton; they also sought to restructure the *political* relationship between the Qing court and the outside world. The British sought revisions in diplomatic practice, the elimination of the kowtow, and direct access to the court (Horowitz 2020).

But more fundamentally, they sought concessions on tariffs, how foreign powers could access domestic markets, permission to invest directly, and corresponding rules to assure that access would be sustained and debt repaid. Moreover, they pursued these objectives through formal treaties that were clearly imposed. In the wake of the Opium War Treaties of Nanking (1942, Britain) and Tientsin (1858, to which the United States, France, and Russia as well as Britain were parties), a host of others followed in the nineteenth century involving other imperial powers. To cite but a few, these included the Supplementary Convention of Peking (1880, with Germany), the Treaty of Saint Petersburg (1881, Russia), the Treaty of Tientsin (1885, ending the war with France), the Treaty of Peking (1887, with Portugal ceding Macao), and the Treaty of Shimonoseki (1895, with Japan, ending the war and ceding Formosa). But the pattern continued right through into the twentieth century. In the 1890s, Nield (2015) documents a total of fifteen episodes of new agreements on treaty ports, territorial settlements, and concessions, including in the form of leases. The Boxer rebellion (1899–1901) set off another round of concessions. In the two decades following the rebellion, Nield identifies another seven treaties or administrative agreements marking new concessions. According to Kayaoglu's (2010, 1) count, as late as 1926, twenty-six British, eighteen American, and eighteen French courts operated in China's ports and cities.

For IR scholars, the central concept undergirding these relations was extraterritoriality or what Turan Kayaoglu (2010) calls "legal imperialism." His definition highlights the interdependence of law and power:

> Legal imperialism is the extension of a state's legal authority into another state and limitation of legal authority of the target state over issues that may affect people, commercial interest, and security of the imperial state. Extraterritoriality was quintessential legal imperialism: it extended Western legal authority into non-Western territories and limited non-Western legal authority over Western foreigners and their commercial interest. The production and maintenance of extraterritorial legal authority required both a legal framework to deny non-Western law and sovereignty and also the material capability to defend these extraterritorial courts systems against the non-Western elites and populations who became increasingly uncooperative and even hostile to these courts. (p. 6)

As Saeyoung Park (2020) argues in the first volume of this project, it was not just force that undergirded this change in diplomatic relations. Imperial powers exercised a kind of discursive power. The appropriate way of interacting took the form of legalized interactions between sovereign entities but legal interactions in which the outcomes were foregone conclusions.

The protectorate provides yet another example of a hybrid political form (Wolfers 1971). As support for formal empire waxed and then waned in the late nineteenth century, the British pursued a more minimalist strategy with respect to acquired territories. In lieu of direct rule, they sought other arrangements designed to achieve free trade and to prevent other European powers from declaring sovereignty. Protectorates and protected states – although subtly different in legal form – varied in the extent to which the Crown intervened. But in principle, protected states were ceded some or even significant domestic authority – albeit subject to steerage – while metropoles maintained control over foreign policy and defense matters, including immigration. Protectorates were the favored form of rule in Malaya (including with respect to its individual states), Sarawak, North Borneo, and a number of Pacific Islands (e.g., Tonga and the Solomons). France similarly used the protectorate mechanism with respect to Laos, Cambodia, Annam, and Tonkin.

These political forms were not confined to the bilateral relationships between metropoles and colonial subjects. They were also managed multilaterally through the mandate system (following World War I) and the trust territories (following World War II). Mandates were legal entities that were effectively administered by colonial powers, but nominally under provisions established under the covenant establishing the league. In Asia, they included the South Pacific Mandate – administered fatefully by Japan – New Guinea, Nauru, and Western Samoa. In the early years of the United Nations, eleven territories were placed under the International Trusteeship System, including Western Samoa, New Guinea, Nauru, and the peculiar Strategic Trust Territory of the Pacific Islands which – for strategic reasons – fell under American jurisdiction. In this volume, Corbett and Wallace detail the rise and fall of these institutional forms as a reflection on the wider question of the limits of sovereignty and the blurry line with what David Lake (2024) calls "indirect rule."

1.4 Theme II: Time, History, and Periodization

A second analytic theme that preoccupies many of the papers in this volume is competing conceptions of historical time and periodization. The contributions repeatedly point out how the dates that animate Western views of world politics and the region often bear little resemblance to those that are important within it. Moreover, these historical differences are not merely academic; they shape national narratives in ways which are surprisingly enduring (see Simpser, Slater, and Wittenberg 2018 on historical "legacies"). These divergent periodizations center on the differences between Westphalian and colonial and postcolonial tropes, on the significance of World War I and the Wilsonian moment, how we think about the timing of war in the Asia-Pacific, and the meaning – and timing – of the Cold War.

One narrative in the IR literature is how Westphalian norms gradually diffused and by the early twentieth century had become the de facto normative foundation of international order. Yet for virtually all countries in the region, the storyline focuses not on Westphalian norms but on the issue of imperialism and colonialism addressed in the previous section. The Opium Wars were fought in 1839–42 and 1856–60, but the cycle of foreign pressure, violence, and treaty concessions extended well into the twentieth century. Extraterritoriality in China did not end until 1943.

We know that the idea of a "century of humiliation" served domestic political purposes in China (Wang 2008). China, perhaps more than any other country in the region, has managed to keep the resentments of the colonial era alive precisely as it has enjoyed unprecedented growth and a rise in international stature (Wang 2008; Miller 2013). More broadly, we know that such legacies are almost always manufactured by political elites. Yet, are those preoccupations any less accurate than the Westphalian mythology of equal sovereign states?

To say that regional views of the current security architecture, international institutions and law, and key bilateral relationship were shaped by colonial history is an understatement. Asia's "history issues" – particularly those related to Japan – have spawned a rich literature in political science, including on the logic of apologies (Dudden 2008; Lind 2010; Berger 2012; Smith 2015, Chapter Three; Kimura 2019). We are still learning how events such as the Tokyo war crimes trials are read very differently – and were read very differently at the time – by victors and vanquished (Bass 2023). Whatever domestic sources nationalism in Asia has tapped, it always posits itself in part as the antithesis to a thesis posed by foreign powers: China vis-à-vis the European powers; Southeast Asia in its struggle for independence against the British, French, Dutch, and Americans; and the persistent role of Japan as an historical protagonist across the region but particularly vis-à-vis China and Korea. The social and political forces carrying and advancing these historical narratives are to be reckoned with, and they continue to locate contemporary conflicts within an imperial, postimperial, or neo-imperial frame.

The imperial era is by no means the only example of these divergent views of well-known historical markers. Consider the case of World War I, typically taught as an object lesson on how wars can start inadvertently. In terms of impact, World War I was significant because it finished off three long-standing land-based empires – Austro-Hungarian, Ottoman, and Russian – fundamentally reshuffled territory and constituted a failed US effort to rewrite the rules of global governance. The direct effects of the Versailles settlement were more consequential for Europe than for Asia, however, where it redistributed a handful of German holdings. The imperial order also shifted in East Asia, but because of new challengers to the aging colonial powers there: the British, French, and Dutch. New histories emphasize how it was World War I that ushered in the era of US dominance that is usually seen as a feature of the post-World War II order (Tooze 2015); that holds in East Asia as well. Japan, however, was also a beneficiary of these shifts and its rise and expanding imperial ambitions are arguably the most important consequence of World War I in Asia.

As Erez Manela (2009) and other historians have shown, the flag of self-determination that Wilson held out – as well as the Soviet identification with anti-colonial struggles – provided a rallying point for nationalist movements across Asia no less than they did in Europe (Aydin 2007; Mishra 2012; Streets-Salter 2017; Guan 2018, Chapter One; Harper 2020). These nationalist forces were disappointed at Versailles and by the capitulation of the United States to European imperial interests. Nonetheless, the crucial concept of self-determination was now on the table.

An interesting question about periodization is whether there was a post-Versailles liberal moment in Asia as there was in Europe, and if so whether it bears consideration as a precursor or comparator to the postwar liberal order. As a latecomer, the United States had a somewhat different colonial project than the European states, for example, in its nominal commitment to "open door" norms of nondiscrimination and the potential for multilateral solutions to the region's security problems. These included the League itself but also the projects set in train by the Washington Conference in 1921–22, the Four- and Nine-Party Treaties, and the nod to negotiating tariff autonomy for China. Iriye (1965) outlines the rise and fall of that project but Dickinson (2013) goes farther, making the case for a "new Japan" in the 1920s that moderated the country's imperial ambitions. We are skeptical, seeing more continuity across the period, including US support for the European colonial powers in Southeast Asia (Foster 2010). But the 1920s does raise the complex counterfactual of whether the more overt tensions and conflicts of the 1930s might have been avoided and if so how.

Collective memories of war also operate on very different timelines across the Pacific. Pearl Harbor may have been the triggering event in the onset of the Pacific War for the United States. But when that war – or wars – really started remains a matter of debate to this day. At a minimum, we need to go back to the typical dating of the Second Sino-Japanese War in 1937. But a strong case can be made that the onset of regional wars should be pushed back to the Mukden incident of 1931. S. C. M. Paine (2014) titles her overview of what might be called the long interwar period *The Wars for Asia: 1911–1949*, a subversive periodization whose beginning and end dates are associated with two Chinese revolutions. But why not go back further to the incorporation of Korea as a protectorate in 1905 – a prelude to its annexation in 1910 – or Japan's initial push to exercise more decisive influence in Manchuria? Yoshihisa Tak Matsusaka (2001) opens his history of the making of Japanese Manchuria by claiming that "Japan's subjugation of Northeast China . . . began in 1905," with the rail concessions secured in the wake of the Russo-Japanese war (see also Young 1998; Matsusaka 2001; Chapter 4, this volume).

Finally, we are continually reevaluating the Cold War, mining it for comparative insights into the growing polarization between the United States and China and Russia. But while the Cold War trope may appear a logical – and even self-evident – framing for our understanding of the postwar period, it is by no means as obvious as Western scholars might think. Such periodization is not innocent. Under the Cold War narrative, the defining puzzles center on American grand strategy and the idea of a "postwar settlement" or "order" (Chapter 2, this volume). This framing naturally poses questions about the components of that order and how states allied, aligned, or hedged vis-à-vis great power patrons; in effect, what the lineup of the red and blue teams looked like.

But for virtually the entire developing world, the arc is quite different. The global South's timelines focus on the emergence of nationalist movements, which reached back into the 1910s and 1920s, and in a number of cases in Asia only achieved their goals well into the postwar period. In these colonial narratives and their postcolonial successors, the problems are not the preoccupations of the great powers and the emergence of competing Cold War coalitions. Nor are they completely captured by those interpretations of the Cold War that rightly focus attention on the developing world as the main arena of great power competition (e.g., Westad 2005).

Rather they center on a much longer arc and literatures that were central to political science at one point but have wrongly dropped from the research radar: the articulation of national identities, the mobilization of opposition to colonial rule, the civil wars that are at the heart of virtually all national movements, and the efforts of newly independent states to manage risks emanating from all large powers, regardless of their ideological camp. There is little doubt that World War II had decisively corrosive effects on the European empires. But those processes were by no means automatic, and the US role was by no means always a liberal progressive one; it sided with nationalist forces in Southeast Asia in some cases (such as Indonesia) while supporting European allies in their effort to reenter the region, most fatefully with respect to the French in Indo-China (e.g., Lawrence 2005).

The important point to make here is that these temporal-cum-analytic frameworks have important interpretive consequences. The Cold War narrative of the postwar period naturally hones in on such important developments as the alliance systems, to which political scientists have made important historical as well as theoretical contributions (Christensen 2011; Henry 2022). Yet it sits uncomfortably with other aspects of the historical record in which large swaths of the developing world – including key Asian states at the time such as Indonesia and Burma – were in fact nonaligned or seeking a third way (Lee 2010; Miskovic, Fischer-Tine and Boskovska 2014; Getachew 2019). The implications carry through all the way into the present. The current controversy about hedging in Southeast Asia is little more than a replay of strategic debates in developing countries about how to carve out independent foreign policies in the early Cold War era (Goh 2007; Kuik 2008).

1.5 Themes III: The Domestic Political Foundations of Regional Order

Domestic political factors are a recurring theme in any consideration of regional order, but which ones and how should they be theorized? At the most basic level we are interested in those political factors that generate capabilities and weaknesses. One of the great puzzles of the period under review is the divergence between the political and economic trajectory of China and Japan. That divergence sets the stage for the central conflict of the interwar period – Japan's inextricable commitment to its mainland empire, which in turn drew in the United States. Coe and Wolford return to this fundamental problem in the conclusion, and we summarize their take in more detail next.

Here, however, we complicate the picture. In this volume, Sawasdipakdi shows how the Thai court pursued reforms that gave it bargaining leverage vis-à-vis the imperial powers. However, "reform" is not typically of a single piece. Joe Esherick's (1976) classic treatment of the 1911 revolution in Hunan and Hubei suggests how hard it is to get these domestic political stories right:

> There has always been, in American historiography of Asia, a certain partiality toward reform. The gradualism inherent in reform is preferred to radical revolution, especially if the model for reform is borrowed from the West. The bias is most visible in studies of the Meiji reforms in Japan where American historians have found an Asian success story while Japanese historians have discovered the roots of Japan's twentieth century imperialism, yet the closing years of the Qing saw her most vigorous efforts to reform from above on the Japanese model. (p. 106)

Esherick points out that in the context of China, "reforms" tended to benefit elites while exposing the masses to extraordinary risks, most notably in higher taxes and price inflation.

Nor is the "traditional and modern" binary necessarily useful for understanding the choices made by reforming elites. New accounts of the Meiji era such as Ravina (2017) show that far from Meiji reforms mimicking Western models, they drew on highly traditional justifications and reflected odd amalgams. And there is certainly no way that crude factors such as a regime type were decisive; Japan was also oligarchic. The failure of republicanism to take root and rapid descent into what would now be called competitive authoritarian rule and ultimately warlordism is also clearly more complicated than that.

It goes far beyond the scope of this volume to litigate an historical comparison of the complexity of Japan and China from the late nineteenth century into the early twentieth. But the international causes and consequences are worth underscoring. First, as Horowitz shows, the problems China faced lay in the contradictions of the imperial system itself: that outside powers made demands on the Chinese system that made it less rather than more capable, even with respect to defending imperial interests. The imperial powers simultaneously wanted a Qing court that could protect foreign interests yet was not strong enough to stand up forcefully to imperial depredation. This ambivalence arguably persisted into the KMT era on the mainland and into the deepening civil war.

Second, the contribution by King highlights the role of economic factors in the Sino-Japanese relationship. Perfectly aware of the threat Japan posed, the Nationalist government had little choice but to accommodate continued trade and investment from Japan because of the need for capital, inputs, and technology. As with any international economic relationship, imperial ties generated their own sources of political support.

Domestic political factors play an equally important role in our consideration of Cold War dynamics, and we can think of them most broadly in coalitional terms: who held power, to whom were they accountable, and what were the foreign policy implications of these political relationships? We observe significant heterogeneity in the governments that emerged in the postwar period. In Northeast Asia – Japan, South Korea, and Taiwan – conservative anti-communist governments dominated and allied with the United States; in South Korea and Taiwan, these governments were authoritarian, labor-repressive right-wing dictatorships. In China and North Korea, virtually opposite regimes emerged, led by Communist parties that were aligned with the Soviet Union. We do not need to imagine the counterfactual: if the Nationalists had prevailed in the Chinese Civil War and the United States had occupied the entirety of the Korean peninsula, we would have had completely different alignment patterns.

Southeast Asia by contrast was characterized by much greater diversity and generated more diverse foreign policies as a result. These ranged from the socialist commitments of the Democratic Republic of Vietnam and its subsequent ties with the Soviet Union and China, through the nonaligned cases of Burma and Indonesia to the conservative coalitions that assumed power in Singapore, Malaysia, South Vietnam, Thailand, and the Philippines. This latter group clearly tilted toward Europe and the United States. Ngoei makes the case that these domestic political alignments constituted the political foundations for American hegemony in the region. It is worth noting that political convergence in the region also provided the foundation for the formation of ASEAN in 1967, which subsequently played a surprisingly important role in structuring the organizational architecture of the entire region. In their contribution on the Pacific Islands, Wallis and Corbett play out how domestic political alignments similarly influenced the extent to which semi-sovereign states would pursue closer or more arm's-length ties to the United States and more recently with China as well.

However domestic political forces aligned, it is worth noting how the strategic environment could generate bargaining leverage for governments in their relationships with the great powers. James Lee makes this point most clearly in his political economy take on the alliance system. To be sure, the conservative political coalitions that emerged in the Cold War era were more likely to gravitate toward close relations with the United States, including through the conclusion of formal alliances in mutual defense treaties. But he shows that they also used concerns about domestic subversion to extract aid commitments. Moreover, the appearance of patron–client relationships did not imply that the Asian alliance partners moved in lockstep with American policy preferences. A second important theme of Lee's paper is how the economic models adopted by newly independent governments were by no means liberal in orientation; to the contrary, the region proved a test bed for interventionist economic policies that were subsequently identified with developmental states (Haggard 2018).

1.6 Theme IV: Ideational Factors and the Role of Race

A fourth and final theoretical theme that follows on the first volume is the renewed effort to give due weight to ideational factors in international relations. We argued that normative structures were not only crucial to the Sinitic order but were also equally important in sustaining subsequent imperial projects. In that volume and here, we note the role that treaty law and extraterritoriality played in that regard and – following Park (2020) – see them as embodying a kind of discursive power.

Here we add an additional dimension into the mix: the role that race plays in international politics and in relations between Europe and the United States and Asia in particular. As with the literature on imperialism, the topic is not a new one: classic works on colonialism and race can be found in the interwar and early postwar period (e.g., Du Bois 2014; Fanon 1965); the "colonial turn" noted here has deep roots. Moreover, prominent historians have highlighted the role of racial tropes as a handmaiden to wartime mobilization (e.g., Dower 1986). Yet attention to race in international relations has lagged, in part because of the difficulty of incorporating it into models in which states – rather than their polities and societies – are conceived of as the dominant actors (Freeman, Kim and Lake 2022; Brown 2024).

In this volume, Han and Kim provide a political economy explanation for the emergence of anti-Chinese racism in the United States, focusing on the migration that accompanied the opening of China, the demand for labor arising from the gold rush and railroad-building in the United States, and the inevitable conflicts that arose with American labor as a result. They trace the politicization of race in the second half of the nineteenth century that culminated in a succession of exclusionary acts, first passed in 1882 and not ultimately repealed until 1943.

However, they are clear that material factors were not the only ones at work. We can do no better than to cite from their contribution:

The political success of anti-Chinese political rhetoric was facilitated in large part by the growing popularity of scientific racism and social Darwinist approaches to race in late-19th century Europe and America. While ethnocentric beliefs in the superiority of one's own group have been found in a wide range of different human societies dating as far back as the ancient imperial states of Egypt and Rome, the advent of modern racial thinking in the 19th century was distinguished by its adherence to new "race science" of can be sustained. The differences between the United States and China are increasingly seen as fundamental differences in economic system that may not be amenable to negotiated settlement. Rather, we are seeing a turn in the direction of state intervention and protectionist policies as the United States and Europe confront the negative externalities of China's increasingly statist growth strategy.

However, the economic geography is also shifting in ways which limit decoupling. Not only does the United States remain dependent on China – and vice versa – the countries in the region are rapidly integrating with each other in ways that only partly engage the United States. Southeast Asian nations in particular were never as engaged in a bipolar competition as was the case in Europe (Chapter 2, this volume) and continue to engage in close relations with both the United States and China. Even more than during the early Cold War period, we expect domestic political alignments in the countries of the region to continue to shape the nature of the post-Cold War order.

Second, Coe and Wolford provide a promising way to think about the emerging ideological conflict that is occurring between the United States and China. They are worth quoting at length:

In game-theoretic terms, ideologies do not only describe why adhering to a set of social roles, beliefs, and strategies are better than provoking punishment by deviating from prescribed behavior. They also explain why the equilibrium entailed by those social roles, beliefs, and strategies is better than *other* equilibria defined by other sets of social roles, beliefs, and strategies – i.e., by other ideologies. In other words, a theory of ideological competition is a theory of competition between equilibria; a successful ideology represents (a) one idea among many of how to organize politics and (b) survives by convincing its adherents that other equilibria aren't as attractive, whether by suppressing comparisons or outlasting others.

Throughout this project, we have sought to give due weight to shifting power balances while always paying equal attention to the complicated and sometimes idiosyncratic ideational factors that sustain order: in the tribute system, in the complex negotiations and coercions of the European and Japanese imperial orders, in the racial ordering of interactions across the Pacific, in the early postwar Pax Americana, and now in the increasing Chinese commitment to reforming global and regional governance. Given political developments in both the United States and China, we see few reasons to believe that the ideological jousting outlined by Coe and Wolford is likely to attenuate; the analytic task is to map its evolution.

2 The Myth of the San Francisco Settlement: Understanding Post-World War II East Asian Order

Evelyn Goh

US hegemony structures many contemporary debates about the rapidly changing international order, not least in East Asia.[1] One notable way in which US hegemony manifests itself is the common starting assumption that contemporary East Asian order was created as part of the post-World War II settlement at San Francisco in 1951, which provided a stable, rules-based order that is now being challenged by China, authoritarianism, and myriad other threats. By taking a large step back and also expanding the time horizon, this chapter critically tackles the question: *What is the best way to understand the post-World War II order in East Asia and its evolution?*

This chapter challenges two tropes about post-World War II East Asian order. The first is the twentieth-century "US as resident Pacific power" trope that draws a trajectory from Pearl Harbour, via the Pacific campaign, through to the US Occupation of Japan, and the hub-and-spokes bilateral alliance system that sustains US forward positioning in the region today. While US power projection and imperial expansion in the Pacific obviously has a longer trajectory, this post-Pearl Harbour phase emphasizes the notion of the United States as a somewhat reluctant and defensive offshore power becoming an indispensable part of the region with legitimate and long-standing interests as justified by various formal postwar treaties. The second is the "San Francisco System" trope that emphasizes how the great power victors designed a broad and enduring set of postwar settlements for East Asia and the world after 1945, including the 1951 San Francisco Treaties, as well as the United Nations and Bretton Woods international institutions. While these were all clear and very ambitious elements of a victor's peace, the emphasis of the trope is on how, through

---

[1] I thank Emirza Adi Syailendra and Nayoung Lee for their capable and enthusiastic research assistance, and Steph Haggard and Rosemary Foot for their comments and suggestions that helped to improve this chapter.

29

liberal institutionalization, they constituted the legitimate and therefore indefinitely sustainable peace, overriding a myriad of unresolved issues.

These tropes arise from the essential productive power that a hegemon wields: the ability to define and circumscribe collective understandings about the region in order to further the hegemon's own agenda. Without disputing the very significant role of the United States in winning the Allied war in the Pacific, and in fostering prosperity after that war and during the Cold War, these are "tropes"[2] because they miss out very major elements of the history, and by these omissions create a partial and misleading account of regional order, its disruption, creation, and evolution.

These reflexive ways of understanding post-World War II East Asian order are inadequate because they explain little about regional order apart from the US hegemonic enterprise. Those omissions would only be justifiable if we accept that US hegemony and US interests are all we need to know about East Asia in international relations.[3] If we are unable to accept this proposition, then we need to move beyond the myth of the San Francisco "settlement." The rest of this chapter explains why and how to do this.

The following analysis develops in three parts. The first explains the partialness of war settlements in East Asia after 1945. In particular, the San Francisco treaties were only a very partial reckoning. The United States exacted the 1951 Treaty of Taipei from Tokyo, but other signatories to these treaties crucially excluded the People's Republic of China (PRC, Communist China) and the two Koreas, as well as the Soviet Union. With the exception of Nationalist China and Japan, many other East Asian states or polities involved in the region's wars and conflicts were excluded from negotiating settlements.

The second part then shows how the San Francisco treaties helped to create the five key territorial conflicts that endure today in East Asia (Taiwan, the Kuriles, Takeshima, the Senkakus, and the disputes in the South China Sea). These treaties repudiated or fudged prior secret agreements at Yalta and the subsequent Cairo, Potsdam, and Japan Surrender declarations. The San Francisco settlement myth was also used to discipline regional contestation over territorial claims, until the past fifteen years or so when these contests resurfaced with a vengeance.

The third part of the analysis addresses how acknowledging the myth of the San Francisco settlement can change our basic understanding of East Asia's past and present. Here, the chapter provides an alternative way to understand East Asian order and its evolution. "Regional order" is not

---

[2] I thank Steph Haggard for suggesting this term and angle.
[3] Drawing from Gramsci, I use the term "hegemony" in its classical sense, meaning unequal power backed by a greater portion of consent than coercion. For a fuller analysis of US hegemony in this region, see Goh 2013b.

synonymous with "US strategy in Asia." The idea of the San Francisco treaties "settling" East Asian conflicts and creating a new postwar order is a myth. The end of World War II (really, for the United States, the start of the Cold War) is the wrong watershed for understanding contemporary East Asia.

Instead, the transition of order in East Asia we are dealing with is really the longer and as-yet unfinished transition out of the Sino-centric order that was crumbling by the mid-1800s under domestic dissent and Western imperialism, and then fatally challenged by Japan from the last quarter of that century onward. At the same time, for East Asia as a whole, the parallel transition was also a transition out of Western colonization, and the shorter-lived Japanese imperialism, toward a regional system of sovereign states struggling for independence and autonomy. This struggle to create a stable regional order is still ongoing – China and Japan have not reached a viable settlement, Korea remains divided, China's unification dreams are unfulfilled, Japan's boundaries are not agreed, and peace settlements between vital regional countries are incomplete. Even as those items of unfinished business are unresolved, East Asian states have had to grapple with unfolding dilemmas of the current power shifts as US hegemony weakens.

This chapter's analysis and argument make at least two significant contributions. First, by extending the temporal frame both backward and forward, it disrupts the de facto US hegemonic lens often used in the literature to frame discussions of East Asian order. Second, by fleshing out East Asia's innate, longer- and bigger-order transition since the mid-nineteenth century, it properly contextualizes US hegemony and the US-centric debates and literature on US strategy in Asia. While the US role in recent East Asian history is very important in (and to) itself, US hegemony in East Asia is more appropriately understood as an interregnum, rather than as part of the "natural" order of things.[4] Especially in the contemporary era when history is both constitutive of and instrumental to international relations, such challenges to the dominant tropes about post-World War II East Asian order should not be treated simply as hectoring from the sidelines. They ought to be recognized as significant contestations of US hegemonic narratives and – particularly with growing willingness and wherewithal to pose these challenges from within the region – revelations about the interim nature of this hegemony. East Asian order has been and remains *in transition*: The nature of the new order is yet uncertain and unlikely to be determined primarily by US interests.

---

[4] On the interregnum nature of post-Cold War US hegemony in East Asia, see Goh 2013b.

2.1 A Very Partial Settlement: The San Francisco Treaties

When discussing the so-called San Francisco System, historians focus on two treaties[5] signed in that city on September 8, 1951, providing the terms for restoring vanquished Japan's independence: (i) the multilateral Treaty of Peace with Japan that forty-eight allies signed; and (ii) the bilateral US-Japan Security Treaty, under which Japan granted the United States the right to "maintain armed forces … in and about Japan" and the United States supported and encouraged limited Japanese rearmament. Both treaties came into effect at the end of the US occupation of Japan, on April 28, 1952.

Two major issues stand out in these treaties: First, they were partial settlements only; and second, they were contingent, that is, not final and subjected to subsequent revisions, additions, and other alterations.

On the glaring partialness of the "San Francisco peace," I can do no better than John Dower's elegant and parsimonious description of what he called its "contorted origins"[6]:

[T]he San Francisco settlement was a " *separate peace.*" The omissions from the list of nations that signed the peace treaty were striking. Neither Communist China nor the Chinese Nationalist regime that had fled to Taiwan were invited to the peace conference, despite the fact that China had borne the brunt of Japanese aggression and occupation beginning a full decade before Pearl Harbor and the US entry into the war. Both South and North Korea were excluded, although the Korean people had suffered grievously under Japanese colonial rule and oppressive wartime recruitment policies between 1910 and 1945. The Soviet Union attended the peace conference but refused to sign the treaty on several grounds, including the exclusion of the PRC and Washington's transparent plans to integrate Japan militarily into its Cold War policies.

Viewed from the perspective of the separate peace, the San Francisco settlement thus laid the groundwork for *an exclusionary system that detached Japan from its closest neighbors.* In the months following the peace conference, the United States tightened the screws on this divisive policy by informing a dismayed and reluctant Japanese government that Congress would not ratify the peace treaty unless Japan signed a parallel treaty with the Chinese Nationalist government in Taiwan, thus effectively recognizing that regime as the legitimate government of China. Failing this, the US occupation of Japan would be perpetuated indefinitely. Japan acquiesced to this ultimatum in the

---

[5] There are different understandings of what constitutes the San Francisco "system" (SFS). In the Introduction, I alluded to the broadest understanding – within the US trope – that wraps the US-Japan treaty in with the US-led postwar international institutional order. Apart from that, some historians (including those cited in this section) focus on the 1951–52 treaties when referring to the SFS, while others include the US security pacts with Australia and New Zealand as well as the Philippines to take into account the hub-and-spokes regional alliance system. For a critical discussion, see Buszynski 2011.

[6] Dower 2014, 3; emphasis mine.

famous "Yoshida Letter," dated December 24, 1951 (from the Japanese Prime Minister Yoshida Shigeru to John Foster Dulles, the US emissary in charge of the peace settlement). The ensuing peace treaty between Japan and the "Republic of China" ensconced in Taipei was signed on April 28, 1952 – the same day the peace and security treaties signed in San Francisco came into effect.

In effect, therefore, San Francisco was a settlement of the war between the United States and Japan, on terms that were sharply influenced by Washington's new imperatives in the developing Cold War against the Communists.

Why is this a problem? The trouble arises less from the fact that this was very much a victor's peace than because of its glaring partialness. San Francisco was a separate peace in two crucial ways: The United States settled its war with Japan separately from the Allied settlements in Europe and elsewhere in the world, *and* Japan settled its war only with the United States and some of its allies but not with Japan's other adversaries and victims, especially not its neighbors in East Asia.

Why is this a particular problem for understanding East Asia's postwar order? Because in East Asia, what Americans imagine as "the Pacific War" or even "World War II" was actually a messy conflation of the Second Sino-Japanese War, the Chinese Civil War, *as well as* the Pacific theatre of World War II. Strikingly, neither of the two regional conflicts was or has been settled by some grand peace treaty.[7]

The 1951 San Francisco Peace Treaty and the Treaty of Taipei extracted terms of peace from Japan, but this "settlement" with Japan excluded the PRC and the two Koreas, as well as the Soviet Union. China was left out of the San Francisco conference because Britain and the United States could not agree on whether the PRC or the Republic of China (ROC) would represent it, and Korea was excluded because of the ongoing war on the peninsula. The preceding war crimes trials conducted under the International Military Tribunals for the Far East (IMTFE) delivered a similarly partial reckoning – not only because of the US decision not to prosecute Emperor Hirohito as head of state but also because of the exclusion from the indictments of Japanese Class B and C war crimes conducted against Asians.[8] Two Japanese were found guilty at the Tokyo Trial

---

[7] Readers schooled in the modern history of East Asia are likely to be very familiar with the details of the discussion here and in Part II. These readers may wish to proceed to Part III for an analysis of how knowing this (and broader regional history) helps to change significantly our entry points for understanding the nature and evolution of East Asian order since 1945.

[8] The discussion here and in the next two paragraphs draws from material I previously published within the IR literature – for a detailed analysis of these issues, the complicity of East Asian leaders and governments, and the implications for regional order, see Goh 2013b, 166–194. Significant controversy surrounds the 1946–68 Tokyo Trial particularly, at which twenty-eight Japanese war leaders were tried for Class A "crimes against peace." Military tribunals were also

in connection with atrocities committed in the southern Chinese city of Nanjing, but no charges were brought in any tribunals against those responsible for the enslavement of Chinese forced laborers and "comfort women" from Korea, China, and other Asian countries, or for experimentation on mainly Asian victims at Japanese chemical and biological warfare facilities.[9]

By definition, the US-centric nature of the San Francisco treaties excluded peace negotiations and settlements between key East Asian states and polities involved in the region's major wars and conflicts between China and Japan, within China between the Nationalists and the Communists, and resulting from the dismantlement of both the Qing and the Japanese empires. The United States has stood in the way of these regional reckonings at different junctures. In 2000, South Korean comfort women victims filed a suit in a US law court, but the George W. Bush administration set an important precedent by issuing a "statement of interest" in May 2001, arguing that these lawsuits would affect negatively US-Japan treaty relations. The District of Columbia court and appeal judges subsequently dismissed the case on the grounds that it was a "nonjusticiable political question" and "inimical to the foreign policy interests of the United States."[10]

Viewed from Japan's neighborhood therefore, San Francisco was very far from a settlement. It did not bring about the complete cessation of conflict – given that the Chinese Civil War continued to produce crises across the Taiwan Straits, for example. Neither did it assist with negotiating or creating real channels for the resolution of several complex territorial claims among regional states and polities that were transitioning from colonialism toward independence or that were engaged in civil war and division. Overall, there was no San Francisco "settlement" in the sense of producing decisive terms for peace, or for a new regional order.[11]

That the San Francisco treaties themselves were contingent is clear from the important evolution of the Japan–US Treaty between 1951 and 1960. The 1951 treaty delivered on the most important aspects of the postwar bargain that Washington wanted: the right to establish bases in Japan and a forward military presence in Northeast Asia, as well as Japan's commitment to support "the free world" in the developing Cold War divide. However, the 1951 treaty was notably vague on at least three counts: it did not clearly commit the United States to Japan's defence, it left open the possibility that the United States could

convened throughout Asia to try Class B (conventional war crimes) and C (crimes against humanity) war criminals.

[9] On the collusion of US occupation forces in marginalizing Japan's war atrocities in China and Korea, see Conrad 2003.

[10] Dudden 2008, 92. Similar rulings were passed for related Asian forced labor cases.

[11] Indeed, the general IR literature tends to focus mainly on disruptions wrought by major war, and the opportunities for renegotiating order presented by postwar peace-making settlements – e.g., Holsti 1991; Osiander 1994.

use its bases in and around Japan for any purpose it saw fit, and it was an explicitly provisional arrangement that lacked specification about its duration and the conditions under which it would cease or be renegotiated. The treaty stated that "Japan desires, as a provisional arrangement for its defence, that the United States of America should maintain armed forces of its own in and about Japan," and the United States would expect that "Japan will itself increasingly assume responsibility for its own defence."[12] Left unstated were the level of Japan's economic or military capability that would constitute a change in the circumstances, and what the resulting reduction of US forces or commitments would have to be.[13]

By the 1960 Treaty of Mutual Defence and Cooperation, Japan continued to provide basing rights for US forces, but in exchange for a clearly articulated US commitment to the defence of Japan.[14] The stipulation that the treaty could be abrogated with notice after ten years provided a time frame for reviewing the evolution of Japan's defence capabilities. Importantly, it required the United States to consult with Tokyo regarding the use of US forces in Japan, allowing Tokyo potentially to veto US military action from bases on mainland Japan.[15] The US right to intervene in domestic riots was curtailed in an important return of sovereign recognition. The other important aspect of restoring Japanese sovereignty – the reversion of Okinawa from United States to Japan's control – took another nine years. Subsequent updates and revisions of Japan-US defence cooperation in the 1980s, 1990s, and 2000s would produce elaborations and expansions of Japan's defence interests and potential military contributions with ramifications for the region more broadly. These included Japan's responsibility for the security of sea lines of communication, ability to respond to military contingencies in surrounding areas, including Taiwan, and the scope of its military assistance to neighboring countries.[16]

Similarly, but on a broader scale, it took another three decades for some of the major inadequacies of the partial settlement in 1951 to be addressed in subsequent vital negotiations between Japan and its immediate neighbors. By the 1951 Treaty of Taipei, the ROC on Taiwan had followed the San Francisco convention of waiving reparation claims against Tokyo. But it was not until normalization of relations two decades later, in 1972, that Japan and the PRC issued a joint statement affirming the same terms of peace. There is no treaty to acknowledge the end of Japanese colonial rule in Korea, even though Japan did

---

[12] Security Treaty between Japan and the United States 1951.   [13] Ishihara 2023, 47–65.
[14] See, e.g., Swenson-Wright 2005; Schaller 1997; Buckley 1992.
[15] There was one secret exception: Tokyo would approve the use of these bases to defend South Korea against a North Korean attack. For an analysis of how the form of the new alliance agreement reflected Tokyo's fears of becoming entrapped by the United States in an unnecessary conflict with China over the Taiwan Straits, see Henry 2022, Chapter 5.
[16] See Buzan and Goh 2020, 161–177; Liff 2023. Further details are beyond the scope of this chapter, but my point about the contingency of the 1951 treaty should be clear.

sign a Treaty on Basic Relations with South Korea during their bilateral normalization in 1965. This itself was a drawn-out process for, from the San Francisco Peace Treaty coming into force in 1952, "it took another 14 years, seven rounds of negotiations and some 1500 official meetings to reach the final agreement in 1965."[17] Japan still has no peace treaty with North Korea, and though the two sides agreed in 2002 to work toward normalization, no progress has been made to date.

Thus, anyone wishing to focus on postwar peace settlements involving Japan in Northeast Asia would need to know at least about these agreements. In Southeast Asia, where the newly independent ex-colonies of the allies did not waive their rights to reparations, we would need to study the separate peace treaty and reparations agreement Japan signed with Burma in 1954, the Philippines in 1956, and Indonesia in 1958.[18]

In order to fully comprehend the major transition for regional order that accompanied the Communist victory in China's Civil War from 1949, we would also need to know about regional negotiations of terms of recognition and coexistence with the PRC. For this, we need to add knowledge of the key agreements establishing diplomatic relations with the PRC, recognizing the long timespan between the first Southeast Asian state to normalize relations with the PRC (Indonesia in 1950) and the last (Singapore in 1990). Moreover, we would need knowledge about the various agreements surrounding the Sino-American rapprochement and normalization from 1972 into the 1980s (which are being re-contested by both sides in significant ways today, especially with regard to the mutual understanding on Taiwan).[19]

In other words, there was no definitive "war settlement" in East Asia after World War II. Instead, East Asia's change of regional order after 1945 has been a long-drawn saga, with movements and revisions at different junctures, and in significant parts still without an actual ending to conflicts or beginning of a coherent new arrangement. At this juncture, there is usually a strong impulse to focus on the US-centric reasons for why it turned out this way – with prime factors located at the start of the Cold War, including US intervention in the Korean War from June 1950, and in domestic political developments, especially McCarthyism. In contrast, this narrative has emphasized the outcome of non- or prolonged war settlements when one privileges a region-centric perspective. Section 2.2 helps to unpack how US-centric reasons to do with its

---

[17] Togo 2010, 157–158.
[18] Burma received from Japan US$200 million in war reparations and $50 million to support economic cooperation, and an additional $140 million in 1966. The Philippines received $550 million in reparations and $50 million for economic cooperation, and Indonesia $223 million in reparations and $400 million for economic cooperation. Aung 2019.
[19] For a useful analysis, see Liff and Lin 2022; e.g., Fukuda 2023.

The Myth of the San Francisco Settlement 37

early construction of the Cold War with the Soviet Union interacted with the longer, underlying order and power transitions in East Asia itself.

2.2 Regional Disputes and the San Francisco Myth

The very partialness and contingent character of the San Francisco System engendered serious lasting effects for East Asia. Most notably, the San Francisco treaties helped to create the five key territorial conflicts that endure today in East Asia. Writing about the postwar international relations of Northeast Asia, Calder observed:

> Lack of clarity in the treaty over what constituted the Kuriles estranged Japan and the Soviet Union, for example. Similarly, ambiguity as to who held sovereignty over Takeshima/Tokdo, in the middle of the Japan/East Sea, complicated Japan-Korea relations. Lack of clarity regarding whether the Senkaku/Diaoyutai islands were part of Okinawa or Taiwan likewise estranged Japan and China. The treaty also failed to resolve North-South territorial divisions in Korea, not to mention relations across the Taiwan Strait. It thus enhanced prospects for future intra-regional conflict along multiple geopolitical dimension.[20]

There is a long, slightly technical, and certainly unresolved history in each case, the details of which are well-covered in the existing literature on the recent history and international relations of East Asia.[21] Essentially, the 1951 San Francisco Treaty repudiated or fudged earlier drafts of this treaty, prior secret agreements at the "Big Three" Allies' conference in Yalta in February 1945, as well as the Cairo, Potsdam, and Japan Surrender Declarations. The San Francisco settlement was also used by the United States to discipline Japan and to sustain regional divisions at the start of, during, and beyond the Cold War.

The following text summarizes briefly each of five ongoing disputes across East Asia, highlighting their connections with the San Francisco Treaty and the limits of the US–Japan settlement in 1951.

Northern Territories (Japan)/Southern Kuriles (Russia)

This dispute centers on four islands or island clusters north of Hokkaido, and whether they are part of the Kurile islands chain handed over to the Soviet Union in 1945, or part of Japan's territory off its northernmost main island of Hokkaido.[22] At Yalta, in part to gain Soviet entry into the Pacific War, President Roosevelt had promised Stalin the Kurile Islands, which Soviet forces duly

---

[20] Calder 2004, 139.
[21] See especially Hara 2007. Hara suggests here and in other essays that US ambiguity about these territories in the San Francisco Peace Treaty was deliberate. For a detailed discussion from an international law perspective, see Lee 2002.
[22] This summary draws mainly from Hara 2001.

took upon Japan's defeat. In the San Francisco Treaty six years later, Japan renounced its rights and claims to the Kuriles – but without detail regarding the composition or extent of this island chain, and without stating to what country Japan was ceding the claim. In any case, the Soviet Union was not a signatory to the SFT and like for Japan's other neighbors, a separate process of settlement would be required in subsequent years.

During crucial bilateral diplomatic negotiations between Japan and the Soviet Union in 1956 – when the two established diplomatic relations – the United States intervened when it seemed that the Japanese were amenable to the Soviet suggestion of a compromise that would see the return of two of the four disputed islands to Japan. US Secretary of State John Foster Dulles threatened his Japanese counterpart Foreign Minister Shigemitsu Mamoru that the United States would accordingly claim full sovereignty over Okinawa if Japan reached such an agreement with the Soviet Union. The subsequent Japanese stance that all four islands had to be returned scuppered the war settlement negotiations, and Japan still has no peace treaty with Russia to this day.

Liancourt Rocks: Dokdo (Korea)/Takeshima (Japan)[23]

The dispute over this group of two islets and over thirty outcrops located in the Sea of Japan, between Korea and Japan, centers on whether they are included in the "Korea" that Japan renounced and recognized as independent in the San Francisco Treaty.[24] It is also intertwined with Korea's process of decolonization from Japan and emergence out of the old Sinic tributary order. Korea exerts a historical long claim to these features, while Japan's claim dates from its establishment of a protectorate over Korea in 1905. This dispute is most affected by contradictions across multiple drafts of the treaty, as helpfully summarized by Lee and Van Dyke:

> The first five and the seventh draft of the Treaty included Dokdo in the Article 2(a) list, thereby providing that the islets would be returned to Korea. The 6th, 8th, 9th and 14th drafts explicitly stated that the territory of Japan included Dokdo. The 10th through 13th and 15th through 18th drafts, like the final text of the Treaty, were silent on the status of Dokdo.[25]

---

[23] This summary draws mainly from Hara 2001; and Lee and Van Dyke 2010.
[24] There is an intertwined story about the undetermined status of Korea: at Yalta in February 1945, the Allies agreed informally joint trusteeship of the peninsula in its transition from Japanese colonization to independence, but at Japan's surrender six months later the peninsula was divided at the 38th parallel and separately occupied by the Soviet Union and the United States. In 1948, two separate governments were set up without going through the trusteeship arrangements, leading eventually to the North's invasion of the South in mid-1950 and the US-led countercampaign that was still ongoing when the SFPT was signed the following year.
[25] Lee and Van Dyke 2010, 744–745.

This dispute was also very much shaped by growing US Cold War imperatives in Asia. Earlier US inclinations to recognize Liancourt Rocks as Korean were reversed after the Communist victory in China in December 1949, with documentary evidence that the outcrops' potential for US radar and weather stations began to be emphasized by key US officials as the prelude to emphasizing US maritime control in the area. Additionally, after the outbreak of the Korean War in June 1950, Washington worried about the loss of South Korea to the communist North. The San Francisco treaty drafting was simplified to exclude extraneous details (including references to these rocks) partly to facilitate quick agreement and the redeployment of US troops from Japan to the peninsula. Korea was not represented at San Francisco, but US Secretary of State Dean Rusk had already informed the Korean Ambassador in Washington that the United States regarded the islands as Japanese. In early 1952, South Korea explicitly claimed Dokdo as its territory via Presidential decree and has physically exerted control and patrolled the maritime features since 1954. The 1965 ROK-Japan Peace Treaty did not address or resolve the dispute; the disagreement indeed helped impede the drawn-out negotiations. The United States has largely stood aside and sought neither to further the dispute nor assist with its resolution.

Senkaku islands (Japan)/Diaoyutai (China)

Over this clutch of islets and rocks in the East China Sea, the dispute focuses on whether these are part of Japan's Okinawa Prefecture, or part of Taiwan; at different junctures dispute has also arisen about whether Okinawa is part of Japan or China. The Senkaku islands were declared *terra nullius* and annexed by Japan in 1895, following Japan's victory in the First Sino-Japanese War, by which Taiwan was ceded to Japan in the Treaty of Shimonoseki. Qing China's defeat itself had come twenty-three years after Japan annexed the Ryukyu kingdom in 1872 and turned it into Okinawa in 1879. From 1895, the Senkakus were treated as part of Okinawa Prefecture by both the Japanese and the Americans – under the San Francisco Treaty's Article 3, the Senkakus together with Okinawa were separately placed under US administration and existed as US military territory until their return to Japan together with Okinawa in 1972.

During the 1940s, Republican China under President Chiang Kai-shek had tried – unsuccessfully – to stake Chinese claims to Okinawa and Tsushima, as remnants of the Ryukyu kingdom that had been part of the Qing dynasty's tributary system. During that decade, the wartime conferences among the Allies in Cairo and Potsdam had included the ROC alongside the Americans, British, and some junctures in the Soviet Union. The December 1943 Cairo Communiqué stipulated that "all the territories Japan has stolen from the Chinese, such as Manchuria, Formosa, and the Pescadores, shall be restored to the Republic of China,"[26] the July 1945 Potsdam Proclamation confirmed that the Cairo terms would be carried out, and the September 1945 Japanese Instrument of Surrender wrought Japan's acceptance of the Potsdam Proclamation. The Chinese have subsequently relied upon these earlier conferences to stake their claim to both Taiwan and Diaoyutai (as part of Taiwan), rather than the very different outcome in San Francisco in 1951 at which China was not represented, and the Senkakus were not mentioned and thus retained by Japan.

Be that as it may, the dispute was postponed by the PRC when negotiating bilateral normalization with Japan in the 1970s, despite the ROC resurrecting historical claims to Diaoyutai in preparation for oil exploration on the adjoining seabed. During the September 1972 summit meeting, Premier Zhou Enlai declined to talk about the Senkakus,[27] while during the 1978 peace treaty talks, Premier Deng Xiaoping suggested "shelving" the issue and possibly pursuing joint development.[28] While Japanese governments have resisted the "shelving" formulation because it implied Tokyo's acceptance that a dispute existed over the Japanese-controlled islands, they did in practice "put the topic to one side" for the greater purpose of stable relations with China.[29] During the escalation of the dispute in the 2010s, the Chinese also saw the Americans as having reneged on their long-standing position of neutrality on the territorial dispute, when in 2014 President Barak Obama declared that the Senkaku Islands were included in the US-Japan defence treaty.[30]

Taiwan

Unlike the others on this list, this infamous dispute is not about largely barren rocks; it is a sovereignty dispute and a divided nation situation more akin to the North–South separation in Korea or previously in Vietnam. The Taiwan dispute arose from the combination of Japan's wars against China, Japanese decolonization, and the Chinese Civil War. The island was invaded by Japan during the First Sino-Japanese War and ceded by Qing China in the 1895 Treaty of Shimonoseki to Japan, remaining a Japanese colony for fifty years. As already indicated, one of the agreed conditions of Japan's surrender was the return of Taiwan and neighboring Penghu island to China. However, Taiwan was taken

---

[26] Formosa and the Pescadores refer, respectively, to Taiwan and an adjacent archipelago of islets in the Taiwan Straits named Penghu in Chinese. Roosevelt et al. 1943.
[27] "Record of the Third Meeting between Prime Minister Tanaka and Premier Zhou Enlai" 1972.
[28] For the official Chinese account in English, see MOFA (PRC), "Set Aside Dispute and Pursue Joint Development," n.d., www.fmprc.gov.cn/mfa_eng/ziliao_665539/3602_665543/3604_66 5547/t18023.shtml.
[29] See Buzan and Goh 2020, 154–155, 169–170.
[30] The Trump and Biden administrations subsequently echoed this stance that Article V of the Treaty includes the Senkakus in US obligation to help defend Japan. See, e.g., US Congressional Research Service 2021.

over by Chinese Republicans who fled the mainland during the Chinese Civil War at the end of 1949. Upon their victory and creation of the PRC on the mainland, Communist Chinese forces were prepared to rout the Republicans on Taiwan to end the war.

Like some of the other disputes already discussed, references to Formosa and the Pescadores disappeared from the San Francisco Treaty after Dulles' "simplified" the treaty contents following the "loss" of mainland China to the communists and the outbreak of the Korean War. At the time of the San Francisco conference, the United States was the occupying force in Japan, and also provider of aid to Taiwan and South Korea. In the latter, it was one of the main combatants in an ongoing war against the North and its Communist allies the PRC and the Soviet Union. Two days after the outbreak of war in Korea, on June 27, 1950, Washington ordered the imposition of the US Seventh Fleet in the Taiwan Straits to prevent a CCP invasion and defeat of the Chinese Republicans, and thus to forestall unification of Taiwan with the mainland.

Correspondingly, as discussed in the previous section, the US–Japan Security Treaty signed at San Francisco facilitated a lasting US forward positioning in the region that, among other purposes, included intervention to avoid Taiwan falling into communist Chinese hands – a purpose that has increased in salience in the intervening decades. At the same time, Washington also required Tokyo to sign the Taipei Peace Treaty with the ROC on Taiwan. This move reinforced the US policy of separating the two Chinese regimes, but also rendered Japan complicit in denying Taiwan to the mainland again. In these ways, potential conflict over Taiwan became a major premise of the United States' San Francisco "settlement."[31]

Because of this feature, the Taiwan dispute has essentially become a triangular one involving the United States as a key third party, while Japan plays a secondary but vital role both in peace and in a potential war. In the September 1972 Joint Communique establishing diplomatic relations with the PRC, Japan stated that it "fully understands and respects" the PRC's stance on Taiwan, and "firmly maintains its stand under Article 8 of the Potsdam Proclamation," which had obliged Japan to return Taiwan to China. In essence, Japan set the formula for others wanting to open diplomatic ties with Communist China, for how to assure the PRC that the Taiwan question was an internal affair and they would not support Taiwanese independence.[32]

The Spratly and Paracel Islands in the South China Sea

Further south, the PRC, Taiwan, and several Southeast Asian states stake rival territorial and resource rights claims to three groups of islands, atolls, and

---

[31] Dower 2014.   [32] Kokobun et al. 2017, 95.

maritime features – the Paracel Islands claimed by Vietnam and Taiwan and occupied since 1974 by China; the Spratly islands claimed in their entirety by China, Taiwan, and Vietnam and in part by the Philippines and Malaysia; and Scarborough Reef and Macclesfield Bank, disputed by the Philippines, China, and Taiwan.[33] Currently, China controls all of the Paracels, but the other two groups are variously occupied by each of the claimants. These disputes gained particular notoriety after the Cold War, and are covered in a steadily expanding set of scholarly and policy analyses.[34]

Once again, these disputes were created or exacerbated by the combination of Japanese and French decolonization, and the Chinese Civil War. Similarly, the San Francisco Treaty presented a lost chance to negotiate rival claims and helped to obfuscate the disputes. Chinese, Japanese, and French agents staged rival expeditions and annexations to these features in the opening decades of the twentieth century.[35] Both the Chinese Nationalists and Communists made sovereignty claims to these maritime territories in the late 1940s (indicated by the now-infamous "dashed lines" on official maps), and Japanese forces occupied some of the larger islands during the Pacific War. Upon Japan's surrender, Chinese Nationalist forces took over and occupied key islands in the Paracels; and in 1947, the ROC incorporated Macclesfield Bank, the Paracel, Spratly, and Pratas Islands under the administration of the Hainan Special Administrative Zone. ROC forces withdrew when Communist forces routed them in mainland China in 1949. In the San Francisco Treaty, at a French request, Japan renounced the Spratly and Paracel Islands by name, though again, without stating to whom they belonged thereafter. Among claimants present at San Francisco, Vietnam stated its claims to both island groups (with no response from other states present), and the Philippines did not. The ROC was not present but subsequently argued that it had never renounced its 1945–47 de facto and de jure sovereign claims over the islands despite troop withdrawals in 1949, and had also ensured that the Treaty of Taipei stipulated ROC recognition that Japan had renounced these islands along with Taiwan.[36] As with the other conflicts, by 1951, the Americans clearly avoided designating recipients of such renounced territories because they would have included Communist China and the Soviet Union.

The forgoing brief survey substantiates Dower's view that the ambiguities regarding territorial and sovereignty dispensations in the SFPT did not result from "simple inadvertence or oversight. On the contrary, much of it was deliberately introduced in the final drafts of the peace treaty by the United States, in conformity with Washington's overall strategy of thwarting communist influence in Asia."[37] Observing that earlier treaty drafts prepared by US officials between 1945 and 1950 were "long and detailed, providing clear

---

[33] See Smith 2010. [34] For example, Emmers 2009; Hayton 2014; Taylor 2018.
[35] See Hayton 2014, Chapters 2–3. [36] See, e.g., Chen 2014. [37] Dower 2015, 217.

border demarcation," including grid references and names of small islands, Kimie Hara concluded from her definitive scholarly study of these territorial disputes that

> [t]he equivocal wording of the [San Francisco] treaty was neither coincidence nor error; it followed careful deliberation and multiple revisions. Earlier drafts were, as a whole ... consistent with the 'punitive peace' plan and the Yalta spirit of inter-Allied cooperation. However, with the emergence of the Cold War in the immediate postwar years, Japan was given central status in the US Asia strategy, and the peace terms changed from punitive to generous as US strategic thinking focused on securing Japan within the Western bloc and assuring a long-term US military presence in Japan, particularly in Okinawa.[38]

This is not to say that there was an alternative, fully worked out "Plan A" determining whom would have gotten which territories. From 1945 to 1950, there had been an unfolding process of negotiation and evaluation about how to resettle regional boundaries and authority structures in the wake of the dissolution of the Sinic order, Japan's defeat and withdrawal, the (partial) end of (some) European imperialism, and the (ongoing, contested) creation of new political entities within the region. This was an ongoing process, with multi-agentic stabs – not only by US officials on paper, but also by various East Asian forces on the ground – at a new order post-Chinese hegemony, post-Sino-Japanese War, post-World War II, semi-post-colonial, post-Chinese Civil War. This transition, already messy and already dominated by the United States as the victorious and undiminished power after World War II, was hijacked by the developing superpower conflict and by US impositions of its rapidly changing strategic imperatives.

The years between Cairo and Yalta (1943–45) and San Francisco (1951) were vital in remaking Washington's threat perceptions and reorienting US priorities in Asia. Japan's elevation to the position of prime US supporter state as a result of the triumph of communism in mainland China and North Korea's invasion of the South entailed quite deliberate *reversals* of US peace settlement policies. By 1951, these went in favor of Japan and against the interests of its neighbors who had been victims of Japanese aggression – especially in Korea, China, and Taiwan. Japan's centrality for US Cold War strategy in Asia was deliberately constructed out of the fear that the communists would win everywhere else and so the United States had to keep hold of as much of Japan as broadly defined as possible, and to keep Japan "wedged" away from its neighbors[39] and therefore as dependent on the United States as possible.[40]

---

[38] Hara 2006, 2–3. Lee and Van Dyke 2010 agree with this assessment based on their detailed review of the numerous draft versions of the treaty.

[39] This is Hara's assertion across her publications.

[40] Or, as another author put it: "The intra-regional conflicts among Northeast Asian nations provoked by treaty ambiguity ultimately enhanced the geopolitical leverage of the United States, particularly with an anxious and defensive Japan." See Calder 2004, 139.

Buttressing this new US strategy was the myth that the treaties at and around San Francisco "settled" the war in East Asia, and created a new "system" centered on the United States as hub and hegemon. The mythical dimension was the notion that US hegemony was sufficient to subsume and to subdue outstanding, unresolved conflicts and struggles within the region itself. The latter was rendered less important, unstrategic, because the key struggle had become redefined as the superpower-centric, "global" Cold War. Against this context, it was a system in which US strategy in Asia became equated with East Asia's order per se.

2.3 How to Understand East Asia's Evolving Order

How does acknowledging the myth of the San Francisco settlement affect or change our basic understanding of East Asia's past and present? In itself, this is a fascinating question that might spawn many new dissertations. Here, I briefly suggest some important entry points into building understanding of East Asian order and its evolution. To begin, it is vital to recognize that "regional order" *is not synonymous* with "US strategy in Asia." More broadly, regional order is not reducible to great power ordering efforts at the end of a systemic war, planning the world that they "won," drafting and then simplifying treaties to codify defeat and victory. Essentially, East Asian order is determined by regional states undergoing complex transitions on the one hand, interacting with the choices and strategies of great powers on the other. At this juncture, it would be a mistake to approach this dynamic asymmetrically, for example, by thinking that it is a matter of how regional states *respond* to great power strategies. We would be in a better position to take regional agency seriously if we asked instead how regional and domestic political transitions and imperatives within East Asia *interacted with*, or were *pursued in the context of*, great power ordering efforts. What do we mean by complex transitions in East Asia? There are at least two ways to understand these bigger and deeper transitions: via the unfinished business between East Asia's two regional great powers, and through the ongoing struggle with nation-building and development within and across East Asian states.

2.3.1 East Asia's Unfinished Great Power Transition

The foregoing dissection of the San Francisco myth demonstrates why the end of World War II (really, for the United States, the start of the Cold War) is the wrong watershed for understanding contemporary East Asia. Yes, there was a wider transition of the international order from the post-World War II period into the creation of the Cold War. At the same time though, there was a parallel transition of order in East Asia: that longer and as-yet unfinished transition out of the Sino-centric order that was crumbling within itself by the mid-1800s, unable to compete against Western imperial encroachment, and then fatally challenged by Japan in the last quarter of that century.

The 1945–51 negotiations about peace settlement in East Asia did not – indeed could not – address a deeper power transition in Northeast Asia, which stretches back at least to the antagonistic alienation between China and Japan from the mid-nineteenth century onward. Throughout their long, shared histories, Japanese polities spent long periods as ambivalent side players in the Sinic order, generally keen on trade but not on tribute or obeisance (most famously, Tokugawa Japan effectively denied China's political supremacy from the seventeenth to the mid-nineteenth century). But the outright rupture in their relationship, and in the regional order, only came in the second half of the nineteenth century, following Japan's self-removal from the Sino-centric regional society and adoption of Western norms, technology, arms, and practices following the Meiji Restoration, including Japan's adoption of Western-style imperialism in Asia. From this base, modern Japan successfully challenged both Russia and China on the Korean peninsula, with the First Sino-Japanese War of 1894–45 further exposing Qing China's decline in the face of domestic dissent and Western technological competition and imperialism.[41] This rupture also culminated in Japanese imperialism: its spoils from the First Sino-Japanese War included Taiwan in 1895 and the Ryukyu kingdom in 1897; the annexation of Korea followed in 1910, the gradual settlement and then invasion of Manchuria in 1931, and then all-out war with China between 1937 and 1945, during which the China-centered tributary order finally and decisively disappeared.

But, as already discussed, Japan's subsequent defeat by the United States saw a peace process that kept China and Japan from a bilateral peace settlement. More than that, the intervening Cold War and US strategy held Japan and China apart and alienated from each other for decades, preventing a deeper process of mutual reckoning. In the preceding seventy years or so, both China and Japan had undergone radical and traumatic changes in their sociopolitical character and national-cultural identity and purpose. These two East Asian great powers had confronted each other at great cost, but with no defined outcome in terms of what their new mutual relationship would be, or what the regional political order was within which they had to locate themselves as new political entities. The partialness of the San Francisco peace exacerbated the "fundamental dissonance in Chinese versus Japanese understandings about the socio-normative structure of [their bilateral] relationship, and the nature of the regional order" that had been ravaged by Japan's challenge and China's imperial collapse.[42] I have argued elsewhere that without an important process of recovering and negotiating these

---

[41] For a treatment of the multiple causes of state failure in Qing China during this period, see Chapter 7.
[42] Buzan and Goh 2020, 148.

constitutive understandings, East Asia's regional order will remain crippled and strange. This is because "Japan's defeat in the Second World War and its subsequent subordination to the US did not so much draw a line under the old imperial era, as it interrupted the power transition between China and Japan that had been brewing since the nineteenth century."[43] During and still after the Cold War, this unresolved power transition between China and Japan left East Asia without indigenous great power leadership, while growing swathes of the region were grafted onto first the superpowers' and subsequently United States', strategic preoccupations.[44]

This is not to say that if left to their own devices, China would have gradually overtaken Japan or challenged it; or that Japan should now be supported to complete its challenge to China. Following World War II, Japan's defeat and China's descent into civil war and exclusion from US-led international society prevented not only mutual settlement between these vital adversaries but also a more organic or indigenous reordering of East Asia. These twin vacuums make more dramatic and unstable the current ongoing transitions involving China's recovery of great power and the weakening of US hegemony.[45]

So what? First, recalling this unfinished power transition between China and Japan suggests that, when considering East Asian order, a focus on Japan is certainly apt. However, too often, focusing on Japan translates automatically and myopically into looking only at the US-Japan alliance or their bilateral relations. Instead, we need to pay crucial attention to the relationship between the two indigenous regional powers with the unresolved transition – Japan and China. The changing relationship between these two regional powers drove war and peace in East Asia in the first half of the twentieth century, and as discussed in this chapter, their economic, political, and security relations continued to set important parameters for regional order during and after the Cold War.[46] One of the most important consequences of recognizing this is that it enables us to consider more clearly Japan's vital position as a potential "swing state" in the East Asian order, rather than simply assuming that it will forever remain beholden and yoked to US interests. Put simply, by altering its current US dependency, and/or by seeking rapprochement with China, Japan can significantly alter the nature of East Asia's order.[47]

Second, understanding the troubled postwar non- or partial settlements between Japan and most of its immediate neighbors draws attention to the

---

[43] Buzan and Goh 2020, 149.
[44] On this curious deficit in indigenous great power management in East Asia, see Goh 2014.
[45] Note that I am not positing a simple causal connection between the two.
[46] See also Chapter 8 for an analysis of the unexpected relationship between war and economic interdependence between China and Japan between the 1930s and 1960s.
[47] For a detailed analysis of how adopting a Japan–China-centered view can significantly change our efforts at future scenario-building for East Asian security, see the four scenarios developed in Buzan and Goh 2020, Chapter 7.

long-standing puzzle of Japan's role in Asia. From US perspectives, Japan may well be regarded as the lynchpin or cornerstone of US alliances and strategy in Asia – but for Japan and its neighbors, Japan is the troubled member of the regional community. Japan's problematic history of relatively recent aggression has not been fully redressed; it has had a demonstrated desire since Meiji times to emulate the West, to exit Asia without being able to leave Asia; and since the 1990s Japan was the regional lead economic goose that suffered decades of ignominious stagnation. Given these circumstances, the wonder is the extent to which Japan has nevertheless managed to salvage its regional role since 1945, and to buy and to repair its diplomatic, social, and cultural standing in East Asia. Again, from a US perspective, the explanation tends to revolve around Cold War exigencies and the superiority of the US-led "liberal order." Privileging East Asian viewpoints, we would need to recognize that there has been a great deal of hard-headedness among Japan's neighbors that usually goes unacknowledged. For their own good reasons – usually to do with regime legitimacy, economic growth, and other domestic political imperatives arising from nation-building requirements after independence – many East Asian countries quite quickly chose to put aside their history problems with Japan. For many decades, such choices were also made by the hardest cases in the region – this includes the complicity from regimes in China and Korea in sustaining the partial postwar settlements I referred to in the previous sections. In this sense, Japan's acceptability to regional constituencies predates the recent preferences for Japanese sources of investment, developmental aid, or infrastructure lending as an alternative to China's.

2.3.2 *East Asia's Broader Ongoing Transitions in Political Order*

By the time the Second Sino-Japanese War had logrolled with Japan's Pacific War and the Chinese Civil War, East Asia as a whole also faced the parallel, dramatic transition out of Western colonization and shorter-lived Japanese imperialism, toward a regional system of sovereign states struggling for independence and autonomy.[48] In terms of systemic political transitions, this worldwide process of decolonization and universal nation-state formation was the most significant change in international relations since the technological transformations of the early nineteenth century. On top of these, enormous changes were superimposed on the United States' efforts to fight the new Cold War, partly by developing a strategy for maintaining a forward presence in East Asia beyond the end of the world war it had just won. Washington largely

---

[48] On how these very radical changes in global and regional ordering took place in compressed time and space as Northeast Asia transitioned from empires to modern nation-states, and grappled with the intrusions of Western imperialism, see Buzan and Goh 2020, pt. 2.

achieved its purposes over the four decades after the San Francisco peace conference. But, as the two previous sections show, East Asia's struggle to create a stable regional order is still ongoing. US imperatives did not cause these struggles to disappear. China and Japan have not reached a viable settlement, Korea remains divided and at war, China's unification dreams are unfulfilled, Japan's boundaries are not agreed, and postwar peace agreements are incomplete.

Looking at it through a more East Asian-centered lens like this extends the temporal frame both backward and forward, helping to contextualize US Cold War strategy in Asia against the deeper currents of change in the region itself.[49] It is not only that San Francisco did not resolve much for the region (beyond establishing US hegemony). The key issue is that major elements of East Asia's two transitions – the end of the Sinic order and Japan's failed challenge, and the painful and often violent decolonization and nation-building processes – took decades to unwind. Some of that vital process remains stubbornly unresolved today in the form of divided countries, disputed territories, and seemingly irreconcilable differences over history between neighbors. These points become obvious when we consider two key examples: Korea and Vietnam. Both have had to transition out of the Sinic order *and* out of subsequent complex histories of colonization into modern statehood. Each presents a fascinating case of how national or regional histories or international relations might be told using a series of partial treaties or agreements – but each story also shows the stark flaws in the assumptions about "peace settlements" creating "order" at a single point in time.

Lying as the bridgehead in between Japan and mainland China, the Korean peninsula has been called the "vortex of empires"[50] and since 1876, Korea has often been the trigger for great power war and the site of incomplete efforts at settlements. Japan's late nineteenth-century attempt to impose a new regional order began with war with China over intervention in Korea. Their unsuccessful efforts to transfer Korean suzerainty led directly to the First Sino-Japanese War in 1894–95. A decade later, Japan's unsuccessful efforts to delineate its exclusive sphere of influence in Korea helped precipitate Japan's victorious war against Russia, and outright colonization of Korea thereafter. When the Soviet Union entered the Pacific theatre of the war in 1945, Soviet forces advanced onto the peninsula with alacrity, and in 1945 Korea was carved up at the 38th parallel for postwar administration by the Soviet Union and the United States.[51] The subsequent war when North Korea invaded the South in

---

[49] For a helpful analysis of how understanding this interconnection casts new light on Southeast Asian support for the United States during the early Cold War period, see Chapter 14.
[50] Key-Hiuk 1980, 350.
[51] For the argument that the initial division of Korea had less to do with the Soviet Union or Cold War dynamics than might be expected, see Chapter 10.

1950 ended in 1953 with an armistice but no peace treaty, and the two Koreas remain partitioned to this day.

The experience of postcolonial Vietnam after 1945 was similarly fraught and long-drawn. From an American perspective, it is common to talk about "the Vietnam War," referring to the period roughly between 1965 and 1973 when the United States intervened with combat troops in the conflict between North and South. Among historians and within Southeast Asia, it is more common to think about the "Indochinese Wars" as three sets of conflicts spanning the 1950s to the 1990s. From a Vietnam-centric perspective, it took three wars and forty years for it to make the transition out of the old Sinic order and into the Westphalian one. The First Indochinese War was fought by Vietnamese independence fighters against the French colonizers, and by the Geneva Accords of 1954, the Vietnamese got the French out, but at the price of a North–South division à la Korea. The Second Indochinese War was subsequently fought between the Viet Minh and Viet Cong, each supported by external great powers during the Cold War. By the Paris Agreement of 1973, the North Vietnamese got the Americans out and unified the country. The Third Indochinese War involved Vietnam invading and occupying neighboring Cambodia to defeat the genocidal Khmer Rouge regime in 1978 and China briefly invading Vietnam in 1979 to "teach it a lesson," followed by over two decades of diplomatic campaigning by non-Communist Southeast states against Vietnam for its continued occupation of Cambodia. Only with the end of the Cold War and the drying up of Soviet aid could the Paris Accord of 1991 be negotiated, finally opening the door for Vietnamese withdrawal, Cambodian independence, and Vietnam's habilitation as a normal nation-state in its own region.

What does knowing about these wider processes of order transition in East Asia do for IR scholarship? Importantly, this knowledge should undermine the significance of common questions like "who will dominate East Asia next?" or analyses of East Asia that fixate solely upon the United States and/or China. Such approaches do not make sense unless we assume that the rest of East Asia is simply a blank-slate arena for great powers. As other chapters in this volume clearly demonstrate, this assumption is wrong. When analyzing or debating order in East Asia, we need to resist the reflexive tendency to assume some linear power transition involving one declining hegemon having its baton wrested away by a rising challenger, and the whole region then tumbling into a clearly discernible "new order."

As already established, East Asia has been living through a broader, long-term, systemic transition away from a decayed and disintegrated Sinic order, via the Cold War and interrupted nations-building processes and a post-Cold War interregnum of US hegemony, toward a new order that remains unclear. The outcome of this order transition will not be determined solely by which great power dominates. Instead, as Buzan and Goh argued strenuously, the new regional order will have to be an arrangement that

> reconciles – or at least finds an equilibrium among – three sets of unresolved contradictions: the overlay of the Westphalian system emphasizing sovereign equality as well as great power privilege onto the remnants of hierarchical, civilizational modes of relations in the region; the penetration of external powers, especially the US, versus the role of indigenous great powers, especially China and Japan; and the strategic and political alienation among the major indigenous states in [the region] alongside their rapid economic integration.[52]

In other words, East Asian states have had a lot of other fundamentally important work to do as their governments and leaders stepped up to the contemporary tasks of becoming nation-states; they have not operated solely in response to the Cold War or great power competition. At the same time, East Asia's indigenous great powers have existed in a state of unresolved mutual antagonism and alienation since the late nineteenth century. They have not had an opportunity to reach a mutual settlement, not just of territorial claims, but also of mutually acceptable political relations and modus vivendi for dispute resolution. For at least sixty years after San Francisco, China and Japan could postpone this mutual reckoning by focusing on how to optimize their positions and benefits within the US-led order. But as US hegemony weakens and challenges to its attendant order grow, the need for Tokyo and Beijing to negotiate and reconcile their bilateral relationship and their mutual rights and responsibilities within the region becomes more urgent and necessary.

2.4 Conclusion

This chapter set out to bust the myth that the 1951 San Francisco treaties "settled" East Asian conflicts and created a new postwar order for the region. In so doing, it sought to destabilize and disrupt the de facto US hegemonic lens often used in the literature to frame discussions of East Asian order. By fleshing out East Asia's innate, longer, and bigger order transitions since the mid-nineteenth century, the chapter also tries to properly contextualize the recent interregnum of US hegemony and the US-centric debates and literature on US strategy in Asia.

It is important to note that the post-World War II nonsettlements in East Asia have not posed a problem for the United States either during the Cold War or in its pursuit of the liberal US hegemonic order after the Cold War. Indeed, the perpetuation of each of these conflicts, divisions, and unresolved disputes undergirds and helps to justify continued US forward positioning and US leadership or dominance in East Asia. In this sense, US hegemony in East

---

[52] Buzan and Goh 2020, 129.

Asia is built upon, and relies upon, regional disputes continuing to fester. US leadership in East Asia was not constructed upon the settlement of war or conflict or division – quite the opposite.

Some of these observations have already been made very persuasively by historians, including the so-called revisionist or leftist historians of US foreign policy epitomized by the Wisconsin School.[53] The latter critiques and the influence of revisionist historians, especially during and following the Vietnam War in the United States, reminds us that the trope of the US provision of order, stability, and prosperity in East Asia has been actively challenged from within the US establishment too. In the foregoing, I have endeavored to complement these critiques – which remain largely US-centric in their purpose of challenging and improving US national awareness and conduct – by offering an analysis that is East Asia-centric. This analysis might be read alongside revisionist accounts of the United States' Cold War to help move discussions beyond what these days may appear to be an esoteric consideration of "alternative" interpretations of US foreign policy motivations toward deeper consideration of vital dynamics in a core world region.

Where does all this leave us? At the very least, it should lead scholars to focus on Japan as a pivotal player in East Asia and the Sino-Japanese relationship as equally vital, if not more important in the long run than the Japan-US one. We also ought to investigate more thoroughly the puzzle of Japan's recovery as a regional power in the postwar decades. Tied to that, we should be asking more sophisticated questions if we are interested in East Asian order, questions that reflect the intertwined and ongoing transitions at the international, regional, and domestic levels within which 1951 was but one (often indeterminate) landmark. Better questions ought to reflect how the countries in the region have exercised their own agency to shape the emergent order, not at a singular landmark like a peace conference, but in a process extending over long decades since 1951.

Furthermore, knowing the minimal additional knowledge about East Asia outlined in this chapter will help shed light on why US allies do not often see eye to eye with Washington, and may not always be persuadable to do certain things because they have their own, complex interests. In turn, knowing this could help explain the increasing feeling of talking at cross purposes across a number of partnerships. There will be other implications that I hope this chapter can help to spur others into considering, and I look forward to lively debates that will help push forward the fields of international relations and international history as they relate to East Asia.

---

[53] Especially the works of William Appleman Williams, Walter Lafeber, Lloyd Gardner, and also Akira Irye and Bruce Cumings.

Meanwhile, the contents of this chapter are very likely to make a US-focused audience uncomfortable. This discombobulation will arise because this is an analysis that does not have the United States or its strategy or its interests at the center of it. More importantly, it does not conflate "US strategy" with "East Asian order." In other words, this chapter has approached East Asian security and politics in a way that does not assume that it revolves around the United States. My contention is that this type of analysis is urgently and explicitly required, given the post-US hegemonic lived reality in East Asia (and perhaps, to some extent, in the world at large).

Part II

The Imperial Era

3 Survival through Reforms: Siam and Its Escape from Colonialism

Pongkwan Sawasdipakdi

By the end of the nineteenth century, Siam, now known as Thailand, was surrounded by colonial powers on all fronts. To the south, British control extended over Penang, Singapore, and Malacca. In the west, the entirety of Burma fell under the British rule in 1886. To the east, Cambodia became a French protectorate in 1864, following the French capture of three southern Vietnamese cities in 1862. However, Siam maintained its independence until the end of the colonial era. This raises the following questions: How could Siam avoid colonialism, while other surrounding countries succumbed to their colonial fate? More specifically, why did the British and the French choose a policy of restraint over Siam while not doing the same for others?

In this chapter, I demonstrate how Siam maintained its independence amidst the challenges of colonialism. I argue that Siam's accomplishment was a testament to an intricate interplay between the country's geographical location and the strategic implementation of political and economic reforms. Situated at the heart of the region, Siam afforded the invaluable advantage of time, granting it an opportunity to prepare for the inevitable encounter with Western powers. However, devoid of successful reforms, Siam could have posed a potential threat to Western interests, thereby justifying colonization similar to other Southeast Asian nations.

In the following section, I provide a brief overview of the history of European colonial expansion in mainland Southeast Asia, starting from the nineteenth century. I then turn the focus to Siam and its interactions with Western nations, particularly the British and the French. This section delves into Siam's territorial disputes with these powers, rooted in differing interpretations of concepts such as boundary, territory, and sovereignty. Finally, I explore the various reforms undertaken by Siam to establish itself as a modern state deserving of equal recognition and respect with Western counterparts. The case raises the interesting question of the extent to which Thailand maintained its independence or was, in fact, an informal colony.

3.1 Colonial Expansion in Mainland Southeast Asia: An Overview

Western traders were no strangers to Southeast Asia, particularly maritime Southeast Asia, as it has been integrated into the European trade routes since the sixteenth century. In the mid-sixteenth century, Portugal became the first European power to conquer territory in maritime Southeast Asia. Soon after, the Netherlands and Spain followed suit. However, during this initial wave of colonization, mainland Southeast Asia, encompassing Burma, Siam, Laos, Cambodia, and Vietnam, remained largely unaffected. Even when the British arrived in the late eighteenth century, their focus was primarily on establishing trade posts and ports in Penang, Malacca, and Singapore rather than venturing into the mainland territories.[1]

In the early nineteenth century, mainland Southeast Asia became a target for colonial powers, in part as a result of strategic concerns about border areas and later as a result of competition between the British and French for influence and, ultimately, territory. In 1824, the first Anglo-Burmese War erupted due to conflicts along the southeastern border of British India and the western border of Burma. Despite the detrimental impact on the economic stability of British India due to the war's high cost, the British emerged victorious. The Treaty of Yandabo, signed to end the war, forced Burma to cede several northeast provinces, including Assam, Arakan, and Tenasserim, to the British. Furthermore, the treaty stipulated that the Ava Kingdom, the dominant kingdom in Burma then, establish diplomatic relations with British India and immediately sign a trade agreement with the British. The British also demanded that Burma pay indemnity payments as a condition for withdrawal. Subsequently, in 1853, the British annexed the delta region in Lower Burma following their victory in the Second Anglo-Burmese War, which was fought over allegations of discrimination against British merchants.[2]

After the British successfully annexed Lower Burma, the French were motivated to secure their position in terms of trade and colonial expansion in mainland Southeast Asia. While the British approached mainland Southeast Asia from the west, the French did it from the east. The prosecution of French missionaries in Vietnam justified French intervention in the country. With assistance from Spanish forces, the French launched a war in 1858 that lasted until 1861, when they successfully occupied Saigon and three additional provinces in the Mekong Delta.

The Treaty of Saigon, signed in 1862 to officially end the war, guaranteed the freedom to practice Catholicism and opened the Mekong Delta in southern Vietnam, along with three northern ports, to free trade. Furthermore, the treaty

---

[1] See Hall 1979, 598–621.   [2] See Bastin and Benda 1986, 38–41.

formally recognized the French occupation of several provinces in south Vietnam and demanded reparations from the Nguyen dynasty to the French. Motivated by their interest in exploring the Mekong River, the French expanded their occupation to other provinces in the south. By 1867, the French had effectively occupied the entire southern region of Vietnam and the Mekong Delta, in addition to declaring Cambodia a French protectorate in 1864.

The French exploration of the Mekong River and their annexation of the entire southern region of Vietnam and the Mekong Delta alarmed the British. With the onset of the Opium Wars and the subsequent opening of trade opportunities with China, the French and the British eagerly sought a secure passage to connect their colonies with the Chinese market. Initially, the French considered establishing the Mekong River as their connecting route. However, they later discovered a more convenient passage via the Red River, which ultimately led to the French conquest of Tonkin and other northern cities in Vietnam in the 1870s and 1880s.[3]

While the French enjoyed trading privileges in Vietnam and successfully established a trade route, the same cannot be said for the British. The British failed to develop a secure trade route connecting Lower Burma to western China and encountered commercial difficulties with the Ava Kingdom despite a trade agreement signed in 1867. Furthermore, the growing influence of the French within the Ava Kingdom, invited by the Ava court to counter the British domination, added to the existing obstacles. As the French expanded their control over Indochina, particularly in the north and westward regions, the British deemed it necessary to strengthen their influence over Burma. Consequently, in 1885, the British initiated the Third Anglo-Burmese War and subsequently occupied Burma's remaining territories, solidifying their control over the country.

Where did Siam fit into this grand scheme of colonial competition? Up until this point, only indigenous governments situated at the rim of mainland Southeast Asia had succumbed to Western colonization. Siam, located in the heart of the region, managed to avoid sharing the same fate in part for geographical reasons. Siamese relations with the British and, notably, with the French sometimes escalated into armed conflict, and its influence over other kingdoms in Southeast Asia significantly diminished. However, the conflicts solidified power over its defined territory and led to the emergence of a modern Siam that embraced Western concepts of government and law.

---

[3] See Hall 1979, 787–803.

3.2 Siam's Struggles with the West

Unlike other kingdoms in Southeast Asia, Siam's primary struggles with the West did not directly arise from the trade domain. Siam was not coerced into opening its trade, as Burma and Vietnam were. After persistently refusing to give up trade monopolies, the Siamese court finally changed its attitude toward commercial relations with the West in the late nineteenth century.

In 1855, Siam invited John Bowring, the governor of Britain's Hong Kong, for a new round of trade negotiations in Bangkok.[4] The negotiations led to the conclusion of the Treaty of Amity, Commerce, and Navigation, which reduced Siam's import duty to a fixed rate of 3 percent and allowed the import of opium and bullion duty-free. This agreement made Siam the first country in mainland Southeast Asia to establish a trade agreement with Western powers. Subsequently, Siam also entered into similar trade agreements with Japan and other Western nations.

However, opening its door from within did not exclude Siam from having conflicts with Western countries; it merely excluded Siam from conflicts based on trade. Instead, the most prevalent source of misunderstanding between Siam and the two neighboring Western powers revolved around disputes concerning territorial and sovereignty issues. These disputes primarily stemmed from the vastly different conceptions of sovereignty and territory held by Western and Siamese elites.

In contrast to the modern notion of sovereignty, which emphasizes the importance of the exclusive power of a specified entity over a fixed territory, "the sovereign of a state [in premodern Southeast Asia] was neither single nor exclusive. It was multiple and capable of being shared – one for its own ruler, another for its overlord – not in terms of divided sovereignty but rather a sovereignty of hierarchical layers."[5] Under this system, inferior kingdoms were required to demonstrate allegiance by regularly sending a tribute mission to the overlord. Additionally, they were obliged to send workforce, troops, goods, and other supplies to the overlord when required. If tributaries were received regularly, the overlord rarely intervened in a tributary's domestic business, including matters regarding succession.

It is noteworthy that the concept of hierarchical order in premodern Southeast Asia also vastly differed from the one in East Asia. While the order in historical East Asia emphasized a formal recognition of unequal status and a clear ranking,[6] the order in premodern Southeast Asia involved considerable fluidity within the hierarchical structure and constant competition to establish dominance at the top. Due to the relatively small power disparity among major regional powers, "overlords" from these superior

---

[4] Baker and Phongpaichit 2022, 49.   [5] Winichakul 2009, 88.   [6] See Kang 2010; Kang 2020.

states, traditionally consisting of Siam, Burma, and Vietnam, competed to extend their influence over small states and each other. These disputes sometimes ended with one side achieving complete victory over the other. However, it was also typical for the competition to result in the multiple overlords sharing their sovereignty over a tributary state. Some small towns at the juncture of Laos, Burma, and China today could submit to three overlords simultaneously.[7]

The phenomenon of shared sovereignty in premodern Southeast Asia was underpinned by at least two factors: one was strategic, and the other was spiritual. Strategically, the tributary kingdoms sought protection from one or more overlords for survival reasons. In some cases, survival meant seeking protection from one overlord against another. In other cases, however, survival meant seeking protection against another domestic faction. During internal disputes within a tributary court, each faction sought support and backing from a supreme overlord against the influence of the other faction.

The action of Wichaichan, Siam's heir presumptive, in 1874 is a perfect example of the survival strategy employed during internal disputes but now extending to the imperial powers. Wichaichan, nicknamed "George" after George Washington, sought support from the British consul to mediate his conflict with King Chulalongkorn (r. 1868–1910). The Siamese king had initiated economic reforms that detrimentally affected Wichaichan's revenue. Despite being unaffected by these reforms, the British sent a gunboat to the mouth of the Chao Phraya River to back Wichaichan's cause. This crisis prompted Chulalongkorn, whose thinking aligned more with Western ideas than most of Siam's old elites, to appeal to Paris and London through letters, seeking European neutrality to maintain his undivided sovereignty over Siam.[8]

The other factor undergirding the phenomenon of shared sovereignty was spiritual. As explained by Thongchai, the desire of supreme overlords to extend protection over smaller kingdoms was fueled by their aspiration to gain Buddhist merit and fulfill their religious mission of becoming spiritual kings. "In Theravada Buddhist polity of the region, the righteous kingship, the universal monarch was obliged to protect the religion from declining."[9] To fulfill this righteous mission, overlords imposed protection on smaller states. The more power the leaders wielded, the more merit they accumulated. In this sense, a submission was "unavoidable compulsory rather than voluntary."[10] Small states in premodern Southeast Asia, therefore, were rarely able to enjoy their sovereignty without being shared with the supreme overlords.

Another attribute that sprung from these political and religious differences was the lack of clear boundaries and the lack of interest in border demarcation.

---

[7] Thongchai 2009, 73.   [8] Wyatt 2003, 178.   [9] Thongchai 2009, 83.
[10] Thongchai 2009, 84.

While Europeans and East Asians regarded a boundary as a line, Southeast Asians saw it as a corridor. The territory of each town "was determined primarily by the extent of the surrounding area it could protect,"[11] leaving the areas outside the border as a corridor that belonged to no one. Sometimes, a town might have a common border that connected with another town. Still, more often than not, two towns were usually separated with some uninhabited areas or corridors in between. This meant that "a kingdom [in premodern Southeast Asia] was composed of political-territorial patches with much blank space in between."[12]

The lack of a common border between countries confused officials from the Western world in three ways. First, because the borders were unconnected, premodern Southeast Asian rulers did not find it necessary to agree on where the borderlines should be drawn. And even if the countries shared a common border, Southeast Asian countries were comfortable defining their sovereign authority independently, without the need for agreement or ratification from another country. Sovereignty could be shared.

Second, as premodern Southeast Asian states valued the actual exercise of authority over people over the control of land,[13] a piece of territory, especially those areas far from the city center, could, therefore, be given as a gift to another friendly state as a gesture of collegiality.[14] The lack of interest in controlling forest and inhabited areas was evident in how Southeast Asian states protected their borders. Local guards were only responsible for protecting border corridors that consisted of roads and places heavily used by travelers. The unused border areas were not regarded as areas under one's sovereignty and, therefore, were often left unwatched.

Finally, because lines did not strictly delimit borders, people of different countries could travel freely through the areas between frontier towns and even earn their living in these unowned corridors. Moreover, they were permitted to settle indiscriminately close to others' frontier towns without permission. Only when the two countries engaged in hostile relations would subjects be prohibited from crossing into the areas under the other's authority. This fact certainly raised a question about who was subjected to which rulers and who could and could not cross into the areas under others' authority.

The Southeast Asian understandings of boundary, territory, and sovereignty brought confusion to the colonial powers who wished to settle in mainland Southeast Asia. Sometimes, these misunderstandings turned into full-blown conflicts, such as the one between Siam and French Indochina in 1893. In contrast to the French, the British took a much gentler approach when dealing with issues surrounding the uncertainty of borders. The subsequent part of this

---

[11] Thongchai 2009, 75.   [12] Thongchai 2009, 75.   [13] Read Mead 2004, Chapters 1–2.
[14] See Thongchai 2009, Chapter 3.

section demonstrates how the territorial disputes, rooted in the differing conceptions of state, between Bangkok and London and Bangkok and Paris unfolded and how these conflicts triggered reforms on the part of Siam.

3.2.1 Great Britain: Living with the Shared Sovereignty

Siam's initial interactions with Great Britain concerning territorial matters can be traced back to the first half of the nineteenth century. During the First Anglo-Burmese War, from 1824 to 1826, Britain's East India Company assigned Captain Henry Burney to lead an envoy to Siam in 1825. The primary mission of the envoy was to discuss issues concerning the domestic affairs of the Malay states, which had informally come under British protection since the early nineteenth century. However, following Britain's triumph in the war and its subsequent acquisition of the southern region of Burma, Burney's responsibilities were expanded to address the boundary issue between Lower Burma and Siam. For decades, Siam and Britain lived with what amounted to shared sovereignty.

On the issue of the Malay states, the two countries settled the matter relatively smoothly. Burney successfully secured a commitment from Siam to abstain from sending military forces to the Malay states as long as they continued to provide tribute to the Siamese court. The matter of delineating boundaries between Lower Burma and Siam was more complicated. During negotiations, Siamese officials willingly retracted claims to border territory as a goodwill gesture. Nonetheless, Siamese officials clearly lacked interest in establishing fixed boundaries between these towns and Siam. When faced with pressure from the British, Siamese officials directed their counterparts to consult with the residents inhabiting the frontiers of these towns. Ultimately, Burney relinquished the pursuit of boundary demarcation. As a result, the language addressing the boundary in the treaty signed by both countries in 1826 was deliberately kept vague and broad. The subsequent British efforts to establish clear boundaries between Lower Burma and Siam encountered similar responses. Siamese officials consistently steered the British toward engaging with local inhabitants and officials to resolve the matter of boundary demarcation.

Siam's stance on this matter did not shift until the late nineteenth century, particularly under the reign of Chulalongkorn, who had received considerable Western education. The complexities arising from the timber industry operating along the unsettled borders of Lower Burma and the Kingdom of Lanna, a vassal state of Siam situated around the city known as Chiang Mai in present-day Thailand, forced Siam to take proactive steps. In 1874, Siam entered into a boundary agreement with British India to establish clear demarcations between Lanna and Lower Burma.

3.2.2 France: Rejecting the Shared Sovereignty

In contrast to the disputes with the British, which often concluded with uncertain outcomes favoring Siam, conflicts involving the French tended to escalate into a military one until a clear winner emerged. As the French gained control over Indochina, Siam's influence over the area, especially in Cambodia and Laos, diminished. Despite Indochina falling, Siam managed to escape France's direct control, in part because its relations with the British acted as a check on the French. Situated in the middle of Southeast Asia, Siam was treated as a buffer between the French and British colonies. Ultimately, the French and the British reached an agreement designating Siam as a buffer zone between the British and French empires.

France's initial challenge to Siam's sovereignty arose in 1863 when the French, after colonizing the southern provinces of Vietnam, sought to extend their influence into Cambodia based on Vietnam's historical rights. A French representative proposed to Norodom, the king of Cambodia, that France would safeguard Cambodia's sovereignty from any intervention by Siam. Although initially hesitant, Norodom, who had recently ascended the throne following his father's death and grappled with internal uprisings, eventually welcomed the French proposal.[15]

While the French were correct about Vietnam's historical protection of Cambodia, they overlooked the fact that Cambodia was also a tributary of Siam. Cambodia's situation perfectly exemplified the practice of shared sovereignty in premodern Southeast Asia discussed earlier. As a small state situated between the two major regional powers, Cambodia submitted to both countries to guard against the influence of each other. Factional disputes within the Cambodian court further contributed to the decision of Cambodian rulers to seek protection from both powers. Hence, when Norodom concurred with the French proposal, he did not intend to sever all ties with the Siamese court.

Upon learning about the French proposal, the Siamese court, backed by the British, immediately opposed it, asserting that Cambodia, as their contributory, should communicate with the French through Siam. Amidst the ongoing disagreement, Norodom reinforced Siamese suzerainty by entering a secret agreement with Siam. To solidify Siam's status over Cambodia, Norodom's coronation and allegiance ceremony were planned in Bangkok. However, during Norodom's journey to his coronation in Bangkok in 1864, French troops occupied Norodom's palace and hoisted the French flag atop it, prompting him to forsake the coronation in Bangkok, hastily return to his palace, and accept French protection. Despite Mongkut's humiliation, Siam persisted in negotiating with the French over shared sovereignty in Cambodia. Nevertheless, in

---

[15] Hall 1979, 790–791; Wyatt 2003, 170.

1867, Siam ultimately acknowledged the French protectorate over Cambodia in exchange for the French ceding two western Cambodian provinces to Siam.

Following the annexation of Cambodia and northern Vietnam, the French turned their attention toward Laos in the mid-1880s. The desire to establish a protectorate over Laos was driven partly by the need to counterbalance the increasing British influence in Burma and the Siamese court and partly by sympathy for the mistreated Lao people. In 1889, despite Siam's protests, Luang Prabang, one of the three Lao kingdoms, officially came under French protection.[16] Additionally, the French claimed other parts of present-day Laos. Responding to French assertiveness, Siam strengthened the authority of royal commissioners and increased military presence in those areas.[17] Tensions escalated in 1893 with the appointment of Jules Develle as French foreign minister, who advocated for more aggressive measures against Siam.

With favorable public opinion, the French mobilized more troops and demanded that Siam withdraw its forces from disputed areas. Simultaneously, they dispatched gunboats up the Chao Phraya River toward Bangkok,[18] which prompted the British to send their gunboats to Bangkok to protect their citizens and assets from potential clashes. Worrying that the British presence would make Siam more resistant to their demands, the French sent additional gunboats to the river's mouth and ultimately crossed the no-cross line. In response, the Siamese fired at the French gunboats. After a brief exchange, the two French gunboats broke through Siam's defense line.

While docked in front of the French Embassy in Bangkok,[19] the French presented nonnegotiable demands to Siam.[20] Among these, the French requested that Siam cede control of disputed areas on the eastern side of the Mekong River and grant French protégé status for Vietnamese, Laotian, and Khmer individuals in Siam. This curtailed Siam's authority over these ethnic groups, diminishing its control over the workforce. Initially resisting, Siam

---

[16] In contrast to the case of Cambodia, Luang Prabang initiated a request for French protection itself following Siam's failure to help defend the city against Haw rebels in 1886. Since the mid-1860s, groups of Chinese refugees known as Haw rebels had been causing disturbances and unrest in some regions of northern Vietnam and northern Laos. Despite receiving a warning from a French vice-consul in Luang Prabang about a potential Haw attack, Siamese troops sent to protect the city against the rebels retreated to Bangkok after successfully capturing Lao princes, leaving the town vulnerable and undefended. In the middle of the chaos, the French vice-consul stepped up to safeguard the king of Luang Prabang and his Siamese advisor. Subsequently, the French sent additional troops to Luang Prabang, contributing to the rebels' surrender.

[17] Wyatt 2003, 188.   [18] Peerapol 2012, 48–50.

[19] Wyatt 2003, 188; Peerapol 2012, 50–51; Baker and Pasuk 2022, 64.

[20] These demands included a call for Siam to (1) pay an indemnity for the clashes near the Mekong River and during the gunfire exchange at the river's mouth; (2) cede control of the disputed areas on the eastern side of the Mekong River; (3) punish officers responsible for the death of a French officer; and (4) grant French protégé status for Vietnamese, Laos, and Khmer individuals living in Siam.

yielded to French pressure, which included a port blockade. Siam's concession was partially due to inadequate support from the British, who were simultaneously negotiating with the French over the possibility of establishing Siam as a buffer state. Siam reluctantly conceded to France's demands.[21]

The French annexation of areas on the eastern side of the Mekong brought their border close to the British border in the upper Mekong River region. Due to British concerns over potential territorial disputes escalating into a broader European conflict, the two powers agreed in 1896 to establish the Mekong River as the boundary between British Burma and French Laos after six years of negotiations. The Anglo-French Convention assured Siam's sovereignty along the Chao Phraya Valley, although the exact extent of this area remained ambiguous.[22] Both nations agreed to withhold activities that established exclusive advantages over the areas along the Chao Phraya Valley. However, certain regions like the Malay Peninsula, areas near the Mekong River, and western Cambodia were deliberately excluded, suggesting the possibility for both the British and French to seek exclusive advantages within these areas. Siam later entered agreements with Britain and France to rectify the unsettling boundaries, resulting in Siam losing influence over the Malay Peninsula to the British and areas near the Mekong River and western Cambodia to the French while reclaiming some territories. Siam emerged as it is seen on the map today.[23]

While the imperial rivalry between Britain and France contributed to the survival of Siam as a state, it only partially explains the puzzle. Throughout its interactions with Western powers, Siam actively pursued a series of reforms to align with Western notions of statehood, a topic I will delve into in the next section. Not only did Siam participate in formal negotiations for boundary demarcation – the concept originally foreign to the Siamese elite – with both the British and the French,[24] but it also reformed its administrative and judicial

---

[21] The French subsequently presented a new set of demands to Siam. These included a demilitarized zone of 25 kilometers (approximately 15.5 miles) along the east bank of the Mekong River and the western region of Cambodia, where the French shall enjoy unrestricted trade rights, and control of Siam's eastern border provinces, Chanthaburi and Trat, which were used as leverage and hostages until Siam fully complied with the demands (see Wyatt 2003, 188–189). It was not until around a decade later that these two provinces eventually returned to Siam.

[22] Loos 2010, 83.

[23] In 1897, Great Britain and Siam entered into a secret agreement to prevent any third power from engaging in activities in peninsular Siam (see Wyatt 2003, 190). Similarly, Siam reached a deal with France in 1904 to ratify the boundary between Siam and Laos in a manner favorable to the French. In addition, Siam abandoned its sovereignty claim over Luang Prabang and agreed to participate in a boundary demarcation committee for the Siamese-Cambodian border in exchange for the recovery of Chanthaburi (See Hall 1979, 851). In 1907, the French and Siamese reached another agreement, clarifying their rights over specific territories. Siam agreed to cede Battambang and Siam Reap to France while receiving the territories in Laos acquired by the French in the 1904 agreement in exchange.

[24] Thongchai 2009, 94.

systems to gain Western acceptance. Finally, in 1904, the French agreed to remove the protégé status over their Asian subordinates. In 1909, the British relinquished extraterritorial rights in Siam, thereby enhancing the Siamese government's capacity to hold foreign citizens accountable and strengthen its rule over the kingdom.

3.3 Siam's Political, Economic, and Cultural Reforms

The previous section explored how geography played into Siam's ability to maintain its independence. In this section, I explore Siam's extensive reforms across political, economic, diplomatic, and cultural domains in response to the challenges posed by Western colonial powers. These reforms were crucial in shaping Siam's ability to navigate the pressures of colonialism. Without these reforms, it remains uncertain whether the French and British agreement to establish Siam as a buffer zone would have been sufficient to safeguard Siam's territorial integrity, as reflected on today's map. Furthermore, suppose Siamese rulers had not demonstrated their competency in governing the country in a manner that aligned with Western interests. In that case, it raises doubts about whether the British and French would have been confident in designating Siam as a buffer zone in the first place.

3.3.1 *The Bowring Treaty and the Beginning of Siam's Economic Reforms*

In 1855, Siam experienced a pivotal moment in its economy and subsequent modernization. This marked the year Siam entered into its first commercial agreement with the British, effectively bringing an end to the Siamese court's trade monopoly. Multiple attempts by the British to negotiate trade agreements with Siam in the early nineteenth century had faced substantial resistance from Siamese elites. The resistance, in part, stemmed from the significant contribution of trade monopolies to the income of the Siamese court and ruling elites.[25]

The Siamese court's shifting stance toward free trade can be attributed to at least two primary factors: China's defeat in the Opium Wars and the increasing gains from trade with the West. The aftermath of the Opium Wars served as a lesson to Siam about the consequences of defying British demands for free trade. Moreover, China's defeat prompted Siam to seek an alternative trading partner to replace China, which had been its predominant trade partner since the sixteenth century.[26] The West emerged as the most promising alternative. As

---

[25] The only time the two countries successfully penned a document close to being a trade deal was in 1822, when Siam agreed to guarantee British rights to trade in the Malay states of Kelantan and Terengganu without third-party interference. In exchange, the British acknowledged Siam's claims over the five northern Malay states: Kedah, Kelantan, Perlis, Terengganu, and Pattani.

[26] Kullada 2004, 25.

previously noted, Siam concluded the Bowring Treaty with the British in 1855, effectively reducing Siam's import duty and export tax and granting extraterritorial rights to British citizens, allowing them to be subject to Britain's legal jurisdiction.

Indeed, this commercial agreement initially hurt Siam's economy. After all, the long-standing warehouse monopoly had been a cornerstone of the country's financial system. However, both Mongkut and Sri Suriyawong, the Prime Minister of Southern Siam and Chancellor of the Military,[27] were confident that they could implement measures, such as expanding tax farms and extending monopolies over the domestic consumption of certain products,[28] to offset the resulting loss. Moreover, accepting the short-term setback was a more favorable option than succumbing to Western pressure, which could lead to the signing of an even more disadvantageous trade agreement and the loss of sovereignty, akin to what happened with China.

Siam's economic structure underwent a rapid transformation due to its linkage to the Western market. Junk trade experienced a sharp decline, and the influence of long-dominating Chinese business families diminished.[29] Despite the loss of some economic sectors, Sri Suriyawong, a key figure in the negotiations with Bowring, emerged as a beneficiary of this trade reconfiguration. As the proprietor of a Western-styled shipbuilding enterprise in Siam, he was better prepared to compete with British traders.[30] Benefitting from trade, he advocated for deeper integration into the global economy by expanding Siam's domestic production for the global market. However, such an expansion would require the use of free labor, which was nonexistent in Siam at that time due to the practice of slavery and unpaid labor (corvée).

Sri Suriyawong's advocacy for free labor aligned with the vision of the young king Chulalongkorn (r. 1868–1910), who ascended the throne after Mongkut's passing in 1868. Despite facing strong opposition from Siam's noble families, whose power rested in controlling unpaid labor and domestic slavery,[31] Chulalongkorn initiated a gradual plan to abolish these practices. Drastic measures were enacted toward the end of the reforms when some of the old nobles had already aged or passed away to mitigate strong objections. Implementation began in the mid-1870s, with notable steps such as shifting from compensating nobility with manpower to monetary stipends in 1877 to reduce reliance on unpaid labor. In 1905, the court enacted new legislation

---

[27] Before the administrative reforms, Siam had two prime ministerial positions: the Prime Minister of Southern Siam and the Prime Minister of Northern Siam. The Prime Minister of Southern Siam, who concurrently held the position of the Chancellor of Military, was responsible for the affairs of the southern provinces. The Prime Minister of Northern Siam, concurrently serving as the Chancellor of Interior, managed the affairs of the northern provinces.

[28] Wyatt 2003, 169.   [29] Baker and Pasuk 2022, 101.   [30] Kullada 2004, 28.

[31] The status of Siamese nobles was determined by the extent to which they were granted land and labor by the king.

emancipating all offspring born into slavery and reducing freedom-price caps and age limits. By the turn of the twentieth century, the practices of corvée and domestic slavery came to an end, paving the way for a free labor force essential for producing agricultural products for the global market.

3.3.2 Strengthening the Centralized Power: Siam's Political Reforms

Despite its efforts to accommodate Western interests in free trade, Siam continued to face pressure from Western powers, particularly concerning territorial boundaries, as already discussed, and its outdated governance and justice systems. After all, Siam was forced to forgo its exterritorial rights to all trade partners bound by treaties. Marked as the "other" by the West, Siam found itself subjected to harsh comparisons with the standards of civilization. If it persisted in upholding its traditional practices, Siam would inevitably remain subordinate to Western nations and could inadvertently invite Western interventions, often justified to promote progress and civilization.

In response to the pressure from the West, Siamese rulers initiated a comprehensive project to transform Siam into a modern nation-state, where a centralized government emerged as the authority with complete control over its territory. These reforms included the creation of function-based ministries, a meritocracy-based bureaucratic system, a tax collection system, and legal reforms inspired by Western practices. Whether these changes were directly prompted by Western pressure or emerged as an indigenous, creative response to foreign influences continues to be a subject of ongoing debate.[32] Nevertheless, it is not an exaggeration to argue that these transformative changes, at times undertaken in the face of political resistance, played a vital role in establishing the foundation of modern-day Thailand.

The first area of reform focused on establishing a new tax collection system. In 1873, Chulalongkorn established the Treasury Department to centralize the administration of tax collection and export and import duties under the direct control of the Siamese court. This marked a departure from the previous tax farming system, in which designated individuals, typically nobles, were responsible for collecting taxes on behalf of the state. The former system had encouraged issues of corruption and prevented the central administration from collecting the appropriate amount of taxes.

In the subsequent year, Chulalongkorn intensified his efforts to further consolidate the court's authority by establishing two new administrative bodies – the Council of State and the Privy Council – with himself as the leader of both councils. These two councils, comprised of princes and nobles handpicked by Chulalongkorn, were entrusted with the task of enacting

---

[32] Rajchagool 1994, 82.

written legislation – a novel practice in Siam. The establishment of these two institutions posed a further threat to the positions of old nobles, who found themselves with diminished influence over the governance of the state.[33]

Among those who vehemently objected to the administrative reforms were Sri Suriyawong, Chulalongkorn's former regent, who had aligned with him on the creation of free labor, and Wichaichan, the son of Mongkut's brother. Both were financially and politically affected by the establishment of the Council of State, the Privy Council, and particularly the Treasury Department. Wichaichan resisted by mobilizing military forces within his palace, leading to a confrontation between him and Chulalongkorn, known as the Front Palace Crisis, in 1874. As a close friend of the British consul in Bangkok at that time, Wichaichan sought refuge at the British consulate and requested British mediation. Concerned about Western intervention, Chulalongkorn eventually decelerated his reform efforts, which he later resumed when Sri Suriyawong, Wichaichan, and other old elites aged or passed away between 1882 and 1888.[34]

Within this window of limited opportunity, Chulalongkorn directed his attention toward less sensitive educational reforms. These included establishing schools in Bangkok and sending royal and noble sons to study in foreign countries. In 1872, around twenty royal family members began their education in Singapore, with the most accomplished later selected by Chulalongkorn to continue studies in London.[35] Over subsequent years, more members of the royal family, primarily Chulalongkorn's sons, and elite sons were sent to various European countries to pursue studies across multiple disciplines. The objective was to acquire Western knowledge and bring Siam on par with the Western nations.

After a decade of slow-paced reforms, Chulalongkorn resumed his reform agenda when most of what he referred to as "ancient" nobles either retired or passed away. In 1888, Chulalongkorn delivered a speech on reforms, criticizing the inefficiency of Siam's administrative and judicial systems. In 1892, he established a council of ministers, with each minister tasked with responsibility over specific issues ranging from defense to finance to transportation. These ministerial positions were primarily occupied by Chulalongkorn's brothers and half brothers, who shared his vision of reforms. Additionally, he recruited foreign advisors to advise the operations of each ministry. For Chulalongkorn, these foreign advisors not only brought expertise on Western knowledge but also provided "ready-made textbooks" to assist Siam in navigating the threat of colonization.[36] Consequently, as tensions with the French over the areas on the

---

[33] Sattayanurak 1995, 132–134. [34] Wyatt 2003, 183. [35] Loos 2016, 21.
[36] Baker and Pasuk 2022, 76.

east bank of the Mekong escalated, the number of these foreign advisors increased.

Once the consolidation of the central administrative system was complete, the next step targeted the consolidation of the court's authority over other parts of Siam. Starting in 1893, the newly established Ministry of Interior appointed officers from Bangkok to replace semi-hereditary governing families holding administrative offices outside of Bangkok. For tributary states, such as Lanna, the Issan Plateau, and the south, commissioners, often royal princes, were sent to administer these regions and redirect tax revenues to the treasury in Bangkok. Following Britain's colonial practices, local elites, who had ruled these regions, were offered fancy titles and generous allowances.[37] This reform gradually detached local elites from administrative roles, enhancing the centralization of the Siamese court's authority over its territory.

In parallel with the administrative reforms, Siam began revolutionizing its justice system to eliminate the grounds for Western extraterritorial rights. Prince Ratchaburi, upon returning from Oxford, led the task of judicial reforms. Although he personally favored the common law system, Ratchaburi yielded to others' persuasion for the codified law approach, deemed more impressive to foreigners. By 1897, Ratchaburi founded a law school and began rewriting Siam's Criminal Procedure Code. The drafting committee comprised not only Siamese experts but also individuals from France, Britain, and Japan. They extensively studied legal codes from ten modernized countries, including Great Britain, India, and Japan, to inform the revision.[38]

Alongside the administrative and judicial reforms, the Siamese court also implemented a collective identity promotion scheme to foster shared awareness among people of different races. The absence of collective identity encouraged numerous Siamese populations to identify themselves as Lao or Khmer – races that warranted French protégé status – instead of Siamese to avoid corvée or tax payment to Siam.[39] Furthermore, the lack of a collective identity among the Siamese was precisely why the French claimed Siam's rule over Laos and Cambodia was unjust. To the French, Siamese, Lao, and Khmer were distinct races, and it was the French's responsibility to liberate the Lao and Khmer from Siam's oppression.

To foster a collective identity in Siam, the Siamese began giving Sanskrit names to the newly formed provinces – a tradition that continues today. Previously, provinces were named based on the majority race and ethnicity, such as Lao or Malay. Additionally, the commissioners overseeing the outlying provinces and former tributaries were instructed to downplay distinctions between Siamese and other races, particularly in discussions

---

[37] Baker and Pasuk 2022, 60–61.   [38] Baker and Pasuk 2022, 73.   [39] Wyatt 2003, 190.

with foreigners.[40] Finally, in 1913, the Siamese government passed the Nationality Act, allowing individuals born within Siam's borders to claim Siamese nationality, ending the issue of unclear nationality.

These transformations, along with changing international factors, contributed significantly to the concluding agreements with the British and French at the beginning of the twentieth century that resolved the issue of extraterritoriality. In 1907, Siam ceded three provinces in western Cambodia to France in exchange for the French abandoning their jurisdiction claims over their Asian subjects. Two years later, Siam gave four Malay states to Britain in exchange for the British conceding extraterritorial claims in Siam. From this point onward, the boundary of the Siamese state became fixed. Siam successfully transformed into a modern nation-state, demonstrating its capacity to govern and uphold territorial integrity. In a way, it won "grudging acceptance of its right to self-administration within its newly constricted, Western-defined borders."[41]

3.3.3 The Quest for Westernization (Civilization): Siam's Cultural Reforms

Alongside political and economic reforms, Siamese society also underwent significant cultural transformations. These changes included a transition toward adopting Western scientific methods of inquiry, alterations in royal household etiquette and daily routines, and changes in clothing styles. While these cultural changes may not have been the sole determinants of Siam's ability to resist colonialism, they played a role in facilitating interactions between Siam and the Western powers. At the very least, Westernization among Siamese elites helped mitigate potential misunderstandings stemming from cultural differences, as seen in the case of the court of Ava's interaction with the British.

While Siam's pursuit of Westernization became more pronounced following the signing of the Bowring Treaty and subsequent agreements with other countries, signs of a shift toward Western modes of thinking among Siamese elites had already been apparent before that time. The catalyst of this changing attitude toward Westernization was a familiar event: China's defeat in the

---

[40] In private, however, they were told to maintain the ethnic categorization as Siamese officials believed that people from different ethnicities and classes possessed different capacities to civilize and progress. Siam's officials classified its population into three broad tiers. The lowest tier comprised hill peoples perceived as beyond the capacity to progress. The middle tier consisted of people in lowland agricultural communities deemed economically valuable but simple-minded. At the top stood princes and governing elites, who possessed the capacity to civilize and progress, thus qualifying to dominate others. Unfortunately, remnants of this people stratification still endure in modern Thai society, casting some minor frictions among people of different regions (see Baker and Pasuk 2022, 72).

[41] Harrison 2010, 13.

Opium Wars. Witnessing the decline of Asia's traditional powerhouse, prominent Siamese elites like Mongkut and Sri Suriyawong recognized the necessity to "acquire knowledge about the Western people to be prepared for future eventualities."[42]

In his quest for Western knowledge, Mongkut sought guidance from European missionaries before ascending to the throne in 1851. While ordained as a monk, Mongkut dedicated himself to studying Western modes of inquiry and honing his proficiency in Western languages.[43] Among the various subjects he delved into, science, particularly astronomy, became his expertise. Mongkut did not keep his remarkable skill in the field a secret. Quite the opposite, he made efforts to showcase his expertise to garner respect among Western representatives. For example, in 1868, he invited British and French colonial officers to attend an eclipse-viewing event, which he had accurately predicted even though the viewing location ultimately resulted in him contracting malaria and an untimely death.

As Siam embraced Westernization, it distanced itself from the Chinese-led international order. At the beginning of Mongkut's reign, Siam still observed Sinicized rituals of tributary and investiture. For instance, during a period of domestic disorder, Mongkut wore a Chinese robe, took a picture, and sent it, along with a tribute mission to China to gain legitimacy to rule. Unfortunately, the mission never reached the Chinese emperor due to rebel activities within China, prompting Mongkut to abandon the practices of investiture and tributary altogether. This realization of China's diminishing power occurred relatively earlier than in other kingdoms in Southeast Asia, as evidenced by the Ava court's request for Chinese protection against Great Britain as late as the 1870s.

The shift toward Westernization became significantly more pronounced and accelerated during the rule of Mongkut's son, Chulalongkorn. Guided by his father, Chulalongkorn received a Western-style education from European teachers, particularly British teachers, who were hired to educate the young princes in the palace. By the time Chulalongkorn ascended to the throne in 1868, he was already well-equipped with Western knowledge, Western cultures, and European languages. However, due to his young age, the initial years of his rule were heavily overlaid by Sri Suriyawong, who acted as his regent. His revolutionary mindset only began to shine after his second coronation in 1873.

Upon assuming full regal authority, Chulalongkorn wasted no more time. One of his first acts was the abolition of the practice of prostration.[44] In the past, individuals of lower social status were required to prostrate themselves before those of higher rank, a custom prominent in the interactions between the king and his subjects and between nobles and their subordinates. Chulalongkorn saw

---

[42] Quoted in Kittiarsa 2010, 65.   [43] Pattana 2010, 65.   [44] Wyatt 2003, 177–178.

this custom as a form of oppression where "the inferior had to suffer the fatigue of prostration in order to honor the superior."[45] For the first time, Chulalongkorn's audience stood and bowed to him instead of lying low on the ground, reflecting a symbolic change in the power dynamics within the Siamese society.

The decision to abolish the practice of prostration not only reflected Chulalongkorn's beliefs about social norms but also served as an instrument to bridge the cultural gap between Eastern and Western traditions. Chulalongkorn intended for Westerners to perceive Siam as civilized, thereby positioning the country on par with the European powers. By eliminating these seemingly "backward" practices, Siam could potentially forestall conflicts arising from disparities in cultural etiquette, as demonstrated in the Ava Kingdom-Great Britain "shoe question" incident. In the 1870s, a British representative in Mandalay refused to remove his shoes before an audience with King Mindon of Ava, thus violating a display of respect in the Eastern tradition. As a result, the British representative was barred from ever entering the Ava court, thereby disrupting diplomatic ties between Ava and Britain.[46]

In addition to transforming social etiquette to align with Western values, Chulalongkorn aspired for the new generation of Siamese officials to genuinely experience Western society and education, a path he had not taken. The goal was to get Siamese as civilized as Westerners while maintaining the Siamese identity. The emphasis on preserving their Siamese identity reflected Chulalongkorn's belief in the ability of the Siamese to selectively adopt favorable elements from other cultures and seamlessly incorporate them where appropriate.[47] In conversations with his sons, Chulalongkorn emphasized how education could get Siam on par with the Westerners:[48]

[European] are no different from us; they are humans, just as we are. We must acknowledge our shared humanity and reject any sense of inferiority based on birth. We are misjudged because of our lack of knowledge. It is heartening, however, that [the Europeans] do not withhold wisdom from us. If we wish to know something, we can pursue the knowledge just as they can. All that is required is an unwavering dedication to be outstanding, just as they are.

The ultimate objective of becoming civilized was for Siam to gain Western recognition as an equal partner and to establish itself on the global civilizational map. After all, political and cultural transformations were deemed futile without acknowledgment from foreign entities. Siamese students, educated abroad, once again played a pivotal role in this endeavor. Their proficiency in Western languages and understanding of Western worldview allowed direct communication with Western representatives, setting Siam apart from other Southeast

---

[45] Kullada 2004, 44.   [46] Hall 1979, 763–770.   [47] Harrison 2010, 15.
[48] Quoted in Krairiksh 2018.

Asian countries like the Ava Kingdom, whose king relied on translators for communication.

Siamese students not only facilitated diplomatic communication at home but also played a key role in establishing Siam's diplomatic channels abroad, especially in Europe. In 1882, Chulalongkorn appointed former student Prince Prisdang as Siam's first resident envoy extraordinaire to Europe. Prisdang oversaw Siam's relations with major European countries and the United States, enabling direct engagement with metropoles and bypassing communication with colonial officers who often held location-specific interests distinct from those officials in the capital cities. This strategic move allowed Siam to cultivate more consistent relations with Western countries, avoiding reliance on unpaid European honorary consular officials who might misrepresent Siam's interests or special envoys dispatched only during crises.

Beyond establishing consistent communication, Siamese representatives, like Prisdang, were directed to present Siam as a civilized nation. Educated in London, fluent in English, and familiar with British culture, Prisdang regularly socialized and networked with European heads of state and royalty. He engaged in adept diplomacy, mastering the nuances of negotiation with each European nation. For instance, he understood that the French "would always demand a quid pro quo in their negotiations with Siam and that international law and diplomacy might appear 'universal' but consistently benefited its European progenitors."[49] Thus, for Siam to achieve its goals, concessions might be necessary. For instance, when attempting to revise Siam's alcohol treaties with European partners and join the Universal Postal Union and International Telegraphic Union, Prisdang navigated a French demand for Siam to hire Frenchmen for the telegraphic line between Bangkok and Saigon. Complying with this demand allowed Siam to revise its alcohol treaties and join the Universal Postal Union in 1884 and the International Telegraphic Union in 1885,[50] making it the second Asian country, after Japan, to participate in Western-led international networks.

With Siam recognized as a nation, the next step was to introduce the Siamese king as a legitimate and civilized ruler to the world. In 1897, Chulalongkorn undertook a nine-month state visit across several European countries, including Italy, Switzerland, Austria-Hungary, Russia, Sweden, Denmark, England, Belgium, Germany, the Netherlands, France, and Spain. However, this ambitious journey faced initial objections from both the British and French governments. Britain's reluctance was rooted in concerns that the hosting of Chulalongkorn could cause potential conflicts with France, as they had signed an agreement designating Siam as a buffer state.[51] In France, colonial expansionists and journalists fueled hesitancy by spreading reports of clashes

---

[49] Loos 2016, 35.   [50] Loos 2016, 35.   [51] Jeshurun 1970.

between Siamese and French troops near the Mekong River. They also alleged that Siamese individuals had attacked villages within the French protectorate and killed a priest, a crime that justified the intervention in Vietnam.[52] Despite these challenges, with Tsar Nicholas II's assistance,[53] Chulalongkorn successfully visited every country on the itinerary and met with each head of state.

Chulalongkorn's journey to Europe in 1897, as observed by a French colonial minister, aimed to convey "the impression that the kingdom of Siam, whose sovereign [had] been received in the manner due to a European head of state, [was] a civilized country which should be treated like a European power."[54] At the dawn of the twentieth century, a British postcard featured a photograph of Chulalongkorn alongside other reigning monarchs from Europe, Japan, China, and Servia – all dressed in Western-style military uniforms. While Siam may not have been considered an equal partner yet and was still seen as a secondary power, the evidence suggested that it was, at the very least, included within the semi-inner circle of the world's ruling monarch. Siam's effort to establish itself on the global civilizational map had succeeded.

3.4 Conclusion

This chapter has examined how Siam successfully avoided colonialism while its neighboring countries succumbed to this fate. Despite a debate on the relative importance of external factors versus internal reforms in Siam's colonial evasion, I argue that these two factors are interdependent. Without the synergy of both external factors, such as Siam's geography and British–French strategic competition, and Siam's comprehensive political and economic reforms, it remains uncertain whether Siam would have successfully steered clear of colonization. After all, Siam was not immune to pressures exerted by Western powers like the British, who appeared to accept looser conceptions of sovereignty, and the French, who engaged in conflicts with Siam to increase their influence in Laos and Cambodia.

Despite these pressures, Siam did not fall under the direct control of either the French or the British, in part because of its geographical location. Situated at the heart of mainland Southeast Asia, Siam functioned as a natural buffer for the British and French empires, which initially approached Southeast Asia from its rim. While the two Western powers attempted to exert influence over Siam, they also carefully avoided a clash with each other, recognizing the potential for a larger conflict in Europe. Being situated in the center also meant that Siam had the luxury of more time than its neighboring countries to prepare

---

[52] Quoted in Naksuk 2022. [53] For more detail, see Posrithong 2009–2010; Phiramontri 2016.
[54] Quoted in Baker and Pasuk 2022, 77.

itself for such eventualities. The combination of geography, Siam's strategic concessions, and Britain's and France's own interests in avoiding a clash provided Siam with some breathing room, enough for it to actively devise strategies to avoid its colonial fate.

However, Siam's triumph over colonial pressures was not solely contingent on external dynamics. Internal transformations, spanning political, economic, and cultural spheres, played a crucial role. Economic reforms demonstrated Siam's openness to Western commercial interests, while administrative and judicial reforms signaled an intent to be a "responsible holder," aligning with Western practices. Without these reforms, it remains uncertain whether the British and French would have been confident in leaving the Chao Phraya River Valley under the rule of the Siamese court and designating Siam as a buffer state. It was these reforms that contributed to Siam's resilience against colonial encroachment and gave rise to the modern state of Thailand as seen today.

4 The Russo-Japanese War, 1904–1905

Scott Wolford

Contemporaries quickly recognized the significance of the Russo-Japanese War.[1*] For eighteen months in 1904 and 1905, two major powers – a vigorous, industrializing upstart and an aging dynastic empire – waged a large-scale interimperial war on the territory of an even older empire bottoming out after two centuries of decline. Japan's unexpected military victory secured grudging membership in the great power club (Chapter 6) and spheres of influence in Korea and northeast China. It also captured the imaginations of Chinese reformers[2] and revolutionaries,[3] inspired Indian independence activists,[4] and, by cementing Japan's position in Manchuria, posed the first of several challenges to American interests in the Asia-Pacific. Ground combat, which saw battles of historic scale and destructiveness, also offered a prescient glimpse of modern warfare.[5] Yet well over a century later, IR scholars underestimate what we can learn from the Russo-Japanese War, thanks to its occurrence a decade before World War I and, perhaps more significantly, outside the European imperial core.

International relations scholars are generally familiar with the war's origins. Russia attempted to boost its military power in northeastern China, which threatened Japan's imperial project in Korea. Japan then attacked to prevent the growth of Russian power in the region after the latter dismissed the former's threats to address the problem with war. But the Russo-Japanese War makes additional contributions to the modeling dialogue between the theory of war and the historical record.[6] The modern theory of war understands the outbreak,

---

[1] * Thanks to Terry Chapman, Andrew Coe, Alexis Dudden, David Fields, Steph Haggard, Dave Kang, Amy King, and Harrison Wagner for helpful comments and suggestions, and to Crown & Anchor Pub, Lazarus Brewing II, Pinthouse Pizza, and Workhorse Bar in Austin, Zhang Men Brewery in Kaohsiung, Lab Gastropub in Los Angeles, Bravo Beer and GBA in Taichung, as well as Jup Jup Bikini Café Bar and Zhang Men Brewing in Taipei, for inspiring work environments.
[2] Esherick 2012, 3; Ichiko 1980.   [3] Gasster 1980, 484–489.   [4] Jacob 2017, 65–67.
[5] See Kowner 2006; Paine 2017, 50.
[6] On "modeling dialogues" in general, see Myerson 1992 and in IR, see Powell 1999, 24–29.

prosecution, and termination of war as a bargaining process.⁷ First, fighting is wasteful in terms of death, displacement, and destruction, which creates incentives to avoid or end it. Second, opponents choose fighting over negotiations when some bargaining friction, like incentives to renege or disagreement about relative power, stands in the way of a cost-saving settlement. Third, belligerents make peace once fighting eliminates that friction, rendering commitments credible by stabilizing the distribution of power⁸ and/or resolving uncertainty about the relative attractiveness of fighting to the finish.⁹ As a result, wars typically end before one side's elimination, just as disputes are typically resolved without fighting. Explaining how war begins requires identifying what prevents states from resolving disputes with other methods, like peaceful negotiations, that they know to be cheaper than fighting. Explaining how war ends requires showing how fighting solves these bargaining problems, making settlement possible where it wasn't beforehand.

After describing the course of the Russo-Japanese War from the imperial competition as its heart to crisis diplomacy and military campaigns to wartime diplomacy and termination, I discuss its place in the modeling dialogue between history and the modern theory of war. First, Russia's dismissals of Japan's threats to fight show how uncertainty about the chances of preventive war can lead a state to try to increase its power and bring about just such a conflict. This insight also identifies a means by which fighting can make commitments credible that weren't beforehand – that is, disabusing a rising side of its optimism about the declining side's willingness to fight – and facilitate war termination short of one side's total defeat. Second, the modern theory of war can resolve a puzzle related to the discrepancy between Japan's impressive military performance and its disappointing gains in the Treaty of Portsmouth. Japan dominated the seas and defeated the Russian army in the field, but thanks to disparities in access to credit provided by the other great powers, Russia could fund military defeats much longer than Japan could pay for victories, giving the former an advantage in a longer war. The Treaty of Portsmouth reflected beliefs about the *future* course of fighting, not just the war to that point. Next, I argue that the outcome of the Russo-Japanese War is a proximate cause of World War I, showing how Germany's infamous Schlieffen Plan was a response to Russian defeat in 1905 and the still-more-infamous – and casually critical – "blank check" given to Austria in 1914 was a response to Russian recovery from that same defeat. I close with an argument

---

⁷ Wagner 2007, Chapter 4; Thomas Schelling wrote that wars are "essentially bargaining situations" (1960, 5), and that's great. It is! But it took decades of advances in noncooperative game theory and a recognition that war is mutually costly to get us to the point of using Schelling's insight to say more than "Hey, bargaining!" Facile assertions of some IR scholars aside, it's not the case that "[i]t all goes back to Schelling."
⁸ For example, Leventoğlu and Slantchev 2007. ⁹ Filson and Werner 2002.

that Japan's rise helps explain one of the enduring puzzles of the early twentieth century: how a long era of great power peace and relatively limited conflicts gave way to decades of total war and a fundamental reordering of international relations.

4.1 Overview

The crisis that escalated to war in 1904 grew out of two previous conflicts, themselves products of Qing decline and interimperial rivalry. First, Japan's 1895 victory in the First Sino-Japanese War secured influence in Korea against looming Russian encroachment.[10] China's forced recognition of Korean independence and neutrality pulled the latter out of the Tributary System[11] and into a set of nominally European imperial legal forms Japan exploited as part of its Meiji reform project.[12] Japan also captured the Liaodong Peninsula, but a Russo-German-French threat of war forced its return to China.[13] Over the next three years, Russia exploited the Liaodong Retrocession to extend its own empire, securing twenty-five-year leases on Liaodong and Port Arthur, as well as rights to build the Chinese Eastern Railway (CER), which would link Port Arthur to the Trans-Siberian Railway.[14] Second, under cover of the multilateral Boxer Intervention, Russia invaded and occupied three Manchurian provinces in 1900, ostensibly to protect the CER from Boxer attack. After signing the Boxer Protocol with the Qing empire in 1901, Russia promised to withdraw by 1902, so long as the railway remained secure. This qualification only opened the door to sustained Russian presence; allegations of Qing weakness would allow Russia to stay in Manchuria indefinitely, honoring the letter but violating the spirit of the agreement. Indeed, by 1903 Russians were collecting customs duties at Beijing's port of Tianjin,[15] leading Japan to infer that Russia intended to stay in Manchuria, much as it had in other parts of China, like the Ili Valley, that Russia had peeled off in recent decades.[16]

Russian consolidation in Manchuria promised deeper economic penetration and faster military deployments, both of which threatened Japan's imperial interests in Korea.[17] For Prime Minister Katsura Tarō and Foreign Minister Komura Jutarō, "the root of the problem lay in the fact that neither [Japan nor Russia] could allow either Korea or Manchuria to fall into the hands of the other."[18] Japan pursued a Russian promise to respect spheres of interest, making a series of proposals that culminated on January 13, 1904, with a generous offer of Manchuria for Russia and Korea for Japan.[19] Such a free hand in Korea would've allowed Japan to consolidate its position against future

---

[10] See Park 2020b. [11] See Kang 2010; Lee 2017. [12] Park 2020b; Dudden 2020, 189.
[13] See Zachmann 2006. [14] Paine 1996, 186, 220, 309. [15] Paine 1996, 212, 220.
[16] Kim 2004; Paine 1996, 110; White 1964, 118. [17] Katō 2007, 101–102.
[18] White 1964, 100. [19] See Koda 2005, 24–25.

Russian encroachments, maintaining the regional balance of power by pouring troops into Korea yet avoiding the need to fight.

Yet Russia effectively ignored these proposals, bolstering its military and civilian presences in Korea, securing a lease to the port of Yongampo,[20] and sending a half-hearted response through British and French intermediaries that arrived in Tokyo only after Japan had decided to fight.[21] Throughout the crisis, Tsar Nicholas II's advisors insisted that Japan wouldn't go to war, even after Japan withdrew its ambassador to Russia on February 6, 1904, with an announced intention "to take such independent action [read: war] as ... necessary to defend [its] menaced position."[22] Yet Russia's Viceroy to the Far East insisted that Japan was "bluffing," even after observing signs of mobilization in Tokyo and hearing from Japan's Foreign Ministry that its "patience had been exhausted."[23] Attempts at compromise rebuffed, Japan opened hostilities on February 8 with a naval attack on Port Arthur, several hours before the Russian government received the declaration of war.[24] Early naval efforts to secure supremacy in the Yellow Sea were indecisive, leading Japan to besiege Port Arthur at the tip of the Liaodong Peninsula. A sizable Japanese force also landed at Incheon on the western Korean peninsula, from where it would cross into Manchuria to complete the encirclement of the port.

Russian forces played defense, attempting to break the siege and, failing that, to hold the line until reinforcements could arrive from European Russia. One naval breakout attempt led to the August 10 Battle of the Yellow Sea,[25] during which the Japanese Navy sank several Russian ships, including the First Pacific Squadron's flagship. These early naval losses prompted Russia to redeploy its Baltic Fleet all the way from the eponymous sea.[26] It wouldn't set sail until mid-October, and by the time it arrived the following spring, Japan's supremacy in the Yellow Sea forced the Russians, running low on supplies and needing maintenance after their long journey, to make a desperate – and fateful – northward dash between Korea and Japan toward Vladivostok. On land, Japan's victory at the Battle of Mukden in April and May 1905 severed the CER's links to Liaodong, shattered Russia's Manchurian Army, and forced a Russian retreat into northern Manchuria. And with the Tsar diverting reserves to deal with revolution at home, reinforcements weren't forthcoming. Yet Japanese forces, at the limit of their supply chains and reeling from heavy

---

[20] White 1964, 104. [21] Nish 1985, 222. [22] White 1964, 128. [23] Connaughton 2004, 24.
[24] This dismissal of the legal niceties of war notwithstanding, Japan risked its opening campaign by refusing to fire on Russian ships at Incheon because of proximity to the ships of neutral powers (Connaughton 2004, 27–30; Wolford 2019a, 807).
[25] See Koda 2005, 30.
[26] You read that right. *All the way* from the Baltic Sea to the Yellow Sea, which meant that the battleships too large for the Suez Canal had to sail around the Cape of Good Hope. That's a historically long way to travel just to get your ass kicked.

casualties, halted their pursuit of retreating Tsarist formations. Major land campaigning came to an end, and Japan – stretched to its military and financial limits – asked the United States for mediation.[27]

Later that month, Russia's long-traveled Baltic Fleet, rechristened the Second and Third Pacific Squadrons, met the Japanese Combined Fleet in the waters between Korea and Japan. In the Battle of the Tsushima Strait, which took place over May 27–28, 1905, Japan effectively annihilated the Tsar's navy.[28] Japan was now supreme in Korea, southern Manchuria, and the Yellow Sea, but the final act of the war played out only on July 8. At American President Theodore Roosevelt's suggestion, Japan landed troops on Sakhalin Island, hoping that a direct threat to Russian territory would force the Tsar to negotiate.[29] Russia agreed to peace talks three days later, and formal negotiations began the following month in – and with the good offices of – the United States.

The Russo-Japanese War lasted eighteen months, which is about five months longer than the mean post-Napoleonic interstate war and a year longer than the median.[30] It killed tens of thousands on the battlefield, came close to bankrupting Japan, forced Prime Minister Katsura Tarō from office, and nearly toppled the Tsar. Land and naval campaigns also disrupted the lives and livelihoods of the Chinese and Korean populations unlucky enough to have a war fought near their homes. The Treaty of Portsmouth, signed on September 5, 1905, recognized Japanese dominance in Korea, transferred the Russian lease on the Liaodong Peninsula to Japan, reduced Russia's sphere of influence to northern Manchuria, and divided Sakhalin Island between the two belligerents. Japan secured its Korean flank and gained in Manchuria and Sakhalin, while Russia retained more than its battlefield performance would warrant. Yet terms like these weren't just available but *explicitly proposed* during prewar bargaining! Both belligerents would've been better off reaching that same deal without all the death and destruction, Russia neither defanged nor (from the Tsar's perspective) liberalized, and Japan preponderant in Northeast Asia but less indebted. Yet Japan and Russia, reeling from the social, economic, and political costs of war,[31] could look back on such forgone settlements with only regret.[32]

---

[27] Paine 2017, 69. [28] See Koda 2005, 32–36. [29] Connaughton 2004, 343.
[30] Calculations conducted with data from Sarkees and Wayman 2010.
[31] Jacob 2017, 47–55, 74–77.
[32] The *existence* of deadweight losses, not their size, creates ex post regret. Had the same outcome been available for free, belligerents hoping to minimize death, destruction, and displacement would regret not reaching it before the war (Fearon 1995). Victory is great, but unless it generates private benefits that can't come from peaceful transfers, it's still inefficient.

4.2 Outbreak

Why did Japan and Russia go to war in 1904, only to end eighteen months of bloodletting on terms they'd considered beforehand? Streich and Levy argue that two bargaining frictions – a commitment problem and an information problem – stood in the way of a war-averting bargain.[33] First, Russia couldn't credibly commit not to undermine Japan's position in Korea after completing the China Eastern Railway, which encouraged Japan to attack before power could shift further against it.[34] Indeed, Japan's "operating principle" was that "time was on the side of Russia," whose ability to project power into the region would only grow with the CER's completion.[35] Second, the strategic setting prevented a credible revelation of Japan's privately known willingness to go to war.[36] A heavy dose of anti-Asian racism,[37] which fed into the popular view of Japan as an inferior military power,[38] as well as an awareness of incentives to dissemble during crisis bargaining, led Russia to dismiss Japan's threats as bluffs. Streich and Levy maintain that this information problem provides a causal sufficiency for the Russo-Japanese War that the commitment problem lacks, explaining why Russia refused to make concessions even as Japan's threats of war turned out to be genuine.[39] With cheap-talk diplomacy exhausted, Japan used war to change Russian beliefs about its military prowess and, as a result, what it required in lieu of war.

Streich and Levy's reasoning implies that accurate beliefs would've led Russia to accept Japan's proposed war-averting settlement. But this leaves open the question of why Russia would entrench in southern Manchuria in the first place if, in this counterfactual world, it knew that Japan would use war to stop it. First-generation crisis bargaining models show that sufficiently large and rapid prospective shifts in power can cause war,[40] but second-generation models recognize that states typically *choose* how much power to pursue. And if certain decisions will provoke a costly war, states have strong incentives *not* to take them.[41] Indeed, prospective shifts in power that cause preventive wars, from the Austrian plan to dismember Serbia in 1914, which drew Russia into

---

[33] Streich and Levy 2016. [34] See Powell 2006.
[35] White 1964, 125; Also consistent with the commitment problem was Russia's willingness to entertain foreign proposals of good offices, thereby further delaying a resolution, while Japan was less patient (Nish 1985, 222); rising powers see only benefits from dragging out negotiations, while declining powers want to stabilize the distribution of power quickly. Emphasizing Japan's view that Russian power would only grow if diplomacy continued, White (1964, 146) notes that "[i]t is ... a factor of the greatest military significance that this railway was then unfinished and single-tracked, and that its services were still inefficiently organized."
[36] See also Fearon 1995, 398–400. [37] See Koda 2005, 37.
[38] Streich and Levy 2016, 501–503. [39] Streich and Levy 2016, 508.
[40] For example, Powell 2006.
[41] A reader might say: "But states can never credibly promise to limit their power!" That reader would be wrong. Consider Germany's release of conscript classes during the Moroccan Crises of 1905 and 1911, which directly limited its military power ahead of potential clashes with

the July Crisis,[42] to the suspected (yet abandoned) Iraqi pursuit of weapons of mass destruction that prompted American invasion in 2003,[43] are often conscious policy choices. Any explanation of why prospective shifts in power – of which power transitions, like the one occasioned by China's return to great power status, are a special case – cause war must reckon with this observation.

Why do states pursue increased power only to provoke preventive wars they'll ultimately regret fighting? Second-generation crisis bargaining models answer this question by invoking leadership change,[44] the challenges of arming against multiple enemies,[45] and secret arming.[46] The Russo-Japanese War offers an additional solution to this puzzle: The rising side may simply doubt the credibility of the declining side's threat of preventive war. In 1904, Russia's inaccurate beliefs about Japan's willingness to fight made the scheme to build railways in Manchuria attractive in the first place.[47] Yes, the CER portended a shift in relative power at Japan's expense, but if Japan wouldn't push back, why not forge ahead? Information and commitment problems rarely need each other to bring war about.[48] But the Russo-Japanese War is a case in which one bargaining problem depends on the other: absent uncertainty about Japan's willingness to fight, building the CER made no sense, and uncertainty about Japan's willingness to fight was irrelevant absent an opportunity for Russia to entrench itself in Manchuria. Contra Streich and Levy, information and commitment problems were individually insufficient but jointly sufficient to cause war in 1904.[49] Stated in terms of the modeling dialogue, the Russo-Japanese War shows how wars caused by commitment problems result not only from (a) sufficiently large and rapid shifts in power, as given by the first-generation account[50] but also (b) whatever stands in the way of states limiting those shifts in power – in this case, uncertainty about whether a declining side will launch a preventive war.

4.3 Termination

Why did the Russo-Japanese War end *when* it did, with both belligerents still standing, and *how* it did, with Japan securing less than its military performance warranted? In the modern theory of war, politics doesn't stop once the shooting

---

France and made for effective de-escalation (see Stevenson 1997). See, inter alia, Chadefaux 2011; Debs and Monteiro 2014; Fearon 1995, 406–407.

[42] Wolford 2019b, ch. 4. [43] Debs and Monteiro 2014. [44] Wu et al. 2021.
[45] Chadefaux 2011, 243–244. [46] Debs and Monteiro 2014.
[47] Completion of the CER also entailed commercial benefits, and these opportunity costs of peace might represent a "costly peace" explanation for the war (Coe 2011), provided Russia couldn't have been compensated from the benefits of any peaceful settlement for not completing the CER. I'm grateful(ish) to Andrew Coe for this point.
[48] See Wolford, Reiter and Carrubba 2011. [49] Streich and Levy 2016, 508.
[50] Fearon 1995; Powell 2006.

starts, nor does the shooting typically produce something like colloquial understandings of "victory" and "defeat."[51] Blood and waste notwithstanding, war entails the "authoritative allocation of values" whether it ends in one side's disarmament or a negotiated settlement.[52] War *is* politics. And the Russo-Japanese War is a useful case in point, helping us understand how belligerents form and react to shared expectations about the outcome of a fight to the finish and how those expectations shape war duration and termination. I show in this section that (a) fighting solved Russia's commitment problem by disabusing it of the notion that Japan would tolerate competition for influence in Korea, resolving a key puzzle in the modern theory of war, and (b) that Japan's gains at Portsmouth fell short of its battlefield performance because of its relative weakness in securing credit for a long war, using the modern theory of war to resolve a historical puzzle about the Russo-Japanese War.

4.3.1   Solving Commitment Problems

War ends when fighting solves the bargaining problem that prevented settlement in the first place, saving the costs of further fighting. Most work on war termination focuses on how battlefield events can reveal private information about capabilities and resolve[53] or secure private benefits for the leadership.[54] But fighting can also make commitments credible that weren't beforehand. If war begins when a rising side can't or won't limit a prospective shift in power, then settlement requires either slowing the shift or changing the rising side's willingness to exploit or continue it.[55] Most work envisions war stabilizing the distribution of power via conquest, regime change, or forcible disarmament,[56] but conquest and disarmament are exceedingly rare. The Russo-Japanese War shows how fighting can solve a commitment problem short of total war.

Fighting began because Russia doubted Japan's willingness to wage a preventive war, encouraging the former to increase its power in Manchuria. Therefore, ending the war required preventing Russia's rise, by persuasion or by force, or disabusing it of the notion that Japan wouldn't fight. And as it happened, the war did all three, wrecking Russia's military power in East Asia, changing its beliefs about Japan's relative capabilities, and securing Japanese preponderance in territory – Manchuria below Mukden – that Russia could've leveraged in future bargaining. By the end (and because) of the war, Russia's willingness to encroach on Japanese interests in Korea was substantially reduced. British critic Syndey Brooks noted in *The North American Review*: "Sooner or later, ... Russian expansion will resume its course. Whither will that course lie? ... [I]t will lie

---

[51] See Wagner 2007, Chapters 3–4.   [52] Easton 1985, 134.   [53] Filson and Werner 2002.
[54] Goemans 2000.   [55] Leventoğlu and Slantchev 2007; Wolford 2019b, Chapter 11.
[56] For example, Reiter 2009; Wolford, Reiter and Carrubba 2011.

along the line of least resistance. But there can be very little difficulty in proving that Manchuria and the Far East are the line, not of least but of greatest resistance."[57]

Settlement was possible in 1905 because the war ejected Russia from southern Manchuria and dashed its optimism about Japan's power and resolve: consolidating the eastern reaches of the Tsar's empire wasn't worth fighting a powerful, resolute Japan intent on expanding its own sphere of influence.

Power, both its pursuit and its exploitation, are choices, and those choices can be shaped by war.[58] Fighting itself can alter the expected value of continued fighting, whether by redistributing resources, destroying value, or – as it did in the Russo-Japanese War – changing beliefs about relative power and resolve. And if fighting can rearrange incentives or change beliefs enough to make war less attractive, then states can use war to solve others' commitment problems short of conquest or disarmament, some prominent claims notwithstanding.[59] Criticisms of the commitment problem mechanism often ignore the agency behind changes in military power, and eliding this substantive point limits our ability to explain why wars caused by commitment problems typically end in negotiated settlements.[60] Solving commitment problems via fighting need not entail total war, nor need it set states permanently back on long-run growth curves.[61] Russia made credible postwar promises not to encroach on Japanese interests precisely because fighting had reduced its willingness and ability to compete with Japan. The two erstwhile enemies agreed in 1907 to a division of influence that proved nearly identical to what Japan had proposed back in 1903,[62] and this agreement was possible only because of what Japan did to both Russian beliefs and capabilities during the war.

4.3.2 The Terms of Settlement

Foreign Minister Komura had an ambitious remit at the peace talks in Portsmouth, requiring "that [Japan's] rights in Korea be absolute; that Russia leave Manchuria; that the spoils of war [i.e., Japanese conquests in Manchuria] be confirmed; the cession of Sakhalin; the granting of fishing rights along the Russian coast; and the payment of an indemnity to reimburse Japan for the costs of the war."[63]

After Japan knocked Russia's army halfway across Manchuria and sent its fleet to the bottom of the Tsushima Strait, these demands didn't look

---

[57] Brooks 1905, 591–592; The same issue also sees Andrew Carnegie praise the Anglo-French *Entente Cordiale*, which he ranks equal "in importance with the appearance of Japan as one of the great World Powers," and argues that the United States should be part of a broader understanding between these liberal-minded nations (Carnegie 1905, 510).
[58] See also Beard 2019.   [59] For example, Gartzke 1999; Walt 1999, 28.
[60] See also Leventoğlu and Slantchev 2007.   [61] Cf. Organski and Kugler 1977.
[62] Matsui 1972; Paine 2017, 82.   [63] Connaughton 2004, 343.

unreasonable. Peace is sustainable when parties receive at least as much as they expect to secure by fighting,[64] and Japan had proved itself more than capable of besting Russia militarily on land and at sea. Yet the Portsmouth terms came in below popular Japanese expectations, which were based on a strong if costly military performance.[65] Russia would retain influence in northern Manchuria after a mutual evacuation, hold on to northern Sakhalin, and – of special note to Japanese nationalists[66] – pay no indemnity. Per the *New York Times*, "A nation [Russia] hopelessly beaten in every battle of the war ... dictated her own terms to the victory."[67] Why did Japan fare so poorly at Portsmouth, given its demonstrated ability to rout Russia's armies and sink its warships?

Battlefield outcomes are only part of the war termination equation; fiscal and financial factors also come into play. By summer 1905, belligerents agreed not only on Japanese operational superiority but also on Russian advantages in securing funding – and insensitivity to casualties – for a longer war. As Japan's military prestige increased, its creditors grew wary of enabling it to dominate China.[68] This was, after all, the era of the Open Door,[69] and Japan's creditors had no desire to enable it to secure exclusive concessions. Japan's creditworthiness wasn't in doubt, but nor was its opportunity to dominate northeastern China. By mid-1905, Japan's credit had nearly dried up, but now-underdog Russia's was surprisingly more robust. Battle outcomes and beliefs about relative access to credit worked together, the former an advantage for Japan and the latter an advantage for Russia and its larger but slower-moving reserves. Operational superiority notwithstanding, Japanese leaders judged winning a long war an "impossibility."[70] Russia could lose battles indefinitely, but Japan couldn't fight forever. Even with additional credit, Japan wouldn't be able to strike much beyond Mukden.[71] This recommended peace even if it meant withdrawing from Manchuria, because Russia's revised beliefs about Japan's military prowess rendered promises not to encroach on Korea credible. The war's underlying commitment problem had been solved. Some accounts emphasize the personal politics of the peace conference,[72] but Russian diplomat Sergei Witte's deft management of public opinion won little more for Russia than what Japan agreed it could get from continued fighting: the current battlefield situation as the new status quo.

Beliefs about the outcome of a fight to the finish depend as much on fiscal capacity as they do on operational strengths revealed on the battlefield. In the Russo-Japanese War, lenders on Wall Street and in the City of London[73] played a key role in war termination, structuring expectations about what a continued war would look like and, ultimately, influencing the terms on which peace

---

[64] Powell 1999, 85. [65] Jacob 2017, 47. [66] Jacob 2017, 54–55.
[67] Quoted in Connaughton 2004, 344. [68] Connaughton 2004, 342; Miller 2005, 480–481.
[69] See Jacob 2017, Chapter 5. [70] Connaughton 2004, 341. [71] White 2015, Chapters 11–12.
[72] For example, Connaughton 2004, 343–344. [73] Miller 2005.

could be had.[74] Russia could rely on lines of credit in France and Germany, but Japan's credit was limited when it requested mediation. Japan's creditors, once concerned that it might be flattened by the Russian steamroller, now had to make sure that it didn't beat Russia too badly. We can see echoes of this in Roosevelt's changing views of the war, which began pro-Japan but tilted toward Russia once Japan proved a formidable military power. Ultimately, Roosevelt aimed to ensure that neither Japan nor Russia gained so much that it could close the Open Door.[75] The key question for war termination – how belligerents will fare if they fight to the finish – depends on both battlefield outcomes and access to the sources of military power.

4.4 The Asian Roots of World War I

Japan's victory over Russia was a sensation in what we now call the Global South,[76] but it also led other great powers to renegotiate their relationships with the newest member of the great power club. The United States, for example, exchanged recognition of Japanese dominance in Korea for acknowledgment of its own position in the Philippines[77] and shifted strategic focus from gaining a foothold on the Chinese coast to defending Pearl Harbor, given Japan's displacement of Germany as the key regional competitor.[78] But the war's impact was truly global, and the unexpected nature of its outcome allows us to draw causal linkages between Russia's defeat and the outbreak of World War I in Europe nine years later.

States are typically effective at guessing who's likely to win any given war.[79] As a result, the effects of a war's outcome on other states' decisions about armaments, alignments, and military strategies – even war and peace – may be censored out of the empirical record: the postwar actions of states that guessed a war's outcome correctly may appear, falsely, to be unaffected by it. But when states fail to anticipate a war's outcome[80] and retain the same freedom of action before and after the war,[81] we can be confident in observing causal effects on subsequent choices. The Russo-Japanese War is a useful example. Against observer expectations, it boosted estimates of Japan's military prowess, diminished Russian capabilities, and downgraded third-party estimates of Russian competence.[82] Policies that would've remained in place after an anticipated

---

[74] For more on how states finance wars, see Zielinski 2012.
[75] Jacob 2017, Chapter 5; Third parties also prevented the war from expanding. China stayed neutral under (often heavy) pressure from other great powers (Hsu 1980, 139) despite battles raging on its own territory, and the Anglo-Japanese alliance kept Russia diplomatically isolated, because no other power wished to risk war with Britain – least of all Russia's French ally, itself in the process of moving closer to England under the threat posed by Imperial Germany.
[76] Esherick 2012; Gasster 1980; Ichiko 1980; Jacob 2017.   [77] White 1964, 268.
[78] White 1964, 219–220.   [79] See Gartner and Siverson 1996.   [80] Sun and Tyson 2019.
[81] Slough 2023.   [82] Seligmann 2006, 116–117.

Russian victory now changed, and those changes chart a straight course from 1905 to 1914.

World War I scholars often ask why 1914's July Crisis, as opposed to previous crises in Algeria, Morocco, Bosnia, and the Ottoman empire – to say nothing of two Balkan Wars – brought the great powers to war in 1914.[83] Unlike prewar crises, the assassination of Archduke Franz Ferdinand in Sarajevo gave Austria pretext for preventive war against Serbia, which proved only the first domino to fall. The prospective fall of Serbia pushed Russia to protect its interests in Southeastern Europe, which then gave Germany the opportunity to wage its own preventive war against Russia.[84] Germany's preventive motives helped expand an Austro-Serb war into a general one, yet we often overlook *why* Russian power was rising fast enough to worry Germany in the first place. The answer is Russia's unexpected 1905 defeat. For years before 1904, Germany had endeavored to keep Russia, newly allied to France and part of any potential encircling coalition, out of Europe as much as possible. Kaiser Wilhelm II, hostile to the rise of a non-European imperial power in Asia, hyped the burgeoning "Yellow Peril" in the East and pushed the Tsar to confront Japan in defense of Christendom rather than pursue imperial ambitions along the fraying frontiers of the Ottoman empire.[85]

Far from getting merely tied down in East Asia, the Tsar saw his navy destroyed, his army revealed to be poorly organized and even less well-led, and his government vulnerable to explosive popular unrest. German policies changed in response to this new information, with Chief of the General Staff Field Marshal Alfred von Schlieffen reasoning that (a) rearmament notwithstanding, the Russians would remain inferior to other great powers pound-for-pound and (b) they wouldn't reemerge as a serious threat for years.[86] The result was 1906's "Schlieffen Plan," which outlined how to defeat the Franco-Russian alliance by first knocking out France and then turning East to deal with what, thanks to Japan's performance in Manchuria, Schlieffen believed would be a large but poorly trained and slow-to-mobilize Russian Army. Therefore, a war plan that looked like an audacious gamble in 1914 – especially once it failed to win the war – was a clear response to new information about Russian logistical, organizational, and operational limitations revealed in 1905.

Yet Russia wasn't idle in defeat. Turning away from the "line of greatest resistance" in Manchuria, the Tsar refocused his ambitions on Southeastern Europe; reformed the army's organization, mobilization, and personnel policies; used French financing to upgrade his rail network; and increased military spending in 1912's *Grand Programme*. If Russia had its way, post-defeat weakness would be temporary. German leaders watched carefully, discussing

---

[83] See Levy 1990–1991; Levy and Mulligan 2021. [84] See Wolford 2019b, Chapter 4.
[85] McLean 2007, 26; Seligmann 2006, 111. [86] Seligmann 2006, 119–120.

the attractiveness of preventive war at what the Chancellor dubbed a "war council" weeks after the announcement of the *Grand Programme*. By the summer of 1914 – not long before the assassination in Sarajevo – the best guess held that Russian growth would "[b]y 1916–1917 . . . nullify the calculations embodied in the Schlieffen Plan."[87] When Austria then requested German support for war against Serbia in retaliation for Franz Ferdinand's assassination, Germany granted the now-infamous "blank check," promising to support its partner if Russia entered on Serbia's side. German leaders calculated that if the Tsar stayed neutral, Russia could be shut out of the Balkans and its rising power blunted on the cheap; and if Russia entered the war, Germany could work at cutting it down with otherwise-uncertain Austrian help.[88] Even with French and British involvement, "the Germans believed that in 1914 they had a better chance of defeating any Entente combination than they would ever enjoy again,"[89] which made exploiting Austrian involvement in the Balkans all the more urgent. Thus did Austria go to war against Serbia, which gave Germany a chance to stop Russian recovery from 1905 in its tracks.

Seligmann argues that World War I was "not the inevitable consequence of the Russo-Japanese War" but "partially inspired by it."[90] I disagree. If we accept that German willingness to countenance war with Russia in 1914 was driven by fears of continued Russian rearmament, then the outcome of the Russo-Japanese War is a proximate cause of World War I. Russia's fall down the ranks of military powers was directly responsible for the later shift in capabilities – its determined recovery – that made the July Crisis unique among other prewar crises, during which Russia had been widely known to be unable to fight a major war.[91] Absent a weakened Russia in 1906, the Schlieffen Plan wouldn't have banked on a slow Russian mobilization. Absent a rising Russia in the summer of 1914, Germany would've had little reason to give Austria *carte blanche* against Serbia. And linking it all together, Russia's strength wouldn't have cratered in 1905, only to be recovering as it was in 1914, had Japan not beaten it bloody in Manchuria. Japan's victory over Russia in 1905 didn't just unhinge the balance among imperial powers in East Asia. By creating a temporary shock to Russian strength and a longer-term redirection of its interests along "the line of least resistance," it also set the stage for Germany to attempt the same in Europe in 1914.

4.5 Conclusion

Superficial similarities to World War I – imperial rivalries, industrial warfare, domestic revolution, and belligerent financial ruin – notwithstanding, the

---

[87] Clark 2012, Chapter 6. [88] See Wolford 2019b, 85–93. [89] Hastings 2013, 78.
[90] Seligmann 2006, 123. [91] See Stevenson 1997.

Russo-Japanese War probably doesn't merit the provocative label "World War Zero."[92] If anything, that terminology *undersells* the war's influence on international politics. Its global diplomacy, from outbreak through termination and aftermath, reflected a fundamental change in the international system: the emergence of an Asian great power with imperial ambitions, during the era of high imperialism, outside of but competing on equal footing with the European core.

The Russo-Japanese War completed a process by which Japan effected and then exploited first Chinese and then Russian declines in East Asia, upsetting a balance of power that had supported tenuous peace between the European powers for nearly a century after 1816's Congress of Vienna. Russia's defeat at Japan's hands helped cause World War I, ending the ostensible golden age of economic interdependence that preceded it – and that was widely presumed to make war too costly to contemplate.[93] But the late nineteenth century's high-water mark of globalization didn't collapse into decades of global war, trade restrictions, and superpower confrontation solely because of a German bid for world power,[94] or even the interlocking commitment problems of the July Crisis.[95] It collapsed because the rise of a new great power in Asia upended relations between the others. With the imperial frontier all but closed, not by a scramble for colonies but by the emergence of a powerful, ambitious, and homegrown East Asian empire, great power competition had become a truly global affair. The Russo-Japanese War marked the transition from one world, where provincial European powers believed they could decide matters of war and peace for themselves, to another in which new, dynamic powers like Japan, the United States, and, eventually, a resurgent China would define a new, truly global balance of power. The transition had only begun when the Treaty of Portsmouth was signed in 1905, but that treaty's effective redefinition – and globalization – of membership in the great power club would help cause World War I and set the terms for the second, when the bloody termination of Japan's imperial ambitions would herald still more changes to the global order.

---

[92] Cf. Steinberg et al. 2005.   [93] See Gartzke and Lupu 2012.   [94] Fischer 1967.
[95] Wolford 2019b, Chapter 4.

5   The Chinese Exclusion Act

Enze Han and D. G. Kim

The Chinese Exclusion Act of 1882 was the first – and, to this day, the only – American law to single out and restrict a specific group of people from migrating to the United States.[1] Putting the brakes on the influx of Chinese gold miners and laborers looking for economic opportunities in the American West, this explicitly race-based immigration policy was later expanded to exclude all immigrants from Asia in the 1924 Immigration Act. Set within the context of the post-Civil War Reconstruction politics, the exclusion laws epitomized the intense politicization and consolidation of a white-dominant racial hierarchy in the United States. Along with the continual segregation of the black population, surging anti-Chinese racial resentment highlighted the widely shared vision of America as a nation of the "Anglo-Saxon race."[2] The exclusion of Chinese, however, also had its sources and consequences that extended far beyond the American domestic racial politics. In this chapter, we revisit the major historical events of Chinese exclusion in America within the *global* political context of the time. Specifically, we propose that the exclusion laws emerged from the collapse of Sino-centric regional order in nineteenth-century East Asia. To begin with, many of the background forces behind Chinese emigration – the forced opening of China by Western imperial powers, the discovery of gold in white settler societies, including California, and America's westward expansion and newfound commercial and imperial interests – were all integral to the ascendance of a new West-centric order in East Asia and later Anglo-American global dominance.[3]

As historian Mae Ngai puts it, these transitional forces brought the "first mass contact between Chinese and Euro-Americans" in the American West that basically stood as one of the *"international contact zones"* on the frontiers of Anglo-American settler societies."[4] Chinese immigration sparked a fierce debate over what came to be known as the "Chinese Question": do Chinese

---

[1] Ngai 2021, 4.   [2] Rosenblatt 2018, 255. See also Omi and Winant 2014, 12.
[3] Chapter 6 focuses specifically on the early twentieth century rise of the Anglo-American international order and the historical significance of Japan's failed attempt to include a racial equality clause in the Covenant of the League of Nations.
[4] Ngai 2021, 3. Italics added.

pose a racial threat to these "white, Anglo-American countries," or should they be embraced based on liberal principles of freedom and equality?[5] This "Chinese Question" therefore closely reflected the apparent contradiction between the Westphalian principle of sovereign equality and the prevailing notion of civilizational and racial hierarchy. As we will see, decades of political mobilization of mass anti-Chinese racial resentment eventually led to the American decision to ban Chinese and subsequently all Asian immigration, signaling the predominance of what W. E. B. Du Bois called the "color line" as an organizing principle of modern international relations.[6] Finally, the exclusion laws also played an important role in shaping China's forced – and contested – entry to the new global order that had thus become deeply racialized by the early twentieth century. We will pay particular attention to the Six Companies and transnational networks of late Qing reformers and revolutionaries who were the first to promote modern Chinese nationalism and diplomatic practices.[7] After cultivating a deep sense of humiliation and racial awareness in the face of Chinese exclusion – a trope maintained to this day – this new generation of Chinese elites laid key intellectual and political foundations for a modern *nation*-state for *Chinese people*.[8] Heralding the biggest change in thousands-of-years of Chinese history that had previously been maintained by the Sino-centric worldview of *Tianxia*, the rise of modern Chinese nationalism became the driving force behind the 1905 anti-American boycott movement and by 1912, the eventual collapse of the Qing empire. We will highlight the historical significance of the boycott movement as China's first mass nationalist protest and the mobilization of anti-foreign sentiment and national victimhood – a political force as alive in today's China as it was 100 years ago. The Chinese Exclusion Act's later expansion to exclude Japanese also became a catalyst for the increasingly racial overtones of Japan's own nationalist and imperial projects for the next decades.[9]

The chapter proceeds as follows. In the next section, we provide a brief overview of key historical events surrounding the Chinese Exclusion Act and trace their effects on the actual flows of US immigration from East Asia. We then examine the multilayered international political sources and implications of the exclusion laws, dividing them into (1) the historical pulling factors for Chinese emigration in the emergent nineteenth-century international order, (2) the subsequent rise of racialized violence and identity politics in the "international contact zones" of the American West and their far-reaching global

---

[5] Ngai 2021, 4.
[6] Du Bois 1903, 33. Similarly, Alexander Barder uses the term "global racial imaginary" to describe the prevailing racial thinking and racialized international hierarchy of the time that was based on scientific racism and white supremacist beliefs. See Barder 2021.
[7] Qin 2009.   [8] Wang 2001; see also Zhu 2021, 863–890.
[9] See Chapter 6 for a more detailed exploration of this issue.

implications, and finally (3) the ramifications of Chinese exclusion for modern Chinese nationalism and the contested arrival of modern international order in East Asia. We then conclude by discussing an important parallel we can draw between the global politics of Chinese exclusion in the early twentieth century and contemporary, post-pandemic US–China relations that have once again become characterized by mutually reinforcing racial identities, resentment, and Chinese sense of national humiliation.

5.1   Historical Overview

Before delving into the sources and consequences of the Chinese Exclusion Act, we first provide a brief historical overview of the decades-long development and demise of the Chinese exclusion laws in the United States. Figure 5.1 visualizes the evolution of US immigration flows from China and Japan along the timeline of major historical events surrounding Chinese immigration and exclusion in America. Signed on July 28, 1868, the Burlingame Treaty established friendly diplomatic relations between the United States and the Qing dynasty, lifting any formal restrictions on trade and immigration between the two countries. As shown in the graph, the Burlingame Treaty ushered in the era of large-scale Chinese overseas emigration that had begun during the gold rushes of the mid-nineteenth century. By 1880, there were over 105,000 Chinese across the United States, most of whom lived in the American West and accounted for over a tenth of California's burgeoning population.[10]

This dramatic change, however, was soon followed by a series of mass protests and legal restrictions against Chinese immigrant workers, culminating in the Page Act of 1875, one of the first major exclusion laws. Enforced primarily against Chinese, the Page Act prohibited the importation of "unfree" laborers and women brought for "immoral purposes."[11] In 1880, the Angell Treaty was signed to revise the Burlingame Treaty, allowing America to restrict and eventually suspend the flow of Chinese immigration. The landmark Chinese Exclusion Act, signed into law by President Chester A. Arthur in 1882, placed a ten-year ban on Chinese immigration and was later renewed for another ten years by the Geary Act. In 1888, the Scott Act prohibited the reentry of most Chinese immigrants to the United States after leaving the country. The Chinese Exclusion Act was then made permanent in 1902.

After years of unsuccessful resistance against the exclusion laws, the Qing court signed the Gresham-Yang Treaty in 1894 that acknowledged Chinese exclusion in America at the international level. As the treaty was later due to expire, the large-scale boycott of American goods erupted across both overseas

---

[10] Source: US Census Bureau and Department of Homeland Security.
[11] Immigration and Ethnic History Society, n.d.

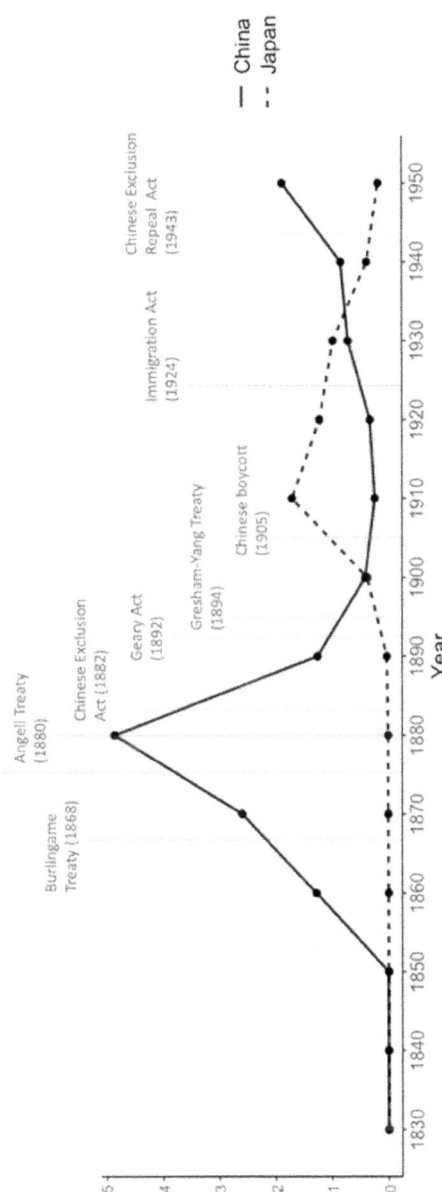

Figure 5.1 US immigration flows from China and Japan by timeline.

Note: Each dot represents the proportion of new immigrants from China or Japan as a percentage of total new immigrants to the United States for the previous decade. For example, from 1860 and 1869, around 2.6 percent of new immigrants came from China. Immigration flows from China and Japan are distinguished by straight and dotted lines, respectively. The figure also shows major historical events on Chinese immigration and exclusion in the United States. Source for immigration data: US Department of Homeland Security.

and local Chinese communities in 1905, as we will discuss later in this chapter. As shown in Figure 5.1, the exclusion laws had direct effects on the actual immigration flows. Chinese emigration significantly dropped following the Chinese Exclusion Act in the 1880s until the trend was slowly reversed in the 1940s when the Act was eventually repealed in 1943. After the short-lived uptick in Japanese immigration in the early 1900s, the 1924 Immigration Act expanded upon the Chinese exclusion laws to ban immigration from all Asian countries, including Japan.

5.2 Chinese Migration and the Arrival of Modern International Order

To understand what led to the first mass contact between Chinese and Euro-Americans in the frontier of the white settler society in nineteenth century America, we can trace three key trends that were all integral to the emergence of a new order in Asia as well as later Anglo-American global hegemony.[12] These international political sources included the opening of China by Western imperial powers, the discovery of gold in Anglo-American settler societies, and America's westward expansion and newfound commercial and imperial interests in East Asia. As Barry Buzan and George Lawson note, it was not until this century of "global transformation" did the world become a truly global system – one that came to replace multiple regional international systems, including the millennia-long Sino-centric order in East Asia, with an international system whose center of gravity clearly resided in the West. Unlike the previous "polycentric world with no dominant centre," the modern international order was being shaped by dominant Euro-American states that "could quickly and decisively project the new mode of power around the world."[13] Against this crucial international backdrop, the forced opening of China by Western powers was the first trigger for Chinese global emigration and the mass contact between Chinese and Euro-Americans.

5.2.1 The Opening of China

During the Ming (1368–1644) and Qing (1644–1911) dynasties, maritime trade and emigration were periodically limited or forbidden outright for Chinese

---

[12] Mae Ngai's reference to the first mass contact between Chinese and Euro-Americans makes an interesting parallel with Alexander Wendt's well-known discussion of the "First Encounter" between the Spanish and the Indigenous peoples of the Americas. These two historic "First Encounter" cases, both with far-reaching implications for modern international order we still live in today, exemplify "the Hobbesian dynamics resulting from radical alterity." See Wendt 1999.

[13] Buzan and Lawson 2015, 1–2.

subjects to curb piracy and insurgency along the southeast and southern coasts. Any returnees from overseas could even face execution. Trading relations with Western countries were heavily restricted and only permitted in the thirteen factories outside of Canton (Guangzhou). It was after the defeat of the Qing by the British in the First Opium War (1839–42) that opened the floodgate for Chinese out-migration, predominantly from the southern provinces of Fujian and Guangdong. Hong Kong, which was ceded to the British after the war, together with Portuguese Macau and other port cities such as Xiamen (Amoy) and Shantou (Swatow), became major exit ports for Chinese labor in Southern China. The Second Opium War (1856–60) signaled the continued violent opening up of China by the West. To exploit cheap Chinese labor and replace African slaves, Britain and France forced the Qing court to allow the international migration of low-skilled Chinese workers. As a result, amidst domestic political chaos in the wake of the Taiping Rebellion (1850–64), which was extremely devastating for southern China, a growing number of Chinese sought livelihood overseas.[14] Most of the Chinese out-migration followed the trails of European imperialism and expanding world markets in East Asia and around the globe. Decades after the abolition of the slave trade in the Americas, Chinese workers came to fill the vacuum as cheap labor in agriculture and mining.[15]

Meanwhile, labor recruitment companies saw high profit for exporting Chinese labor overseas, and as a result tens of thousands of low-skilled Chinese, predominantly men, went abroad as contracted workers. These labor recruiters used all sorts of means to entice potential migrants, including violence and intrigue. Indeed, the most destitute of these laborers were often captured and sold as part of the coolie trade that led them to work in plantations in the Caribbean and Latin America. Most of the Chinese emigrants would incur debt to pay for their passages overseas and thus came to be called indentured laborers or "coolies." While often being accused of being slaves, the majority went abroad of their free will, seeking new economic opportunities during this uncertain time.[16] Particular opportunities were found in the American West, with the discovery of gold in California in 1849 and the construction of the trans-continental railway in the mid-1860s.

5.2.2   The Gold Rush and American Westward Expansion

If the forced opening of China by ascending Western powers provided the first major pulling factor for Chinese migration, it was the gold rushes in mid-nineteenth-century California, Australia, and South Africa that accelerated the "first mass contact between Chinese and Euro-Americans." Importantly, the

---

[14] Macauley 2021, 26.   [15] McKeown 1999, 315.   [16] Ngai 2021, 150.

discovery of gold in these Anglo-American settler societies signaled the decades-long shift of global economic and geopolitical power to Great Britain and the United States. For the latter, the gold rush in the American West further pushed the country's territorial expansion to its western frontier. Driven by the growing cultural belief in America's Manifest Destiny,[17] this westward expansion soon evolved into the country's newfound commercial – and later imperial – interests in East Asia. Decades after its claim to the Western Hemisphere as its sphere of influence with the Monroe Doctrine, in 1898, the United States gained control of the Hawaiian Islands, the Philippines, Puerto Rico, and Guam as spoils of the Spanish–American War.

Behind America's expansion in Asia were the East Coast industrialist Republicans, such as the New York Senator William H. Seward, who later became the secretary of state from 1861 to 1869. Seward was one among a group of cosmopolitan expansionists who saw tremendous potentials for trade, investment, and evangelical mission in China.[18] For Seward, "the free migration of the Chinese to the American and other foreign continents will tend to increase the wealth and strength of all Western nations."[19] He saw in the Chinese abundant cheap labor that would help raise "the status of white laborers and helped to bring prosperity to the U.S. West."[20]

Meanwhile, across the Pacific, news of goldmines in California quickly traveled to China and inspired many Chinese to seek fortune in the "Gold Mountains." Later, with the discovery of gold in Victoria, Australia, "Old Gold Mountain (*jiujinshan*)" became the name for San Francisco, which continues to be used in Chinese today. At the time, California was not yet part of the United States and came into its possession only after the Mexican–American War (1846–48), joining the federation as a newly admitted state in 1850. In a sense, the Chinese gold seekers were among the first of many groups of people who rushed to California to seek gold in the mountains of Sierra Nevada. Although there were many indigenous gold diggers, and many from Mexico, Peru, and Chile, increasingly it was the tens of thousands of Euro-Americans who came over by land and by sea, known as "forty-niners," who became the dominant group of gold seekers in California.

Most of the Chinese gold seekers came from four counties in the Pearl River delta in Guangdong province, and the vast majority came from the county of Xinning, currently known as Taishan. Through chain migration these Chinese brought with them mostly men to the gold mountains in California and competed with others for the valuable mineral. Within a year, 325 Chinese joined the gold rush, and this number increased to 20,026 only four years later.[21] The

[17] Stephanson 1996. [18] Lew-Williams 2018, 24. [19] Lew-Williams 2018, 26.
[20] Lew-Williams 2018, 27. [21] Lew-Williams 2018, 21.

Chinese accounted for 10 percent of the population in California by the late 1850s and up to 25 percent in the mining districts.[22]

Besides working in the gold mines, many Chinese also took on other professions, such as gardener, cook, launderer, cleaner, farmer, shop keeper, nannies, maids, prostitutes, and others. Importantly, thousands of Chinese also worked for the construction of the Transcontinental Railroad in the 1860s – one of the most important facilitators and symbols of American westward expansion. Similar to the British and French moves to replace African slaves with cheap Chinese labor in their colonial plantations after the Opium Wars, it was the difficulty of securing white workers that led to the hiring of Chinese immigrant workers for the railway construction. There were over 20,000 Chinese laborers, accounting for about 90 percent of workforce for the Central Pacific Railroad Company (CPRR), which built the line from Sacramento in California, over the high peaks of Sierra Nevada.[23] Leland Stanford, the company's president, former California governor and founder of Stanford University, testified to Congress in 1865 that without these Chinese workers, "it would be impossible to complete the western portion of this great national enterprise."[24] The railroad eventually reached Promontory Summit, Utah, where it joined the Union Pacific line built westward from Omaha, Nebraska. From 1864 to 1869, these Chinese worked for the CPRR in the most difficult conditions receiving significantly lower wages than their white peers, yet their contribution to this historic American national project was not recognized until much later.

5.3 The Rise of Chinese Exclusion

These nineteenth-century transnational political forces – the forced opening of China by Western powers and the rise of Anglo-American global hegemony marked by the discovery of gold and American westward expansion – brought about the mass Chinese migration to white settler societies, including the American West. Spurred by the growing popularity of new "scientific" theories of race, anti-Chinese racial resentment soon became a prominent source of political mobilization in American society that was already deeply divided along the color line. The rise of virulent anti-Chinese racism and exclusion in America further confirmed that despite the façade of sovereign equality, modern international order was organized by the prevailing notion of global racial hierarchy – what Barry Buzan and George Lawson describe as "an apparently contradictory feature of the nineteenth century ideational landscape."[25] In such a "bifurcated international system," the rules-based

---

[22] Ngai 2021, 16.   [23] Chang 2019, 2.   [24] Cavalier 2005, 189.
[25] Buzan and Lawson 2015, 121.

international order appeared to be reserved only for "white" countries that claimed and exercised their right to colonize, control, and exclude "colored" populations.[26]

5.3.1 Politicization of Racial Resentment

From the early days of the gold rush in California, competition in the gold mines was fierce among different groups of people making claims over their findings. Violence and threat of violence were common in the gold mines, and white settlers were especially aggressive toward the Chinese, who were basically chased off from most prolific sites. In the end, the Chinese found a small digging site passed over by others, which was later named Chinese Camp. The Chinese gold seekers thus gathered around the Chinese Camp, together with many others who conducted other professions. Their numbers grew very quickly, further leading to the unease of the white population in California.

As a new state in the union, many white people went to California not only for gold but also for political ambitions. The first governor of California John Bigler saw a political opportunity in the Chinese migration issue and used it to excite the populous mining districts to his side during his electoral campaigns in 1853.[27] Most importantly, Bigler framed the Chinese as unfree "coolie" labor. He accused the Chinese labor were under control by their masters to mine gold for pitiful wages, and they removed the gold from the United States to send money back to China. Such messages were powerful at the time when many white workers in the gold mines were not making enough money for digging gold and became wage labors for others themselves. Bigler's portrayal of the Chinese labor as unfree "coolie" labor, comparable to black slaves in the American South, stoked white fear against Chinese immigrant workers as a monolithic threat to their own sense of independence and economic security. As a result of Bigler's campaign, miners railed against the industrialists who tried to "flood the state with degraded Asiatics, and fasten, without sanction of law, the system of peonage on our social organization."[28]

Bigler was therefore the first politician to use the issue of Chinese migration to elected office, and this association of Chinese labor as unfree "coolie" labor became a doctrine for the Democratic Party in California that would be used whenever there was need for a racial scapegoat. In 1852, California imposed a Foreign Miners' Tax of $3 a month, which was believed to be the amount Chinese "coolies" earned a month so as to make mining unprofitable for them. Violence toward the Chinese miners and expulsion were common throughout the state. For many whites in the American West, the growing Chinese population posed an existential threat to their vision of a free white republic in the

---

[26] Buzan and Lawson 2015, 3. [27] Ngai 2021, 86. [28] Ngai 2021, 86.

settler colonies in the Western states and territories, from California to Oregon and Washington.[29] For them, the arrival of the Chinese would hamper the westward expansion of the United States, and the "filthy, vicious, ignorant, depraved, and criminal" Chinese would be a menace to the republican form of government for the white people.[30]

The completion of the Transcontinental Railroad in 1869 further integrated the newly incorporated western states and brought even larger numbers of white workers from the East Coast. Many were in fact recent migrants from Western Europe themselves, particularly the Irish who came to the United States after the Irish famine during the mid-nineteenth century. At the time there was no restriction of Western European migration to the United States, and they could also easily naturalize as American citizens because they were white. The mass arrival of white labor in search for jobs led them in direct competition with the Chinese. Coinciding with an economic recession in the 1870s, the surplus white labor fermented anti-Chinese rhetoric and racial violence. They claimed that white labor could not compete with the Chinese, because they were too cheap and frugal, and they also should not compete with Chinese, because they were inferior. Led by the Workingmen's Party of California, founded by Denis Kearney, who was himself an Irish immigrant, called for violence and demanded the ridding of the Chinese from California with the slogan "The Chinese Must Go!" Calls for violence met with strong popular support among the white settler communities and led a series of purges of the Chinese along the Western states and territories.

5.3.2 Modern Racism and the Chinese Question

The political success of anti-Chinese political rhetoric was facilitated in large part by the growing popularity of scientific racism and *social* Darwinist approaches to race in late-nineteenth-century Europe and America. While ethnocentric beliefs in the superiority of one's own group have been found in a wide range of different human societies dating as far back as the ancient imperial states of Egypt and Rome,[31] the advent of modern racial thinking in the nineteenth century was distinguished by its adherence to new "race science" of the time.[32] Centered on the belief that all humankind can be divided into distinct races that are subject to the same Darwinian laws of natural selection and "survival of the fittest," emerging racial theories quickly gained popularity among Westerners as a convenient explanation for their colonial rules in Africa and Asia. As historians have shown, such words as "racist" and "racism" were in fact first coined during the 1890s and 1900s to designate those who

---

[29] Lew-Williams 2018, 29. [30] Lew-Williams 2018, 29. [31] Isaac 2004.
[32] Rosenblatt 2018, 254. See also Buzan and Lawson 2015, 122.

subscribed to scientific racism and promoted a *global* hierarchy of human races.[33] In international law, the idea of racial hierarchy became formalized in the concept of the "standard of civilization" that was frequently invoked to defend the European states' right to colonize and exploit non-European societies and populations.[34] Theories of white supremacy and global racial hierarchy thus became widely accepted in the United States as the country, coupled with the myth of America's Manifest Destiny, sought its own expansionist missions across its western frontier and into the Asia-Pacific. The idea of *Anglo-Saxon* white supremacy soon prevailed in American society where some influential figures like Andrew Carnegie went further to suggest a "racial confederacy" between Britain and America to bring peace and order to the world inhabited by other "barbaric" and "inferior" races.[35]

After centuries of European subjugation of African slaves in the plantations of the New World, the continued Western expansion into East Asia gave rise to the "first mass contact between Chinese and Euro-Americans" in white settler societies. Under the growing influence of modern racial thinking, the American West thereby turned into the site of "racial formation" – what Michael Omi and Howard Winant define as "the sociohistorical process by which racial identities are created, lived out, transformed, and destroyed."[36] Competing with white workers in gold mines and fast-increasing in their numbers, Chinese immigrants were soon viewed as a threatening racial *Other*.

In addressing this "Chinese Question," Americans quickly subscribed – and eventually contributed – to the social Darwinist view that the world is inhabited by the ruling white race and the subordinate non-white races, including the Asian ("yellow") race. Treated as a biologically distinct race, Chinese immigrants were considered inferior, slavish, but also cunning and threatening. On the one hand, Chinese represented a degraded form of manhood for the white people. In the aftermath of the American Civil War, the number of white wage workers increased significantly. No longer could one claim moral self-sufficiency as property-owning men and many had to compete for employment as cheap labor under economic recessions and widening income gaps.[37] Known for working hard for lower wages, the Chinese labors were deemed a threat to the white workingmen's manhood. The Chinese were thus viewed with contempt as "rice-eating men" who had "neither the rights nor responsibilities of masculine 'beef-eating' men" – aka the white men.[38] On the other hand, there was fear of the fast-increasing size of the Chinese population. A common slur was that the Chinese were like "devouring locusts" that could easily overrun the settler societies. The idea that there were endless Chinese migrants who

---

[33] Bethencourt 2013, 6. See also Buzan and Lawson 2015, 119; and Taylor 2022, 56.
[34] Linklater 2016. [35] Rosenblatt 2018, 254–256. See also Bell 2014.
[36] Omi and Winant 2014, 109. [37] Lew-Williams 2018, 31.
[38] Lake and Reynolds 2008, 27.

would come in hordes and wipe out everything on their path stoked fear among whites who were also recent arrivals to the American West themselves.[39] In this view, the Chinese were cunning and ruthless, and the white people simply could not compete with them.

The racialized views of the Chinese were also heavily gendered. Because the overwhelming number of Chinese migrants were men, there was also widespread view in the American West that the Chinese men were queer, and thus did not have the same type of manhood as the white. Indeed, white working class men highlighted their bravery, pugnacity, and their manliness in direct opposition to the servile Chinese.[40] At the same time, the small number of Chinese women who made their way to the United States were often prostitutes. As a result, they were often blamed for the spread of venereal diseases, which were believed to be hereditary to Chinese women according to the medical science of the time. Chinese women were considered one of "the most abject and satanic conception of human slavery and the source of contamination [s] and hereditary disease."[41]

5.3.3 From Restriction to Exclusion

Indeed, the first federal legislation to restrict Chinese immigration specifically targeted the Chinese women. In 1875, at the urge of California, the Congress passed the Page Act that "prohibited the immigration of any Chinese woman who was not a merchant's wife and any 'Mongolian' woman who entered the country for the purpose of prostitution."[42] The Page Act intended to prevent Chinese women from migrating to the United States, and to force thousands of men to return to China. After the passing of the law, the overall ratio of Chinese females to males fell from 78 per 1,000 in 1870 to 47 per 1,000 in 1880.[43] This significantly reduced number of Chinese women meant there would be much less Chinese children born in the country and thus no future for a settled Chinese community in the United States.Threats of violence toward the Chinese and additional measures to stop their migration soon came to the center of American national politics. In the 1876 federal election, both Democrats and Republicans vied for anti-Chinese votes in the face of such threats of white racial violence and working-class revolt. The Workingmen's Party of California openly declared "Treason is better than to labor beside a Chinese slave," and "The people are about to take their own affairs into their own hands."[44] Such threats of violence forced the Republican Rutherford Hayes administration to seek China's approval for a revision of the Burlingame Treaty to restrict Chinese immigration. Viceroy Li Hongzhang,

---

[39] Ngai 2021, 117. [40] Lew-Williams 2018, 129. [41] Pfaelzer 2007, 98.
[42] Pfaelzer 2007, 101. [43] Pfaelzer 2007, 105. [44] Lew-Williams 2018, 45.

who believed that America could be a useful ally when China was facing encroachment from both Russia and Japan in Manchuria, agreed to the Angell Treaty. Ratified in 1881, it reversed the language of the Burlingame Treaty, and granted the United States the right to "regulate, limit, or suspend" Chinese migration.[45]

More bills were proposed in the Congress to limit Chinese migration further. In the end, in 1882 President Chester Arthur signed into law the first of a series of laws that together would be called "Chinese Exclusion Acts." The one signed in 1882 did not in fact exclude the Chinese from immigrating to the United States but set to restrict its scope. Its duration was also set to be ten years. In order to preserve commercial and diplomatic ties with China and the façade of open door, the act provided a set of exemptions for Chinese elites, including diplomats, merchants, students, and tourists.[46] It allowed the Chinese government to determine who would be able to receive such exemptions, which according to San Francisco customs at the time were defined very loosely. It also allowed return of migrants from China and even their passage through the United States to other destinations. Furthermore, the law did not create a specific immigration bureaucracy to task with immigration control, nor was there additional funding. Rather this onerous task fell on the shoulders of the Department of Treasury and its customs houses. In reality, with limited funding and manpower, it was very difficult to enforce such restriction. Overall, the act thus did not significantly slow Chinese immigration, despite the fact that it made life of the Chinese migrants much more difficult.Because of the perceived ineffectiveness of the Act, popular vigilante against the Chinese grew. In the summer of 1885, *Seattle Call* declared that "[t]here is no longer any hope of obtaining relief from this Chinese curse through the laws enacted by Congress. ... Their inefficiency to prevent Chinese immigration has been demonstrated. ... Since the federal government had failed, we must protect ourselves or be overrun by these heathens."[47] Violent expulsion of thousands of Chinese spread across towns and cities in the American West. They were expelled from Tacoma, Washington, and Eureka, California. They were met with violence and massacre at Rock Springs, Wyoming. Indeed, such violence toward the Chinese persons and their properties created a shockwave among national political elites. Facing an impending white racial revolt, the Congress would have to further exclude Chinese migration. In 1888, President Cleveland signed the Scott Act that prohibited the return of Chinese laborers after leaving the United States. In 1892, the Chinese Exclusion Act was extended in the Geary Act that further required Chinese people to carry a resident permit. Failure to do so would lead to their deportation or a year of hard labor. The

---

[45] Lew-Williams 2018, 47–48.   [46] Lew-Williams 2018, 56.   [47] Lew-Williams 2018, 88.

Chinese were also not allowed to bear witness in court and could not receive bail in habeas corpus proceedings.

Years of restriction and exclusion left a deep mark on the remaining Chinese community in the United States. The number of Chinese admitted to the United States fell to a very small trickle. While the number of Chinese who arrived in 1852 was around 20,000, that number dropped to 1,716 by 1891. Most of these were returned migrants anyway, which fundamentally hampered the organic growth of the Chinese community in the United States. The exclusion also created a pattern of their segregation and migration within the country. Because of the anti-Chinese violence in much of the American West, many decided to migrate to the East, while others stayed in those Chinatown enclaves. Most of the Chinese, even though they were legal and entered the country before 1882, remained perpetual aliens, because they were not eligible for citizenship because of their race. The registration card that they were made to carry would later become the green card that still certifies one's permanent residency status within the United States. Indeed, the whole concept of "resident alien" is a legacy of the exclusion era. The exclusion of Chinese also created a powerful precedent to racialize and exclude other "undesirable aliens" from America's gate.[48] For example, southern and eastern European immigrants were later denounced as "coolies, serfs, and slaves" as well, and the Foran Act of 1885 prohibited the immigration of all contract laborers. Similarly, the Page Act created a precedent to exclude individuals who were perceived as immoral or guilty of sexual misdeeds.[49]

As the United States expanded to take on more overseas territories, the Chinese Exclusion Act was made applicable to new territories of Hawaii and the Philippines that were annexed in 1898, and to Puerto Rico in 1899, and Cuba in 1902.[50] Touting the exclusion of Chinese as a benevolent act, the federal government argued that it was a policy to protect the natives in these overseas territories from Chinese encroachment. Such policies proved disastrous for the Chinese communities, particularly in Hawaii and the Philippines, where there already had been a large number of Chinese migrants, and many were in fact native born and settled through mixed marriages with local populations. In 1902, the Congress extended the Chinese Exclusion Act into perpetuity. Later on, the 1924 Immigration Act further expanded the exclusion laws to prohibit all Asians, including the Japanese from migrating to the United States. This act infuriated the Japanese government, as it violated the previous "gentlemen's agreement" between Washington and Tokyo that exempted the

---

[48] Lee 2003, 30.
[49] The Immigration Act of 1891 excluded women on moral grounds, including adultery, fornication, and illegitimate pregnancy. All prostitutes were excluded in the 1903 Immigration Act. See Lee 2003, 30–31.
[50] Lew-Williams 2018, 210.

Japanese. As a rising power with imperial ambitions and which also believed itself one of the modern great powers, the Japanese government took this as an insult to its national pride. The law led to strong anti-American sentiment and retaliation in Japanese foreign policy. In 1934, through the Tydings-McDuffie Act or the Philippine Independence Act, Filipinos were also excluded from migrating to the United States despite their being US nationals. Instead of letting the Filipinos have free access to the US mainland, the federal government would rather let the Philippines gain independence.

5.4 Chinese Nationalism and the Boycott Movement

By the early twentieth century, the West-centric international order, now also led by self-identified white Anglo-American powers, was deeply divided along the color line. After decades of forced racialization as a subordinate "colored" people, both overseas Chinese and those in mainland China came to redefine their own collective identity. As Seo-Hyun Park describes it, the period saw a "complex transition in East Asia, during which the ideational and institutional boundaries of national, regional, and global identity were being reframed."[51] While previously distinguishing among themselves on the basis of different regions and dialect groups of the multiethnic Qing empire, the Chinese now saw themselves as a unitary national group[52] that is simultaneously subjected to racialization as a yellow race within the new international system. After cultivating a deep sense of humiliation and racial awareness in the face of Chinese exclusion, both overseas and domestic Chinese elites through their transnational ties started envisioning modern Chinese nationalism – and ultimately a new *nation*-state – as a tool for resistance against the dominant "white" nations. A key actor in this transnational rise of Chinese nationalism was the Chinese Consolidated Benevolent Association, or more popularly known as the Six Companies in San Francisco, who were traditional Chinese home associations or *Huiguan* that served as socioeconomic support groups for merchants and immigrant workers from different regions of China. They facilitated the Chinese passage to the United States, provided assistance to the newcomers, functioned as mediators among the Chinese, and acted on their behalf to the outside world.[53] While *Huiguan* originally stood for respective home regions of China from which each individual derived his or her social identity, the Six Companies came to integrate the disparate Chinese communities in America, most importantly by adopting collective strategies to counter racism and lobbying against the exclusion laws as a representative of the Chinese people and nation. The Six Companies thus played a crucial role in promoting the sense of collective Chinese identity and worked closely with the Qing legation

---

[51] Park 2013, 281–307. [52] Wimmer 2008, 1035. [53] Chang 2019, 46.

in Washington – which was established years after the Burlingame Treaty and mass Chinese migration in 1875 – by helping the Qing officials learn the new techniques and practice of modern national diplomacy.[54] Not satisfied with the Qing legation's protest against the 1892 Geary Act that extended the Exclusion Act for another ten years, president of the Six Companies confronted Secretary of State John W. Foster, arguing that the bill "proposed to treat Chinamen like animals." The Six Companies also distributed a poster calling for solidary among all Chinese and petitioned the Qing emperor to act on behalf of "your children in this country."[55]

A watershed moment to such Chinese national awakening arrived in 1904, when the 1894 Gresham-Yang Treaty, which placed the Geary Act on a proper treaty basis between the American and Chinese governments, was due to expire. By the spring of 1905, Washington made it clear that Chinese exclusion would continue, and even get more stringent, by authorizing the Bureau of Immigration to carry out arbitrary deportations of Chinese residents.[56] As over twenty telegrams by Chinese Americans protesting the treaty renewal poured into the Chinese Foreign Office in May,[57] the leadership of the Shanghai Chamber of Commerce passed resolutions urging all Chinese in Shanghai not to buy American goods. It then called upon the chambers of commerce of twenty-two other treaty ports to join the anti-American boycott movement, signaling the onset of the transnational Chinese boycott movement of 1905. As direct targets of exclusion and decades-long pioneers of modern Chinese nationalism, overseas Chinese in America turned out to be the most generous financial donors to their fellow boycott participants in Shanghai, Guangdong, Hong Kong, as well as overseas Chinese communities in Singapore and Malaya.[58] Perhaps more importantly, their vivid descriptions of life under exclusion and racial violence were widely circulated in Chinese newspapers, read aloud at boycott rallies, and thus supplied a key source of nationalist sentiments and racial resentment. At the same time, Chinese American leaders such as the first Chinese Christian minister and publisher Ng Poon Chew were joined by prominent Qing reformers like Kang Youwei in their American tours delivering fervent speeches against exclusion and inspiring in broader masses new experiences of nationalism and political activism.[59] While the boycott activists eventually achieved little in influencing actual American immigration policy and treatment of Chinese, they successfully transformed the movement into China's first mass mobilization of anti-foreign sentiment and the sense of national humiliation – a political force as alive in today's China as it was 100 years ago.[60]

[54] Qin 2009, 1. [55] Qin 2009, 121, 123. [56] McKee 1986, 174. [57] McKee 1986, 175.
[58] Wong 1998. [59] Larson 2007.
[60] IR scholars have closely examined the influence of anti-foreign nationalist protests and the discourse of national humiliation on Chinese foreign policy, particularly after the end of the Cold War. Gries 2004; Wang 2008; Weiss 2014.

Through their speeches and popular writings, the boycott leaders also drew on the ideas of social Darwinism and instilled in both overseas and mainland Chinese the view that "the world was ... a Hobbesian battleground where the strong preys on the weak ... if the Chinese were unfairly treated, it was because China was weak, and weak races would become extinct in the ruthless competition for survival."[61] Originally serving as the legitimizing myth of dominant whites, such racial theories and worldviews provided an ideological template for the construction of modern Chinese identity and statehood. This convergence of racial awareness and nationalism during the boycott movement, therefore, can be understood as a direct antecedent to the ethno-racial nationalism in modern China. Many boycott leaders and followers in fact became central players in the revolutionary movements that led up to the collapse of the Qing empire in 1912.[62]

5.5 Chinese Exclusion Then and Now

The historical significance of the Chinese Exclusion Act extends far beyond the single context of America's domestic race relations and should be understood within the global landscape of the emerging modern international order in "the long nineteenth century" and extending into the twentieth. Driven by the technological and military superiority of peoples of European origin, the first fully integrated international system was being ostensibly shaped not only by power dynamics but also by the logic of global racial hierarchy. Within this turbulent making of the modern world, the exclusion acts played a critical role. Brought by the forced opening of China and the expanding Anglo-American spheres of influence, the large-scale international contact between Chinese and Euro-Americans soon produced what Wendt would call a Hobbesian dynamic of interaction *and* co-constitution between Self and (racial) Other.[63] From the 1875 Page Act to the 1905 Chinese boycott movement, a spiral of mutually reinforcing racial resentment and identities became a powerful driver of this essentially *transnational* intergroup security dilemma.[64] Triggered by economic anxiety, opportunistic elites, and the new vocabulary of scientific racism, European Americans increasingly subscribed to their white racial identity while viewing Chinese and subsequently other peoples of Asian origin collectively as the "yellow peril."[65] The Chinese, in turn, as they went through decades of forced racialization, marginalization, and eventual full-blown

---

[61] Wang 2001, 145. [62] Ts'ai 1976, 96. [63] Wendt 1999. See also Wendt 1992.
[64] For a pathbreaking discussion of the relationship between racism and security dilemmas in international politics, see Johnston, forthcoming. Here Johnston points out that the intensification of identity difference, especially in terms of racial identities, is one of the behavioral components of the life cycle of security dilemmas.
[65] Lee 2015.

exclusion, now engaged in the construction of their own collective identity that was likewise to be defined in interlocking terms of race, ethnicity, and nationalism. Heralding "the biggest change in the Chinese three thousand years' history,"[66] the rise of modern Chinese nationalism subsequently contributed to the 1905 anti-American boycott movement against Chinese exclusion and the collapse of the Qing empire in 1912. There is also an important parallel between the global politics of Chinese exclusion in the past and contemporary international relations that are now characterized by rising ethno-racial nationalisms, populist elites, and resentment between groups both within and across borders.[67] Today's US-China geopolitical tensions in particular are articulated increasingly in terms of mutually exclusive and reinforcing identities – be they ideological, civilizational, or, importantly, ethno-racial.[68] Similar to how national and racial identities shaped and were shaped by the transnational Hobbesian dynamic between Chinese and European Americans during their "First Encounter,"[69] growing discourses of identity and resentment have once again become central to contemporary Sino-American security dilemmas.[70] Moreover, the recent rise of anti-Asian violence since the global pandemic has not only revealed the deep-seated and recurring American animus toward the "yellow peril" but also simultaneously convinced the Chinese that the world is still dominated by the same "white" countries responsible for China's continued national humiliation.[71] As 100 years ago, transnational Chinese communities have been playing an important role in promoting collective identity and anti-foreign sentiments – to an even greater and faster extent via cyberspace – by sharing their firsthand experiences of racial discrimination, affecting both overseas and mainland Chinese opinion and thereby pressuring the government in Beijing.[72]

Seen in this light, the United States and China today face each other in a world "defined predominantly by the downstream consequences of the nineteenth-century global transformation."[73] The Chinese exclusion was America's past answer to the "Chinese Question" after long debates between proponents of racial hierarchy on the one hand and liberal inclusion and diversity on the other.[74] And these two opposing forces, recently termed by Zoltán Búzás as "traditional" and "transformative coalitions" in international

---

[66] Qin 2009, 138.
[67] For a theoretical discussion of the centrality of identity politics and resentment in post-Cold War international politics, see Fukuyama 2018.
[68] For one of the most prominent discourses today on China's civilizational identity, see Weiwei 2012.
[69] Wendt 1999.
[70] For a discussion of identity discourses and US–China security dilemmas, see Breuer and Johnston 2019.
[71] Gries 2004; Wang 2008. See also Kim, forthcoming.   [72] See also Callahan 2005.
[73] Buzan and Lawson 2015, 5.   [74] Rosenblatt 2018.

politics,[75] have survived to this day and are still contending to steer the world toward more racially exclusive or inclusive directions. Which side prevails to shape future international order will have far-reaching effects on the prospect of peace and conflicts among both great powers *and* different groups of people in our society – as it did a century ago.

[75] Búzás 2021.

6 Race and Great Power Politics: The Japanese Racial Equality Proposal of 1919

Erez Manela

In recent years, international relations scholars have begun to note and critique the "norm against noticing" race in the contemporary IR literature.[1] In the early part of the twentieth century, however, the use of racial lenses in the analysis of international affairs was commonplace. Indeed, World War I was often framed at the time as a fratricidal conflict within the "white race," giving rise to perceptions that the war had destabilized international order not least by challenging the assumptions of racial hierarchy on which it was founded. In Europe and North America, these perceptions gave rise to anxieties about rising threats to "white world supremacy."[2] Elsewhere around the world, perceptions of Western decline served as an accelerant behind the numerous anti-colonial revolts that broke out in the immediate aftermath of the conflict.[3]

Moreover, the war's aftermath saw the first time that the problem of racial prejudice and its solution, the principle of racial equality, were directly broached at a major international forum, via a proposal made by the Japanese delegation to the Paris Peace Conference of 1919. As the victorious Allies gathered in Paris to negotiate the peace, Japan was recognized as one of the five "great powers" at the conference, alongside the United States, the British empire, France, and Italy. The Japanese government came to Paris with some territorial desiderata, but it also sought to use the opportunity to enshrine the principle of racial equality in the postwar international order. Thus, Japan proposed inserting a provision to that effect in the Covenant of the League of Nations that was to be negotiated at Paris – a document widely seen at the time as a new "constitution" for the world.

For the Japanese public, the inclusion of such a provision in the League Covenant was not merely symbolic. Rather, it would help ensure the principle

---

[1] Freeman 2022. On this critique, see also Acharya 2022; Zvobgo and Loken 2020a; forum on Zvobgo and Loken 2020b; Vitalis 2015; and the section on "Race and International Relations: Introduction" in the *Cambridge Review of International Affairs*, 26 (1): 1–4 (Bell 2013).
[2] Stoddard 1920.
[3] Manela 2009. Although these revolts were largely suppressed in a wave of imperial reassertion, the interwar era saw rising challenges to the racial basis of the imperial world order, from Garveyism to Pan-Asianism and beyond.

of equal treatment for Japanese residing abroad, particularly in the United States and the white dominions of the British empire. The discriminatory treatment of Japanese there was viewed in Japan as a profound humiliation and ending it was a long-standing goal of Tokyo's foreign policy.[4] Despite common perceptions at the time and since, the Japanese proposal was not designed as a broad challenge to racial hierarchy in international society – the global color line – or to the imperial order that this hierarchy supported.[5] Japan, after all, was by this point itself a colonial power, ruling over Korea and Taiwan and seeking to gain further territories at the peace table. Indeed, even as Tokyo was pursuing the racial equality proposal in Paris, its forces were engaged in the violent suppression of a Korean uprising on the peninsula.

The Japanese delegates first approached the US delegation discretely and asked for their help inserting language on racial equality into an article in the League Covenant. The Americans were initially sympathetic but the British delegation, spurred by vehement opposition from Australia, scuttled the idea. As the negotiations dragged on, the Japanese proposal became public and raised fierce domestic opposition in the United States, further complicating the position of the US delegation in Paris. Scaling back their ambitions, the Japanese eventually proposed to insert a vague statement about the equality of nations into the covenant's preamble. Even that effort, however, eventually failed.

The story of the Japanese racial equality proposal has often been cast as a simple narrative of an initiative against racism foiled by a racist US president.[6] In this telling, a proposal challenging white supremacy in international relations received majority support at the League of Nations Commission – the body charged with drawing up the League covenant – but was rejected by the commission's chair, President Woodrow Wilson, who conjured for this purpose a novel requirement for unanimity. Wilson racist views are well known, and his administration had infamously introduced segregation in the federal government for the first time since Reconstruction. Thus, the rejection of the Japanese racial equality proposal of 1919 becomes yet another example of Wilson's personal racism and, more broadly, of the influence of US racism in the international arena.

---

[4] A prominent example of such discrimination was the California Alien Land Law of 1913, which imposed severe restrictions on Asian immigrants leasing or owning land. For the rise of anti-Asian policies in the British dominions and elsewhere, see Lauren 1988, 51–58.
[5] Lake and Reynolds 2008.
[6] For example, Freeman et al., cited in n.1, write that although the Japanese proposal "received broad support" in Paris, President Wilson, "who himself had resegregated the US civil service ... summarily declared that such an important change required unanimity, which effectively killed the proposal." With no other reason for the rejection offered, this formulation implies that it was simply Wilson's racism that explains the rejection. The fact that no citation accompanies this description suggests that the authors view this explanation as widely accepted.

While Wilson certainly did hold racist views and implement racist policies, careful histories of this episode have found little evidence that these views were decisive in this case.[7] Instead, two factors stand out as important in explaining the failure of the Japanese proposal. The first and most important was the resistance of the British delegation in Paris, and especially from the Australian prime minister, Billy Hughes, who worried about the domestic implications of any concession to the Japanese demands. Hughes' vociferous opposition prompted the British delegation to emerge in Paris as the strongest opponent of the Japanese proposal. A second, contributing factor was the opposition that met the Japanese proposal in the United States, particularly among key senators from western states whose votes Wilson needed in order to get the peace treaty, of which the League Covenant was a part, ratified in the US Senate.

The story of the Japanese racial equality proposal has important implications, then, for our understanding of the intersection between the role of race in international relations and its influence in domestic politics. It shows how racism embedded in domestic politics shaped the foreign policies of major powers and, by extension, the dynamics of international society. At the same time, it suggests the complexity of the role of that race has played in international relations. While in retrospect the failure of the Japanese proposal may have appeared inevitable, the chain of events as the historical actors experienced it at the time was in fact more contingent. With the horrors of the war having challenged assumptions of white supremacy and President Wilson's ringing endorsement of the equality of nations echoing around the world, it did not at the time seem impossible that the Japanese racial equality proposal, in one form or another, might succeed.

6.1   Japan at the Paris Peace Conference

International relations in the early twentieth century were structured through an imperial world order built on foundations of white supremacy of which Japan, too, had initially been a victim. After its forcible "opening" to outside commerce and influences in 1853, Japan was subject to many of the same imperial depredations as other nations in Asia (and elsewhere), including unequal treaties that circumscribed its legal and economic sovereignty. Earlier than other non-European nations, however, the Japanese managed to extract themselves from these shackles. In 1899, after winning a war against China, Tokyo got the European treaty powers renounce their extraterritorial privileges. By 1911, after its shocking defeat of the Russian empire in the war of 1904–05,

---

[7] The standard work is Shimazu 1998. Also useful is Guoqi 2016, 185–210. Paul Gordon Lauren's pioneering article is still worth consulting for its deep research and vivid quotes, though its interpretative frame lacks the nuance of the later works. Lauren 1978.

Japan also won back its tariff autonomy. By 1919, then, virtually alone among nonwhite nations, Japan had ostensibly met the so-called standard of civilization that qualified it for recognition as a fully sovereign power in international society.[8]

At the peace table in Paris, Japan's status as the world's leading nonwhite power was confirmed when its delegation was allotted five seats at the conference's plenary table. This was the same number allotted to the other four great powers in attendance: the United States, Great Britain, France, and Italy. No other power got more than three seats; most got only one or two (see Figure 6.1).

The plenary session, to be sure, was of largely symbolic significance, as most important decisions at the conference were made in deliberations among the great powers. The so-called Big Five were eventually reduced to three – the United States, Britain, and France – since the Japanese delegates opted not weigh in on issues that did not directly concern their interests and the Italians left in a huff midway through the conference. Yet this seating chart provides a clear illustration of the hierarchy among the participating nations, signified in both the number of seats and in their location around the table. The US delegation is seated to the host's right, reflecting its preeminent status. The British delegation is seated to the host's left, the second ranked position, though there were separate seats, in addition to London's five, allotted to the white dominions and to India (two each except for New Zealand, with one). All told, the British empire occupied an extraordinary fourteen seats at the table, a reflection of its broad influence in the negotiations.

The seating location of the other major powers also denoted their relative status. France and then Italy were placed beyond the US delegation to the host's right. Japan was on the left side, past the British empire's fourteen plenipotentiaries, marking it as the least among the five major powers. This position, of course, reflected a host of considerations, not least the fact that Japan saw far less fighting than other powers and contributed little to the Allied war effort. Still, the seating arrangement signaled that though Japan's was now among the great powers, it was not fully their equal.

Moreover, unlike the delegations of the other great powers, Japan's was headed not by a head of state – as was the case with the US delegation – nor even by a head of government, as were those of Britain, France, and Italy. Its formal head was Marquis Saionji Kinmochi, a former prime minister who by 1919 was effectively in retirement and in ill health, and so did not take an active

---

[8] Gong 1984. As Xu Guoqi points out, it took Turkey until 1923 and China until 1943 to fully abrogate the extraterritorial privileges of foreign powers. Xu 2016, 185. For Japan's unusual position within the racial hierarchy of the era, see Merida 2023.

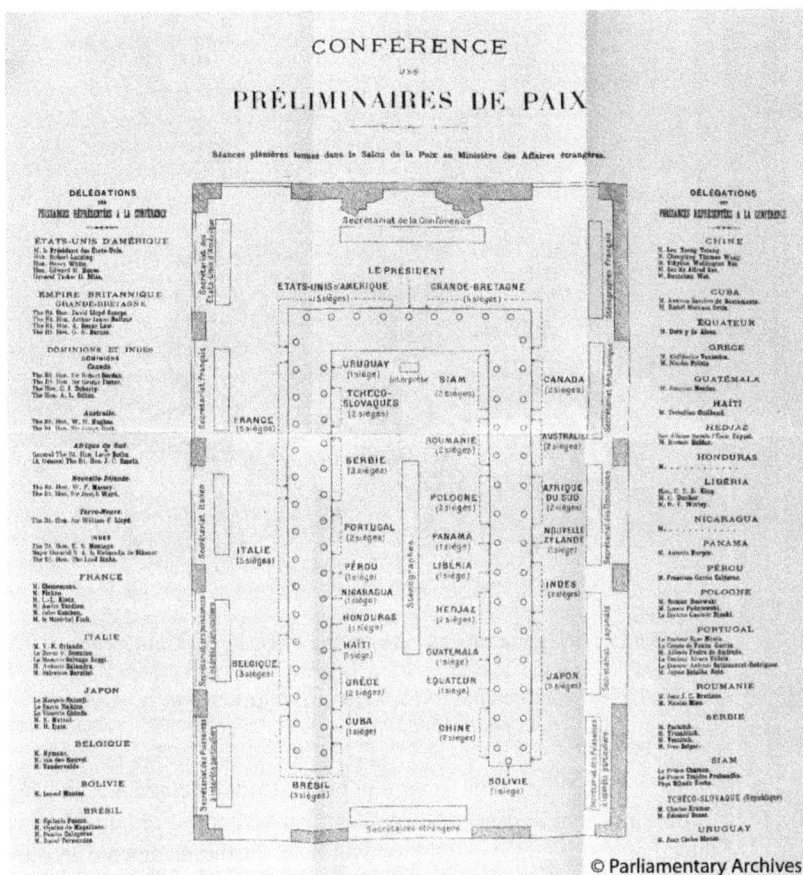

Figure 6.1 **The seating chart for the plenary session of the Paris Peace Conference in 1919**. The major powers – the United States, Britain, France, Italy, and Japan each had five seats at the table, whereas all other participants got three or fewer. With the British Dominions and India occupying their own seats at the table, the British empire as a whole had a grand total of fourteen seats. Japan was clearly the highest status nonwhite power at the table; China and Siam, the only other participants from East Asia, had only two seats each.
Source: Courtesy of UK Parliament, "Seating Plan of the Paris Peace Conference," www.parliament.uk/about/living-heritage/transformingsociety/private-lives/yourcountry/collections/paris-1919-vers/par-peace-sp/.

part in negotiations (Figure 6.2). The de facto leader was his deputy, Baron Makino Nobuaki, who had served a brief stint as Japan's foreign minister before the war but had long since stepped down. Neither Japan's prime minister

Figure 6.2 **The Japanese delegates to the Paris Peace Conference**. Marquis Saionji, the delegation head, is seated front and center. Baron Makino, the second-in-command, is seated on the left. *Source: Courtesy of Library of Congress, public domain.*

at the time, Hara Takashi, nor his foreign minister, Count Uchida Kōsai, made the journey to Paris. The Japanese delegates in Paris, then, were outranked by those of the other major powers, and their work was further hampered by slow communications between Tokyo and Paris and by the government's frequent indecision – the Hara cabinet had only been in power a few months and its political position was tenuous.[9]

From the start, then, the Japanese position in Paris was ambivalent – included among the great powers but as the least among equals. Still, this disadvantage was counterbalanced by the fact that Japan came to Paris with a far more limited agenda than the other major powers. It had little interest in the complex and consequential debates over the postwar territorial settlements in Europe and the Middle East or in the discussion about German war guilt and reparations. In fact, Tokyo instructed its delegates to avoid embroiling themselves in these issues, a dictate they followed so faithfully that Japan came to be ridiculed in Paris as "the silent partner," involving itself only in issues that touched on its own self-interest.[10]

---

[9] Shimazu 1998, 15–16.   [10] Minohara 2020.

The Japanese desiderata in Paris were largely limited to three points: first, obtaining control over Germany's island possessions in the Pacific that it captured during the war, which the conference would indeed eventually award to Japan to govern under the League of Nations mandate system. Second, Tokyo wanted to obtain formal recognition of its wartime occupation of the German concession territories in China's Shandong Province, centered on the city of Qingdao. The final desideratum, and the one that concerns us here, was to insert language opposing racial discrimination into the League Covenant.

6.2   Japan Makes a Proposal

On February 4, 1919, shortly after the conference opened, Makino and Count Chinda Sutemi, the ambassador to London and a fellow delegate, approached President Wilson's close adviser, Colonel Edward M. House, a member of the US delegation. They came, they said, to ask for advice on "what Japan had best do regarding the race question." The Japanese public, they explained, demanded that the League of Nations Covenant then being prepared express "some broad principle of racial equality," and they hoped that the United States could help having such language included in the text. House asked them for two versions of the resolution they wanted – "one which they desired, and another which they would be willing to accept" – and promised to see what he could do. House added that in his view race prejudice was "one of the serious causes of international trouble" and should therefore be confronted in some way at the peace conference.[11]

The Japanese returned to House the next day with the two versions of a draft article, the one they wanted and another they were willing to settle for. House showed them to the president that afternoon. The first version, House reported breezily in his diary, was "discarded at once,"[12] but the other version "the President thought might do" and made some edits to it in his own hand. House showed Chinda the amended text later that evening. Chinda, who had served as ambassador to Washington from 1912 to 1916 before moving to London, seemed pleased with the result, though he said he wanted to discuss it with his colleagues before he accepted the changes.[13]

---

[11] "From the Diary of Colonel House, February 4, 1919," [henceforth House Diary] in *The Papers of Woodrow Wilson* [henceforth Link, *PWW*] 54: 484–485.

[12] House apparently meant this literally since the editors of *The Papers of Woodrow Wilson*, the definitive collection of Wilson's papers, noted that they could not find this text in the archival record. Link, *PWW* 54: 500 n. 2.

[13] "House Diary, February 5, 1919," in Link, *PWW* 54: 499–500.

The text of the draft article that the Japanese proposed, with Wilson's edits (deletions in parentheses and additions in italics), was as follows:

> The equality of nations being a basic principle of the League, the H.C.P. agree that concerning the aliens in their territories, they will accord them, (as far as in their legitimate power,) *so soon and so far as practicable*, equal treatment and rights in law and in fact, without making any distinction on account of their race or nationality.[14]

The language of the proposal, then, was quite specific: Its focus was guaranteeing equal rights to aliens already resident in other states, not a right to free immigration into those states. Moreover, the Japanese delegates accepted Wilson's substantial weakening of the text with his edits, which left to the discretion of each government when and how it might implement the call for "equal treatment and rights." Tokyo, knowing it could not get a binding commitment to equal treatment to their citizens, was willing to accept something less: a statement of principle that could be presented as an achievement to the public at home and perhaps built upon in future diplomatic negotiations.

Yet even this request for, as House called it, a "mild and inoffensive" gesture quickly met with fierce resistance at the peace conference. This came mainly from the British empire delegation. The chief instigator was the Australian prime minister, Billy Hughes. Other members of the British delegation either agreed with Hughes' position or, even if they did not, were unwilling to challenge him on this issue.[15] For Hughes, the Japanese proposal was a clear threat to his policy of a "White Australia" and resisting was crucial to his chances in the general elections there that were expected later that year. So, Hughes became the proposal's most determined opponent in Paris, protesting that the proposed clause would impinge on the domestic affairs of Australia and threatening to speak against it publicly if it were to be included in the League Covenant presented to the plenary.[16]

6.3 Domestic Politics and International Context

For some weeks afterward, it seemed that the Australian (and therefore British) opposition meant the end of the line for the proposal. Yet the Japanese were not

---

[14] "A Draft Article for the Covenant," in Link, *PWW* 54: 500.

[15] House Diary, February 13, 1919, in Link *PWW* 55: 155. The British foreign secretary, Arthur Balfour, told House that he "did not believe that any of the English-speaking communities would tolerate a great Japanese flow of immigration" and, if that was the case, inserting in the covenant language implying otherwise would be counterproductive. Balfour cited in Shimazu 1998, 18–19. Canada prime minister, Robert Borden, took a more moderate approach, seeking to preserve both restrictions on Asian immigration and good relations with Japan, but his efforts to broker a compromise failed. See McKenzie 2017.

[16] Shimazu 1998, 23–27. The Australian position and its influence on the British Empire delegation in Paris is discussed in detail in Chapter 5 of Shimazu's book.

ready to give up. Influential groups among the Japanese public had come to expect that, as a result of its wartime support for the Allies, Japan and its people would, finally, achieve the respect they were due in international society. Fearing the domestic repercussions of failure, Tokyo was keen to meet that expectation.[17]

In early March, with President Wilson back in the United States for a brief visit, the Japanese ambassador in Washington, Ishii Kikujiro, asked to see him. Told that the president had already left for New York City and would head directly back to Paris from there, Ishii left a letter from his government instead. In it, Tokyo thanked Wilson for his efforts for peace and for the "sympathy and support" he and the American delegation gave to the Japanese effort to do away with "race discriminations." It then proceeded to lay out the most explicit argument so far that support for the principle of racial equality was crucial for the preservation of world peace.

The spirit of the League of Nations, the letter said, required establishing the principle "that the difference of race should in no case constitute a basis for discriminatory treatment under the law of any country." Failure to do so would bring about constant friction "among nations and races," which would hamper the work of the League. Therefore, Japan would continue to pursue its proposal and it hoped for the president's support. But, the letter added, Tokyo would not insist on the format or wording of its original proposal; instead, it would be happy to entertain any suggestion the president may have on this point.[18] By signaling its flexibility on wording and format, Tokyo again suggested that it did not demand a legal commitment. It wanted a gesture that would satisfy domestic opinion and national honor.

Ten days later, Ishii escalated the campaign by taking it public. Speaking at a dinner meeting of the Japan Society at the Hotel Astor in New York City on March 14, he announced that his government wanted "the inclusion of a provision against racial discrimination" in the covenant of the League of Nations.[19] Ishii insisted in that address that this provision need not mean equal treatment for Japanese nationals in immigration, and indeed, as we saw, the text of the proposal focused on equal treatment to aliens already in the country rather to on the right to immigrate. Still, the speech created a furor in Congress and in the press among supporters of the long-standing discrimination against Asians on matters of immigration and citizenship. And, though Ishii did not say that his government would reject the League Covenant if this provision was not included in it, this notion, too, spread quickly, not least among senators in

---

[17] Shimazu 1998, esp. 50–66.
[18] Breckinridge Long to Woodrow Wilson, March 4, 1919, in Link, *PWW* 55: 436–437.
[19] "Ishii Looks to End Race Prejudice," *NYT*, March 15, 1919.

western states who rushed to issue sharp denunciations of this supposed Japanese demand.[20]

The furor raised by Ishii's speech in the United States was such that the Japanese delegates in Paris felt compelled to reassure their US counterparts, telling House that while they reserved the right to take the issue of racial equality up with the League on a future date, they would not seek to block the covenant over it.[21] Meanwhile, some within the US delegation hoped that the British opposition to the proposal would scuttle it without requiring the United States to oppose it openly. Indeed, by late March this appeared to be happening, as the Japanese delegates agreed to table their proposal while reserving the right to renew it at a later date.[22]

Back in Washington, Ambassador Ishii was busy managing the fallout from his March 14 speech. In an interview published on March 21, Ishii averred that his speech did not reflect the official position of his government but was simply his attempt to reflect Japanese public opinion. Nor did it represent an attempt to alter the status quo on immigration. Tokyo, he said, was satisfied with the so-called gentlemen's agreement, an arrangement dating back to 1907 through which the Japanese government voluntarily enforced strict limits on the emigration to the United States and the US federal government, in return, worked to ensure the rights of Japanese already resident in the United States.[23] Still, Ishii said, support for "race equality," just like support for the principle of government by the consent of the governed, was "a matter of simple justice," and the inclusion of this principle in League Covenant would make Japanese people more enthused about it. He therefore hoped for a friendly and favorable settlement of question.[24]

Ishii's reference to the "consent of the governed," a favorite phrase in Wilson's wartime speeches, sought to frame the principle of racial equality within the broader horizon of Wilsonian principles. In this way, the Japanese move to advance a proposal for racial equality intersected with the broader historical conjuncture that I have elsewhere called the "Wilsonian moment," defined as the widespread mobilizations in the immediate wake of the war behind the notion that the principles that Wilson had articulated for the peace

---

[20] "Ishii's Plea Stirs Western Senators," *NYT*, March 16, 1919.
[21] "From the Diary of Dr. Grayson," March 18, 1919, *PWW* 56: 59–60.
[22] "From the Diary of Dr. Grayson," March 22, 1919, *PWW* 56: 164, and April 11, 1919, *PWW* 57: 239–240.
[23] The 1907 agreement emerged from the so-called "California Crisis," which was ignited by the decision of the San Francisco School Board to segregate Japanese children in a separate school. On this episode, see Merida 2023, Chapter 5. As Merida points out, although Japan in this period sometimes enjoyed the status of an "honorary white" nation for the purpose of interstate relations (e.g., receiving great power status at the peace conference), Japanese individuals living in the United States and other white settler societies remained marked as nonwhite and subject to discriminatory treatment.
[24] "Polk to American Commissioners," March 22, 1919, *PWW* 56: 187–189.

could lay the foundation for a radically new international order.[25] As peoples in many parts of the world mobilized behind calls for equality and self-determination, the Japanese press and civil society also mobilized around the demand for racial equality.[26]

This broader context meant that despite the limited aim of the Japanese proposal itself – to claim equal rights for Japanese residing abroad – some at the time saw in it the potential to deliver a broad blow against white supremacy writ large. Already in the early months of the war, the African American activist and intellectual W. E. B. Du Bois expressed the hope that "the fact that black Africans and brown Indians and yellow Japanese are fighting for France and England" in the war might lead the latter to emerge from the bloodletting with "new ideas of the essential equality of men."[27] When the war ended, Du Bois, like many other nonwhite activists, headed to Paris to try to advance the rights of what he called the "darker races." So, he and others interpreted the news about the Japanese proposal and the debate around it within the context of that wider struggle.

The Japanese press, moreover, initially encouraged this view, calling on Japan to champion the principle of racial equality for all. Indeed, it seems that at least some in Japan thought that their country ought to play that role.[28] The Japanese government and its delegates in Paris, however, were more circumspect. When representatives of African American groups and delegates from Liberia and Ireland approached the Japanese delegation with expressions of gratitude for their proposal, they met with a cool reception. Japan, Makino told a Liberian delegate, could only represent its own interests at the peace table. If Liberia wished to take up the matter of racial discrimination in Africa, it should do so itself.[29]

6.4   Things Come to a Head

By April, after the furor that followed Ishii's speech, the Japanese government and its delegates in Paris decided to change tack. Giving up on the idea of inserting a separate article on racial equality in the League Covenant, they decided instead to propose inserting an amendment to that effect into the preamble of the covenant. A clause in the preamble would be less binding in international law than an article in the body of the covenant. This change, they hoped, would help soften the opposition in Paris while still getting a statement of principle into the text that would help satisfy domestic opinion.[30]

As the members of the League Commission met yet again on April 11 to finalize the text of the League Covenant, time was of the essence. The

---

[25] Manela 2009.   [26] This is covered extensively in Xu 2016.   [27] Gallicchio 2000, 18.
[28] Merida 2023, 153–157.   [29] Dickinson 2013, 254.   [30] Shimazu 1998, 27–33.

negotiations among the allies had already gone on for far too long, dragging into their third month even as the situation in Europe and elsewhere appeared increasingly unsettled. The chaos in Russia, prompted by the Bolshevik seizure of power the pervious November, was spreading westward. Communist factions had come to power in Hungary and Bavaria and the recently established republican government in Germany seemed on the verge of collapse. Upheaval was also rising in the colonial world, including in Egypt, India, and Korea. If stability was to be restored, the League Covenant, a cornerstone of the new international order, had to be finalized.

The meeting lasted well past midnight as the members of the commission discussed and approved twenty-five articles, one-by-one. Toward the very end of the meeting, when they came to the text of the preamble to the covenant, Makino rose to read a prepared statement.[31] He had already raised this issue previously, he said, but in a different form. Given that it was an issue of great concern to "a considerable part of mankind, and especially to the nation" that he represented, he would take the liberty of raising it again. He continued:

The League is intended to be a world instrument for enforcing righteousness and defeating force. It is to be the highest Court of Justice. It will, besides providing for social reforms, also look after the welfare and interests of the less advanced peoples by entrusting their government to mandatory States. It is an attempt to regulate the conduct of nations and peoples toward one another according to a higher moral standard than has obtained in the past, and to administer fairer justice throughout the world. These ideas have touched the inmost human soul and have quickened the common feelings of different peoples scattered over the five continents. It has given birth to hopes and aspirations, and strengthened the sense of legitimate claims they consider as their due.

The sentiment of nationality, one of the strongest human feelings, has been aroused by the present world-wide moral renaissance, and is at present receiving just recognition in adjusting international affairs. In close connection with the grievances of the oppressed nationalities, there exist the wrongs of racial discrimination which was, and is, the subject of deep resentment of the part of a large portion of the human race. The feeling of being slighted has long been a standing grievance with certain peoples. And the announcement of the principle of justice for peoples and nationalities as the basis of the future international relationship has so heightened their legitimate aspirations, that they consider it their right that this wrong should be redressed.

It is here that Makino came closest to invoking an argument for racial equality not only for Japan or for Japanese nationals abroad but also in the name of the nonwhite world writ large. How else are we to interpret the connection he makes between "the grievances of the oppressed nationalities" and the "wrongs of racial discrimination" which has been "the subject of deep resentment" among "a large portion of the human race"?

---

[31] Makino's address is printed in *PWW* 57:259–261. All the following quotes from it are taken from that source.

Of course, the expansive scope of Makino's critique of racial discrimination harbored a contradiction. After all, among those then expressing most strongly the "sentiment of nationality" and demanding an end to their oppression were the people of Korea who had, about six weeks earlier on March 1, 1919, launched a popular uprising against Japanese rule. Chinese nationalists, too, were aggrieved by Japan's history of interference in their affairs, including, most immediately, Tokyo's demand to take over the former German concessions in Shandong Province.[32] That Makino chose to frame his demand in that way, and that no one present challenged him on this point, suggests that everyone in the room understood that this universal language actually embodied a demand particular to Japan.

Still, Makino continued to unspool the argument for the Japanese amendment in universal terms. The support of the peoples of the world, and not merely of governments, was needed for the work of readjusting international affairs, he said, and their support would be necessary for the future success of the system being put in place. Given this, he continued:

> I think it only reasonable that the principle of equality of nations and the just treatment of their nationals be laid down as a fundamental basis of future relations in this world organisation. If this reasonable and just claim is now denied, it will, in the eyes of those people with reason to be keenly interested, have the significance of a reflection on their quality and status. Their faith in the justice and righteousness, which are to be the guiding spirit of the Covenant, may be shaken.

One dangerous possibility, noted Makino, was that peoples' faith would be so shaken that they would refuse to carry out their obligations under the covenant, most notably those related to collective security. For why would such disillusioned nations submit "to a call for heavy and serious obligations" to come to the "defense of those at whose hand they are refused a just treatment"? The peacemakers must bear this danger in mind, he cautioned, "for pride is one of the most forceful and sometimes uncontrollable causes of human action." Humiliation, in other words, would be detrimental to cooperation. Failure to address the question of equality would undermine the legitimacy of the League.

A dozen years later, in 1931, Japan would invade and occupy Manchuria, in China's northeast. It would sever it from Chinese rule, establish there the puppet state of Manchukuo, and then respond to the League's injunction to withdraw by withdrawing not from Manchuria but from the League itself. The Japanese invasion of Manchuria in 1931 did not, of course, flow directly from the rejection of the racial equality proposal in 1919. Still, one cannot help but wonder: Had the principle of racial equality been included in the covenant in

---

[32] Manela 2009, esp. Chapters 5 and 6.

1919, would Japan have been less likely to withdraw from the League fourteen years later?

Finally, as if to soften the impression left by his remarks thus far, Makino noted that the Japanese proposal intended simply to "lay down a general principle" that would govern relations between "the nationalities forming the League." That is, the principle would not apply to nonmembers, for example to colonial territories. He also emphasized, significantly, that his amendment was not meant to "encroach on the internal affairs" of any nation but rather to set forth a "guiding principle for future international intercourse." The amendment, he added, did not fully meet Japan's wishes but was a compromise that accounted for "various aspects and realities of present international relations" – that is to say, the discriminatory policies and practices of the United States and the British Dominions.[33]

Having laid down this groundwork, Makino finally put forward the new, and final, Japanese proposal. The text of the covenant preamble as it then stood (and as was eventually approved) was as follows:

THE HIGH CONTRACTING PARTIES,
In order to promote international co-operation and to achieve international peace and security
 by the acceptance of obligations not to resort to war,
 by the prescription of open, just and honourable relations between nations,
 by the firm establishment of the understandings of international law as the actual rule of conduct among Governments, and
 by the maintenance of justice and a scrupulous respect for all treaty obligations in the dealings of organised peoples with one another,
 Agree to this Covenant of the League of Nations.

Makino's proposal, he said, was to add after the words "relations between nations" above the following clause: "by the endorsement of the principle of the equality of Nations and the just treatment of their nationals." With this, he rested his case. Notably, though he had referred explicitly to the "wrongs of racial discrimination" in his remarks, the word "race" was nowhere found in the actual text of the amendment, presumably in the spirit of compromise Makino had invoked. Instead, the phrase "equality of Nations" was used as an implicit stand in for racial equality.

The British delegate, Lord Robert Cecil, was the first to respond. Makino, Cecil later confessed to his diary, had given "an extremely effective paper." Moreover, Jan Smuts, the South African statesman (and soon to be prime minister) who was the other British empire delegate on the Commission, had

---

[33] See chapter on the Chinese Exclusion Acts in this volume.

"fled," abandoning Cecil in an uncomfortable spot.[34] A committed internationalist and leading advocate for the League, Cecil could hardly gainsay the justice of the Japanese demand. The equality of nations, everyone around the table agreed, was a foundational principle of the League as they were conceiving of it. And who could object to the "just treatment" – Makino was not asking for "equal treatment," only just treatment – of the nationals belonging to nations already recognized as equals? Yet Cecil represented the British empire, with its panoply of exclusionary laws and practices, and the instructions from London were clear: the proposal must not pass. So, he prevaricated.[35]

Cecil regretted, he said, that he was not in a position to support the Japanese proposal. The "racial question" was admittedly important, but it could not be resolved by the Commission without encroaching on the sovereignty of member states. One of two things must be true, he argued. Either the proposed amendment was ineffective, in which case why bother with it, or it was effective, in which case it would interfere with the sovereign rights of member states. There were many things that nations *ought* to do – he mentioned, by way of example, advancing the rights of women – that were not and could not be enumerated in the preamble. Besides, Japan, as one of the great powers, would have a spot on the League's Executive Council (the rough equivalent of the Security Council in the UN system). Its presence there would signal its full equality with the other powers and would also allow it to bring the matter of "equality of races and of nations" before the Council at a later date.

Chinda, the second Japanese delegate present, responded to Cecil's objections. The Japanese proposal, he reminded Cecil, mentioned neither race nor immigration. It asked only that the covenant acknowledge the equality of nations and support the just treatment of their nationals. Was this principle not as important as other issues addressed in the covenant, such as labor conditions, public health, control of the arms trade, and so on? Japanese public opinion, he added, was strongly behind this amendment, and some in Japan even argued that it should not join the League if the amendment was not included. He asked, therefore, that it be put to a vote.

At this juncture, several other members of the League of Nations Commission spoke in favor of the amendment. The Italian prime minister, Vittorio Orlando, said that perhaps the question of equality of nations should not have been raised, but since it was it had to be supported. Cecil's objections

---

[34] "From the Diary of Lord Robert Cecil," April 11, 1919, *PWW* 57: 247.
[35] This and the discussion that follows is in *PWW* 57: 261–263. David Hunter Miller, the American lawyer most closely involved with the drafting of the League Covenant, wrote later that it seemed "that Cecil felt that he was performing a difficult and disagreeable duty" and added that "[a]fter making his statement Cecil sat with his eyes fixed on the table, and took no part in the subsequent debate." Miller 1928, I: 461.

might have carried weight if this was a separate article in the covenant, which would have implied specific legal obligations. But as part of the preamble, it would simply be a general statement of principle, and rejecting it would go against the spirit of the covenant. The French delegate Léon Bourgois, a veteran politician who would win the Nobel Peace Prize in 1920 for his internationalist work, also expressed support as the amendment "embodied an indisputable principle of justice." His fellow delegate Ferdinand Larnaude, Dean of the Faculty of Law of Paris, added that the Japanese proposal now came in an "entirely different form" – referring to the fact that no mention was now made of race – and that it was to be part of the document's preamble, which "ordinarily lay down broad declarations of principle" and "did not impose obligations so strict" as those of the enumerated articles. For those two reasons, he said, the Commission must vote in favor.

The Greek prime minister, Eleftherios Venizelos, also highlighted the Japanese compromise in eschewing any explicit reference to racial equality. As now phrased, the amendment could hardly be rejected, especially since Makino had pointed out that it would not compel any state to take any specific measure with regard to immigration. Karel Kramář, the prime minister of the new state of Czechoslovakia, thought the amendment to be in harmony with the rest of the preamble and supported its adoption. Only the Polish delegate, Roman Dmowski, seconded Cecil's opposition. He was in sympathy with the Japanese proposal, he said, but did not think a principle should be included in the preamble that was not enforced with specific articles in the body of the document.

The Chinese delegate, V. K. Wellington Koo (Gu Weijun), spoke next. A cosmopolitan figure fluent in both English and French, Koo held a doctorate in international law and diplomacy from Columbia University. Barely thirty-years-old at the time, Koo had already served as the Chinese minister (i.e., ambassador) to the United States. Alone among the speakers except Makino, he read a prepared statement and asked that it be included in the protocol. Wishing neither to appear to support Japan, China's chief antagonist at the conference, nor to oppose racial equality, Koo found himself in an uncomfortable spot. His response, therefore, was both deliberate and ambivalent.

The principle contained in the Japanese amendment, Koo began, involved "a number of questions to which time alone" could give a "universally satisfactory solution." This rather evasive opening highlights just how pained Koo was to find himself forced to agree with Japan. He was also well aware of China's dependence on the major powers, and on the United States in particular, for support in the ongoing diplomatic struggle with Japan over the fate of the former German concessions in Shandong Province. Still, Koo could not go on the record opposing the principle of the equality which, after decades of unequal treaties, was as dear to the Chinese public as it was to the Japanese.

So, he added blandly, he would be "very glad indeed to see the principle itself given recognition in the Covenant."[36]

6.5 The Final Rejection

Finally, it was President Wilson's turn to speak. As commission chair, he had waited until others had their say. Surprisingly, perhaps, given how this episode is typically remembered, there is evidence that the US president was initially inclined to support the Japanese amendment as it was presented that day, presumably calculating that accepting the amendment would help keep Japan within the League and yet, in its revised form, was innocuous enough to pass muster at home. However, once it was clear that the British empire delegation was still determined to oppose it, Colonel House convinced Wilson to stand with Cecil. Accepting the amendment, House told Wilson, would "raise the race issue throughout the world." Moreover, Hughes would surely make "an inflammatory speech" at the plenary session if the amendment passed, and this sort of public display of division among the allies was best avoided.[37]

Wilson followed House's counsel. No one could deny the merit of the principles that Japan proposed, he began. The League, after all, was based on the principle of the equality of nations, and its collective security arrangements were designed to vindicate precisely that principle. Yet, some "others of our colleagues" – a clear allusion to Hughes – saw things differently, so accepting the amendment risked unpleasant "discussions" at the plenary session. It was better to "quiet discussion that raises national differences and racial prejudices," to keep it in the background rather than give it center stage. Makino and Chinda were doing their duty in raising the proposal and yet, Wilson said, in rejecting it he was sparing them "the very embarrassments which I think they have in mind." In other words, the president was claiming that in rejecting a reference, however veiled, to racial equality in the League Covenant, he was sparing Japan, and the conference more generally, a public display of precisely the sort of prejudice the amendment was intended to combat.[38]

Makino interjected that he did not wish to prolong an "unprofitable discussion." On behalf of the government of Japan, he insisted that the proposed amendment be put to a vote. A vote was then taken, and eleven of the seventeen

---

[36] Link, *PWW* 57: 263.
[37] House Diary, in Link, *PWW* 57: 285. Miller noted that "the form of the proposal was such that to formulate any objection to its language was not an easy task," since no one could say "that he objected to the principle of equality of Nations or that he favored unjust treatment of any nationals." Nevertheless, he added, the "very vagueness" of the words meant "that they were a sort of curtain behind which was the question of White Australia and of immigration of Eastern peoples into countries which regarded the possibility of such immigration as impossible to discuss." Miller 1928, I: 461–462.
[38] "Remarks upon the Clause for Racial Equality," in Link, *PWW* 57: 268–270.

delegates present voted in favor.[39] Wilson, as chair, then declared the amendment rejected because, he said, passage required unanimous consent or, at the least, that no one register an objection to its passage. Given that "at least one objection" – that is, the British – was "insisted upon," he deemed that the amendment had failed. The president then concluded with a statement that, in retrospect, is steeped in historical irony: no one, he said, would "ever interpret the result of this evening's discussion as a rejection on our part of the principle of the equality of nations." Makino then asked that the result of the vote be recorded in the minutes. He would take the issue up again, he said, at the "first appropriate occasion."[40]

In the end, then, Wilson came down on the side of the British, as House had advised. Had he not done so – had he instead ruled that the support of the majority was sufficient – the Japanese proposal, in its latest form, would have become part of the covenant. Even so, Cecil was not pleased. He had wanted more fulsome support for the British position, not the invocation of a technicality to get it through. The president, he confided to his diary, "did not show quite as much courage" as he had hoped, since Wilson, in alluding to Hughes' recalcitrance as his reason for rejecting the amendment, lay the blame for its failure at the feet of the British delegation. Wilson, Cecil noted, was "a very curious mixture of the politician and the idealist," concluding: "He is not to me very attractive."[41]

If Cecil saw the US effort to blame the British for the failure of the Japanese proposal, he was right.[42] The US delegation, and House in particular, had from the outset tried to accomplish just that. House had clearly concluded that the price of accepting the proposal was too high, but at the same time did not wish to appear as opposing the principle of the equality of nations. This principle, after all, had been central to Wilson's wartime rhetoric and was now, in theory at least, at the core of the new League of Nations the president was laboring to construct.

This US delegation approach was reflected clearly in the press release that it put out the following day. It outlined the Japanese proposal and commended Makino and Chinda for presenting it "admirably." It described the discussion in the commission – the same one that Cecil in his diary had called "incoherent" – as

---

[39] "From the Diary of Lord Robert Cecil," April 11, 1919, in Link *PWW* 57: 247. Cecil writes that he and Dmowski voted no, though House claimed (*PWW* 57:571) that "the vote in the negative was not demanded." It is possible that Cecil considered the fact that he and Dmowski spoke against the amendment in the discussion as de facto no votes.
[40] In Link, *PWW* 57: 264–265.
[41] "From the Diary of Lord Robert Cecil," April 11, 1919, in Link, *PWW* 57: 247.
[42] Hughes reciprocated in kind, issuing a statement to the Japanese press denying that "Australia alone" was responsible for the failure of the Japanese proposal at the League Commission and noting that Australia itself had no representative on that commission. See Link, *PWW* 57: 570–571.

"marked by breadth of thought, free and sympathetic exchange of opinion and a complete appreciation by the members of the commission of the difficulties" involved in either accepting or rejecting the proposal. It then noted, as Cecil had done during the discussion, that Japan would be a member of the League's highest body, its Executive Council, so the rejection could not be construed as diminishing the prestige of Japan. The press release then explained the rejection in the vaguest possible terms, noting that "various members" felt they could not vote "for its specific inclusion in the covenant" and the commission therefore could not give the amendment the "unanimous approval" that was required. In fact, no coherent explanation is given for the amendment's rejection, as none could be without admitting that it was done to protect the practice of racial discrimination at home.[43]

6.6 Conclusion

Why, then, did Tokyo pursue so doggedly a proposal that, in retrospect, seems to have been destined to fail? At the time, some members of the US delegation in Paris believed that Japan had never expected the proposal to pass, but rather proffered it as a bargaining chip to gain negotiating leverage on other Japanese desiderata, particularly the Shandong question. According to this view, the Japanese calculated that the rejection of the proposal would put more pressure on the Western powers to relent on the territorial issue.[44]

However, given the long-standing salience of the question of racial discrimination in the Anglophone countries in Japanese diplomacy in this era, it seems unlikely that Tokyo made the proposal in Paris merely to gain leverage on another issue. It is certainly possible that the government felt compelled to raise it regardless of the expected result in order to appease domestic public opinion, as failure to do so would have exposed them to harsh critiques at home. But it is also possible that, from the perspective of early 1919, the Japanese government had reason to expect that their proposal could succeed. The language of equality had been central in Allied rhetoric, particularly in Wilson's. In that context, it was possible to imagine that a proposal to include in the covenant the principle of the "equality of nations" would find broad support. In fact, it did find broad support among the members of the League Commission, including from two of the major powers: France and Italy. After all, as several of the

---

[43] According to Ray Stannard Baker, Wilson's press secretary in Paris, he prepared the statement and asked Wilson to sign it, but the president demurred, saying he "had no right to report what went on in the meeting." Still, he approved the text, and it was published in the *NYT* and elsewhere on April 13.
"From the Diary of Ray Stannard Baker," April 12, 1919, in Link, *PWW* 57: 286. The text of the statement itself appears in Link, *PWW* 57: 286, note 1.
[44] This theory is discussed in detail in Shimazu 1998, 143–148.

speakers at the crucial commission meeting described above noted, a rejection of the Japanese proposal was inconsistent with the foundational principles of the League of Nations.

The chain of events that led to the Japanese proposal's eventual failure, seemingly so inevitable in retrospect, would not necessarily have been predictable in advance in the heady international atmosphere of early 1919. Could things have gone differently? The vehemence of the Australian opposition; London's decision to allow Hughes to dictate the British position as a whole; and, finally, Wilson's decision to support the British – each was an inflection point where things might have gone differently. Moreover, Ambassador Ishii's attempt to address reservations in the United States may have made things worse, inadvertently inflaming US public opinion against the Japanese proposal.[45] Had events taken a different turn at any of these points, history might well have recorded that the Japanese racial equality proposal was accepted and made part of the League Covenant, even if perhaps in the attenuated form of the April compromise.

In short, despite the entrenchment of racial hierarchy in international affairs at the time, the rejection of the Japanese racial equality proposal was not foreordained. In the heady atmosphere of 1919, with the language of equality having permeated Allied wartime rhetoric, rejecting the Japanese call for that selfsame equality was not a simple thing. At the same time, we would do well to recall that, as consequential as the debates over the text of the League Covenant might have appeared at the time, much of it soon proved to be a dead letter as events unfolded over the next decade and beyond. There is little reason to think that a vague reference to the "equality of nations," as requested in Japan's final proposal, or even a bolder promise, as their initial text demanded, to accord all people "equal treatment" without "distinction on account of their race or nationality," would have been any more effective in shaping international affairs in the interwar years than other, more central elements of the League Covenant had been.

As IR scholars seek to shed the "norm against noticing" the role of race in international relations, the story of the Japanese racial equality proposal helps us think about this role in at least two ways. First, it shows how domestic politics, specifically in this case around the questions of immigration and the treatment of aliens, drove the behavior of all the major actors and created what amounted to an international crisis. It was domestic pressure that compelled the Japanese government to raise the racial equality proposal in the first place and to continue to pursue it for months despite initial rejection and growing tensions around it. It was, too, considerations of domestic politics that led the Australian prime minister, Billy Hughes, to oppose the proposal so strongly.

---

[45] Shimazu 1998, 23, makes a similar assessment of the impact of Ishii's speech.

Finally, opposition in the Senate and its implications for the future of the League likely played a part in Wilson's eventual decision to throw his lot with the British and reject the Japanese amendment. At bottom, then, this story was one of a tug-of-war between domestic politics in Japan, on the one hand, and in the United States and Australia, on the other.

Second, this story invites us to make nuanced assessments of the challenges posed to the role of racial hierarchy in international society. Although the Japanese proposal was sometimes seen, both at the time and later, as a broad salvo against racial discrimination in international affairs, Tokyo's intent was more specific, to assert Japan's equality among the world's great powers. As the Japanese delegates in Paris made clear, their proposal was fully compatible with the racialized Mandate system being put together in Paris and did not extend to colonial peoples, whose sovereignty was not internationally recognized. Japan pursued the principle of the "equality of nations" in Paris even while suppressing an uprising against its colonial rule in Korea and seeking further expansion in China and the Pacific.[46]

Japan, in short, aimed to move its seat closer to the head of the proverbial table of international society. What it discovered, however, is that despite a decades-long effort to shed the humiliation of unequal treatment and join the ranks of the great powers, it had hit a racial glass ceiling. This realization would eventually help to lead Japan, in the ensuing years, to withdraw from the Western-dominated international order and attempt, through war and conquest, to construct an alternative one on the basis of a pan-Asian ideology.[47] In a racialized international order, even the circumscribed equality that the Japanese demanded for themselves proved to be out of reach, let alone the more expansive version of racial equality – the complete erasure of the global color line – that some of Japan's admirers across the nonwhite world had imagined that they were after.

---

[46] Critics in China and elsewhere, including in Japan itself, pointed out the hypocrisy of Japan's position at the time. See Merida 2023, 152–153.

[47] On this, see Aydin 2007.

Part III

To the Pacific War

7 Reform, Revolution, and State Failure in Early Twentieth-Century China

Richard S. Horowitz

On October 10, 1913, Yuan Shikai, recently sworn in as the President of the Republic of China, declared in an inaugural speech to the National Assembly in Beijing:

The attitude of the foreign powers towards us has always been that of peace and fairness, and whenever occasion therefor has arisen they have rendered us cordial assistance. In this is furnished ample evidence of the civilization of the world, and such exhibitions of good will from friendly nations arouse in us sentiments of deep gratitude. It is most important that all citizens of the Republic should clearly understand this, in order that with sincerity of purpose they may endeavor to strengthen the friendship of our international bonds.[1]

At first glance, this statement is curious. During the preceding seventy-five years the Qing empire had fought five major conflicts and innumerable smaller ones with foreign powers. The two-year old Republic of China had inherited a regime of unequal treaties and economic privileges largely extracted at gunpoint. But inaugural speeches are political statements. President Yuan was speaking to two audiences: foreigners he needed to placate, and Chinese nationalists whom he worried would provoke foreign ire. In a speech focused on promoting China's economic development, Yuan apparently wished to set China's foreign relations aside.

Yuan's hopes would prove futile. The advent of World War I in Europe freed Japan to demand further concessions from Yuan's Republic. The government's acceptance of these demands fueled popular anger in the cities. A little more than two years after this speech, Yuan Shikai badly misread the public mood, and made himself emperor. Within months even his allies were deserting him, and Yuan's shaky hold on power disintegrated.

In the ensuing decade, from 1916 to 1927, the division of China among many regional military satrapies – with only a figurehead government in Beijing – meant

---

[1] US Office of the Historian 1920.

133

that there was no functioning foreign policy, and no ability to resist the rising influence of Japan. Chinese students and workers launched waves of protests from boycotts of Japanese imports to the May Fourth protests in 1919 to the May 30 protests in 1925, with little effective response from the government. The transfer of German concessions in Shandong province to Japan, the cause of the 1919 protests, was a case in point. This arrangement had (we now know) been agreed to by the warlord-controlled government in Beijing months before the Versailles conference.[2] The weakness of Chinese politics likewise prevented China from ending the unequal treaties with European powers, and at a time when Turkey ended the similar regime of capitulations and Siam was able to negotiate the end of extraterritoriality[3] State failure in China had profound consequences both for Chinese politics and for the country's foreign policy.

The causes of the failure of the state in the early twentieth century were complex. Provincial officials felt less and less beholden to Beijing. Military reforms created numerous new armies with provincial loyalties instead of an integrated national hierarchy; there was little consensus around what kind of constitutional system should replace the monarchy.

But at the center of many of these problems was the foreign presence itself. William Kirby has remarked that in the Republican Period "everything important had an international dimension."[4] Yuan Shikai, like others before him, discovered that while foreign pressure required close attention, caving to foreign demands came at a high cost. This chapter explores the collapse of the state in China in the 1910s as the endpoint of a two-decade-long historical process. Moving on from the military and financial issues that have been the focus of much historical research, I concentrate on the ways that the foreign presence contributed to the collapse of the state in China, with its myriad international consequences.

7.1 The Failure of the State in China, 1900–1916

China's road to revolution in 1911, and the repeated crises of the following five years began with the defeat by Japan 1895. The Treaty of Shimonoseki that ended the first Sino-Japanese war ceded Taiwan to Japan and granted Japan a set of unequal treaty arrangements in China similar to the major Western powers. China was forced to keep out of Korean affairs and pay a massive indemnity to Japan. In the ensuing years, there was a "scramble for concessions" in China: One power after another demanded investment concessions and naval bases or what were called "spheres of influence." In 1898, the Guangxu emperor stepped out of the shadow of his aunt, the Empress Dowager Cixi, and at the urging of a group of young reformers led by Kang

---

[2] Elleman 2002, Chapter 1.   [3] Chapter 3, this volume.   [4] Kirby 1997, 433.

Youwei issued a blizzard of reform edicts. But after three months, a coup supported by senior officials placed the Guangxu emperor on involuntary medical leave and brought back Cixi. The reforms were largely reversed.[5]

The Boxer War in 1900 was a swing in the opposite direction and a mistake of epic proportions on the part of the Empress Dowager. The Boxers United in Righteousness was a popular martial arts movement that attacked Chinese Christians as the purported cause of drought. The Boxers spread rapidly in rural north China in late 1899. Initially, the movement was supported by some conservative officials who were sympathetic to its anti-foreign attitudes and suppressed by officials more experienced with dealing with foreigners. By spring, the Boxers began to attack foreigners. By May, rapidly growing groups of Boxers converged on Beijing and Tianjin. Ignoring the demands of foreign diplomats that the movement be suppressed and foreigners and Chinese Christians protected, the Empress Dowager Cixi endorsed the movement. Through the summer of 1900, Boxers and Imperial Troops besieged the foreign legations in Beijing and the foreign community in Tianjin. But Boxer claims to have charms that made them invulnerable to bullets proved false. In August, an army of eight foreign powers relieved the legations and launched months of violent reprisals in areas said to be supportive of the Boxers. Qing officials signed another expensive and humiliating treaty to end the conflict.[6]

By 1901 anyone remotely conscious of politics in Qing China understood the need for major changes. Social Darwinist ideas were in the air. As journalist/reformer Liang Qichao warned, China was in imminent danger of becoming a "lost country" like Poland or Hawaii, swallowed up by larger empires.[7] Within the Qing government as well, there was urgency about the need for change. After the Boxer disaster, the Empress Dowager – ever the political survivor – reversed course, and now called for wide-ranging reforms, encouraging officials to make proposals for thoroughgoing change, initiating what historians call the New Policy Reforms.

Among politically engaged people two distinct tendencies developed. Reformers sought change within the framework of the Qing state. Many pointed to the constitutional monarchies in Europe and Japan, and believed this was the right direction to go in. In China, many officials and members of the literati elite were clearly in this camp. Outside of China, Kang Youwei, Liang Qichao, and others involved in the 1898 reforms (who remained political refugees) called for the return of the Guangxu emperor to the throne, and the resumption of the reforms. The "Restore the Emperor Society" actively campaigned and raised funds among overseas Chinese communities. Until perhaps

---

[5] The Hundred Days Reforms have been much debated – this represents a fairly conventional view following Wong 1992.
[6] On the Boxers see Esherick 1988, Cohen 1997, and the essays in Bickers and Tiedemann 2007.
[7] Qichao 1936.

1909, the reformers were the predominant group among political activists and included people both in and out of government.

Revolutionaries on the other hand, like Sun Yatsen, focused on overthrowing the Qing dynasty. In their eyes, the Manchus had failed to defend China against foreign aggression. Only ending Manchu control would free the Chinese people to become a modern nation. The revolutionary movement was fed particularly by students who studied abroad in Japan and were both energized by the model of Japan's dramatic transformation in the Meiji era and exposed to anti-Manchu ideas that were suppressed within the Qing empire. Initially, the revolutionaries were on the political fringes. But after 1908, the other groups became frustrated with the self-serving activities of Manchu elites and the inadequate pace of reforms. Revolutionary ideas began to secure a growing foothold among politically active Chinese.[8]

At the beginning of the twentieth century, there was widespread agreement among both reformers and revolutionaries that China's government and society needed to be transformed. One area of concern was educational reform, particularly replacing the Neo-Confucian curriculum (which dated back to the Song era) with a curriculum that would prepare China's elites for the modern world (which was much harder to define). A movement began to end the practice of foot-binding and improve the education of women: A strong nation could not cripple half its population. Government needed to be modernized and better able to mobilize resources without the corruption endemic to the old system. Reforming the legal system and abolishing outdated practices, like the use of torture to extract confessions, was also a priority. The Qing needed new armies, equipped with the latest weaponry, led by a well-trained officer corps, and organized on European lines.

The New Policy Reforms of 1901–10 began many of these changes. The exam system for recruiting officials was reformed. When it proved impossible to create a new curriculum, including modern subject matter, the exam system was abolished. The structure of central government administration was reorganized, law codes were rewritten to abolish torture and cruel punishments in order to meet European expectations, new armies were created and trained in the Western style, and efforts were made to reform local government and introduce modern systems of budgeting.[9]

Efforts were made at multiple levels to create avenues for greater political participation. These included establishing Chambers of Commerce in major cities. In some provinces reforming governors created local councils in the early 1900s, a movement that later expanded nationally. In 1909, by imperial

---

[8] A still useful survey of this period is Wright 1968a.
[9] On the New Policy (*xinzheng*) reforms, see Wright 1968b; Reynolds 1993. On legal reform, see Bourgon 2003.

decree, provincial assemblies were created and elected. Although participation was limited to men of wealth or who had examination degrees, this reform gave voice to a broader population. The provincial councils quickly became prominent voices for change. There was discussion of the drafting of a constitution (planned for 1916) and a national assembly was created in 1911.[10]

But the ethnicity issue became unavoidable. The Empress Dowager died in 1908 and the Guangxu emperor mysteriously predeceased her by a day. The last emperor, Xuantong (Puyi), was a baby, and the Manchu princes who ruled in his name made foolish decisions that exacerbated tensions. Manchu princes with limited experience and qualifications were appointed to influential official positions. Prominent Han Chinese officials were pushed aside. Zhang Zhidong, who had promoted industrial development and created a modern army in the Wuhan area, was kicked upstairs to Beijing to the largely ceremonial post of Grand Secretary and Yuan Shikai, the creator of the Northern Army, was forced into retirement. Qing decisions to nationalize railroads in Sichuan funded through public subscription generated intense resistance. The Chinese political public was increasingly sensitized to arguments made by revolutionaries that the Manchus did not care about the well-being of the Chinese nation. In this context, the pattern of decision-making at the top gave many reasons to support, or at least not to oppose, the cause of outright revolution.

7.2 The Revolution, the Early Republic, and the Road to State Failure

In the end, the revolution began with a random development: the discovery of lists of revolutionary alliance members by British police in Hankou, including the names of some Qing soldiers. Officers at the nearby Wuchang garrison – facing likely criminal trial for treason – rose up in rebellion. Within weeks the revolutionary fever spread as provincial assemblies, particularly in the south and central coastal provinces, declared support for the revolution. Fighting between loyalist troops and the revolutionaries was fierce but inconclusive. In desperation, the Qing throne accelerated moves toward representative government and summoned Yuan Shikai out of retirement to suppress the rebellion. Meanwhile, Sun Yat-sen – the most prominent revolutionary leader – returned from a sojourn in the United States at the end of the year and was named provisional president by the revolutionaries. A National Council was convened in Nanjing, with delegates from each province, to provide a rudimentary form of unified governance for the revolution.[11]

The return of Yuan Shikai would turn out to be the Qing throne's final misjudgment. Initially, Yuan endorsed an accelerated move to a constitutional monarchy, a position unacceptable to the revolutionary side. But Yuan quickly

---

[10] Meienberger 1980; Thompson 1995.   [11] Dutt 1968; Esherick 1994.

realized that there was little support for maintaining the Qing monarchy among military officers and civil officials. Rather than fighting, he negotiated the end of hostilities with the revolutionaries, and took control of the Qing government himself, declaring the end of the dynasty. In February 1912, the emperor abdicated, Sun Yat-sen had stepped aside and Yuan was acclaimed as the president of the Republic. Sun became a cabinet minister, symbolizing a unified transitional government. A new provisional constitution was written and approved by the National Council. After months of debate, the National Council voted to move the provisional government to Beijing in April, formally merging the governmental structure of the revolutionaries and Yuan Shikai's post-Qing government.

While in retrospect, this rapid development may seem surprising, at the time it made sense. Yuan was a figure who was widely respected: a leading figure in the New Policies, a capable administrator, and the creator of the Northern Army. He had experience dealing with the foreign powers, who respected him. His forced retirement in 1909 gave him some distance from the Qing court. Even among revolutionaries he was seen as acceptable. The developments of early 1912 embodied a compromise between Yuan and the revolutionaries, who had established their political center in Nanjing. Yuan assumed the position of president and would lead the government of the new republic. Meanwhile the National Council created by the revolutionaries in Nanking would write the provisional constitution which would govern the new republic.[12]

The provisional constitution called for a bicameral parliament, with the upper house elected by provincial assemblies and the lower house elected proportionately by the population. Adult men who held property of $500 or paid taxes of $2 and had at least an elementary school education – about forty million men – were granted the vote. Elections were held in December of 1912 and January of 1913.

China's democratic transition failed. On one side the revolutionary alliance was reorganized into a national political party and renamed itself the Nationalist Party (Guomindang or Kuomintang). Under the leadership of Song Jiaoren – one of the most able of the early revolutionary alliance leaders – the Nationalists focused on winning elections, and fielded candidates and campaigned throughout China. Yuan Shikai, with little conception of how to manage electoral politics or organize at the grassroots, ineffectively tried to undermine the Nationalists. The Nationalists won a substantial plurality in both the upper and lower houses at the ballot box. But Yuan Shikai was not interested in sharing power. On March 20, 1913, Song Jiaoren, who was expected to lead the Nationalists to power in the National Assembly, was assassinated at a train station in Shanghai. It was widely believed that Yuan

---

[12] Young 1968.

Shikai was behind the assassination. Those involved had connections to Yuan's cabinet, but in the ensuing weeks all were either killed or mysteriously disappeared, leaving no clear resolution of whether the president had been directly involved. But the assassination shattered the already tense relationship between Yuan Shikai and the Nationalists.[13]

Meanwhile, Yuan proceeded to conclude a huge foreign "Reorganization Loan" and refused to submit it to the National Assembly for ratification (where it almost certainly would have been rejected). In May, facing sharp criticism from the Nationalist Party, Yuan Shikai moved decisively to enforce his own authority by firing pro-Nationalist Party governors, and replacing them with his own appointees, another step in expanding his authority at the expense of the elected representatives.[14]

In June, the Nationalists turned to military resistance to Yuan, and a three-month-long civil war followed, referred to at the time as the "Second Revolution." Yuan was able to marshal more effective military forces and benefited from the support of the British and most other foreign powers. The role of the Japanese government is confusing. Diplomatically, the Ministry of Foreign Affairs supported Yuan's government, but individual Japanese subjects quite prominently supported the Nationalists. By early September, Nanjing, the major resistance stronghold, had fallen to forces loyal to Yuan and Nationalist Party leaders scattered abroad.[15]

Yuan Shikai proceeded to solidify his authority. He forced the National Assembly to elect him and was inaugurated as the first president (as opposed to provisional president) of the Republic on October 10, the second anniversary of the Wuchang Uprising. Yuan governed by fiat for the next two years, benefiting from help from the foreign powers that knew him well, and thought him to be a more reliable choice than his opponents. But his government, based in Beijing, while firmly in control of north China had more limited influence in other parts of the country and particularly in the south.[16]

Throughout his presidency, Yuan was willing to compromise with foreign interests, but the beginning of World War I presented new challenges. Since the Opium War Britain had been the dominant foreign power. The Great War forced Britain to pull resources out of Asia, offering new opportunities for Japan, ostensibly Britain's ally. With the beginning of World War I, Yuan's government was confronted with an aggressive set of demands for foreign

---

[13] Young 1968; Koji 2013, 920–922.   [14] Koji 2013, 923–927.
[15] Young 1968, 129–137. While Young asserts that the Japanese supported the revolutionaries, this paragraph follows Koji 2013, 932–933, based on Japanese diplomatic documents.
[16] Young takes a contradictory position suggesting on the one hand that "by mid-1914, Yuan had an extraordinary grip on the administration of the country" at the same time pointing that Yuan's administration was unable to introduce even "modest programs for social and institutional change." See Young 1968, 177.

concessions: Japan's infamous Twenty-One Demands. Some of these demands, including requiring that China purchase arms from Japan and appoint Japanese advisors into government ministries, threatened to turn China into something like a Japanese protectorate. While Yuan's government handled the situation deftly, deliberately slowing negotiations, drawing in other powers to pressure Japan to withdraw the most threatening of the demands, it was clear that Japan was now the major foreign threat. At the same time, the very moderate public rhetoric of Yuan and his government contrasted with public fury. Students initiated a large-scale public movement to boycott Japanese-made goods. The boycott was effective enough to infuriate Japanese diplomats and was the first of many actions in the Republican period where Chinese citizens stood up against foreign exploitation and the unwillingness or inability of the Chinese government to defend the country against foreigners.[17]

In 1915 and 1916, Yuan undertook to transform himself into an emperor. This failed effort would bring on the collapse of the early republican state and the beginning of the warlord era. While Yuan was never a strong advocate of republicanism, the reasons for this decision remain elusive. Perhaps, Yuan was aware of the hollowness of his own regime and hoped imperial dressing would give him a charismatic edge that he lacked. Perhaps, he listened too closely to his Japanese and American advisors who thought that a republic was ill-suited to Chinese civilization. Whatever the reasons, Yuan and his supporters staged a fake grassroots campaign calling on the president to become emperor. Wanting a democratic fig leaf, Yuan created a special assembly of representatives of every county to decide whether such a move was desirable. A unanimous vote called for Yuan to become emperor. On January 1, 1916, Yuan graciously listened to the people, and after staging a coronation with foreign diplomats present, began the Hongxian reign. It was immediately clear he had little support. Two months later, with southern provinces declaring independence, and support from the leaders of the Northern Army (his power base) evaporating, Yuan stepped down as emperor and made himself president again, resisting pressure from even his closest associates to resign from politics. By the end of June Yuan was dead (of natural causes apparently), and China's five-year-old republic was a mess.[18]

Li Yuanhong, the new president, lacked the influence to effectively run the government, and proved unable to influence much outside of Beijing. A year later, General Zhang Xun attempted to restore the Qing dynasty but the effort lasted just two weeks and achieved nothing. Central government power over the provinces was soon close to nonexistent, and the era of the warlords began.[19]

---

[17] On Yuan's response to the Twenty-One Demands, see Shan 2018, 197–200.
[18] Shan 2018, 209–223, the most recent account.
[19] Nathan 1976, esp. Chapter 3 outlines the ongoing role of the Beijing government after Yuan's death.

Scholars have pointed to several structural issues that contributed to the decline of central authority in the first decades of the twentieth century. The military reforms of the New Policy era, while driven by central policy, were implemented through the existing, quite decentralized structure of the Qing state where Governors-General oversaw both civil and military administration within regions of two or three provinces. New military academies were built in several places, but no integrated national military command was established. When the revolution occurred, Yuan Shikai controlled the Northern Army. Because of personal ties – he had been directly responsible for the Northern military academy, which trained the officers, and the creation of the army itself – he had to negotiate with other military leaders to get them to accept his authority.[20] Scholars have also pointed to finances as a major contributor to state breakdown. The late Qing state was struggling with financial shortfalls before the beginning of the twentieth century, and during the New Policy era, provincial officials were in a large part responsible for funding the new armies that were created. Following the revolution, Yuan Shikai pressed for reforms to the land tax, which failed in the face of popular resistance, and was unable to wrest control of military finances from provincial leaders.[21]

7.3 The International Presence and State Failure

While domestic politics and structural issues were important factors in the failure of the early republican state, they are not the full story. The Qing empire and the Republic of China operated in a complex international environment which shaped virtually every aspect of the revolution and the effort to stabilize a new political environment for the Republic. The pervasive nature of external threats and impositions on Chinese sovereignty, financial dependency on foreign-run tax agencies and foreign loans, and the tension between the demands of foreign governments and growing popular nationalism, all contributed to state failure in China.

7.3.1 Foreign Aggression and State Efficacy

Scholars exploring state failure have pointed out that the inability of states to perform core functions is a clear contributor. The failure of the Qing state began with a military defeat. In 1894–95, war broke out between Japan and the Qing empire on the Korean peninsula, and the results were a devastating defeat on

---

[20] On the late Qing military and the advent of warlordism, see McCord 1993.
[21] van de Ven 1996.

land and at sea. The war reshaped the empire's position in East Asia. The Sino-Japanese War, the scramble for concessions, and then the Boxer War, all demonstrated Qing weakness.

In important ways the period after 1895 was different from the era before the Sino-Japanese war. In the 1860s and 1870s, following the Second Opium War with Britain and France, the Qing state had responded effectively to major challenges. New armies were created and equipped with Western style weaponry. Arsenals and shipyards were created, and new taxes on commerce – especially the *lijin* (a commercial transit tax) and the maritime customs – paid the bills. Four major internal rebellions and numerous smaller ones were defeated. Xinjiang was reconquered from the rebel regime of Yakub Beg. In the 1880s, Qing China, while not a power, was able to hold its own. Qing diplomats convinced Russia to withdraw from the Yili valley. A war with France in the mid-1880s over France's advancing control over Vietnam was not altogether one-sided and military conflict netted France little. In Korea, Qing statesmen outdueled their Japanese rivals for influence, and Yuan Shikai was installed as an advisor to the Korean king. It was possible for Qing officials to see themselves as a power that was gradually, and somewhat effectively, adapting to a Western-dominated international system.[22]

But defeat in 1895 changed China's prospects. Multiple defeats at land and at sea had destroyed the most effective Qing armies and left the empire defenseless. The Qing military was now too weak to deter intimidation. In the scramble for concessions, every major power demanded new benefits, including leases on naval ports and exclusive investment opportunities within spheres of influence. One could argue that the concessions were less significant than was feared and the spheres of influence in most cases never developed into significant territorial elements, Yet, at this time the concessions seemed to signal that China was being "sliced up like a melon." The Boxer War in 1900 was an international embarrassment. In attacking foreign diplomats, the Boxers and Qing troops contravened basic ideas of international law and provided ready-made justifications for ongoing interference. The empire was saved from worse consequences by the willingness of officials in central and southern China to ignore Beijing and make separate commitments to suppress Boxer activity in their areas. For political elites, the Boxer War was an obvious political blunder: With no chance for success it saddled China with a perception of barbarism.

In the last decade of the Qing dynasty, the government avoided the worst of the foreign policy disasters of 1895–1900. From the perspective of Chinese political activists – both reformers and revolutionaries – the inability of the

---

[22] For the optimist's view, see Jize 1887. On the Qing revival the classic account is Wright 1957. A recent reinterpretation is Halsey 2015. On late Qing involvement in Korea, see Larsen 2008.

Qing to manage foreign bullying was a constant source of frustration. That the Qing was on the sidelines while Russia and Japan fought a war on Qing territory was another indication of the weakness of the state. Similarly, the Qing government was unable to respond effectively to anti-Chinese discrimination in the United States. So even as the New Policy Reforms made significant progress, the failure of the Qing government with respect to its subjects abroad hollowed out political support.

In China's coastal and riverine cities, the limited capacity of the Qing government to check the demands of foreign powers was on daily display. Foreign influence in China was institutionalized through what was known as the "treaty system." Beginning at the end of the Opium War, the Qing empire signed numerous agreements with foreign powers, key elements of which were not reciprocal (i.e., "unequal"). They included most-favored-nation clauses so concessions that were given to one country usually applied to others. A steadily increasing number of treaty ports were open to foreign residence and the operation foreign businesses. By the turn of the century these numbered more than 100. Tariffs on imports and exports were set by treaties. Foreigners could travel freely within the Qing empire and enjoyed extraterritoriality as they could not be tried in Chinese courts. Foreign missionaries could travel and settle where they wanted, despite the fact that long before the Boxer uprising there had been frequent popular opposition to their activities. In many of the treaty ports open to foreign trade, there were foreign "concessions," areas governed by one country, or sometimes several in combination. These were effectively pockets of foreign territory in China. Shanghai, the center of foreign activity in China, was really three cities: the International Settlement dominated by the British, the French Concession, and the Chinese city. The Boxer settlement added a foreign military presence: Several countries maintained units on call in Tianjin ready to protect the Beijing legations if needed. Foreign gunboats patrolled the Yangzi River ready to protect their nationals if endangered. While the Chinese feared that China would be partitioned, Great Britain, the most influential foreign power prior to 1914, generally sought a stable, unified and compliant government that would promote trade and protect foreign interests.[23]

7.4 Foreigners, Finance, and the State in Early-Twentieth-Century China

China's international debt produced another kind of foreign institutional influence. Prior to 1895, the Qing government had used foreign loans selectively, notably to support the defeat of Muslim rebels, and the reconquest of Xinjiang.

---

[23] An excellent general of the foreign engagement with late Qing China is Bickers 2011.

To pay the indemnities from the Sino-Japanese and Boxer wars, the Qing empire had contracted large international loans, which were guaranteed against customs revenues. The Chinese Maritime Customs Service, manned by foreigners but part of the Qing government, had administered customs duties on imports and exports since the early 1860s, and these revenues had been a crucial element of Qing military modernization measures in the 1860s and 1870s. Under the leadership of Sir Robert Hart, the customs was framed as a Chinese government organization. Customs officers, who were required to learn Chinese, were useful advisors to the Qing government. But with the huge foreign debt, the significance of the customs changed and it became increasingly an institution that served the needs of foreign banks first and the Chinese government second. During the 1911 Revolution, the customs – which had previously only assessed customs dues – also collected them to ensure that debt service would not be interrupted.[24]

During the revolution, Chinese politicians of all stripes were acutely aware of the significance of China's foreign debt, and the concerns of foreign bankers and diplomats that China would default on its loans. The Imperial Government tried in October 1911 to float a large loan from foreign sources, but both British and German bankers demurred and foreign diplomats waited. While smaller loans were floated from French sources, the Qing government was unable to lean on foreign loans to finance suppression of the uprising. On the revolutionary side, Sun Yat-sen tried to reassure European banks that the revolutionaries were not opposed to foreign debt, and tried to float his own loans to support the revolutionary cause. But both the foreign powers and their major financial institutions chose to remain neutral – insisting that a functioning government must be reestablished before they would reopen the tap. Given the very tight fiscal situation, this placed substantial pressure on the various groups to find a compromise.[25]

Once the revolution was over, Yuan Shikai's government initiated negotiations for a major loan, with the now united "Six Powers" (Britain, France, Germany, Russia, Japan, and the United States, although the United States would eventually pull out). Led in the negotiations by the British, the foreign powers insisted on significant financial oversight of the new Chinese government in return for the loan. Negotiations lasted the better part of the year, and Chinese negotiators rolled back the most invasive foreign proposals. Nonetheless, after long negotiation the final agreement included foreign administration of the Salt Tax Inspectorate, which was led from 1913 to 1920 by Sir Richard Dane. The loan agreement was unpopular in China, and Yuan with the

---

[24] Horowitz 2008; van de Ven 2014, Chapter 4.
[25] Foreign Banks and Global Finance in Modern China. Moazzin 2022, 204–211.

support of foreign diplomats and bankers did not seek the approval of the National Assembly, in contravention of the Provisional Constitution.[26]

Foreign financial involvement did enforce a degree of national cohesion in the cause of servicing China's foreign debt. Yuan Shikai, deemed by foreigners to be a stabilizing force, was greatly assisted by the Reorganization Loan in consolidating power. The new foreign Salt Inspectorate proved surprisingly effective, and like the customs brought in consistent revenues. After Yuan passed from the scene, warlord governments in control of Beijing benefited from access to revenues and credit. But while China was unified by foreign banks, it proved hollow as a political force. For Yuan, the loan enabled him to dominate while avoiding the hard work of state-building. For his successors foreign revenue facilitated exploitation.

7.5 Chinese Nationalism and the Foreign Presence

The disaster of the Sino-Japanese war occurred in an entirely new information environment. While China had its own print culture for centuries, newspapers were a new development beginning in the 1870s. By the mid-1890s they were flourishing, and aided by telegraphs and newswires, Chinese had unprecedented access to news. Meanwhile, increasing numbers of Chinese were travelling abroad to study and communicate their experiences to a broader public. The result was a strong public reaction that China was in grave danger. With the growing influence of Social Darwinist thinking, Chinese experienced growing nationalistic fervor. For revolutionaries, saving the Chinese nation from the neglectful Manchus was a rallying point. For reformers, nationalism was by the same token a motivator for reform.

Because of the intensity of Chinese nationalism, the foreign presence was complicating for governments in China both before and after 1911. Growing nationalism produced popular anti-imperialist activities, including the Anti-American Boycott in South China in 1905 and the Railway Rights Recovery Movement between 1907 and 1911. Clumsy efforts at managing railways in Sichuan gave rise to the belief that the Qing government was ready to mortgage Chinese-owned railroads to foreign banks, feeding the rise of revolutionary sentiment in 1911. Similarly, in 1911, unsubstantiated rumors that the foreign powers were planning to partition China fed the belief that radical change was necessary.[27]

Although the "Reorganization Loan" kept the government afloat financially, its terms – the creation of a foreign-run salt revenue administration – made it

---

[26] On the negotiation of the Reorganization Loan, see Koji 2013. On the Salt Administration, see Strauss 2023.
[27] A starting point is Rankin 2002. On rumors in 1911, see Shinji 1994.

unpopular and was one factor that led Yuan to essentially bypass the Provisional Constitution. Foreign powers insisted on enforcing agreements, while doing so opened up criticism that the government was selling out China. Foreign loans and investments might have enabled the Qing and Republican governments but also came at a political cost.

By the mid-1910s, Chinese nationalists had refocused on Japan as the great threat. Here again, the desires of governments ran headlong into the demands of protesters. During and after the negotiations around the Twenty-One Demands, a boycott of Japanese consumer imports organized by students had a noticeable effect. But from the perspective of the Yuan Shikai government, the boycott unnecessarily complicated the already difficult relations with Japan. Yuan worried that a boycott would be a provocation leading to more direct action.[28]

For both the late Qing and early Republican governments, rising Chinese nationalism was complicating. Forced to mediate between foreign diplomatic pressures and popular resistance to imperialism, leaders in both the late Qing and early Republican period tended to sacrifice nationalist desires to avoid potential conflict with foreign powers. This choice in turn tended to undermine their own support.

7.6 Conclusion

Yuan Shikai's fulsome praise of the foreign powers in his 1913 inaugural address makes sense when considered in context. Yuan was the leader of a new republic, and he had just overturned the constitutional system with the assistance of a large foreign loan. In the eyes of foreign representatives, particularly the British, Yuan was a known quantity more likely to deliver what they wanted: a compliant Chinese government that would make sure that the treaties were enforced and foreign lives and investments were protected.

But this fact also points to some of the reasons for the failure of the state in the ensuing years. Yuan's presidency, like the late Qing government before it, failed at the basic task of preventing foreign interference. Dependence on foreign loans and the foreign-collected customs and salt revenues raised concerns about whether the government was more concerned about the well-being of China or maintaining political primacy. Yuan's acceptance of Japan's demands – albeit after much negotiation and growing Japanese pressure – was an embarrassing demonstration that Yuan's Republic remained acutely vulnerable to foreign pressure. Both Yuan and his Qing predecessors found themselves opposing Chinese nationalist movements to avoid conflicts with foreigners.

---

[28] Gerth 2003; Shan 2018, 199.

There were many causes of state failure in early-twentieth-century China, including inadequate systems of taxation, the failure to create a truly national army, and the ethnic tensions around the Manchu identity of the Qing empire. But we shouldn't underestimate the significance of the foreign presence. The failure of the Qing and early Republican states to effectively resist foreign aggression badly undermined their legitimacy in the eyes of the Chinese. The growing foreign financial influence exacerbated these problems. With the advent of the warlords, these had gradually created a hollow Chinese state, functioning primarily to pay foreign loans, but unable to govern.

With World War I, the nature of the foreign imperial presence began to change. British imperial dominance in China was largely focused on maintaining privileges and protection for foreign residents, opening opportunities for foreign businesses, and insuring the servicing of China's debts to foreign creditors. A weak Chinese state served these needs, even as it frustrated Chinese nationalists. But as British influence faded, Japanese aggression grew. The Republic of China, with little popular support, was ill-equipped to combat an empire interested in much more direct control. Chinese popular politics in the 1920s would become focused on how both the Republican government in Beijing and regional warlords who were the de facto power holders had failed China.

8 The Second Sino-Japanese War and Its Aftermath, 1931–1965

Amy King

8.1 Introduction

The Sino-Japanese relationship in the mid-twentieth century is typically characterized by the story of colonization, war, and Cold War alienation.[1*] The key turning points in this narrative are the 1931 "Manchurian Incident," which precipitated Japan's colonization of Northeast China in 1932; the eight-year long "Second Sino-Japanese War" from 1937 to 1945; and the strange lacunae of "abnormal relations" between 1945 and 1972, during which the divided logic of the Cold War prevented China and Japan from resuming diplomatic relations and formally ending the state of war.

Less well known is the fact that in the midst of these decades of war and conflict, China and Japan were also deeply economically intertwined. In 1931, on the eve of Japan's occupation of Manchuria, bilateral Sino-Japanese trade comprised a fifth of Japan's total trade and more than a quarter of China's total trade. These economic ties had been forged in the wake of an earlier war – the First Sino-Japanese War (1894–95) – as the unequal treaties that settled this war forcibly opened China to Japanese trade and investment, and as Chinese officials dispatched students to Japan to absorb the economic ideas, goods, and technology that had underpinned Japan's earlier modernization efforts.

Following Japan's invasion of mainland China in 1937, Sino-Japanese economic ties then increased once again. This was largely a result of Japan's imperial project, which, by 1945, would result in Japanese-occupied China depending on Japan for more than 70 percent of its total trade. However, the economic relationship also reflected Chinese understandings of the constraints under which it operated, and the view that trade with Japan could temporarily alleviate crises in the wartime Chinese economy. Indeed, by 1941, more than half of "free" China's imports were originating in Japan.[2]

[1*] I am grateful to Alicia Turner, Wenting He, and Meira Chen for their excellent research assistance in preparing this chapter.

[2] Much of this chapter's discussion, especially on the industrial and technological dimensions of national security, and on China's post-World War II policy toward Japan, draw from my earlier works. See King 2016b; and King 2016a.

When the war ended in 1945, China and Japan did not reestablish diplomatic relations, but instead remained adversaries, this time on opposite sides of the unfolding Cold War divide. And yet, economic ideas, goods, and technology continued to flow between China and Japan. Although the size of these economic ties remained relatively limited, the two sides signed a host of unofficial trade agreements over the 1950s and early 1960s, and political leaders, business people, and advisers travelling between the two countries exchanged economic ideas. By 1965, Japan had already become China's most important trade partner, well before the diplomatic normalization and Chinese economic liberalization of the 1970s (see Table 8.1).

For China and Japan, economic and security interests have seemingly pulled in different directions for much of the twentieth century. While a rich vein of international relations scholarship has sought to explain the impact of economic interdependence on war (or peace), the Second Sino-Japanese War and its aftermath remains largely at odds with this literature, for it is a story in which economic interdependence grew explosively *during*, *after*, and *because* of war. Moreover, it is a counterintuitive story in which perceptions of *insecurity* have motivated closer economic ties between China

Table 8.1 *China–Japan trade, 1880–1980*

Year	China–Japan trade as a percentage of Japan's total trade	China–Japan trade as a percentage of China's total trade
1880	18.7	3.5
1905	18.7	14.3
1920	21.9	28.3
1930	20.9	24.3
1938	32.3	19.5
1945	91.3	*
1951	0.8	1.4
1965	2.8	11.1
1980	3.5	24.9

Source: Data compiled by the author from *Nihon chōki tōkei sōran* [*Historical Statistics of Japan*], 1987–1988, Tokyo: Nihon Tōkei Kyōkai [Japan Statistical Association], p.69, 77, 80; *Nihon tōkei nenkan* [*Japan Statistical Yearbook*], various years, Tokyo: Mainichi Shinbunsha; Hsiao Liang-lin. *China's Foreign Trade Statistics, 1864–1949*. Cambridge, MA: Harvard University Press, 1974; and Zhonghua renmin gongheguo guojia tongji jubian [National Bureau of Statistics of the PRC]. *Zhongguo Tongji Nianjian [China Statistical Yearbook]*. Beijing: Zhongguo tongji chubanshe, Various years. *Data for 1945 not available.

and Japan.[3] While China understood that its long-run security hinged on developing its internal economic capabilities, it also recognized that doing so required a certain dependence on, and emulation of, its main adversary – Japan – even in times of overt conflict.

In this chapter, I argue that the Second Sino-Japanese War and its aftermath is best explained not through systemic-level analyses of interdependence and war, but rather through the lens of mutually evolving domestic ideas about the relationship between economics and security. I show how Chinese and Japanese ideas about that relationship were fundamentally reshaped by the crisis of Western imperial encroachment in East Asia in the mid-nineteenth century. This crisis forced both states to confront the question of how to ensure national survival in an international economic order designed to advantage Western interests at the expense of East Asian ones. For both states, the answer was eventually to be found in the pursuit of grand strategies that called for economic and military modernization via state-led heavy industrialization. By the 1930s, Japanese ideas about "self-sufficiency" and fascist economic planning would lead to Japan's imperial conquest of Manchuria, and coercive economic dominance over other parts of free and occupied China. At the same time, the Chinese Nationalist government's ideas about state-led industrial modernization as a way to secure China from Japanese and Western imperialism were, perversely, inspired by Japan's own economic modernization model. This, coupled with the Chinese Nationalist government's strategy of placating an expansionist Japan in order to buy time for the roll out of that industrial development model, pushed China into a highly exploitative economic embrace with Japan.

In the aftermath of the Second Sino-Japanese War, I show that although Japanese ideas about "self-sufficiency" and fascist economic planning were delegitimized by the war, Japanese ideas continued to emphasize the economic basis of Japan's national security, and China's ongoing importance to Japan as a source of raw materials and export markets. In China, the Communist Party's reflections on the lessons of the Second Sino-Japanese War, and Japan's own path to modernity, shaped CCP ideas about the industrial and technological foundations of China's national security, and of the critical role that Japan would continue to play in China's path to industrial modernization and national security. These postwar Chinese and Japanese ideas about the importance of either side's economy in securing their own would sustain a deep, ongoing economic relationship between these two states, driven by strategic rather than liberal motivations for interdependence.

The chapter concludes by discussing how the Second Sino-Japanese War and its aftermath helps us to refine International Relations theories about economic

---

[3] For reviews of this literature, see Gartzke and Zhang 2015; King 2018.

interdependence and war, and of the crucial ideational underpinnings of the nexus between economics and security in East Asia. Paying attention to these ideas also highlights the limits of standard periodization in thinking about East Asia: Ideas about economics and security have shaped a continuous relationship of economic interdependence between China and Japan that transcends the typical "break points" of 1931, 1937, 1945, or 1972.

8.2 Economic Interdependence and the Second Sino-Japanese War: Conventional Accounts

In his 2015 *Economic Interdependence and War*, Dale Copeland acknowledged that neither economic realism nor commercial liberalism nor his own trade expectations theory could adequately explain the onset of the Second Sino-Japanese War.[4] This is a stunning observation of the failure of extant international relations theorizing to explain the origins of a conflict that cost approximately twenty million lives, and whose outcome was fundamental in reshaping the domestic politics and societies, international status, and long-term strategic behavior of Asia's two resident great powers.[5] Nonetheless, a review of these conventional IR arguments allows us to consider some of the theoretical alternatives.

According to Copeland, the Japanese side of the conflict *can* be relatively well understood through the lens of both economic realism and trade expectations theory. Realist arguments, emphasizing the vulnerability generated by economic interdependence between states, suggest that if states fear potential trade cutoffs in investment and trade, it increases the chances of military conflict as states seek to reduce their vulnerability by acting to control the source of their dependence.[6] Since the late nineteenth century, Japanese leaders had understood that Japan's drive for industrial modernization and long-term security in the face of encroaching Western powers required access to raw materials, food, and export markets, all of which were sources of vulnerability but could be found in Manchuria and northern China. Japan's growing dependence on China (as well as the United States and other export markets) created a powerful sense of vulnerability among Japanese leaders, who became "obsessed" with the question of how to control these crucial imports and export markets.[7]

---

[4] Copeland 2015.
[5] The 1937–1945 Sino-Japanese War (known in China as the "War of Resistance against Japan") is estimated to have killed between ten and twenty million Chinese, and between two and three million Japanese. For further discussion of these statistics, see Dower 1986, 299; Mitter 2013, 5, 397.
[6] Copeland 2015, 21–22; see also Gartzke and Zhang 2015, 5.   [7] Copeland 2015, 146–147.

Yet, realist arguments are unable to explain the timing of Japan's adoption of particularly coercive policies toward China – notably its occupation of Manchuria in 1932 – despite what had been relatively consistent Japanese dependence for much of the preceding five decades. Instead, Copeland argues that paying attention to a dependent state's *expectations* about its future trade and investment environment enables greater precision about when the "realist logic will kick in."[8] The dramatic increase in the value of the Japanese yen and the corresponding sharp decline in Japanese exports following the onset of the Great Depression in October 1929, Japan's resumption of the gold standard in January 1930, and the passage of the US-Smoot Hawley Tariff in June 1930, together caused a sharp deterioration in Japan's expectations about its future trade environment around 1930–31.[9] The combination of these events "caused havoc to Japan's ability to import the raw materials and food needed for its modern industrial economy," leading to a much greater willingness among Japanese leaders to entertain previously discredited policy ideas about the need for Japan to ensure greater control over Manchuria. Following a coup instigated by the Japanese army against Manchurian warlord, Zhang Xueliang, in September 1931, the Japanese government moved to establish the puppet regime of "Manchukuo" in 1932.[10]

However, while trade expectations theory proves successful in explaining the timing of Japan's occupation of Manchuria in 1932, it is unable to explain how Japan ultimately ended up in the "undesired sideshow" of full-scale war with China in the summer of 1937.[11] In the years between 1931 and 1937, Japanese leaders came to the consensus that their country should protect Japan's economic position in Manchuria while simultaneously taking care to avoid a war with China, so that Japan might undertake the domestic military industrial development necessary to prepare for a future preventive war against the Soviet Union.[12] Japanese leaders were also determined to avoid provoking conflict with the United States, upon whom their country was heavily dependent for trade and raw materials. For Japan, then, a war with China distracted from each of these goals, and was thus something that, Copeland argues, a succession of Japanese leaders in the 1920s and 1930s sought to avoid.[13]

Instead, Copeland suggests that the origins of the Second Sino-Japanese War "lie in Chinese domestic politics" and, in particular, in Nationalist leader Chiang Kai-shek's realization – following the "Xi'an incident" in December 1936, when Chiang was held hostage by exiled Manchurian leader Zhang Xueliang – that his own political survival would depend on the Nationalists joining forces with the Chinese Communist Party (CCP) and confronting Japan.[14] Yet Copeland remains seemingly puzzled that "[i]t was Chiang who sought a war" with

[8] Copeland 2015, 2. [9] Copeland 2015, 159–160. [10] Copeland 2015, 160–161.
[11] Copeland 2015, 172. [12] Copeland 2015, 164. [13] Copeland 2015, 172.
[14] Copeland 2015, 169–170.

Japan at a time when Sino-Japanese trade levels had returned to their pre-1930 peak.[15] Whereas commercial liberal arguments would suggest that economic interdependence should have a pacifying effect on interstate conflict as domestic interest groups lobby states to avoid the costly economic consequences of trade being cut off by war, Copeland notes that "domestic forces within Chiang's regime ... were set loose *despite* the renewal of Sino-Japanese trade."[16]

The inability of realist, liberal, or trade expectations theories to explain the onset of the Second Sino-Japanese War is emblematic of the still-widespread tendency in the historical and international relations literature to focus exclusively on the European and Pacific theatres of World War II, and to downplay or even ignore the Chinese theatre of that war.[17] As Copeland himself notes, his analysis of the Second Sino-Japanese War is included in his 2015 book as a prelude to telling the story of the "lead up to the final year of [US-Japan] diplomacy" in 1940, before Japan's attack on Pearl Harbor and the onset of the Pacific War, the war that remains Copeland's "primary puzzle."[18] But as this book seeks to emphasize, those American timelines do not necessarily correspond with the path of developments internal to the region.

Moreover, in Copeland's telling, China is often rendered as little more than the site of Japanese diplomatic maneuvers vis-à-vis the United States and other major powers, or as a state whose "domestic turmoil" threatened to disrupt Japan's policies toward China.[19] Copeland emphasizes Chinese domestic politics and the "Xi'an incident" as driving Chiang Kai-shek's response to the 1937 "Marco Polo Bridge incident," when Japanese forces stationed in a small village outside Beijing began firing on Chinese troops, precipitating the onset of full-scale war between China and Japan.[20] Yet, situating the origins of the Second Sino-Japanese War in the "Marco Polo Bridge incident," and in Chinese domestic politics more generally, is akin to locating the cause of World War I in the assassination of Archduke Franz Ferdinand.[21] Such an argument overlooks the far more important and longer-standing drivers of this conflict: Chinese and Japanese attempts to respond to the challenge of Western imperial encroachment via late-stage industrial modernization and, in Japan's case, the establishment of a racially stratified East Asian imperial order of its own. Paying attention to these

---

[15] Copeland 2015, 149, footnote 4.   [16] Copeland 2015, 149, footnote 4 (emphasis in original).
[17] For an excellent critique of this tendency in the literature, see Mitter 2013.
[18] Copeland 2015, 145, 150.   [19] See in particular Copeland 2015, 151–162.
[20] Copeland 2015, 169–170. More generally, Copeland fails to appreciate – as does the secondary literature on China – that in early 1936, Chiang Kai-shek and the Chinese Communist Party recognized the growing likelihood of war with an increasingly expansionist Japan and, encouraged by the Soviet Union, had begun productive secret negotiations months before the "Xi'an incident" as a way to prepare for a potential united front against Japan. See Mitter 2013, 63–67.
[21] For a similar argument on the parallels between the Marco Polo Bridge Incident and the assassination of Archduke Franz Ferdinand, see Mitter 2013, 81. Parks Coble also makes clear that Sino-Japanese relations were so strained in 1934–35 that any number of incidents had the potential to escalate into military conflict. See Coble 1991, p. 175.

longer-standing drivers, and the way in which China and Japan *reconceived* the relationship between economics and security in this new imperial order, helps us to better understand how both states ended up in full-scale war in 1937, and why China continued to trade with its adversary, Japan, in the lead up to, during, and in the wake of the Second Sino-Japanese War.

8.3 Domestic Conceptions of Economics and Security on the Eve of the Second Sino-Japanese War

A great deal of the extant IR theorizing on the relationship between economic interdependence and war is drawn from studies operating at the systemic level of analysis.[22] Shifting our gaze both domestically and to the connections between China and Japan, however, allows us to observe two crucial things. First, such a perspective demonstrates how the violent arrival of Western imperial powers in East Asia in the mid-nineteenth century fundamentally reshaped Chinese and Japanese ideas about the relationship between economics and security. Second, it shows how these ideas prompted new domestic strategies in China and Japan, which resulted in dense economic entanglement between the two. The encroachment of Western imperial powers forced China and Japan to reckon with the relationship between industrial development, trade, and military power underpinning this new imperial order: Industrializing countries required access to raw materials and export markets, all of which were available for the taking in militarily weaker, nonindustrialized countries, that were not regarded as sovereign equals by European powers.[23] Contact with Western imperial powers also introduced a host of new Western economic ideas into China and Japan, among which were ideas about "evolutionary modernity" and its attendant notions of "backwardness" versus "progress" and "modernity." These ideas became widespread in depicting Asian states' economic situation relative to that of the Western industrialized powers.[24] Subsequently, over the course of the late nineteenth and early twentieth centuries, successive Chinese and Japanese governments came to recognize that dealing with the challenge of national survival in the face of Western imperial encroachment was a problem that must be solved through economic development and industrial modernization: National security was reconceived as economic security.[25] This new conception of the relationship between economics and security was the ideational foundation for the grand strategies adopted by Japan and China in the late nineteenth and early twentieth centuries.[26] Both states sought autonomy,

---

[22] Gartzke and Zhang 2015. On the limitations of "levels of analysis" as a methodological choice in IR, see Bukovansky and Keene 2023, 13–14.
[23] Suzuki 2009, 59–60. [24] Zanasi 2020, 158–159.
[25] See, for example, King 2016b; King 2016a; Barnhart 1987.
[26] Here, I adopt Nina Silove's conception of "grand strategy" as "grand principles," or the "overarching ideas that are consciously held by individuals about the long-term goals that the

prosperity, and power. Yet the strategies they adopted to achieve these goals – while drawing them into a tight economic embrace – could never simultaneously succeed, relying as they did on Japan's coercive monopolization of Chinese resources and markets, and China's determination to throw off Japanese and Western subjugation.[27]

Imperialism upended the regional economic landscape in which China and Japan operated, forcing them into unequal competition with Western powers now operating in East Asia. Britain's defeat of China in the Opium Wars (1839–60) led to the establishment of the 1842 Treaty of Nanjing, the first of what would be a series of "unequal treaties" imposed by Western powers throughout East Asia. In China's case, these unequal treaties were underpinned by three "Western-sanctioned institutions" – large-scale war reparations payments, the transfer of the Chinese Maritime Customs Service to British control, and extraterritoriality – which, together, resulted in significant outflows of capital from the Chinese central government, the loss of control over the setting of tariffs or collection of customs revenue, and the proliferation of foreign firms within Chinese territory that were not subject to Chinese taxes or import duties.[28] Though Qing China was the first to be militarily defeated by the European powers during the Opium Wars (1839–60), it was Japan that more rapidly absorbed the implications of this new, Western imperial order. Recognizing that Western powers were monopolizing the very raw materials and export markets throughout China and East Asia on which Japan's national survival depended, Japan began deploying its own "unequal treaties." The Treaty of Shimonoseki, signed following Japan's military defeat of Qing China in the First Sino-Japanese War (1894–95), opened China's interior trading ports to Japan, granted favorable foreign investment and manufacturing rights for Japanese firms in China, and brought Japanese trading privileges into line with those already enjoyed by Western powers in China.

The dire economic circumstances wrought by Western and Japanese imperialism, coupled with the older Chinese challenges of large-scale population growth and economic scarcity, "usher[ed] in the notion that the country, as a whole, was deeply in debt and that balancing national finances was an urgent goal for its survival."[29] Over the course of the 1920s and early 1930s, Chinese economists and officials were relatively united around the idea that economic frugality and planning would enable China to mobilize scarce resources and direct them toward nation-building projects.[30] While there were significant differences within the Nationalist cabinet over the desired extent of state intervention in the economy, and whether to prioritize China's economic or military development needs, Chiang Kai-shek's vision of state-led heavy industrial and military development would

---

state should prioritize and the military, diplomatic, and/or economic means that ought to be mobilized in pursuit of those goals." See Nina Silove 2018, 49.

[27] I am grateful to helpful suggestions from Andrew Coe on this point. [28] Zanasi 2020, 138–139.
[29] Zanasi 2020, 111. [30] Zanasi 2020, 159–165.

ultimately triumph over the alternative visions of his Nationalist opponents.[31] Similar ideas were also evolving in Japan in the 1920s and 1930s, where elites and officials had been deeply affected by the lessons of Germany's defeat in World War I. Ideas of "fascist economic planning" and the development of a "total war economy," in which the state would intervene to protect and develop those strategic industries necessary for both military and industrial strength, took hold as Japan recognized that, like Germany, it also suffered the challenge of late industrialization and a lack of access to natural resources. A central pillar in this new Japanese economic model would be Japan's unchallenged access to the coal, iron ore, and agricultural resources found in China's northeast province of Manchuria, which Japanese officials now conceived as a critical "lifeline" for Japan.[32] As both states adopted strategies of greater state intervention in the development of their late industrializing economies, Japan would continue to serve as a model for Chiang Kai-shek's Nationalist government, even as Japan expanded its coercive imperial footprint in China. Facing the threat of growing Chinese Communism at home, and Japan's colonization of "Manchukuo" in 1932, Chiang turned to the fascist economic planning of Japan, Nazi Germany, and Italy for the inspiration behind his 1934 "New Life Movement" (xinshenghuo yundong), a movement designed both to unify China politically and to strengthen China's military-oriented industrial development.[33]

Over the course of the 1930s, Japan would therefore become both an economic model for China *and* China's major economic and military threat. This dual conception of Japan created profound challenges for the Chiang Kai-shek government, which sought to regain Chinese economic autonomy vis-à-vis Japan in the early 1930s while simultaneously trying to avoid provoking a conflict with Japan in order that China could focus first on strengthening itself industrially and militarily. Yet, as Parks Coble makes clear, Chiang's strategy of "first pacification, then resistance" toward Japan was doomed from the start. Japan's objections to even the slightest Chinese attempts to regain some independence for itself, and the unwillingness of other major powers like the United States and Britain to challenge Japan's position in China, severely narrowed the policy space in which Chiang could operate, and ultimately pushed China deeper into an exploitative economic relationship with Japan.[34]

That economic relationship was one that Margherita Zanasi has described as Japan's "economic stranglehold" on China.[35] Japan sought to transform China into what it saw as a natural export market for Japanese goods, flooding the Chinese market with cheaply produced Japanese cotton and other manufactured goods. At the same time, Japanese private firms invested heavily in China, establishing

---

[31] On the differences within the Nationalist party on these questions, see Zanasi 2006.
[32] King 2016b, 30–31; Gao 1997; Mimura 2011; Young 1998.
[33] Zanasi 2020, 161–162, 183–187; Zanasi 2006, 107, 190–192.
[34] Coble 1991, 154–159. See also Mitter 2013, 59.   [35] Zanasi 2006, 43.

cotton mills and other light industries backed by Japanese state capital and commercial associations. This arrangement allowed Japanese-owned industries in China to concentrate their resources and operate at lower prices than their Chinese counterparts, thereby eroding Chinese domestic industries.[36] Japan also used its occupation of Manchuria and the Guandong Leased Territory to source tariff-free imports of food and raw materials, including soya beans, salt, wheat, and coking coal, and its trade with these occupied territories grew steadily over the 1930s, as shown in Figure 8.1.[37] Perhaps the most significant way in which Japan sought to embed its monopoly over the Chinese market was its use of military authorities to support or tolerate the smuggling of goods from Japanese-occupied areas, such as Formosa and Manchuria, into North and Southeast China. Smuggling of cheap sugar, gasoline, cigarettes, narcotics, and other commodities eroded the foreign import duties that the Nationalist government could ordinarily collect on trade in such goods; by one estimate, the customs receipts at the Tianjin Custom House in 1935 were just one-third of the actual value of goods smuggled into the Tianjin region that year. Smuggling therefore undermined the Nationalists' fiscal base and its political morale.[38]

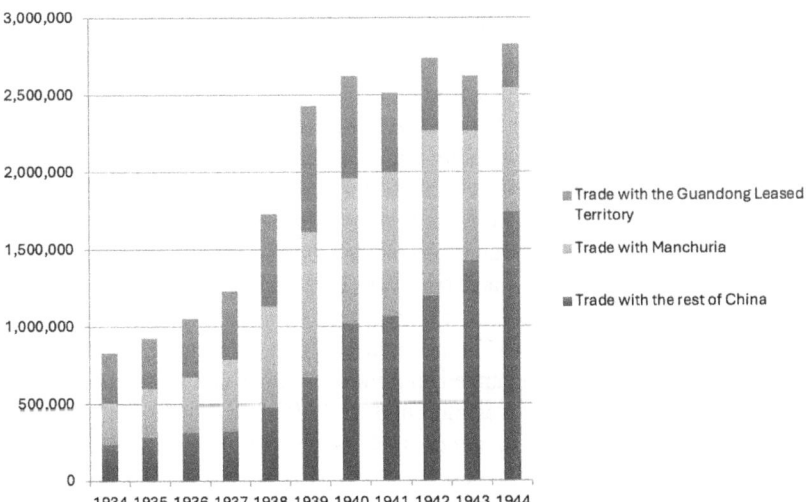

Figure 8.1 **Japanese trade with mainland China, Manchuria, and the Guandong leased territory, 1934–1944.** (1000s of Japanese yen)[39]
Source: King, *China–Japan Relations after World War Two,* p. 35.

---

[36] Zanasi 2006, 136–138. [37] King 2016b, 34–35. [38] Boecking 2017, 159–181.
[39] King 2016b, 35.

In the face of Japan's predatory economic position in the Chinese market, Chinese Finance Minister Song Ziwen embarked on a series of attempts throughout the early 1930s to diversify China's foreign economic partners, including by ending the preferential tariff rates on Japan's chief exports to China, securing US loans for the purchase of American cotton and wheat flour, and attracting aid and technical assistance from the League of Nations. Moreover, Chinese business leaders and the wider citizenry joined forces to boycott Japanese-made goods, successfully disrupting Japanese exports to China in 1931 and 1932.[40] However, Tokyo protested each of these moves as being "anti-Japanese," and as attempts to strengthen Western influence in China, at the expense of Japan. In its constrained environment, the Nationalist government acquiesced to Tokyo, carving out a special three-year extension of low-rate tariffs on some of the most important Japanese exports to China, and suppressing the boycott on Japanese goods in mid-1932.[41] Japan's resistance of Chinese efforts to regain economic autonomy were also symbolized in the infamous 1934 *Amō* Statement, when senior Japanese Foreign Ministry official Amō Eiji argued that Japan would object to any technical assistance or loans by foreign powers made to China because of the political influence enabled by such aid.[42] Instead, Amō urged the West to accept a new "status quo" in which Japan would singularly maintain peace and order in Asia and hold prime responsibility in Chinese affairs.[43] The following year, when the Nationalist government introduced currency (*fa-pi*) reforms to deal with major currency challenges brought about by the Great Depression and the US introduction of the Silver Purchase Act, Japan again protested because of the way in which China had worked with the British government – "without consulting Tokyo" – to introduce the reforms.[44]

On the eve of war, trade between China and Japan stood at a decade-level high, as a result of Japan's occupation of Manchuria and the Guandong Leased Territory, and its smuggling and relatively preferential trade access to "free" China. This exploitative economic relationship continued to increase after the outbreak of war in August 1937 (see Figure 8.2). In "free" China, Chiang Kai-shek's government initially banned all trade with Japan and Japanese-occupied parts of China, but the ban was modified in 1939 and again in 1942 owing to major shortages in China of goods such as gasoline, steel, chemicals, and cotton. As Felix Boecking notes, the Nationalist government's position on trade with Japan and Japanese-occupied territories was, ultimately, an

---

[40] Coble 1991, 74–75. On the boycott movement more generally, see also Karl 2003.
[41] Song Ziwen's efforts also led to his downfall as Finance Minister. Coble 1991, 75, 154–163.
[42] Coble 1991, 154.   [43] Iriye 2013 (1987), 22.
[44] The West's abandonment of the gold standard and the US introduction of the Silver Purchase Act in 1934 led to a near doubling in the value of the Chinese yuan, with severe consequences for China's export markets, and a major currency and liquidity shortage as silver flowed out of China. Coble, 1991, 265.

"ambivalent" one, not only because this trade helped to meet key shortages but also because it helped to dampen spiraling inflation.[45] In Manchuria and other parts of China controlled by Japan or the collaborationist Wang Jingwei regime, Japan established monopolies to extract cheap food and raw materials for export to the Japanese homeland and to the Japanese military operating in China, and placed Chinese industrial plants and businesses in key centers such as Shanghai under Japanese control. At the same time, Japan used Manchuria as a major export market for Japanese manufactured and industrial goods. Absorbing more than 75 percent of Japan's total exports between 1937 and 1941, and exporting 80–90 percent of its soya beans, coal, and grains to Japan, Manchuria had fulfilled its role as Japan's "lifeline" and was directly financing the Japanese war economy.[46]

Yet even at the height of Japan's sustained aggression, Chinese were able to recognize Japan's dual role as both an important model of industrial modernity and as the state whose economic and military predation was preventing China's

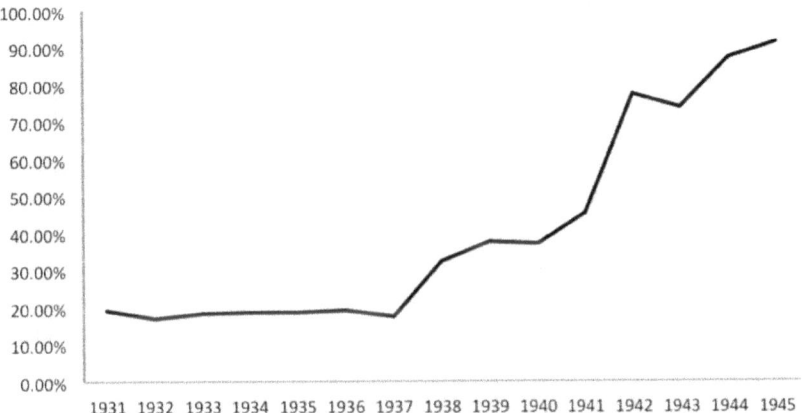

Figure 8.2 **Japanese trade with free and occupied China, 1931–1945.** (share of Japan's total foreign trade)[47] *Source: King, China–Japan Relations after World War Two, p. 38. Note: "Free and occupied China" includes areas in mainland China, as well as Manchuria and the Guandong Leased Territory. Japan's "total foreign trade" includes trade with Korea and Formosa (Taiwan).*

---

[45] Boecking 2017, 213–215. [46] King 2016b, 34–36; Zanasi 2006, 212; Coble 2003, 40–41.
[47] King 2016b, 38. Note: "Free and occupied China" includes areas in mainland China, as well as Manchuria and the Guandong Leased Territory. Japan's "total foreign trade" includes trade with Korea and Formosa (Taiwan).

own ability to industrialize. Writing in the Southwest China Commercial News in 1940, Ma Yinchu, one of China's leading economists, described Japan's "economic invasion" (*jingji qinlüe*) of China:

> Japan's consistent policy has been to prevent China from becoming an industrial nation, ensuring China remains in an agricultural state, and perpetually in a passive position. To achieve this, Japan economically invades China, appropriating China's agricultural products as raw materials for their industry. The Japanese buy cotton from China, weave it into cotton fabric in Japan, and then transport it back to China to sell for profit . . . . In this way, China is constrained by economic shackles and cannot further develop its industry, leaving it vulnerable to unchecked aggression by Japan. As China's industry cannot develop, it is subjected to exploitation by outsiders, which can lead to impoverishment and weakness.[48]

Given Japan's determination to ensure that China remained an "agricultural country" under Japan's control, Ma argued that China had no choice but to "fight to the end" if it were to become a modern, industrially developed, and therefore "autonomous" nation. Nevertheless, in the same article, Ma went on to acknowledge that there were certain aspects of Japan's industrial and commercial model that "would be worth emulating." Ma was critical of the economic and social inequality created by the monopolistic organization of Japanese "*zaibatsu*" – the small number of conglomerates such as Mitsui and Mitsubishi that controlled three-quarters of Japan's industrial and commercial capital. However, he argued that by concentrating their capital and forming large-scale industrial associations, the *zaibatsu* had been effective in negotiating collective benefits for their respective industries, such as lower prices for raw materials. Rather than military strength, Ma suggested, it was the "perfect" organization of Japan's industrial sector that had made Japan "capable of competing and winning" against China.[49] Japan's dual identity – as both a model and threat – placed China in the precarious position of choosing to learn from an adversarial Japan, while simultaneously trying and failing to extricate itself from Japan's exploitative economic embrace.

8.4 Postwar Conceptions of Economics and Security in China and Japan

Japan's dual identity as economic model and threat would continue to shape the Sino-Japanese relationship in the wake of the Second Sino-Japanese War. The resumption of the Chinese Civil War, soon after the ending of war with Japan, concluded in 1949 following the CCP's defeat of the Nationalist government. Despite the many profound differences between the CCP and Nationalists on questions of ideology, foreign relations and domestic political organization, the

---

[48] Yinchu 1940, 3.   [49] Yinchu 1940, 8–9.

state-led heavy industrial model rolled out by the CCP in its earliest years in power was essentially a more radical version of the "frugal modernity" first practiced by the Nationalists during war with Japan.[50]

Alongside these parallel visions of state-led industrial development, the CCP also came to share its predecessors' ideas about industrial power as the basis for national security. By the early 1950s, as the CCP became embroiled in military conflicts that would mark the early years of the unfolding Cold War in Asia, its leaders had to confront the question of how to navigate China's relationship with postwar Japan. During internal Chinese deliberations over Japan's future as a treaty ally of the United States, Chinese Foreign Ministry officials began to discuss their understanding of the nature of the past and ongoing threat posed by Japan. Displaying pronounced continuity with prewar and wartime Nationalist Chinese conceptions of the relationship between economics and security, CCP officials reflected that Japan's rise to power in the late nineteenth and early twentieth centuries underscored the "comprehensive" (*zonghe*) nature of national power, and Japan's success in fusing technological, industrial, and military strength. Contrasting "past wars" as those that required only military planning and a concentration of armed force, the CCP instead emphasized the "industrial" basis of modern warfare (*gongyezhan*), and the imperative of both strengthening China's industrial capabilities, and eradicating Japan's "latent" industrial power.[51] Japan's latent power, the Chinese economist Ma Yinchu had noted just a few years earlier, was already beginning to be revived by US efforts to bring Japan into its "wartime economic system." As Ma warned darkly, "[i]f General MacArthur's headquarters truly intends to restore Japan's industry to the level of 1930–1934, I hope General MacArthur does not forget that it was at this level that Japan followed an aggressive path."[52]

Yet, as in the 1930s and 1940s, the CCP's conceptions of the relationship between economic development and national security resulted in the adoption of some highly counterintuitive policy choices vis-à-vis Japan. To develop the industrial capabilities needed to achieve "comprehensive" national power, the CCP looked to the Soviet Union as a political and economic development model. But the CCP's attempts to follow the Soviet Union's path of rapid industrialization created economic and political problems for China: shortages in key industrial goods, a lack of Soviet expertise with Chinese agrarian

---

[50] Zanasi 2020, 193–194. See also King 2022, 688–690. [51] King 2016b, 68–72.
[52] Yinchu 1947, 1. Though Ma Yinchu had served in the Nationalist government and in various Nationalist-run research institutions, he became increasingly critical of the government's economic policies in the 1940s, was briefly placed under house arrest, and, in 1948, fled to Hong Kong. In 1949, he was invited by CCP Premier Zhou Enlai to return to mainland China, where he served as an economic official and adviser and later President of Peking University. Howard and Howard 1967–1979, 475–478.

economic conditions, and the fear of becoming overly dependent on the Soviet Union. As early as 1949, and increasingly over the course of the 1950s and 1960s, the most senior CCP leaders therefore began to look to Japan as a vital, alternative source of industrial goods, technology, and expertise. Japan, Mao argued, was the only country in Asia to have made the leap from agricultural to industrial country, and its "economy, culture and technology are all relatively more developed than ours."[53]

Japan, editorials in the state-run *People's Daily* argued, remained a security threat to China, particularly because of the way in which the United States had rehabilitated Japan's wartime military-industrial capabilities as the key plank in its wider Cold War containment strategy in Asia.[54] Nevertheless, the very fact of China's insecurity in the face of Japan's growing industrial strength merely increased the necessity for Chinese officials to absorb as much as they could from Japan. Throughout the late 1940s and early 1950s, CCP officials in Northeast China therefore drew on the expertise of thousands of Japanese technicians, scientists, and engineers "left behind" in Manchuria after the Second Sino-Japanese War to repair and restart the coal mines, factories, and other industrial sites previously established by Japan.[55] Chinese officials also reached out to Japanese exporting firms to begin importing steel, chemicals, mining machinery, and other crucial industrial goods from Japan. While Chinese attempts to restart this trade were generally impeded by the US-led Cold War economic embargo on China, the CCP had more success in importing economic ideas from Japan. By the mid-1950s, Chinese officials were travelling to Japan to observe industrial practices at thousands of Japanese factories and large corporations, while hundreds of Japanese politicians, business people, and industrial advisers were travelling to China each year to attend trade fairs, and to provide advice to senior CCP leaders on the nature of the Japanese economy and opportunities for Sino-Japanese trade.[56]

The revitalization of Cold War economic ties between China and Japan was not only motivated by CCP ideas about the relationship between industrial power and national security, and of the ways in which China might therefore learn from Japan. These ties were also driven by continuity in the ideas and individuals that had shaped Japan's imperial project in Manchuria in the 1930s and 1940s, and those involved in shaping Japan's postwar economic policies. Though ideas of "self-sufficiency" and "fascist economic planning" had been discredited by Japan's failed imperial experiments, important elements of

---

[53] King 2016b, 189–191. On how fears of dependence motivated CCP economic engagement with the capitalist world more generally, see Kelly 2021.
[54] During the Korean War, the United States invested heavily in Japanese *zaibatsu*, and US procurements of industrial goods from Japan comprised one-third of Japan's rapidly increasing export trade. King 2016b, 72.
[55] King 2016a.   [56] King 2016b, see Chapters 3 and 4 in particular.

Japan's prewar and wartime development model were successfully retained after 1945, including an interventionist state-led approach to economic planning, and the prioritization of advanced technology and heavy industry in the Japanese economy.[57] These postwar economic plans were being rolled out by individuals such as Saburō Ōkita and Takasaki Tatsunosuke, who had played a role in developing Japan's economic policies in Manchuria, as well as less prominent Japanese who had been responsible for building the infrastructure, running the coal mines, and establishing the Japanese-run salt, cotton, and other industries in China during the 1930s and 1940s.[58] While these postwar Japanese planners believed firmly that Japan's postwar development would continue to rely on heavy industrialization, they also recognized that Japan could no longer use the militaristic policies of the 1930s to monopolize the raw materials, resources, and export markets necessary to build its heavy industrial sector. Instead, they argued that "Japan could secure its future as an advanced industrial power" by relying on the export of technology and industrial equipment to countries like China in exchange for imports of Chinese raw materials.[59] Using their long-standing knowledge of the Chinese economy, and their positions within the postwar Japanese economic and political system, these individuals played critical roles in transmitting industrial expertise to China, creating the Japanese policy conditions that would ensure ongoing complementarity in the Chinese and Japanese economies, and lobbying the Japanese government to normalize economic and diplomatic relations between Communist China and Japan.[60]

8.5 Conclusion

The relationship between China and Japan is emblematic of a wider dynamic in East Asia across the twentieth century, in which deep economic interdependence has coexisted with adversarial political and security relationships between states.[61] Explaining these dynamics requires us to move beyond the still-widespread liberal assumption in the IR literature that interdependence necessarily mutes conflict, as well as beyond mercantilist theories of trade derived largely from European history.[62] Moreover, it requires us to heed calls in that literature to "better understand ... the domestic sources of trade and foreign policy."[63] Paying heed to these calls, this chapter has shown how Chinese and Japanese conceptions of the relationship between economics and security – first developed in response to the crisis of nineteenth-century Western imperial coercion in East Asia, and later amplified in the context of Cold War East

---

[57] Gao 1997; Johnson 1982; Mimura 2011.   [58] King 2016b.   [59] King 2016a, 156.
[60] King 2016b.   [61] Foot and Goh 2018.
[62] For excellent discussions on this point, see Coe and Wolford 2020, 271–274.
[63] Gartzke and Zhang 2015, 419.

Asia – fused the Chinese and Japanese economies in the lead up to, during, and in the decades following the Second Sino-Japanese War.

A wave of recent scholarship on sanctions, statecraft, and "geoeconomics" has renewed our focus on the coercive uses of economic instruments, and of the ways in which foreign aid, trade, and investment might be "weaponized" by states seeking to enhance their own power and national security.[64] These are of course not new developments, but one side of much older understandings of the nexus between economics and security, and exemplified in this chapter's account of Japan's strategic efforts to ring-fence Chinese resources and export markets on its own path to military-industrial modernization and national security.

However, the other, and perhaps more intriguing, side of that nexus is the way in which perceptions of *insecurity* can lead states to choose to engage economically with their chief adversary. Such engagement is not premised on the liberal foundation that trade and investment will transform an adversarial relationship into a more peaceful one. Rather, this engagement is selective and strategic, designed to fulfill a range of domestic economic and ultimately political goals. For the Nationalist and Communist Chinese governments over the twentieth century, economic engagement with Japan was driven by an understanding of the economic foundations of China's long-term security, and the recognition that China could not realize its economic – and therefore national – security without engaging with, and learning from, an adversarial Japan. At the same time, both Japan and later Communist China viewed economic engagement with the other as a way to mitigate the risk of dependence on unreliable and self-interested (Western) hegemonic powers. Understanding the strategic, rather than liberal, foundations of such economic engagement therefore helps us to understand how China and Japan managed the trade-offs posed by strengthening economic ties with an actual or potential adversary. These trade-offs were not conceived in conventional liberal terms as the unintended "negative externalities" of economic interdependence, but rather as calculated choices about the extent of foreign economic integration necessary to achieve self-strengthening and autonomy on the world stage.

The dilemma posed by this understanding is one that is likely familiar to late-industrializing, "backward" countries across East Asia and the wider developing world, whose development choices and grand strategies have always been constrained by the difficulties of "catching up" within an order designed to advantage industrially advanced countries, often at the expense of less developed ones. These constraints help us to understand the prevalence of more "comprehensive," or economically-infused, conceptions of national security in East Asia, and why East Asian states have so often confounded Western IR

---

[64] Nicholas 2022; Farrell and Newman 2019.

theories by tolerating – and finding ways to successfully navigate – the dilemma of economic (and political) engagement with their adversaries.[65] At the same time, the historical developments outlined in this chapter help to excavate the strategic, rather than liberal, foundations of economic interdependence in East Asia.

---

[65] Goh 2013a; Goh 2019.

9 Japan and New Orders in East Asia, 1914–1945

Jeremy A. Yellen

World War II in Asia (1937–45) witnessed the dramatic rise and fall of the Japanese empire, one of the most important but least understood empires in the modern world.[1*] By mid-1942, Japan's wartime new order for Greater East Asia – its Greater East Asia Co-Prosperity Sphere – stretched across Asia and included many former colonial territories in East Asia, Southeast Asia, and Oceania. Japanese leaders and political intellectuals aimed to build a new type of political-economic order, one that reached from the cold northern woods of Sakhalin to the southern tropics of the Netherlands Indies, from the Philippine archipelago to the jungles and deltas of Burma.

Why did visions of a new type of empire and political order rise? Why did Japan advocate a Greater East Asia Co-Prosperity Sphere? And what induced Japanese leaders to take advantage of global instability to advance throughout East and Southeast Asia? This chapter explores the Greater East Asia Co-Prosperity Sphere and Japanese expansionism in the 1930s and 1940s as responses to the challenges of diplomacy and empire reaching back to World War I. It shows how a new type of thinking of empire – total war thought – emerged in the Japanese army in the wake of World War I. This strand of thought emphasized that wars required the total organizational capacities of states (or empires) and favored those that could support and field large armies. Victory or defeat in future wars necessitated total self-sufficiency that could only be achieved by seizing resource-rich territories. Autarky and empire were thus seen as critical to supply a nation's military forces and to fight protracted wars.

This desire for autarky and empire did not influence policy initially. In the 1920s, Japan instead aligned its approach with the emerging liberal internationalist order. But the impending breakdown of that order emboldened groups within the Japanese army to seize Manchuria in 1931 in direct defiance of state

---

[1*] This chapter is adapted from Yellen 2019a.

policies. The staggering popularity of the Manchurian incident confirmed this new course, giving the army and its allies greater power within the Japanese state. But it was war in China from 1937 and the Asia-Pacific from 1941 that led to the ascendance of ideas of self-sufficiency in Japanese political thought. Trends in total war thought reaching back to World War I thus shaped wartime ideas of how to build a new political order in Asia. Japan's wartime expansion and its construction of a New Order in Greater East Asia, in this sense, offers a perfect test case of what happens when empires engage in order building in an era of "total war."

9.1   World War I and Aftermath: A New Order in East Asia

World War I is the natural point of departure for any exploration of Japan's aggressive expansion in the 1930s and 1940s. By the time the Great War began, Japan was a regional power with interests extending across Northeast Asia. This owed to a longer-term effort to transform Japan into an empire and major power, the equal to the "civilized" nations of the West. The pursuit of empire after 1868 emerged out of a keen understanding of power in international relations and a desire to join the ranks of the great powers. Imperialism, supported by international law, was part of the standard of "civilization" in modern international society.[2] Only in possessing a colonial empire would Japan become a "first-class nation," the equal of Great Britain and the United States. Japanese leaders thus became model players in the game of empires, adapting to the mores of international society and retooling their country's domestic institutions to best compete in international politics.[3]

The first phase of empire building was driven largely by strategic concerns, or unease about the potential gains of other imperial powers. Since the 1880s, Japanese elites believed Korea to be a "dagger pointed at the heart of Japan"; Japanese leaders sought to prevent any other power from exercising control over its nearest neighbor. They felt similarly about the Liaodong peninsula, a deep-water port and a gateway to Manchuria. This early strategic push for empire was so successful that by the early twentieth century, Japan had defeated both China in a regional war and imperial Russia in a major war. By 1910, Japan had become a regional power and had a series of formal colonial holdings, from Taiwan to Korea, and Karafuto to the Kwantung Leasehold. These holdings both served as areas that needed to be defended and "imperial gateways" for further expansion: Korea as the gateway to the north and Taiwan the gateway to the south.[4] These two gateways reflected the debates around the

---

[2] See, for instance, Gong 1984.   [3] Pyle 2007, 66–136.
[4] I am adopting the term "imperial gateway" from Shirane 2022. Some scholars see Hokkaidō, the Kuril Islands, and the Ryūkyū Islands as Japan's first colonial holdings. There is merit to such

two directions that shaped Japanese imperialism: defending the south and advancing in the north (*nanshu hokushinron*), or defending the north and advancing in the south (*hokushu nanshinron*), or sometimes referred to as the Northern and Southern strategies.

World War I, however, was transformative in international affairs: It was fought on a colossal scale, led to major shifts in global politics, and provided space for Japan to seize important regional advantages. The Great War was a war of empires. It was also the world's first total war, a conflict fought by mobilizing entire populations and economic resources. It transformed the way wars had been fought, mobilizing state and society to an unprecedented extent. By 1918 much of Europe had been devastated. The Great War dealt the death blow to four major dynastic empires: the Ottoman, Habsburg, Romanov, and Hohenzollern empires. Moreover, it was a global war, with fighting that reached the Asia-Pacific. Japan took advantage of the war to expand its imperial interests in China and the South Pacific, capturing German holdings in Shandong and Micronesia, and leveling the notorious Twenty-One Demands on China. From 1918, Japan also participated in the Siberian Intervention, and staged an extensive occupation of Siberia until 1922.[5] Ultimately, this period gave rise to new thinking about war, transforming understandings of how future wars would be fought.

For Japan, one of the most important impacts of World War I was the rise of total war thought. Staff officers stationed in Europe during the war sent back reports that revolutionized Japanese thinking about modern warfare. Wartime Japanese army surveys on military affairs viewed the conflict as a "national power war." Officers took detailed notes on how belligerent countries tightened controls over all existing resources and facilities to be used in the service of the war.[6] Moreover, the relentless trench warfare and efforts among belligerents to achieve wartime autarky led military strategists to see warfare as dependent on self-reliance in resources and production. Widespread blockades led military strategists to believe that countries that failed to achieve total self-reliance, or those who "could not overcome economic blockades," would lose in future wars.[7]

This new understanding of warfare led military strategists in the army to treat the control over richer territories to the north – China and Manchuria, in particular – as a national imperative. As early as 1918, Ugaki Kazushige,

---

views, but the peoples of these territories over time were incorporated as Japanese subjects with civic rights that were not provided in the formal colonial holdings.

[5] The goals in China and the South Pacific were opportunistic, but the occupation of Siberia had a defensive realist tint. Army leaders like Yamagata Aritomo and Terauchi Masatake, fearing a nightmare scenario of a Russo-German alliance against Japan in 1918, pressed for creating a buffer in Siberia. Kobayashi 2020, 340.

[6] Mori 2020, 3.   [7] Katō 2005, 251.

then a section chief in the general staff, wrote in his diary that a major lesson of World War I was the necessity for "self-sufficiency" (*jikyū jisoku*), and recommended creating a "self-sufficient economic sphere" that forges "China and Japan into a single economic unit."[8] Further army studies throughout the 1920s argued that Japan lacked the resources to meet the needs of modern warfare, and study groups within the army met to discuss how to prepare for future wars. They began studying the broad and massive mobilization of industry and society that would become necessary to fight future wars. Over time, these study groups turned the attention of the general staff and the Kwantung Army to the resource-rich areas of Manchuria and Mongolia, areas of "special interest" to Japan and areas to be kept safe from foreign intervention.[9]

The Great War also led to an ideational shift in international relations. Although many global empires remained intact after the war, aggressive imperial expansion and what William L. Langer and others have called the "diplomacy of imperialism" – wherein the great powers used secret agreements, rival alliances, and threats of force to vie for greater weight in world politics – were no longer viewed as justifiable in the war's aftermath.[10] The winds of change were perhaps best symbolized by the contest of visions between the socialist internationalism championed by Bolshevik leader Vladimir Lenin and the liberal internationalism of US President Woodrow Wilson. Lenin rejected colonialism and foreign domination and viewed class struggle as the preeminent global concern. Wilson, conversely, championed a global peace through a "new diplomacy" of free trade, arms limitation, democracy, collective security, and conference diplomacy, highlighted by his brainchild, the League of Nations.[11] Both leaders advocated a new world order that rejected secretive and imperialist diplomacy in favor of peaceful relations. Both heralded a new globalism in the logic and practice of international relations.

Wilson's vision set the tone for international politics in the 1920s. Scholars have paid specific attention to the League of Nations, the visions behind its emergence, and its efforts at marrying democratic and internationalist ideals with the reality of empire and great power politics.[12] As a global enterprise, however, the League was not only fragile and incomplete but also presided over a dramatic expansion of empire through the mandate system. More pointedly, the League was hobbled by the absence of the world's new great power: the

---

[8] Ugaki 1968, 150. [9] Kurosawa 1985; Barnhart 1987, 22–49; Arima 2002.
[10] See Langer 1935; and Iriye 1965.
[11] Although Wilson has become known for national self-determination, this was originally less important to his international liberalism than his so-called new diplomacy of free trade, arms limitation, democracy, collective security, and an end to secret alliances. Over time, however, Wilson came to champion self-determination above all else. For a work on the international ramifications of Wilsonian thought, see Manela 2009; and Tucker 2004.
[12] Mazower 2012; and Pederson 2015.

United States. Wilson's dream of establishing a new order centered on the League was shattered by Republican intransigence and the US Senate's decision to reject both the Treaty of Versailles and membership in the League of Nations. Wilson died a broken man.

Nonetheless, his internationalist principles found new life in the policies of his Republican successor, Warren G. Harding. It was at the Washington Naval Conference of 1921–22, not Versailles in 1919, that the United States (under President Harding and Secretary of State Charles Evans Hughes) set its Neo-Wilsonian stamp on the new world order.[13] The negotiations at Washington established what is seen as the Washington System, or the Washington Treaty System: an international order in Asia that aimed, first and foremost, to ensure that China did not emerge into a site of great power conflict.[14]

The Washington System was a new enterprise of order making that enshrined Wilsonian principles into the international system. Although primarily focused on the Asia-Pacific, it was global in scope and included power from three continents. It was built upon a series of international conventions signed in 1921–22, from the Five-Power Treaty (naval arms limitation), the Four-Power Treaty (an end to secret alliances), the Nine-Power Treaty (free trade and respect of Chinese territorial integrity and sovereignty), and the Shandong Treaty (Japan's return of Shandong to China). It was later reinforced by other conventions, from the Kellogg-Briand Pact (1928) to the London Naval Treaty (1930), and efforts to negotiate new customs tariffs in China. Peace was to be secured through free economic intercourse, arms limitation, multilateral cooperation and conference diplomacy, and an end to secret treaties. Empires remained (and indeed flourished – no powers were asked to dismantle their existing empires), but the "diplomacy of imperialism" was shunned in favor of open multilateralism and conference diplomacy. In this sense, the new order was an awkward mix: It heralded a future free of imperialism yet remained rooted in the empires of the past.[15]

The Washington System nonetheless signaled a new trajectory in foreign affairs and brought new challenges for diplomacy and empire. Before 1919, Japan had been a model player in the game of empires in Asia, using military might, secret alliances, and territorial expansion to secure national wealth and strength. But the Washington System changed the rules of the game in a way that contained Japan's growing regional power. By the 1920s, aggressive imperialism no longer fit the global standard of "civilization." To participate in this new order, Japan gave up many of the fruits of its participation in the Great War. In 1922, Japan withdrew its troops from the Shandong concession in

---

[13] Iriye 1965; Tooze 2014.

[14] See, for instance, Iriye 1965; Hattori 2001; Hosoya and Saitō 1978; Asada 2006a; Nakatani 2016.

[15] For an overview of the system and its workings, see Yellen 2023.

China and recalled all troops involved in the Siberian Intervention. Moreover, these agreements committed Japan to limiting naval armaments, abandoning the Anglo-Japanese Alliance to participate in multilateral diplomacy, promising nonintervention in Chinese affairs, and making peaceful, economic expansionism the hallmark of its foreign policy.

Most scholarships highlight the skepticism with which Japanese leaders met the new order. The naval disarmament treaties in Washington (1922) and London (1930) generated fierce debate within the Japanese navy and led to the rise of "hot-blooded young officers" who sought to rebel against the treaties. Many officers in the army too, particularly those influenced by ideas of total war, scorned the new situation as little more than imperialism, American style.[16] More often, scholars highlight the scathing critiques written by Konoe Fumimaro, then a fledgling member of the House of Peers, before attending the Paris Peace Conference. Konoe rejected Wilsonian ideals as sugarcoating an unfair status quo among "haves" (*moteru kuni*) like Britain and the United States and "have-nots" (*motazaru kuni*) such as Germany and Japan. "Haves" held an expansive network of colonies, territories, or resources that far surpassed the "have-nots." This led Konoe to see the promotion of the new ideals as a cynical attempt to preserve the unjust global division of land and resources. Prophetically, Konoe argued that unequal access to markets and resources might "compel Japan to attempt to overthrow the status quo as Germany did before the war."[17]

Yet Konoe's earlier concerns were drowned out in the early 1920s by moderates who believed accommodating to the new order served Japan's interests.[18] The ascendant of moderates, historian Kenneth B. Pyle argues, owed to a political culture that was sensitive to the forces controlling the international environment, and one that pursued national power in cooperation with the leading powers of the day. Domestic practices and policies were reshaped in ways that allowed Japan to align itself with the emerging international order.[19] Indeed, some historians have even suggested the overall excitement with which Japan met the new ideals of peace, democracy, and international cooperation. Whatever the case, in the 1920s, Japan chose peaceful economic expansionism in cooperation with the Washington powers. In the process, Japan became a central player in East Asian affairs, and an important participant in global politics – so much so that Konoe himself came to support internationalism as a key to global status.[20] The army and its allies, too, grudgingly acquiesced to the new realities in both international and domestic

---

[16] See Asada 2006b; and Matsusaka 2001, 391.   [17] See Konoe 1918.
[18] As Frederick R. Dickinson argues, however, Konoe tempered his views owing to the excitement among many Japanese in Wilsonian internationalism, which offered opportunities to build a "New Japan." See Dickinson 2013.
[19] Pyle 2007.   [20] Dickinson 2013, 65.

politics. As General Staff intelligence division member Matsui Iwane wrote in 1923: "We must substitute economic conquest for military invasion, financial influence for military control, and achieve our goals under the slogans of co-prosperity and co-existence, friendship, and cooperation."[21]

This Japanese accommodation of the new liberal order in the 1920s has implications for students of international politics, shedding light on what Peter Gourevitch calls "the second image reversed," or what Leopold van Ranke refers to as the "primacy of foreign policy." In the 1920s, domestic politics was not the primary cause or driver of Japanese international politics. Far from it, domestic norms and structures were a direct consequence of the international politics of the day.[22] Yet continued support in Japan for this new standard of "civilization" rested on assumptions of stability, international status, and economic gain. Japan's commitment to the new order and to being a "responsible stakeholder" rested on a commitment among all the major powers to its underlying principles, a commitment that was soon in short supply.

9.2 The Japanese Revolt

This support did not outlive the decade – particularly owing to the inherent weaknesses of the Washington System. When push came to shove, the system proved to be what one historian calls a "house built on sand." It relied too much on economic performance and the "great storage battery of the North American economy," and crumbled under the impact of repeated economic shocks and the global retreat from economic liberalism.[23] Moreover, its international rules remained weak, and regional security in Asia depended on (largely absent) US muscle, so security commitments were soon revealed to be rather thin gruel.

Japan's revolt from the system in the 1930s owed to a convergence of domestic and foreign crises. On the domestic front, a bitter political battle between the Hamaguchi Osachi cabinet and the armed forces over arms limitation in the wake of the London Naval Treaty of 1930 convinced hot-headed officers that the government took national security far too lightly. Young, insubordinate officers began to argue that weakness on defense and empire represented a failure of the political system. This sense of political failure was compounded by a rural crisis and a deepening recession at home. Some groups within the army began to view political change at home and expanded empire in Manchuria as two sides of the same coin. They pressed for both through systematic campaigns of violence that began to undermine the commitment to peace.

---

[21] Iriye 1974, 245.
[22] Gourevitch 1978. See also von Ranke 2011a, 65. See also von Ranke 2011b.
[23] Pyle 2006, 410.

The situation was exacerbated by foreign crises – both economic and political. The global economic crisis in 1929 undermined the economic interdependence on which the Washington System was based. Japan's cooperation in the world system of "free trade" had stemmed from assumptions of vast economic gains. As the major powers undermined free trade in favor of protectionist economic blocs, concerns and dissatisfactions with the order increased in size and scope. The shock of global economic crisis, more than anything else, led Japan on the road to abandoning the Washington System.

The failures of economic diplomacy were exacerbated by power politics and increasing worries over Japanese interests on the continent. Throughout the 1920s, the rise of the Soviet Union and the Kuomintang led members of the Japanese army to fear a so-called Manchuria-Mongolian Problem (*Manmō mondai*). They saw the area as a "problem" in two ways: Japanese "special interests" were potentially threatened by Soviet influence and the possibility of Chinese national unification.[24] A revitalized nationalist movement in China posed an existential threat to Japanese interests in Manchuria and Mongolia. And the Sino-Soviet military conflict of 1929 alerted the Japanese army to Soviet military power and convinced many of the inevitability of a conflict with Soviet Russia.[25] Making matters even more chaotic, media misreporting and overdramatization of the Wanpaoshan Incident (a conflict between Chinese and Korean farmers over irrigation rights in Manchuria) of July 1931 triggered bloodshed and riots in Korea, and increased awareness in Japan of the tense situation on the continent. This security situation was so highly reported that a Tokyo Imperial University opinion survey – held a mere two months before the Manchurian Incident – revealed that a whopping 88 percent of students were in favor of the use of force to solve the "Manchuria-Mongolia problem."[26]

The combination of political and economic crises emboldened domestic actors and gave renewed cogency to empire as a means of solving Japan's problems. It provided the context behind which internal concerns drove external policy. It was at this point that a small group of total war theorists in the military took matters into their own hands. Staff officers in the Kwantung Army led by Lt. Col. Ishiwara Kanji and Col. Itagaki Seishirō exploited the situation on September 18, 1931, initiating what came to be known as the Manchurian Incident, a full-scale invasion of Manchuria in direct defiance of official orders. That the Japanese army itself had run wild became apparent by September 21, when Gen. Hayashi Senjūro, the Commander of Japan's Korean Army, acted without imperial orders and crossed the international border into Manchuria to reinforce the Kwantung Army. The Japanese Cabinet made the retroactive decision to allow it rather than admit to the world that it had lost control over its own army.[27]

---

[24] Arima 2002, 73.   [25] Hattori 2001, 255–263.   [26] Katō 2009, 261–262.
[27] Tobe 2017, 18–19.

Foreign Minister Shidehara Kijūrō nonetheless strove to contain the incident. He persuaded Army Minister Minami Jirō and General Staff Chief Kanaya Hanzō to order the Kwantung Army to stop expanding any further. But the Kwantung Army simply ignored those orders.[28] Making matters even more complicated, the Japanese mass media whipped up a war fever, mobilizing popular sentiment in support of military action abroad.[29] As journalist and ideologue Tachibana Shiraki noted, the power of public opinion made it even harder to back down from the incident. "It was not," he stated, "so much that the military pulled the government along, but that public opinion was spurring government on."[30] Even "liberal" intellectual Yoshino Sakuzō supported the renewed imperialism in Manchuria, and by 1932 advocated for an "East Asian Monroe Doctrine."[31] In the end, Tokyo remained unable to quell the Kwantung Army, which established a new satellite regime (or puppet state) of Manchukuo in March 1932. Six months later, Japanese policymakers had accepted the seizure of Manchuria as a fait accompli. In September 1932, one year after the Manchurian Incident had begun, Japan formally recognized Manchukuo.

The shocks of the depression and corresponding domestic political changes in Japan thus provided the seedbed for "total war" thinking and the desires for autarky to take firmer root. In the 1930s, "go-fast imperialists" in Japan began to seek regional hegemony, and outwardly voiced their disdain for the ideas and institutions that underpinned the old order. For instance, they no longer viewed the League of Nations as serving Japanese interests in East Asia. Japan left the League in 1933 to consolidate its gains in Manchuria and to isolate China from the major powers.[32] The foreign ministry, in turn, became more proactive in asserting Japanese primacy. Foreign Ministry Intelligence Bureau Chief Amō Eiji in April 1934 issued a provocative statement dubbed the "Asian Monroe Doctrine," wherein he declared Japan's "special position" in China and its "mission" to preserve peace in East Asia. This sentiment was by no means new, but it led to an uproar abroad. Foreign Minister Hirota Kōki downplayed and eventually disowned the statement. But the damage had been done – the Amō Statement was understood abroad as less a "declaration" of policy than a "disclosure" of Japan's regional desires.[33]

The military also became more assertive. Japanese field armies in China began several schemes to expand Japanese influence within North China. By 1935, the Kwantung Army and China Garrison Army advocated for a five-province breakaway in North China of Hebei, Shandong, Shanxi, Chahar, and Suiyuan, and by December 1935 had even established two autonomous regimes in the region: the Hebei-Chahar Political Council and the East Hebei

---

[28] Katō 2005, 10–14; Crowley 1966, 123–130. [29] Young 1998, 55–180.
[30] Quoted in Yamamuro 2006, 44. [31] Jiang 2023, Chapter 5. [32] Inoue 1994.
[33] US Office of the Historian 1950, 141.

Autonomous Government.[34] Meanwhile, the Japanese navy repudiated arms limitation altogether at the London Naval Conference of 1935–36. They had sought complete parity with Great Britain and the United States and staged a walkout of the conference when parity was denied. This abandonment of arms limitation was widely recognized for what it was: another denunciation of the Washington System.[35] And as the military moved against the Washington System, it revised Japan's national defense strategy in 1936 – labeling *both* the United States and the Soviet Union as Japan's primary hypothetical enemies and elevating the navy's desire for an advance south to the same priority level as the army's northern advance.

Despite the rise of "go-fast imperialists" in Japan, the crisis in Manchuria did not wholly overturn the post-World War I settlement. A commitment to internationalism in foreign policy continued unabated even after Japan left the League of Nations. Japan remained a party to many international institutions and engaged in widespread cultural diplomacy – sponsoring goodwill missions, garden tours, and even securing the rights to host the 1940 Olympics.[36] More importantly, the creation of an "independent" satellite regime such as Manchukuo highlights the power national self-determination continued to hold in international politics. Even bold new moves toward empires like the establishment of Manchukuo were justified in the language of independence and self-determination. In this sense, Japan served as the vanguard of a "new imperialism" that recast colonialism in the language of self-determination by creating legally sovereign nation-states.[37] Ishiwara Kanji, the planner of the Manchurian Incident, spoke of Manchurian and Mongolian independence in the language of self-determination, noting that both "Manchuria and Mongolia are [the territory of] the Manchurian and Mongolian peoples."[38] This new imperialism reached its peak during the Pacific War. By late 1943, Thailand, the Chinese Nanjing Regime, the Philippines, and Burma had joined Manchukuo as independent regimes within the Greater East Asia Co-Prosperity Sphere. The "independence" of these regimes, however, was little more than a façade that enabled Japanese intervention in their internal affairs.

Over the course of the 1930s, Manchukuo emerged into what historian Louise Young calls Japan's "total empire." Empire building in Manchukuo, she shows, entailed a dramatic and multidimensional mobilization of Japanese state and society in ways that transformed Japan itself. Total empire fed into a war fever at home and changed the mass media into a vehicle of support for imperial expansion. It led to the emergence of "imperial interest groups" that

---

[34] Yellen 2022, 228; Crowley 1966, 231.   [35] Asada 2006b, 172–204.
[36] See, for instance, Collins 2008; Wilson 2001; Gripentrog 2021.   [37] Duara 2007.
[38] Quoted in Yamamuro 2006, 36–37.

called for military expansion abroad and confrontation with Japan's great power rivals. Total empire led to greater state intervention in the economy, polity, and society. And Manchukuo served as a testing ground for revolutionary new ideas, providing intellectuals and bureaucrats with a vast laboratory for enacting social and economic reforms. Disillusioned with liberal capitalism in Japan, intellectuals, radical officers, and military technocrats used Manchukuo as a laboratory to create a managerial state that would allow "have-nots" such as Japan, which lacked as broad a resource base, to compete with the global "haves."[39] The "total empire" of Manchukuo incubated ideas that gained relevance once Japan broke away from the old order.

It was Japan's war in China, however, that impelled this decisive break. The Marco Polo Bridge Incident in July 1937 set Japan on a collision course with the old order and undermined the cooperation upon which the Washington System had been based. Japan's rapid military advance into China, in turn, fed into a sense of destiny of regional leadership, and some intellectuals took to calling the conflict a "holy war."[40] By 1938, Shōwa Research Association (*Shōwa Kenkyūkai*) intellectuals had begun advocating that Japan take advantage of the "holy war" to construct an "East Asian Cooperative Community." Konoe Fumimaro, who by this time was prime minister, followed up in November 1938 by declaring a "New Order in East Asia." This new order, he argued, centered around Japan, Manchukuo, and China, which would work together to "guarantee permanent stability in East Asia." From a short-term perspective, the new order declaration was part of an effort to correct a major blunder from earlier in the year, when Konoe publicly and disastrously announced Japan's refusal to deal with the Kuomintang government. It was part of an effort to gain collaborators like Wang Jingwei within the Kuomintang to help build a new China.[41] But from a longer-term perspective, Konoe's declaration was a rejection of the Washington System. Foreign Minister Arita Hachirō followed up a few weeks later with the final nail in the coffin: He informed the United States that Japan would no longer protect the principle of the Open Door and the commitment to equal opportunity in China.

With this, the Washington System was a dead letter. Thus began Japan's project of imagining the future Asian order, a project that led to the expulsion of the colonial powers from Asia and the establishment of a self-sufficient

---

[39] Young 1998.

[40] Conservative Diet member Saitō Takao saw the empty slogans surrounding Japan's "holy war" as the work of "half-baked intellectuals" who surrounded Prime Minister Konoe Fumimaro. See Kinmonth 1999, 349–350.

[41] See Furukawa 2015, 142. Yet another plot thread was the use of the declaration to explain Japan's "mystifying war" to a domestic audience and to prepare them to commit emotionally to a longer conflict. Arima 2002, 218–219.

political-economic bloc: the New Order in Greater East Asia, also called the Greater East Asia Co-Prosperity Sphere.

9.3 The New Order in "Greater East Asia"

Japan thus embarked on a dramatic new enterprise of empire and order building at the very moment it plunged into total war in China. This convergence of total empire and total war affected all aspects of Japan's new order.

First, at the most basic level, it impelled policymakers and political intellectuals to imagine what Asia would look like under Japanese leadership. Visions for Japanese leadership were highly opportunistic, changing with the developing geopolitical landscape. At first, the new order was limited to East Asia, centering on Japan, China, and Manchukuo. But the Nazi blitzkrieg in Europe from April through June 1940 significantly changed the strategic calculus. As Germany swept through the Low Countries and France and became ascendant in Europe, Japanese leaders began to worry about the implications for Asia. Diplomat Shigemitsu Mamoru recalled that many in Japan were "seized with panic about what would happen to British colonies in Asia and feared what would become of the Japanese Empire once Dutch and French colonies were occupied by Germany." They worried Japan might "miss the bus" to advance south and take advantage of the disposition of European colonies after war's end.[42] This fear, and the belief that Germany might seek to exercise control over Dutch and French colonies in Asia, areas in Japan's own backyard, strengthened calls for an alliance with Nazi Germany and led Tokyo to declare Japanese leadership over "Greater" East Asia.[43]

This was the background behind Foreign Minister Matsuoka Yōsuke's declaration of the Greater East Asia Co-Prosperity Sphere in August 1940. His declaration, like the official announcement of Japan's New Order in Greater East Asia, was an explicit nod south. Matsuoka wanted to use alliances and diplomacy with the great powers to help Japan carve out a pan-region in Asia. Matsuoka further hoped this pan-region would be recognized by both world powers and regional elites alike. In this context, he sought to forge pacts or alliances with Germany, Italy, the Soviet Union, and the United States. His grand design was what I have called "sphere of influence diplomacy," or what historian Kawanishi Kōsuke sees as an effort to create a new world order wherein each great power "respects each other's co-prosperity spheres" (*sorezore no kyōeiken sonchō*).[44] Matsuoka's dream of establishing a world of co-prosperity spheres was ambitious yet naïve. Both US hostility to Japanese aims

---

[42] Shigemitsu 1952, 277–278.
[43] Yellen 2016. Here, "Greater" implied areas to the "South": Southeast Asia, Oceania, and the Indian subcontinent.
[44] Kawanishi 2016, 35–40; and Yellen 2019a, Chapter 2.

and the outbreak of the German–Soviet war in June 1941 made his dream untenable. Yet his foreign policy aims lived on. By the time he was ousted as foreign minister in July 1941, the construction of the Greater East Asia Co-Prosperity Sphere had become the *central aim* of Japanese policy.

After the outbreak of the Asia-Pacific War in December 1941, however, this attempt to imagine Asia anew was given new life. On December 10, 1941, two days after the Pearl Harbor attack, a liaison conference began calling the new conflict the "Greater East Asia War." This new name reflected the fact that Japan was waging "a war that aims to construct a New Order in Greater East Asia."[45] It further legitimized the Greater East Asia Co-Prosperity Sphere as Japan's national policy and central war aim. From this point on, the task to build Japan's new order was taken up by others: from intellectuals to political and military leaders, from bureaucrats to captains of industry. They continued a process of imagining the future Asia under Japanese leadership well into the waning days of World War II.

Second, the fact that Japan built its new order as it plunged into total war meant that Japan needed to exploit Asia. As total war theorists had predicted in the 1920s, Japan required regional autarky for its national survival. Without exploiting the vast resources of its colonial partners, Japan would be unable either to fight a global war or to bring the new order into existence. Even before World War II, Japan was highly dependent on trade with its colonies in Asia – the total value of Japanese exports to its colonies or occupied territories surpassed that of British or French exports to their colonies in absolute terms. By the time total war in China began, Japan was more reliant on its colonies for economic growth than any other imperialist power in Asia.[46] Japan thus looked to pull other resource-rich areas of Southeast Asia (the Netherlands Indies and French Indochina, among others) into a semicolonial relationship to offset Japan's resource needs. This dependence on its colonies only intensified by July 1941, when the United States froze Japanese assets and embargoed all trade with Japan.

As pressure to exploit Asia strengthened, policymakers saw the need to institutionalize exploitation into the political economy of their new Asian empire. This desire also owed to longer-term trends. In the years after the Great Depression, intellectuals and policymakers saw liberal capitalism as nearing collapse. Western capitalist countries had abandoned free trade for protectionism and managed currencies. This ushered in a deep depression that battered much of the world. Japan, which relied heavily on foreign trade to offset its limited resource base, keenly felt the shock of this abandonment of free trade. Faced with the global crisis, Japan turned to industrial policy, bloc economics, and regional autarky. By the early 1940s, policymakers and

---

[45] *Tokyo Asahi shinbun* 1941, 1.   [46] Hori 2009.

intellectuals alike viewed a regional bloc economy under Japanese leadership as necessary for economic growth and hoped to build this with the Greater East Asia Co-Prosperity Sphere. In this sense, trends in total war thought reaching back to World War I shaped later ideas of how to build a new political economy of empire in Asia.

Intellectuals envisioned that the Co-Prosperity Sphere would produce self-sufficiency through a regional hierarchy of production. Japan would account for the highest skill and most capital-intensive production. Lesser-developed nations or areas, on the other hand, would focus on a descending range of economic activities, from lower-skill, labor-intensive production to natural resource extraction. Asia would thus exist as an appendage of the broader Japanese economy, to be exploited for the region's benefit. In this sense, Asia's economic potential was imagined in the context of Japan's national survival – and Japanese intellectuals called for an economy of exploitative development to ensure that Japan survived the war with its empire and regional leadership intact. It was only from late 1943, as the war situation noticeably worsened, that policymakers toned down their dreams of regional autarky.

Third, the convergence of total empire and total war led policymakers to envision expansion into Southeast Asia through a hierarchy of political arrangements. On the one hand, the Greater East Asia Co-Prosperity Sphere witnessed the dramatic rise of a "new imperialism" that supported the creation of nominally independent satellite regimes like Manchukuo, the Chinese Nanjing Regime, Burma, and the Philippines. The rhetorical focus on Asian liberation as well as the establishment of these "independent" regimes have led some scholars to speak of the Co-Prosperity Sphere as "imperialism without colonies."[47]

Yet the old imperialism of direct colonial rule never died out. Korea and Taiwan received no gestures toward independence – they were to be incorporated into Japan proper. By 1945 this imperialism became more inclusive, with Japan planning to offer a greater stake to Koreans and Taiwanese in the politics of Japan proper.[48] Nominal independence was never a possibility for Japan's two most important and long-standing colonies. Moreover, Malaya, Singapore, French Indochina, the Netherlands Indies, and other outer territories were to remain under Japan's direct control. This was so widely understood that on the festivities in Singapore surrounding the emperor's birthday in April 1942, General Yamashita Tomoyuki, often referred to as the Tiger of Malaya, stated that the peoples of Malaya and Sumatra had become "subjects of the Japanese Empire."[49] Japan's new, "anti-imperial" imperialism only applied to select

---

[47] Duus 1996.
[48] This was part of what Takashi Fujitani calls a more inclusionary and culturalist regime of "polite racism," which replaced the "vulgar racism" of earlier years. See Fujitani 2013.
[49] Quoted in Arima 2002, 285.

regimes – so the Co-Prosperity Sphere is better understood as being *both* colonial and anti-colonial at the same time.

This division of the Co-Prosperity Sphere into colonial regimes and nominally independent states continued throughout the war. Japan thus championed a new imperialism that harnessed the logic and sentiment of anti-colonial nationalism, but it never abandoned the old imperialism outright. In this sense, Japanese policymakers perhaps unconsciously mimicked aspects of the British imperial mandate system that emerged after World War I.

Japan sought to meet its strategic objectives and build the new order in Greater East Asia with as little resistance as possible. One way it did so was through ideology: by stressing its effort to build an "Asia for the Asians" and its "liberation of Asia" from repressive European colonial regimes. Yet Japan still suffered from a legitimacy deficit – it struggled to forge an ideology that could bolster its international leadership. Political intellectuals constantly lamented that Japan's "crude" and "unskillful" ideology had little to offer those who were not already believers, and even less to offer colonial subjects. As Tokyo Imperial University Professor Kamikawa Hikomatsu complained in a Naval Intelligence Division meeting in September 1942, Japan's most basic concepts from the *kokutai* (the national polity) to the Kingly Way (*ōdō*), the Way of the Gods (*kannagara no michi*), and *hakkō ichiu* (universal brotherhood, or the "eight corners of the world under one roof") were baffling to foreigners and did little to counter the appeal of liberal-internationalism and "Anglo-American thought."[50] More strikingly, one soldier sent to the Philippines complained about how grueling it was to explain *hakkō ichiu* in English, and how little Filipinos cared about the concept.[51]

This ideological struggle became so pronounced that by 1943, Japan turned back to liberal internationalist values to rally Asia behind Japan's war aims and "to help Japan escape its painful fight for Asia with empire intact."[52] Tokyo held a Greater East Asia Conference in November 1943, and produced a liberal Greater East Asia Joint Declaration, a "Pacific Charter" drafted in response to the Atlantic Charter. Adopted formally on November 7, 1943, the charter called for a new Asian spirit of independence, autonomy, equality, prosperity, and cooperation, thus enshrining Wilsonian (liberal internationalist) values into Japan's war aims. It was part of an unsuccessful ideological and propaganda blitz designed to rally Asia behind Japan's war and to convince the Allied

---

[50] "Gaikō kondankai (Taiheiyō kenshō seitei ni tsuite)" [Concerning the Establishment of a Pacific Charter], September 26, 1942, in Ōkubo Tatsumasa et al., eds., *Kaigunshō shiryō* [Navy Ministry Documents] document 1812: *Shōwa shakai keizai shiryō shūsei* [Shōwa Socioeconomic Document Collection] Vol. 17 (Tokyo: Daitō Bunka Daigaku Tōyō Kenkyūjo, 1985), 132–133.
[51] Shinobu 1988, 194.   [52] Yellen 2019b, 1310.

powers to make peace. In the process, Japan began to share the very same internationalist language employed by its enemies.[53]

The problem of ideology was compounded by a bigger problem: balancing the needs of building legitimacy for the new order and fighting its total war. In the end, the war took precedence. This led Japanese military administrations across Asia to repression, resource extraction, and social control. Military administrations used Japanese businesses to develop and mobilize strategic resources and imposed Japanese discipline and customs on local peoples. Moreover, they maintained social order through widespread use of the military police, which often resorted to brutality and extreme punishments for mild offenses. This has led scholars to view Japanese occupation regimes as "Japanese military dictatorships" and symbolic of Japan's wartime imperialism.[54]

Despite its problems with ideology and repression, Japan still secured transnational elites in the service of its wartime empire. Wherever they went, Japan courted what I have called "patriotic collaborators," nationalist elites who helped Japan administer its new colonial empire, but who did so while using their new overlords for anti-colonial ends. Burmese nationalists accompanied the Japanese military in the invasion of Burma and constructed a pro-Japanese wartime regime; Philippine nationalist leaders in Manila went over en masse to serve as a caretaker regime; and Chinese Nanjing Regime head of state Wang Jingwei sought to use Japan to strengthen his government and to end the unequal treaties imposed on China. Even Indonesian nationalists like Sukarno saw the war and Japanese occupation as offering unique opportunity to gain future independence. Granted, a complex array of motives influenced these leaders, from political opportunism to self-interest, a desire to preserve the social order and perhaps a degree of compulsion. But these leaders – many of whom were caught between two empires – also saw short-term cooperation as a tactical move, done for the sake of achieving or preserving longer-term political freedom.[55]

Many of these patriotic collaborators chafed at Japanese oppression and brutality but saw the Co-Prosperity Sphere nonetheless as offering opportunity. They worked toward nationalist ends, engaging in state-building projects and creating governmental institutions their countries had lacked under colonial rule. They helped make the Co-Prosperity Sphere of use in the colonial present, while operating in a middle ground between collaboration and resistance.[56] This willingness to use the Co-Prosperity Sphere to engage in state-building

---

[53] See also Hatano 1995; Hatano 1996, 161–213, 275–285; and Iriye 1981, 112–121.
[54] See Huff 2020; Roshwald 2023; and Kisaka 1992.
[55] For a useful synthetic work on modes of collaboration, see Dominguez 1979.
[56] For more detailed readings, see Nakano 2019; Kobayashi 2007; Mark 2018; Yellen 2019a, Chapter 4, Chapter 6; Tanigawa 1987; and Nemoto 2010.

efforts did not imply a strong allegiance to Japan, particularly owing to the realities of Japanese rule. Strikingly, by 1945, the patriotic collaborators in Burma – the same ones who accompanied the Japanese invasion in 1942 – revolted against Japan, using the Burmese National Army that Japan built to help British forces recapture the "independent" Burma from Japan. This, more than anything else, shows how nationalist collaborators in the colonial capitals often used the Co-Prosperity Sphere for anti-colonial ends.

9.4   Conclusion

The international history of Japan between the two world wars offers a striking case of a rising power's shift from accommodation to a rejection of the international order, or a shift from being a status quo to a revisionist power. Japan in the 1920s embraced the new international environment, abandoning the "diplomacy of imperialism" and aligning with the new norms of disarmament, peace, free trade, and conference diplomacy. Japanese domestic politics, in turn, reflected and were influenced by this shift – embracing the era of peace, democracy, and free trade. But continuing commitment at home to the liberal order remained dependent on stability and economic gain. By the late 1920s, however (from 1927 in particular), the global commitment to international liberalism had begun to fade, initiating what Robert Boyce refers to as the "great interwar crisis."[57] From this point on, the speed of collapse was striking.

The quick collapse was hastened in part by changes in strategic thought reaching back to World War I. The rise of total war though led military strategists to view self-sufficiency as the prerequisite to success in modern warfare. This understanding of the importance of self-sufficiency did not influence national policy until the Washington System began to break down. But once the old order began to collapse, desires for autarky served as the backdrop behind a series of natural security solutions that gravitated toward establishing a new order in the region. The outbreak of total war – first in China and later in the Asia-Pacific – further compelled Japan to forge Asia into a self-sufficient political-economic order that became known as the Greater East Asia Co-Prosperity Sphere.

At its height, the Greater East Asia Co-Prosperity Sphere represented a dream to reorder the world. In Asia, it would have replaced Western colonial empires with a new, hierarchical community of nations. But it was little more than a failed dream – a battle cry for centrality in world affairs and preeminence in Asia. It epitomized efforts to convey to Asia and the world the benefits of Japanese regional domination. Like Hitler's empire in Europe, however, the Japanese new order never provided a convincing answer to

---

[57] Boyce 2009.

a basic question: Why should the region accept Japanese leadership except under duress? This failure to answer that basic question led Japan to end up producing little more than ideas of "co-prosperity" derided in the Philippines as "prosperity-*ko*," or "me-first prosperity."[58] More pointedly, by late 1943 it was clear Japan simply lacked the wherewithal to match its imperial dreams. By the time of Japan's surrender on August 15, 1945, the Co-Prosperity Sphere was but a distant dream.

The challenges of empire and diplomacy in the wake of World War I led Japan on the road to expansion and global war. The total war of World War II, in turn, shaped the entirety of Japan's new order. In the process, Japan savaged much of Asia, fighting a war that reshaped the international history of the region and initiated the first wave of Asian decolonization. The burgeoning Cold War turned areas of decolonization into theaters of conflict between liberal democratic and communist power blocs. It was these postwar wars of decolonization, internal conflicts, and the gradual stabilization of independence that shaped the region in the ensuing decades. Japan's dreams of creating a new international order were thus relegated to history and memory. The postwar order – taken up by subsequent chapters in this book – would be affected by different processes and guided by different dreams.

---

[58] Friend 1965, 269.

Part IV

The High Cold War in Asia

10 The Division of Korea

David Fields

On the night of August 10–11, 1945, Colonels Dean Rusk and Charles Bonesteel "working in haste and under great pressure" poured over a *National Geographic* map of Korea. They were looking for a natural boundary to propose to the Soviet Union as a dividing line below which they would accept the surrender of Japanese forces on the peninsula. Finding no natural boundary, they suggested the 38th parallel, which was – within a week – worked into MacArthur's SCAP General Order No. 1 outlining which military forces would accept the Japanese surrender where. As Rusk told it years later, the "army did not want to go onto the mainland [of Asia] at all" but the State Department wanted the proposed line as far north as possible. The 38th parallel was a compromise that allowed the United States "a sort of foothold on the Korean Peninsula for *symbolic* purposes."[1]

What symbolic purpose did Korea have in 1945? It would fall to subsequent generations of historians, political scientists, journalists, and opinion makers to explain (or not explain) this historic outcome. Their explanations were invariably shaped by their own context, which for the majority was the Cold War between the United States and the Soviet Union and the two ideologies associated with them: democratic-capitalism and communism. The problem with these subsequent accounts is that too often Cold War ideological tensions between the United States and the Soviet Union become the cause of the division of Korea instead of the division of Korea itself being a cause of the Cold War.

A recent online publication by the History Channel – which surely provides more people with their historical knowledge than any academic publication – entitled "Why Are North and South Korea Divided" is a case in point. In this short piece, which features an interview with historian of Korea Michel Robinson, the division of Korea at the 38th parallel is taken for granted, while the Cold War is offered as the ultimate reason for this division becoming permanent.[2] In the rare cases that the division of Korea is addressed directly, it is often attributed to the Cold War.[3]

---

[1] Rusk 1990, 124.   [2] Pruit 2018.   [3] Cumings 2010, 103–104.

In a sense this confusion is understandable since thwarting a Soviet occupation of the entire Korean peninsula was an American objective. But American policymakers did not conceive of this policy as an effort to contain communism, or even the Soviet Union, per se. In fact, the US military had little interest in making commitments to the Asian mainland in Korea. Rather the US stance was a part of a policy to ensure that Korea emerged from Japanese colonization as a truly independent state. Those more sympathetic with Korea hoped that an American troop presence on the peninsula would give them some influence in ensuring that Korea's future developed along these lines. Not only did the 1943 Cairo Declaration obligate the United States to support Korea's independence, but the Truman administration was also under significant domestic political pressure to do so, as we shall see.

But why did American leaders care about Korea in the first place? Why did average American citizens care enough about Korea to pressure their representatives to act? This chapter will answer these questions, and by doing so, hopefully decenter Cold War competition from our understanding of the division of Korea. It will accomplish this by looking at US–Korean relations in a much broader historical context, one that stretches back to the late nineteenth century, through debates over the Versailles Treaty and the Washington Naval Conference in the 1920s, the alleged appeasement of Japan in the 1930s, the shock of Pearl Harbor, and the tenuous alliances of World War II. In doing so it will show that the future of Korea had become a pressing domestic political issue in the United States by 1945. It was a niche issue to be sure, but one advanced by a dedicated group of activists, which included both Koreans and Americans, was largely Christian of the missionary bent, and was led by Korean nationalist and future president Syngman Rhee. Their cause was aided considerably by allies in the US Congress and the fact they were pushing American foreign policy in the general direction policymakers already wanted it to go. Once the war broke out, Korean claims about the costs of appeasing Japan – which Rhee and others had made since the 1920s – gained much wider salience. It is only in this context that the division of Korea and subsequent events can be properly understood on their own terms, and not merely as the prelude to, or more erroneously, the results of the Cold War.

10.1   Unequal Expectations: US–Korean Relations 1882–1919

Any accurate understanding of the division of Korea, and US–Korean relations as a whole, must begin in the nineteenth century with the Treaty of Peace, Amity, Commerce, and Navigation between the United States and the Kingdom of Joseon in 1882. This treaty (hereafter the 1882 Treaty) for the first time established formal diplomatic relations between the United States and the kingdom. Like all treaties signed between the United States and East Asian nations at the time, this was an "unequal treaty" – perhaps the most unequal treaty the United States ever signed. But what made the treaty so unequal was not the extraterritoriality provisions of Article IV but the unequal expectations and motivations for the treaty by the two parties. For Joseon, the 1882 Treaty was an attempt to address existential threats to their kingdom's independence. For the Americans, the stakes were low, so low that had it not been for the personal ambitions of Admiral William Shufeldt to "open" Korea the way Admiral Perry had opened Japan, there might have been no treaty at all.[4]

These wildly different expectations for the 1882 Treaty led to wildly different interpretations, especially regarding Article I of the treaty, which stated: "If other powers deal unjustly or oppressively with either Government, the other will exert their *good offices* on being informed of the case to bring about an amicable arrangement, thus showing their friendly feelings." The term "good offices" as used in the treaty was a technical diplomatic term that described a sort of mediation well understood among Western diplomats. However, for reasons of mistranslation or wishful thinking or both, at least some in the court of Joseon understood this article to obligate the United States to assist the kingdom should its security be threatened.[5]

Just such a threat materialized in 1904 when the Japanese occupied Joseon during the Russo-Japanese War and then failed to leave once the war ended. In desperation, Emperor Gojong dispatched several secret envoys asking for American intervention based on the 1882 Treaty. One of these was a twenty-nine-year-old Syngman Rhee, an English-speaking protege of American missionaries, who had just been released from prison after serving a seven-year sentence for his championing of political reforms in the 1890s. President Theodore Roosevelt rejected all these entreaties on the grounds that none of these envoys were properly credentialed diplomats and that such requests should come via the Korean embassy in Washington, DC, which he knew was impossible since Japan had already taken control of the Korean Foreign Ministry.

Even had these requests come through the proper channels it would have made little difference. For "good offices" mediation to be successful, both parties had to agree to mediation and there was no desire on the part of Japan to do so. Also, while the snub of Gojong's envoys was justified on technical procedural grounds, there is no doubt Roosevelt viewed the Japanese colonization of Korea favorably and felt that it would remove Korea from being an object of contention between Japan, China, and Russia. Roosevelt would later justify his actions, not on technical grounds, but on common sense, writing in

---

[4] Paullin 1910, 470–499.   [5] Hulbert 1906, 223.

1912 that it was "out of the question" to suppose that any nation should do for the Koreans what they were "utterly unable to do for themselves."[6]

These machinations garnered little attention in the United States at the time. Few Americans had any interest in East Asia or Korea. Those who did, generally agreed with Roosevelt's assessment. This apathy might have continued indefinitely had it not been for the Great Pyongyang Revival of 1907, which resulted in the exponential growth of Christianity in Korea. For a generation of American Christians bent on Christianizing the world in a single generation, this revival seemed to hold out the possibility of Korea becoming the first Christian nation in the most populous region of the globe. Almost overnight, Korea went from being a minor mission field to the focus of much American attention and hopes.[7]

Syngman Rhee was a beneficiary of this surge of interest in Korea. Following his failed diplomatic mission he remained in the United States to get an education. As one of the very few English-speaking Korean Christians in the United States, Rhee became the de facto spokesperson for Korean Christianity following the Pyongyang revival, speaking in hundreds of American churches, social clubs, and universities.[8] While Rhee's activities were religious in nature and superficially apolitical, they were animated by a belief that Korean Christianity and Japanese colonialism were incompatible. Rhee believed that sooner or later they would come into conflict, and he wanted to ensure American sympathy toward Korea when that happened.

10.2 Korea in the 1920s: Versailles and the Washington Naval Conference

On March 1, 1919, just such a clash occurred. Korean nationalists staged nationwide nonviolent protests calling for Korea's independence from Japan. Their "declaration of independence" borrowed heavily on the idealism of what Erez Manela has called the "Wilsonian Moment." The aim of the protestors was to provoke a Japanese backlash that President Woodrow Wilson and the other leaders of the Great Powers meeting at Versailles to create the League of Nations could not ignore. Japanese colonial officials obliged by killing, torturing, and imprisoning thousands of Koreans. They did their best to suppress the news of the "March First Movement," but accounts soon leaked out and received wide media coverage in the United States.

To consolidate the March First Movement and take advantage of the sympathetic coverage it received, Korean activists formed the Korean Provisional Government (KPG) in April 1919. To head this government they selected Rhee. His selection was a direct result of the notoriety he had received in the United

---

[6] Roosevelt 1914. [7] Boone 1910, 136; Gale 1909, 229. [8] Fields 2019, 40–46.

States for his work promoting Korean Christianity. Rhee also had a personal connection with President Wilson – he had been a frequent guest at Wilson's home when Rhee was studying at Princeton and Wilson was president of the university. While Rhee was a logical choice to head the KPG, the hope that his connection with Wilson could further the Korean cause received a severe blow when the State Department refused to grant him a passport to travel to Versailles and instead advised him to seek one from the country "to which you owe allegiance," – Japan.[9]

Rhee was discouraged but not dissuaded by the State Department's response. Meeting with Wilson would have been the most direct way of placing the cause of Korean independence before the world, but it was not the only way as Rhee well knew. American Christians were still keenly interested in Korea, and while the March 1 movement was broader than a Christian movement, the accounts of Christian missionaries often left the impression that the Japanese were targeting Christians. The burning of the "Christian village" of Jeam-ri and photos purportedly showing Korean Christians nailed to crosses fueled outrage among American Christians that Rhee believed just needed to be organized and directed.[10]

And organize he did. Using his existing networks of Americans already interested in Korea, and in conjunction with other Korean expatriate nationalists such as Philip Jaisohn and Henry Chung, Rhee created the League of Friends of Korea, a grassroots organization of American Christians that numbered – so he claimed – 25,000 by 1922 in fourteen branches across the United States. Together with Jaisohn and Chung he also established the Korea Information Bureau in Philadelphia, which published the English language monthly the *Korea Review*, and the Korean Commission in Washington, DC, which functioned as the unofficial embassy of the KPG in the United States.

The hopes Korean nationalists had placed in Wilson and his idealism were completely shattered when the text of the Versailles Treaty was published. Not only had Wilson failed to champion oppressed nationalities, he had also made several compromises to placate Japan, including the transfer of German concessions on the Shantung Peninsula in China to Japanese control. Such compromises not only disappointed Koreans but also divided the US Senate on the question of the treaty's ratification. Ever the savvy lobbyist, Rhee sought to use the contentious fight over the Versailles Treaty in the US Senate to further the cause of Korean independence.

---

[9] Fields 2019, 200n23.
[10] See "The Korean Independence Movement" (1919), www.columbia.edu/cu/lweb/digital/collections/cul/texts/ldpd_7705012_000/; Korea Information Bureau 1919; See also the back cover of *Korea Review*, vol. 1, no. 4. Philadelphia, Pa: Bureau of Information for the Republic of Korea, 1919.

One group of senators would become indispensable to the Korean cause. Known as the "irreconcilables," this faction of fourteen senators was opposed to the Versailles Treaty under any circumstances. Eager to refute the charge of "isolationism" that their opposition invited, the irreconcilables sought out international injustices within the Versailles Treaty that they could use to attack it, while also deflecting isolationist criticism. The transfer of the Shantung Peninsula was one such issue. The brutal Japanese suppression of Korea was another. Rhee worked in tandem with the irreconcilables, providing them not only with evidence of Japanese repression of Korean Christianity but also with a firsthand account of what he now claimed was Theodore Roosevelt's violation of the 1882 Korean American Treaty. This was a serious charge at a time when Germany's regarding treaties as "mere scraps of paper" had been used to justify the US entry into World War I.

Regardless of whether the irreconcilables' championing of the Korean cause (and the Shantung) was genuine, it proved a difficult issue for the pro-treaty senators to address. In addition to arguing that the United States was treaty-bound to aid Korea, the irreconcilables frequently read missionary reports of Japanese brutality in Korea into the *Congressional Record* and argued that the future of Christianity in East Asia was at stake. When irreconcilable Senator Charles S. Thomas proposed an amendment to the Versailles Treaty calling for the self-determination of Korea and its admittance into the League of Nations, it failed by just seven votes. Many senators who voted against it felt compelled to explain that they supported Korea's right to self-determination, and of course the spread of Christianity, and only voted against the reservation because they believed it was a cynical ploy by the irreconcilables to kill the Versailles Treaty. Even had it passed, Thomas' resolution would have been inconsequential since the Senate ultimately failed to ratify the Versailles Treaty in March 1920, but the experience taught Rhee and other Korean activists that American leaders at the highest level could be induced to support Korean independence, at least symbolically, under the right circumstances.

The Washington Naval Conference of 1921–22 gave Rhee another opportunity to present Korea's case to the American public. The conference occurred just as Rhee's lobbying apparatus was hitting its stride: the League of Friends of Korea was growing, Korea-themed speakers were touring the heartland on the Chautauqua Circuit – think early-twentieth-century TED talks – and the Korean Commission had some money to spend, painstakingly raised from the Korean diaspora in the United States and China. From a rented mansion just a few blocks from the White House, the Korean Commission hosted numerous visitors in town for the conference, including luminaries such as H. G. Wells and notable journalists such as Louis Seibold. The commission retained recently retired American political leaders such as former Secretary of

State Robert Lansing and Senator Charles S. Thomas to act as advisers.[11] Perhaps under the influence of these advisers, the Koreans' appeal to the Washington Naval Conference moved beyond concerns over the future of Korean Christianity and the alleged violation of the 1882 Korean American Treaty – though these remained important issues – to include geopolitical arguments such as Korea's existence as an "independent buffer state" being necessary to the peace of Asia.[12] However, despite their best efforts, no delegation to the conference publicly raised the issue of Korean independence although the American delegation assured Rhee they had raised the issue privately with the Japanese delegation.

The failure of Korean activists to change American policy toward Korea during this period masked a real transformation that was taking place. American interest in Korea, which began with the 1907 Pyongyang Revival, was growing. Thanks to a contract with the Luce Clippings Bureau, the Korean Commission was able to report that between March 1919 and August 1920 more than 8,000 newspaper articles were printed on Korea.[13] Philip Jaisohn would later estimate that Korean speakers on the Chautauqua circuit reached an audience of 200,000 in 1920 alone.[14] During its two years in print, The *Korea Review* published examples of local churches or civic organizations passing resolutions – and often forwarding them to congress – calling for the United States to support Korea's liberation from Japan. Perhaps journalist Cyril Player writing in the *Detroit News* best summarized the transformation taking place in the United States regarding Korea when he wrote: "Everyone knows Korea has a case. The American people are by no means unsympathetic toward the Koreans; if there is apathy, it is the apathy of regret, tinged with weariness and impregnated by a miserable feeling of impotence to put matters right."[15]

This sympathy did not change overall American policy toward Korea, but the sentiments player described in 1922 were a world away from those expressed by Theodore Roosevelt in 1912 – that it was unthinkable to do for the Koreans what they were unable to do for themselves. American sympathy had shifted, and with it subtle shifts in policy also became possible. When Rhee applied to the State Department for travel documents in 1932 to present Korea's case for independence at the League of Nations in Geneva, Switzerland, he was not denied as he had been in 1919. He was issued special travel documents signed by Secretary of State Henry Stimson, despite not being a US citizen.

---

[11] Fields 2019, 100.   [12] *New York Times* 1922.
[13] "Editorials, News Items, and Special Articles" in the "Korean Commission" folder, Syngman Rhee Institute (SRI), Yonsei University, Seoul, Republic of Korea.
[14] See "Philadelphia Conference 1919 Addresses and Resolution [Propaganda Report]" in the "First Korean Congress in Philadelphia Conference (1919)" folder, SRI. Although this number seems large, it is estimated that forty million Americans attended Chautauqua lectures in 1924, see Tapia 1997, 32.
[15] Player September 4, 1921.

Surely, the State Department's change of attitude toward Rhee was attributable to many factors, including rising anti-Japanese sentiment following Japan's 1931 invasion of Manchuria. However, it is largely thanks to the work of Rhee and other independence activists that Americans even understood the difference between Koreans and Japanese.

10.3   "A Forgotten Ally": US–Korean Relations during World War II

American policy toward Korea shifted fundamentally during World War II for reasons that, at least initially, had nothing to do with communism or the Soviet Union and everything to do with Japan. The American acquiescence of Japan's colonization and subsequent annexation of Korea in 1910 was predicated on maintaining the stability of northeast Asia and good relations with Japan. Although American sentiments toward Japan had shifted during the 1930s, American policymakers considered the situation of Korea a fait accompli and showed no appetite to revisit it. The attack on Pearl Harbor changed everything. With the United States and Japan at war, the future of Korea suddenly became a live issue.

Korea's cause was also aided by Syngman Rhee's impeccable timing. As US–Japanese relations deteriorated in the late 1930s and early 1940s, Rhee redoubled his efforts to bring the oppression of Korea before the American people in the guise of a warning about Japan. His book *Japan Inside Out*, published in summer 1941, was really as much about the United States and Korea as it was about Japan. It told a story of the decline of American influence and power in East Asia that hinged on the American abandonment of Korea in 1905 in the vain hope it would satiate Japanese expansionism. Rhee argued this appeasement not only failed but also had emboldened Japan to move into Manchuria and China, and now the American people faced the prospect of a war with a much stronger Japan than they would have encountered in 1905 or 1919. Rhee of course mentioned that Koreans had been sounding the alarm against Japan since 1905 but that "our warnings were but voices in the wilderness."[16] *Japan Inside Out* was in its second printing by December 1941.

When Japan attacked Pearl Harbor on December 7, 1941, Rhee was transformed overnight from a "voice in the wilderness" into something of a prophet. For the remainder of the war, he would be a genuine "B-list" celebrity, profiled in *Newsweek* magazine, appearing on radio programs, speaking at universities and conferences, and even, ironically, being invited to the red carpet premiere of the 1944 Oscar-winning film *Wilson* in New York. Eleanor Roosevelt wrote about Korea three times during the war in her nationally syndicated "My Day" column. She referenced the 1882 Korean American treaty, her hopes for Korea,

[16] Rhee 1941, 9.

and, after meeting Rhee personally at the White House, reported on the "beautiful spirit that shines in his face."[17]

With Rhee's transformation the KPG also transformed from a symbolic representation of the spirit of Korean independence into a potential American ally in the war against Japan. Taking full advantage of this new state of affairs Rhee privately offered the services of the KPG and loyal Koreans to any American congressman, military, or intelligence official who would receive him while publicly campaigning for official recognition of the KPG as an ally in the war. Such a move, he argued, would bring millions of Korean allies into the war against Japan.

Rhee's public and private lobbying divided American officials. He generally received a warm welcome from congressmen who were happy to refer him to bureaucrats in the State and War departments and the Office of Strategic Services (OSS). The OSS in particular recognized the potential value of Rhee and the KPG and involved him in at least two schemes to train expatriate Koreans for covert service during the war – neither of which saw action. They also used Rhee to draft and record propaganda broadcasts into Korea during the war.

The State Department was much more wary of Rhee and the KPG. After being importuned by Rhee and two congressmen during the weeks after Pearl Harbor, the Far Eastern (FE) branch of the State Department wrote its first memo on the KPG in which they recommended that recognition be delayed until the subject could be studied further and that the United States should certainly not take any unilateral action on Korea without coordination with "China, Russia, and Britain."[18] This first memo identified what would be the major obstacle regarding recognition of the KPG – coordination with allies. Further FE investigations into the nature of the KPG – now based in China's wartime capital Chungking – and the Korean independence movement as a whole revealed a perilous landscape in which both Nationalist China and the Soviet Union were supporting different factions of Korean fighters with an eye for influence of the Korean peninsula in the postwar period. American recognition of the KPG might bring these tensions to the fore and spark a struggle for influence in Korea before the war against Japan was even won.

Rhee's retort to this was that the apparent Korean disunity was merely a function of their being forced to scrounge for aid from all parties, which often came with strings attached. If the United States recognized the KPG and extended Lend Lease Aid to this government as an ally, then all expatriate Koreans would flock to its banner and out from under the thumbs of Chiang and Stalin. Rhee may well have been right about this, but it was not a gamble the State Department or the Roosevelt administration was willing to take,

---

[17] Fields 2019, 163–164.   [18] Division of Far Eastern Affairs 1941, 895.01/60–11/26.

especially since they knew Rhee's talk of millions of new allies was a gross exaggeration. It would be foolish to risk the cooperation of Nationalist China and the Soviet Union in the war against Japan for a few thousand Korean fighters or for the hope that the KPG might organize a quixotic uprising against Japan on the Korean peninsula.

As we have already seen, this was hardly the first time American officials had disappointed Rhee and, as in previous cases, he did not take their decisions as final, but rather went directly to the American people. Enabled by his reinvigorated celebrity he used his platform to criticize the State Department for failing to recognize the KPG and accept millions of Korean allies against Japan. While his argument about millions of new Korean allies was spurious, it was effective, especially when it was amplified by media coverage and parroted by several US congressmen.[19] To Americans facing the real prospect of losing children in the war against Japan, the argument that Korean blood might be substituted for American blood was an option worth exploring.

Emblematic of Rhee's tactics was the Korea Liberty Conference held in March 1942 at the Lafayette Hotel in Washington, DC, just a block from the White House and the State Department. Held over two days, featuring fifteen speakers, and broadcast live on WINX-AM radio, the conference featured longtime Korean independence activists and prominent Americans (including two congressmen and a former Ambassador), all making the argument that the United States was obligated to recognize the KPG based on the 1882 Korean-American Treaty and that doing so would add millions of Korean allies to the war against Japan. Many of the speakers berated the State Department for continuing a failed policy of appeasement toward Japan, despite the fact Japan and the United States were now at war.[20] One American State Department official who attended the conference called it an impressive "publicity stunt" while complaining that the participants seemed ignorant of the complexities involved in recognizing the KPG and seemed determined to portray the issues as solely "an American problem."[21] Of course, that was their intent.

By 1943 the State Department was perturbed by Rhee's antics – the worst was yet to come – but also facing the necessity of explaining its policy on Korean independence to its critics. Recognizing the KPG was out of the question, but official silence on the issue invited further attack by Rhee and a growing body of Americans concerned about Korea. Slowly over 1943 a policy would take shape to be proclaimed in the Cairo Declaration. In this declaration, the United States – and the other allies – pledged that "in due course" after the defeat of Japan, Korea would become free and independent.

---

[19] Former Senator William F. King, Senator Happy Chandler, Rep John M. Coffee (D-WA) did so at the Korean Liberty Conference. See also Buck 1944.
[20] United Korean Committee in America 1942.
[21] William Langdon Memo 1942, 895.01/84, United States Department of State 1993, 440-445.

This short and simple statement made perfect sense from the American perspective; it put the United States on the record as pledging to restore Korea's independence, but put off the hard decisions that might hamper allied unity until later.

Perhaps the most important aspect of the Cairo Declaration for this chapter is that while the motivations behind this declaration were complex and multifaceted, containment of communism or the Soviet Union were not among them. The FDR administration was both reacting to the popular pressure being brought to make a statement on Korean independence and striving to ensure that Korea did not become a divisive issue among the allies during the war. Soviet actions in Eastern Europe, especially Poland, were still months away. Although Rhee would do as much as anyone to inject anxieties over the Soviet Union into the debate about American policy toward Korea, this was only a very minor part of his discourse up to this date.

In fact, it appears that American concerns over Korea in 1943 were primarily the result of suspicions toward Chiang's postwar policies rather than Stalin's. Chiang, taking the position of his mentor Sun Yat-sen, considered Korea a "lost territory" and there is ample evidence that Chiang hoped to use the KPG to reassert Chinese influence in Korea after the defeat of Japan.[22] After meeting with Chiang, President Roosevelt confidentially informed the British delegation to the Cairo Conference "there was no doubt" that Chiang desired to reoccupy Korea.[23] Roosevelt is widely believed to have sparred with Chiang in Cairo over the future of Korea declaring: "You may have Manchuria. You may have the Pescadores and you may have Formosa, but you may not have Korea, which is to be detached from Japan and is to be given its independence after a period of international supervision."[24] Although American policymakers continued to discuss the Korean issue, the Cairo Declaration would govern their Korea policy for the remainder of the war: Korea would be made independent after the war via a to-be-determined international process. It was not to be part of a new sphere of influence in Northeast Asia, regardless of whether that sphere was Chinese or Soviet.

Far from placating the Koreans and their supporters, the Cairo Declaration only fed their suspicion. A planned celebration of the Cairo Declaration by KPG officials in Chungking was called off after the official text was released. The phrase "in due course" was ambiguous, except for the fact that it ruled out immediate independence, which was the only acceptable outcome for the KPG and Rhee.[25] While it left the Koreans dissatisfied, the Cairo Declaration actually represented the transformation of US policy they had long sought. As the *New York Times* noted in its coverage of the Cairo Declaration, the

---

[22] Liu 1996, 88–90; Lin 2016, 15.   [23] US Office of the Historian 1961, Doc. 263.
[24] Liu 1996, 142.   [25] US Office of the Historian 1963, Doc. 975.

invasion of Korea in 1905 created "hardly a ripple of interest" in the United States and no one at the time "would have dreamed" the United States would ever use force to "undo that act" as it was now committed to do. A similar story syndicated by the Overseas News Agency took Americans through the history of US–Korean relations starting with the 1882 Korean-American Treaty, covering Theodore Roosevelt's approval of Japan's colonization, and noting the lack of an American response to the KPG going back to 1919. It concluded that the Cairo Declaration was proof that "we are now officially ashamed of our former attitude."[26]

While Rhee continued to spar with the State Department over the recognition of the KPG, he had more successes with other government agencies. In addition to his work with the OSS, he consulted with the US postal service on the design of the Korean stamp in the "Overrun Countries Series." Korea's inclusion in this series was remarkable since it was the only non-European nation to be included in the series and since it had been "overrun by Japan" in 1905, decades before the other countries in the series were overrun and before the Axis even existed. The fact that the Korean stamp was issued nearly a full year after what was announced as the "last stamp in the series" seems to indicate that political pressure was involved in its inclusion.[27]

These symbolic victories and sympathetic media coverage buoyed Rhee's spirits, but they were no substitute for the recognition of the KPG, which Rhee believed would do more than anything to establish a firm foundation for Korean independence in the postwar period. After failing to get a delegation from Korea seated at the San Francisco Conference in May 1945, Rhee took his most desperate measure to date by alleging publicly that the now late president Roosevelt made a secret deal with Joseph Stalin at the 1945 Yalta Conference trading Korea to the Soviet Union in return for a Soviet entry into the war against Japan. To this day there is no evidence of any such deal regarding Korea at Yalta, but Rhee made the accusation at a time when rumors of secret deals at Yalta with the Soviets – especially regarding Poland – were swirling and when FDR was no longer in a position to offer any explanation or defense.[28]

Rhee's accusation made front page news across the United States and further energized an already mobilized body of supporters.[29] Concerned Americans wrote letters to President Truman and their congressmen demanding Rhee's Yalta accusation be investigated and the United States take some concrete

---

[26] Hartman 1943, 6; *New York Times* 1943, 26.
[27] Lawrence 1998, 48–74. Perhaps inauspiciously, a flaw in the printing panes caused some of the stamps to bear the name "KORPA" instead of "KOREA." These flawed stamps have their own catalog entry and are significantly more valuable than their nonflawed counterparts.
[28] Crider 1945, 1; *New York Times* 1945a.
[29] Edwards 1945a; Edwards 1945b; Rhee 1945; *New York Times* 1945b.

action to ensure Korea's independence after the war.³⁰ In an attempt to quell the criticism, acting Secretary of State Joseph Grew issued a statement on June 8, 1945, explaining that while the US Government refused to recognize the KPG, this refusal in no way represented a lack of sympathy toward the Korean people or "their aspirations for freedom."³¹ As if to make amends, Grew's statement was followed the next day by an announcement that the State Department was opening a new scholarship program for Korean students in acknowledgment that an independent Korea would need "well-trained men in various fields."³²

If this was an attempt to placate those clamoring for action on Korea, it did not work. Public interest in Korea did not ebb and congressional interest in Korea only increased. In June and July 1945, one representative and two senators – all Republicans – gave impassioned speeches lambasting the Roosevelt and Truman administrations for failing to act on Korea. They accused these Democratic Presidents of creating a situation in East Asia where Korea was ready to fall like a "ripe plum" into the lap of the Soviet Union. Their speeches were not so much anti-communist as they were anti-appeasement, claiming that the executive leadership of the United States had still not learned the lessons of its failed policy of appeasement toward Japan. In his speech Senator Wayne Morse (R-OR) recounted US–Korean relations all the way back to the 1882 Korean-American Treaty, claiming this history placed a peculiar burden on the United States to aid Korea. These congressmen demanded that concrete action be taken by Truman to ensure that Korea emerged from the war a free and independent nation, which, after all, was American policy according to the Cairo Declaration.³³

These Republican congressional outbursts might have been easily dismissed as partisan sniping were it not for one fact: They were saying loudly in public what members of Truman's own administration were whispering in secret. In the closing months of the war, Under Secretary of State Grew, US Ambassador to the Soviet Union Averell Harriman, Secretary of War Stimson, and Ambassador Edwin Pauley, all urged Truman to take urgent action on Korea, either by working out an explicit trusteeship agreement with the Soviet Union or by preparing to occupy a portion of the Korean peninsula as soon as possible should the Japanese surrender.³⁴ Their urgency was linked to Soviet behavior in

---

[30] A handful of these letters were apparently forwarded to the State Department where they were placed in the department's Central Files decimal files where they have been preserved. For a few examples, see United States Department of State, 1995, 美國務省韓國關係文書 [Internal affairs of Korea, 1945–1949, Vol. 8. Seoul: Areum Press], 297–298; Alice M. Butts to Harry S. Truman, May 28, 1945, 895.01/5-2845 CS/D; Lottye B. McMeans to Harry S. Truman, June 4, 1945, 895.01/6-445 CS/D.
[31] Grew 1945, 1058–1059.
[32] "Scholarship Opportunities Open to Students from Korea" 1945, 1059.
[33] Langer 1945, 6580–6581; Morse 1945, 8159–8162; Shafer 1945, 6580–6581.
[34] Matray 1981, 145–168.

Eastern Europe – as Stimson warned Truman on July 16, "this is the Polish question translated to the Far East" but their motivation was not anti-communism or global competition. They were urging action to ensure that American commitments regarding Korea made at Cairo would be kept – commitments that were made in a context of political pressure on FDR to act, that predated concern over Soviet behavior in East Asia, and that were aimed more at Chiang's ambitions than Stalin's.

Scholars, such as James Matray, have long argued that Truman's policy toward Korea experienced a "remarkable transformation" in July and August 1945.[35] This shift was based on the hope that newly developed nuclear weapons might compel Japan to surrender prior to the Soviet entry into the Pacific War, which in turn might have allowed the United States to exclude the Soviets from the Korean peninsula. This is surely the case, but why was Korea so important to the Truman administration in the first place?

For too long, the answer to this question has been, in some shape or another, the Cold War: that ideological and global competition between the United States and the Soviet Union meant that since nuclear weapons allowed American policymakers to claim wider territory and preclude Soviet advances, they did so. While it is impossible to claim that such reasoning played no role at all in the division of Korea, the earlier commitment made at Cairo underlines why this explanation does not capture the entire context in which this decision was made. The American interest in and sympathy toward Korea, which had been cultivated by Rhee and other activists since 1907, was the key factor in shifting American policy toward Korea during the war and in the drafting of the Cairo Declaration. This declaration in turn provided a firm foundation on which Rhee and sympathetic Americans could build political pressure on Truman to act. That this political pressure to act was a key part of Truman's decision-making has been attested to by several veterans of his administration.[36] In Dean Rusk's words, the Truman administration sought a role in Korea for "symbolic purposes" not strategic ones.[37]

That political considerations trumped strategic ones is essential to understanding how American policy toward Korea played out between 1945 and 1950. It is here that the shortcomings of the Cold War paradigm when applied to the division of Korea truly become apparent.

10.4 The Shortcomings of the Cold War Paradigm

If the motivation behind the division of Korea was to ensure that the United States had a "toehold" on the Korean peninsula from which they could engage in ideological and political competition with the Soviet Union, this was never

---

[35] Matray 1981, 161.   [36] Fields 2019, 170–171.   [37] Rusk 1990, 124.

communicated to American occupation authorities. From his first days in Korea, Commanding General of US forces, John R. Hodge was confused as to what his actual mission was, writing that his "preparations for Civil Affairs activities" were far from complete in both terms of personnel and *policy directives*, when he landed.[38] Faced with the need to maintain order, and without instructions from Washington, Hodge made the disastrous decision to announce that Japanese civil authorities would be kept in place temporarily. The backlash from Koreans *and* Americans was so great that Hodge was quickly ordered to reverse the decision and the White House was forced to release a statement pledging that "the Japanese warlords are being removed."[39]

Hodge also received no help from General Douglas MacArthur. Though nominally in charge of both the occupations of Korea and Japan, MacArthur ignored Korea to the extent possible, telling aides: "I wouldn't put my foot in Korea. It belongs to the State Department. They wanted it and got it. ... I wouldn't touch it with a ten-foot barge pole. The damn diplomats make the wars and we win them. Why should I save their skin? I won't help Hodge. Let them help themselves."[40]

Bruce Cumings has argued that the American occupation quickly cohered around the goal of creating a right-wing government in their zone that would forestall a communist revolution.[41] While American occupation forces did eventually cobble together a nonradical provisional legislature for Korea in fall 1946 (the issue of "rightwing" will be addressed below), they did so in possibly the slowest and most cumbersome way possible, by starting from the ground up and, at least for the first several months, *in consultation*, with Soviet officials in Korea.

What is so puzzling about the procedure that Hodge and occupation officials followed is that there already existed a nonradical Korean political regime that could lay a legitimate claim to being a Korean government and even enjoyed at least some popular support within Korea itself – the KPG.[42] Indeed, after only a few days in Korea both General Hodge and the State Department's political officer were calling for the return of the KPG to Korea "as a provisional

---

[38] Supreme Commander for the Allied Powers 1945, 175.
[39] US Office of the Historian 1969, Doc. 780; Truman was also asked about this issue in a September 12, 1945, press conference: www.presidency.ucsb.edu/documents/the-presidents-news-conference-529. That Truman was asked about Korea at all, and that he was asked a question related to Japanese influence there, is a testament to the public interest in Korea at the time.
[40] Bowers 1967.   [41] Cumings 2005. See also, Hart-Landsberg 1998, 43.
[42] Polling by the American military government in their zone after the first two months of occupation indicated that the return of the KPG to Korea was one of the highest areas of concern among Koreans. See Supreme Commander for the Allied Powers 1945, 195.

government" even if they were just to be given a symbolic role.[43] At the same time, apparently unaware of how desperately they were needed in Korea, the KPG was begging American officials in China to return them to Korea, even if they were to serve in menial roles.[44] Had the United States been committed to establishing a nonradical, American-orientated state on the southern half of the Korean peninsula, surely this was the opportunity.

American occupation forces did not take this opportunity. While they did let KPG officials return to their zone as private citizens, they were adamant that Korea's future provisional government must emerge from an international, consultative process with China, the UK, and the Soviet Union – later narrowed down to just the Soviet Union; this was hardly an approach that suggested the later Cold War mentality. They continued to seek cooperation with the full knowledge that Soviet officials were already taking steps to create a communist provisional government in the north and were treating the 38th parallel as a more or less permanent boundary, rather than a temporary demarcation line.

Conventional wisdom holds that even while the United States was still seeking cooperation from the Soviet Union on a trusteeship formula, it was enabling right-wing politicians in Korea at the expense of Korean popular sentiment that was strongly leaning toward the left; the logic being that Cold War imperatives compelled the United States to seek right-wing, anti-communist leaders for southern Korea to ensure it remained anti-communist. Central to this interpretation is American support for Syngman Rhee as an autocratic, but reliably anti-communist strongman.

There is more than a grain of truth to this interpretation. By the time of his election in 1948 Rhee's anti-communism was well-known, but few have recognized that it was also pragmatic rather than ideological. Indeed, throughout his life he had shown a flexibility toward communism that has been mostly overlooked by scholars. His writings in the 1930s reveal an interest in communism and the Soviet Union as potential tools to further Korean independence. Rhee even traveled to the Soviet Union in 1933, seeking Soviet support for the Korean independence movement.[45] During his first days back in Korea in 1945, Rhee made many statements that were quite conciliatory to communism, including telling the *New York Times,* "I believe in some of the Communist ideas" and that he would support communist "economic policies" in any future Korean government.[46] In another interview he went further, saying: "I will do

---

[43] US Office of the Historian 1969, Doc. 781. They also continued to beg for instructions with the State Department political office Merril Benninghoff writing: "[T]his headquarters [of US forces in Korea] has no information in regard to the future policy of the United States or its allies as to the future of Korea. What is going to happen to the nation and what will be the solution of the now almost complete division of the country into two parts? What will be our general policies beyond immediate military necessity?"
[44] US Office of the Historian 1969, Doc. 775.   [45] Fields 2019, 119–126.   [46] Johnston 1945.

all I can to adopt many communist theories – regulate capitalism and abolish the class system, so that farmers will have land and the poor will have food and clothes. In that respect I may be called a communist in sentiment."[47]

Of course, Rhee was hardly a communist, but these statements were exaggerations rather than lies. As I have argued elsewhere, Rhee's policies as the Republic of Korea's (ROK) first president on the economy and the role of the state in Korean's lives were squarely left-of-center, at least by the prevailing American definitions of left and right at the time. Multiple American experts examining the first ROK constitution agreed that the ROK was basically a socialist state. Rhee oversaw a sweeping land reform that fundamentally overturned the highly unequal land ownership structure that had prevailed in Korea since the Joseon Dynasty. Rhee's support for state-owned monopolies and intervention in the ROK economy did not go unnoticed in the US Congress, where a few genuine capitalists ideologues sought to make future aid to the ROK dependent on economic liberalization. Rhee saw off this challenge and for most of his time as ROK president proved quite deft at a complicated two-step that involved proclaiming anti-communism abroad while quietly practicing socialism at home.[48]

If Syngman Rhee was left-of-center, whither the extreme right-wing label? Surprisingly, it originated with the American Military Government that sought to use the label to discredit Rhee and other Korean leaders who were violently opposed to an international trusteeship for Korea. These leaders were so problematic to the American military government for two reasons: They were hampering US-Soviet cooperation on Korea, which in turn was preventing the American withdrawal from the peninsula – something American military leaders desperately wanted (and which again belies a Cold War interpretation of the division of the peninsula).

This labeling of Korean leaders as right-wing caused no end of confusion between Washington and American military leaders in Seoul. When the State Department instructed General Hodge to find some "moderate" Koreans who supported land reform to cooperate with instead of those on the "extreme right," he was forced to explain to them that all Koreans were "socialist and definitely left from the United States [point of view]."[49] A 1948 Central Intelligence Agency (CIA) report attempted to clarify the use of these terms

---

[47] *San Antonio Express* 1945.
[48] All the examples in this paragraph are covered in Fields 2017.
[49] US Army, Historical Division 1953, 859–860. This collection, the *History of the United States Armed Forces in Korea*, is an incredibly valuable resource for understanding US policy toward Korea during the American occupation. It is also difficult to find and cite since it exists in many forms, including manuscript, facsimile publication, and microfilm. Furthermore, each of these forms have different pagination schemes. To facilitate further research, reference is to the archive.org version of this manuscript. The page number cited refers to the electronic page number and not to the printed number on any given page.

by explaining that "[a]s an arbitrary measure coalitions favoring trusteeship have been classified as Left Wing; all opposing trusteeship as Right Wing." It further concluded that socialism is "the common property of the left and right" and that there are "no articulate proponents of capitalism among the Koreans."[50]

What divided Koreans during the postliberation period were not competing ideologies being pushed on Koreans by competing foreign powers, but the agonizing decision about whether cooperation with the Soviet Union or the United States was more likely to result in the true realization of Korea's independence – a question made infinitely more complex by the uncertainty about American and Soviet intentions in the long term. The dividing line among the Koreans themselves was not capitalism versus communism, or any grand ideological difference, but rather which foreign power they *distrusted* more, the Soviet Union or the United States – for there was little trust for either.

This fact is often obscured by the constant use of terms such as "left," "right," "reds," and "communism" in documents from the period. For example, Rhee has often been quoted as saying that he would no more compromise with communism than with small pox or cholera. However, a 1947 letter, in which he likely used the phrase for the first time, is very revealing as to what he meant by it:

> If any one says Dr. R. should unite with moderates or reds or anything else, tell him that Dr. R. will not 'cooperate with small pox'. If I believe it would help our independence cause, I would join hands with uncle Joe[Stalin] tomorrow. But if I do think that would hurt our cause, no one would [could?] persuade me to do so.[51]

He did, and no one could, but the letter reveals that Rhee's opposition to communism was hardly ideological, but rather pragmatic. The letter also reveals that Rhee viewed the struggles for Korea's future in the postliberation period as an extension of the struggle for Korea's independence that he had been waging for most of his life. Only now he was struggling with the Soviet Union instead of the Japanese, with the United States playing its all too familiar ambivalent role. Tragically for the Koreans, there is ample evidence that Kim Il-sung viewed his struggles in a similar way, only with the United States replacing Japan as the main enemy to Korea's independence.

Far from moving quickly to establish a capitalist, right-wing regime in their zone, the American military government, at the insistence of the State Department, sought in vain for a "moderate" Korean leader(s) who had both political legitimacy and would support trusteeship, and thus be acceptable to the Soviet Union. Such an individual or group did not exist. By mid-1947, the

---

[50] US Central Intelligence Agency 1948, I-4, I-7–8. [51] Jeong 1996, 272–273.

American military government had to accept that Rhee, and his brand of left-of-center Korean nationalism, would prevail. In a final attempt to ensure that history would lay the blame for the division of Korea at the feet of the Soviets, the Truman administration orchestrated – with considerable international support – resolutions in the United Nations calling for elections to reunify the Korean peninsula. When UN supervisors were refused even entry into the Soviet zone for discussions, the election was held in the American zone only. Unsurprisingly, Syngman Rhee was elected to the ROK's constituent assembly and ultimately as its first president in 1948.

Subsequent events in 1948 and 1949 offer even firmer evidence that the Cold War paradigm fails to explain American behavior in Korea, as the United States sought to reduce the limited commitments it had made. Immediately after the creation of the ROK in 1948 – the earliest moment the Truman administration could credibly claim to have created an independent (partial) Korean state per the Cairo Declaration – the Truman administration began heading for the exit. They did not do so confident in the knowledge they had firmly planted an anti-communist regime there, but rather beat a hasty retreat from Korea wanting to get out before any eventuality would force them to stay. American forces, with the exception of a few advisers, were withdrawn from Korea in July 1949, despite analysis from the CIA indicating their withdrawal "would in time be followed by an invasion, timed to coincide with Communist-led South Korean revolts."[52]

Such analysis probably only hastened the desire of the Truman administration to leave. As NSC 8/2 explained, the collapse of the ROK was certainly possible, either by "direct military aggression or inspired insurrection," but that "temporary postponement of withdrawal would not serve appreciably to diminish this risk, but would serve rather to perpetuate the additional risk that U.S. occupation forces remaining in Korea might be either destroyed or obliged to abandon Korea in the event of a major hostile attack, with serious damage to U.S. prestige in either case." Fighting *for* the ROK was not even under consideration as the United States had "little strategic interest" in Korea and the withdrawal of American forces would not "adversely affect the U.S. position in Japan"[53] Also, unlike in the summer of 1945, Truman had nothing to fear from congress, who had largely lost interest in Korea – having taken more than six months to deliberate on his $150 million proposed aid package for Korea, only to vote it down in January of 1950.[54] Far from nurturing an anti-communist toehold on the Asian mainland, the United States departed from the ROK hoping Rhee's regime would survive, but confident that its fate was of little strategic importance one way or another.

---

[52] US Office of Reports and Estimates 1949.   [53] US Office of the Historian 1976, Doc. 209.
[54] See "Editorial Note" in US Office of the Historian 1976, Doc. 209.

10.5 Conclusion

If the United States had abandoned Korea in July of 1949, why did it rush back to Korea in June of 1950? This is a puzzling question indeed if Cold War competition with the Soviet Union was the primary motive for the division of Korea. If one starts with the Cold War and works backward, American decision-making from 1945–49 is hard to explain. It is only when one starts in 1882 and works forward that American choices become more comprehensible. The division of Korea and American involvement there from 1945–49 was the result of a complex mix of factors, including guilt over American treatment of Korea, a desire to avoid the charge of appeasing the Soviet Union, and also no small amount of public pressure on the Truman administration to uphold the Cairo Declaration. American involvement had all the hallmarks of a hasty wartime decision taken to uphold an expedient wartime declaration at Cairo, but it was a product of World War II and historical circumstances stretching back to the late nineteenth century. It was not a product of the Cold War.

The American withdrawal in 1949 was the denouement of a long chapter in US–Korean relations that began in 1882; the American return to Korea in June of 1950 was the beginning of a different chapter. In the intervening eleven months much had changed. The victory of the Chinese Communist Revolution, the Soviet Union's first nuclear test, the revelation of a communist spy-ring in Los Alamos, and Senator Joseph McCarthy's Wheeling Speech alleging a vast communist conspiracy fundamentally shifted the assumptions of American leaders. The confidence of the Long Telegram had so given way to the paranoia of NSC-68 that even George Kennan, the author of NSC 8/2 and a staunch advocate for the withdrawal from Korea, insisted that the United States had to go back to Korea to fight. Somewhere in this intervening period the Cold War had begun. American forces returned to Korea in June of 1950 to contain communism, but only then with a singleness of purpose they never had in August of 1945.

11 The Taiwan Straits Crises Revisited

Hsiao-ting Lin

Tensions between the People's Republic of China (PRC) and the Republic of China (ROC) in the 1950s resulted in armed conflict over strategic islands in the Taiwan Strait. On two separate occasions during the 1950s, respectively, in September 1954 and August 1958, the RRC bombed islands controlled by the ROC. The United States responded by actively intervening on behalf of the ROC, but in the context of a broader effort to rein in Chiang Kai-shek's ambitions with respect to the mainland and thus to reduce American risk.

In hindsight, the crises over the offshore islands along China's south and southeast coast momentarily brought America closer to war with the Chinese Communist Party (CCP) while putting the relationship between Taipei and Washington to a serious test. These isles were embedded in the unfinished civil war between Mao Zedong and Chiang Kai-shek, and were resolved in part by the United States asserting its interests vis-à-vis its new treaty ally.

But ironically, the crises also provided an opportunity for secret communications and ultimately a kind of détente between the two supposedly deadly enemies across the Taiwan Strait which proved surprisingly long-lived.

Both the PRC and the ROC had an interest in the offshore islands: Beijing was convinced that the occupation of these islands would eventually lead to liberating Taiwan and Penghu (the Pescadores), whereas Taipei intended to use these islands as a launching pad to recapture the lost mainland. But over time, outside parties (mainly the United States and implicitly the Soviet Union) intervened in ways that raised new issues for both the PRC and the ROC. If Taipei were to give up the islands, both parties realized that it would harden the divide across the Strait. Chiang Kai-shek would lose his foothold along China's southeast coast, and the ROC would end up being entirely restricted to Taiwan. For Mao Zedong, such an all-out withdrawal of the Nationalist presence in the islands carried a series of risks as well: a two-China or one-China, one-Taiwan reality would emerge.

The result was a surprising outcome: After intense crises the conflict essentially died down; shelling was ritualistic and both sides effectively restrained themselves in a way that led to a sort of long peace.

207

11.1 The 1954–55 Offshore Crisis: An Island State Embedded

In late 1949, the Chinese civil war ended with the victory of the CCP, forcing the Chinese Nationalist regime (KMT) under Chiang Kai-shek, and 1.3 million anti-communist supporters, to flee from the mainland. The territory under KMT control was reduced to Taiwan, Hainan, a strip of territory along the China–Burma border, and several island groups along China's southeast coast. In the spring of 1950, the Chinese Nationalist forces evacuated Hainan and Zhoushan Islands off Shanghai, leaving Quemoy, Matsu, and Upper and Lower Dachens the only territorial residues connecting the exiled Nationalists on Taiwan to the mainland they had disastrously lost. The outbreak of the Korean War in June 1950 led the United States to send the Seventh Fleet into the Taiwan Strait to prevent any conflict between the Chinese Nationalists and the Chinese Communists, effectively putting Taiwan under American protection. Washington chose to realign itself to Chiang Kai-shek, the man whom it had bitterly despised not long ago. Now the existence of two political entities across the Strait was pretty much confirmed, although both sides insisted that they solely represented the whole of China and repudiated the other as illegitimate awaiting to be annihilated. Hence, the very definition of "China" would become a thorny issue haunting both Taipei and Beijing, as well as the entire international society.[1]

As the armistice effectively ended fighting on the Korean peninsula in the summer of 1953, Mao Zedong turned his attention southward to Taiwan. Communist Chinese source materials recently made available reveal that by the early summer of 1953, Mao's top military men had worked out a secret five-year plan for the PRC's military endeavors in which the takeover of the offshore islands still under Nationalist Chinese control would become Beijing's top priority. In the eyes of Mao's strategists, occupying the KMT-held isles along China's southeast coast was not purely a matter of national unification, but was closely related to Beijing's national defense and security: The control of these islands had posed a threat as a staging area.[2]

Indeed, after the Republicans regained control over the White House, Chiang Kai-shek and his Nationalist cohorts on Taiwan began pushing hard for a joint military pact with the United States. John Foster Dulles, Eisenhower's secretary of state, welcomed the idea of concluding a general pact of mutual security for Asia, but he had reservations about forging one with Chiang. While Dulles saw the exclusion of Nationalist-held offshore islands in such a treaty as something that would impair Chiang's prestige, he also felt that their inclusion would entail a responsibility that Washington was not as yet ready to assume.[3] Chiang was frustrated, but the many efforts made by his indefatigable

---

[1] Accinelli 1996, 29–54; Bush 2004, 85–99.
[2] Editorial Committee 2000, 848–854; He 2000, 656–660; Zhen 2003, 474–475, 494–499.
[3] Hoopes 1973, 263–265.

subordinates, and all the publicity as well as mass media speculation surrounding these efforts, were quite enough to keep Mao and his top officials nervous and suspicious about America's true intention.[4]

Beijing's extreme anxiety regarding American intentions reached a climax in the fall of 1954. On September 1, 1954, before John Foster Dulles departed for the Philippines to attend the inauguration of the Southeast Asia Treaty Organization (SEATO), he decided to delay setting a date for possible treaty negotiations with Taipei. At this juncture, the Chinese Communists ironically and unwittingly contributed to the final conclusion of a mutual security pact between Taiwan and the United States. In an attempt to forestall the possibility of extending the protection of SEATO to Taiwan, or at least try to keep the geographical scope of such protection to a minimum, on September 3 Mao ordered the People's Liberation Army (PLA) to launch a massive shelling of Quemoy.[5] Mao's actions, however, gave Taipei a perfect excuse to push Washington forward for a desired mutual security treaty. On September 9, during Dulles's five-hour stopover in Taipei on his way back to the United States, Chiang argued strongly that the "fluid situation" of the offshore islands was caused exactly by the absence of a mutual aid pact rather than a reason to forgo such a pact. Although Dulles left Taipei uncommitted, his short visit was widely seen as a strong sign of US support for Taiwan against communism.[6]

As the Communist shelling around Quemoy continued, both Eisenhower and Dulles now viewed a security pact with Taiwan as a feasible way to rein in Chiang, whom they believed should assume a more passive posture and accept a purely "defensive" treaty. Meanwhile, to dissipate apprehension within and outside the administration that defending the offshore islands would bring America closer to war with the PRC, the State Department planned to present the offshore crisis to the United Nations Security Council, where it would seek an injunction against changing the status quo in the Taiwan Strait. Dulles was convinced that a UN-arranged ceasefire, codenamed "Oracle," would secure support from America's Western allies, preserve the isles for Chiang, and avoid a war between Washington and Beijing.[7]

Chiang Kai-shek and his top aides were kept totally in the dark about both Oracle and the US decision to begin treaty negotiations. On the evening of October 12, when the chartered flight bringing Walter Robertson (John Foster Dulles's assistant secretary of state for East Asian affairs slated to open negotiations with the Nationalists) arrived in Taipei, an unprepared Chiang was still in the midst of his retreat outside the capital.[8] In a three-bout negotiation held over twenty-four hours the following day, Chiang vigorously

---

[4] Party Research Center of the CCP 1997, 405; Zhang 2003, 495–496.
[5] Chang 1990, 116–120; Szonyi 2008, 42–49.
[6] CKSD September 8 and 9, 1954; US Office of the Historian 1985, 581–582.
[7] Accinelli 1996, 165–168; Tsang 2006, 121–138.   [8] CKSD October 12 and 13, 1954.

objected to Oracle, deeming an internationalization of cross-Strait issues detrimental to the morale of his people and government. But when Robertson stated that Oracle combined with a mutual defense pact would surely improve Chiang's position, an alert Generalissimo caught the message right away and changed his mind. In other words, Chiang believed he had achieved something more important than the likely internationalization of the supposedly domestic offshore island crisis – a formal security and defense commitment from the United States.[9] A week later, George Yeh, Chiang's foreign minister, was already in Washington for treaty discussion with his counterparts from the State Department.

The opening of negotiations over a mutual defense pact between Taiwan and the United States certainly alarmed the Communist leaders in Beijing. On November 1, the PLA started bombing Upper and Lower Dachen off Zhejiang as a way both to test America's resolve and to influence the ongoing treaty negotiation. As such, the treaty negotiations became the proximate cause of the crisis.[10] During the lengthy process of negotiation, the definition of the territorial scope of American military commitments became a source of controversy. In terms of the territory that was to come under the scope of the treaty, George Yeh tried to prevent specifying only Taiwan and the Pescadores so as to avoid giving the impression that the Nationalist Chinese territory was limited to these two island regions without encompassing the mainland. Dulles refused, only willing to state that the treaty would be "applicable to such other territories [than Taiwan and the Pescadores] as may be determined by mutual agreement." Chiang eventually backed down.[11] Meanwhile, to underscore that the pact was purely defensive in nature, the State Department insisted that, without mutual consent, the Nationalists would not take any offensive action which might provoke retaliation by the Chinese Communists. Yeh initially refused to renounce the right of his government to liberate the mainland, but as the Americans continued to hold their ground on this issue, Taipei again yielded, only requesting that the provision be made secret so as not to cause any damage to the prestige of "Free China."[12]

Before the mutual defense treaty was signed by George Yeh and John Foster Dulles on December 2, 1954, both sides also reached an understanding on the deployment of Nationalist forces within KMT-ruled territory. Worrying that Chiang might provoke Beijing by stationing a huge number of his troops on the offshore islands, thus creating a serious problem for the United States in its commitment to the defense of Taiwan, the State Department insisted on having a strong voice about Nationalist military deployment. In the end, Taipei agreed

---

[9] US Office of the Historian 1985, 728–753.
[10] United States Department of State 1986, reel 4.
[11] CKSD November 7, 1954; Soman 2000, 146–148.
[12] US Office of the Historian 1985, 870–871.

to rephrase the wording in the pact to state that the forces stationed on Taiwan and the Pescadores should not be reduced "to a degree which would substantially diminish the defensibility of such territories."[13] By intentionally not mentioning the offshore islands in the treaty's main text, Washington hoped to deter Beijing from attacking Nationalist positions there while simultaneously discouraging Taipei from using the islands as a springboard to invade the mainland. More significant from a historical perspective, the 1954 mutual defense treaty not only confined Nationalist territorial jurisdiction to Taiwan and the Pescadores (Penghu) but it also virtually shattered any real hope of Chiang's military recovery of the mainland. The content, spirit, and scope of the treaty ultimately provided the groundwork for what would gradually lead to the legalization of an island-based Republic of Chinese state.[14]

Chiang Kai-shek was outwardly pleased when he heard about the conclusion of the bilateral treaty which he saw as a "marvelous achievement" considering the disgrace and humiliation he had endured over the previous decade, as well as from the bitter struggle for his very survival since the Communist takeover of the mainland in 1949.[15] If the Generalissimo was elated that his last power base in Taiwan was now secured and the position of his once-precarious regime consolidated, his arch rivals across the Strait were certainly not. Beginning from early November 1954, the PLA launched a series of assaults against Nationalist-guarded isles off southeast China. On the evening of November 14, the Communists torpedoed and sunk a Nationalist destroyer escort near the Dachens. It became the first positive indication of the PLA's capability to use torpedoes in night work. If the United States wanted to avoid a military clash with the PRC, top brass in the Pentagon argued, withdrawing Nationalist troops on the offshore islands seemed unavoidable.[16]

On January 10, 1955, Mao Zedong ordered a massive attack on the Dachens. Eight days later, about 10,000 Communist forces launched a successful air–amphibious–land operation to occupy Yijiangshan, approximately nine miles north of Upper Dachen, inflicting heavy casualties on the roughly 1,000 Nationalist defenders on Chiang Kai-shek's northernmost island outpost. In the face of the renewed Taiwan Strait crisis, John Foster Dulles proposed a US-assisted evacuation of all the Nationalist-held offshore islands except Quemoy (and later, Matsu) in combination with a defensive commitment for the latter. Despite some strenuous objections from his national security advisors, President Eisenhower stood firmly behind Dulles's idea.[17] To Chiang, abandoning the Dachens, the last territorial hold of his home province of Zhejiang, was certainly distasteful, but he was aware of their vulnerability and their

---

[13] US Office of the Historian 1985, 904–908. [14] Lin 2016, 216–234.
[15] CKSD December 3, 1954. [16] US Department of State 1989, reel 37.
[17] Soman 2000, 130–131; Tucker 2012, 76–78.

diminishing value to the defense of Taiwan. He reckoned that their loss was part of a tacit quid pro quo without which Taipei could not count on US assistance to protect the more strategic Quemoy and Matsu. In addition, refusing to accept Dulles's proposal might generate a very negative influence at the critical moment when Congress was in the process of ratifying the mutual defense treaty already negotiated.[18]

With the Generalissimo on board, President Eisenhower delivered his message to Congress on January 24, now dubbed the "Formosa Resolution." Delegating the president to employ American armed forces to defend Taiwan and the Pescadores, the Resolution provided the authority for the "securing and protection of such related positions and territories of that area now in friendly hands," and the taking of "such other measures as the president would judge to be required or appropriate in assuring the defense of Taiwan and the Pescadores."[19] In Taipei, Chiang viewed the passing of the resolution on Capitol Hill "a blessing for the fate of his nation," something which brought him much comfort and satisfaction.[20] The evacuation of the Dachens was completed by February 11, 1955, and soon thereafter the Communists peacefully occupied the empty isles. The result was undoubtedly a huge propaganda score to Beijing, and Chiang Kai-shek's reputation was badly hurt.

The comfort and satisfaction that the passing of the Formosa Resolution had provided Chiang Kai-shek proved to be short-lived. As tensions across the Taiwan Strait gradually died down in the spring of 1955, the idea that the Nationalists should abandon the offshore islands altogether so as not to drag the United States into war with Communist China became pronounced among Washington's top echelons, including President Eisenhower himself. On April 24, the president sent Walter Robertson and Arthur Radford (Chairman of the Joint Chiefs of Staff) to Taipei to persuade the Generalissimo either to turn the offshore islands into outposts, with a much reduced complement of defense forces stationed there, or to withdraw from them completely and accept a US-policed "maritime zone" that would take the place of the islands as a first-line of warning and defense for Taiwan.[21]

In the end, instead of presenting Chiang with both options, Eisenhower's envoys presented only the latter, the more extreme alternative; if Taipei withdrew from the offshore islands under US naval protection, the United States would join with it in creating an interdiction line running 400 miles through the South China Sea, the Taiwan Strait, and the East China Sea, from Swatow in Guangdong in the south to the port of Wenzhou in Zhejiang. The purpose of the joint interdiction would be to search all ships in the area, foreign or Chinese, and seize all "contraband and war-making materials." The interdiction force

---

[18] CKSD January 20, 21, and 22, 1955. [19] Accinelli 1996, 190–194.
[20] CKSD January 29, 30, and 31, 1955. [21] Taylor 2009, 479–480.

would also replace Quemoy and Matsu as the early line of defense to any invasion force from the mainland. The joint naval action, as Radford stressed to Chiang in their long, arduous meeting at the latter's private residence, would in effect be "a blockade of China's coast," and it would demonstrate to the whole world America's determination to take strong measures, including fighting a war, to defend Taiwan.[22]

Chiang, unprepared for this surprising scheme, was flabbergasted and annoyed. Without first consulting close aides he turned down the envoys' proposal outright, insisting that his government would defend Quemoy and Matsu with or without US help. To jettison the islands would be to lose the respect of the Chinese people, the Generalissimo exclaimed.[23] Privately, Chiang's reaction was much more drastic; he confided in his diary that the Americans were "completely deceiving," and "naïve and ignorant" to think he would believe them. While regarding Radford at least as a "gentleman," Chiang went as far as to call Robertson "a son of a bitch."[24] Apparently, the drawn-out meeting was not a harmonious or pleasant one. Before closing the meeting, Robertson urged the Generalissimo to give "full consideration to all implications" of the interdiction proposal. An agitated and impatient Chiang replied that he had made up his mind and he no long wanted to discuss the matter, reemphasizing that if he pulled out of Quemoy and Matsu, the Chinese people would not support him, and then the Americans "would have to find another Chiang Kai-shek." He was angry that the Americans still did not understand that the loss of the islands would endanger his claims to rule all of China. Unwilling to bear a repeat of what he had already said and heard, and in what by diplomatic standards was considered an incredibly rude act for one's most important ally, the next day Chiang simply ordered his scheduled meeting with the Americans cancelled, leaving his wife and subordinates to keep the American diplomats occupied.[25]

Back in Washington, DC, after reading John Foster Dulles's report on what had happened in Taipei, Eisenhower took a sympathetic stance toward Chiang. The president noted that Chiang's response "made it not only what I predicted but what I think I would have made had I been in his place." While lamenting that Taipei had failed to see the wisdom of the interdiction formula and the unique opportunity to trim its offshore island garrisons down to a reasonable level, the president could not help commenting that, "in a sense, we are still on the horns of the dilemma that you and I have discussed a number of times."[26] It took a relatively three short years to prove that Eisenhower was correct.

---

[22] Lester 1990, reel 6. [23] Lester 1990, reel 6; CKSD April 25 and 27, 1955.
[24] CKSD April 27, 1955. [25] Lester 1990, reel 6; CKSD April 25, 26, 27, and 31, 1955.
[26] Lester 1990, reel 6.

11.2 A Cross-Strait Rendezvous, 1955–1957

Chiang Kai-shek's refusal to accept the American proposal came at a moment when his Communist rivals began to defuse the cross-Strait crisis and change their stance, presumably under pressure from the Soviet Union and other communist bloc and Third World countries. It therefore untangled a diplomatic dilemma for both Taipei and Washington, at least temporarily. During the Bandung Conference in April 1955, the PRC premier Zhou Enlai declared that the Chinese were friendly toward the American people and that Beijing was willing to sit down and negotiate with the US government over how to relax tensions in the Far East, especially in the Taiwan Strait area. In July, Eisenhower and Dulles sent messages through the British that they were prepared to negotiate with the PRC at Geneva at the ambassadorial level. Zhou responded positively, and talks began the following month and would continue on and off for the following one and a half decades.[27]

A little known fact is that when the Chinese Communists expressed their desire to reduce tensions in the Far East, they meant not only by seeking to open a dialogue with the Americans but also with the Nationalists on Taiwan. Beijing entrusted Cao Juren to send three secret letters to the Generalissimo's son, Chiang Ching-kuo. Cao, an old acquaintance to Chiang Ching-kuo who had lived in Hong Kong since 1949, bore private messages from Beijing regarding a settlement of the cross-Strait dispute. Beijing urged Taipei to dispatch a confidant to Hong Kong to receive "important information" about a CCP-KMT reconciliation.[28] Rumors had it that Taipei soon sent Huang Jici (a noted calligrapher who had been the Chinese tutor for Chiang Ching-kuo and Faina Epatcheva Vahaleva, his Belarusian wife) to Hong Kong and Tokyo to contact communist Chinese messengers. This would be the first known cross-Strait contact after Chiang Kai-shek's expulsion from the mainland in 1949.[29]

From the fall of 1955 through the spring of 1957, clandestine communications in the form of the exchange of letters and verbal messages across the Taiwan Strait via Hong Kong were quietly underway.[30] By the early weeks of 1956, newspaper reports concerning cross-Strait contacts had become so prevalent that Chiang was obliged to instruct his propaganda chiefs to clarify

---

[27] Jian 2001, 167–171; Kaufman 2001, 94–95; Tucker 2012, 92–97.
[28] US Central Intelligence Agency 1971, 2–5. Chiang Kai-shek first read Cao's letters on November 23, 1955, and confided in his diary that he could "hardly bear to read them." See CKSD November 23, 1955.
[29] Chiang Ching-kuo was furious at the rumor and soon gathered his trusted advisors to discuss possible ways to cope with it. See CCKD January 7, 8 and 11, 1956; For Ching-kuo's subsequent hot denial, see *Time* 1956.
[30] US Central Intelligence Agency 1971, 6–12; Department of General Political Warfare 1956, 125:437; ROC Embassy 1957, 0046/405.1/2; US Ministry of Foreign Affairs 1957, 0046/405.1/2.

with the outside world that no such contacts were happening.³¹ In June 1956, when the Communists established their "peaceful liberation" posture and formally declared their readiness to negotiate with Taiwan, details of specific steps and terms for negotiations were covertly conveyed to Chiang Kai-shek through secret channels. Cao Juren was reportedly entrusted, this time by the Chiangs, father and son, through a KMT local contact in Hong Kong, to conduct a fact-finding trip to the Communist mainland. Cao gladly accepted the task, and he met with Zhou Enlai in Beijing shortly after the CCP announced its peace overture toward Taiwan.³² Among those confidential messages passed on to Taipei via Cao were Mao Zedong's "heartfelt desire" to reconcile with Chiang and to invite him to return to the mainland, where, Mao asserted, he could stay wherever he liked and would be treated with the highest courtesy and his security guaranteed. Mao also expressed great hope for sincere cooperation between Chiang Ching-kuo and Chen Cheng, the two top political rivals within the KMT, so as to avoid a split in the Nationalist hierarchy.³³ As a result of Cao's clandestine visit to the mainland on behalf of the KMT, Chiang became determined to expand Taiwan's existing intelligence base in Hong Kong, where he felt it imperative to appoint a capable figure to handle matters relating to Communist China.³⁴

Chiang Kai-shek apparently saw it as an advantage to use the widely reported secret cross-Strait communications both as a lever to offset the US-PRC ambassadorial talks and to solicit more military aid from Washington. A few months later, Cao Juren conducted yet another extraordinary visit to Xikou in Zhejiang Province, Chiang's hometown. Ostensibly with permission from Beijing and as a gesture of goodwill, Cao worshipped at the Chiang family's graveyard and stayed in Chiang's former residence. After a while, stories about the imminent cross-Strait peace talks started to find foreign believers, especially in embassies and foreign offices around the world. Secret communications across the Taiwan Strait came to an abrupt halt in the early summer of 1957 when Mao launched his "anti-rightist" campaign.³⁵

Despite the surge of "peaceful liberation" initiatives on the part of the Chinese Communists and the establishment of private contacts across the Taiwan Strait between 1955 and 1957, the situation surrounding the offshore

---

³¹ CKSD January 8, 10, 20, 31, and February 4, 1956.
³² Yi 2009, 149–150. Chiang Kai-shek's diary around May and June 1956 clearly indicates that he was organizing and sending "neutralists in Hong Kong" to mainland to engage in underground activities. See CKSD May 6, 12 and June 14, 1956.
³³ US Central Intelligence Agency 1971, 9–10; ROC Ministry of Foreign Affairs 1956, 0045/405.1/3; ROC Consulate-general 1957, 0045/405.1/3; Lei and Xiaofang 1996, 652–653.
³⁴ CKSD July 21, August 16 and 17, 1956.
³⁵ US Central Intelligence Agency 1971, 10–12; British National Archives (London), Foreign Office RecordFO 371/133354 FCN1022, J. B. Wright (British Consul in Tamsui) to Foreign Office, March 10, 1958.

islands remained very unstable. As has been noted earlier, by mid-1953 top PRC military strategists, mostly hawks in the bureaucracy, had laid out a five-year formula to strengthen Communist China's national defense and border security, including the takeover of the offshore islands. In November 1955, when the cross-Strait political feelers had just begun, Mao vetoed a course of action already approved by the PLA to attack and occupy Quemoy.[36] But a few months later, when Mao's military staff proposed the creation of a new Fujian military region to be carved out of the Nanjing military region for the sake of dealing with Quemoy and Matsu, Mao found it hard to veto again. Mao's hawkish military men began pushing even harder for advancing the Communist Air Force into Fujian.[37]

In the fall of 1956, Nationalist and Communist forces exchanged fire in the Matsu area. Then, in early months of 1957, armed conflict flared again in the waters off Matsu; and in the last week of June, heavy fire was exchanged between Quemoy and Amoy, the fiercest since 1954.[38] During the last months of 1957 several battles were fought briefly in both Matsu and Quemoy waters, with each side claiming victories over the other. On the evening of August 23, 1958, the PLA began a massive artillery bombardment of Quemoy and threatened invasion. Communist patrol boats blockaded the island group against Nationalist resupply efforts. This was accompanied by an aggressive propaganda assault on the United States, threats against American naval ships, and a declaration of intent to "liberate" Taiwan.[39]

11.3   The 1958 Offshore Crisis Revisited

Numerous scholarly works have researched the Taiwan Strait crisis of 1958, but few if any have examined the delicate situation surrounding the secret KMT-CCP channels of communication built up during the previous years. The reasons suggested for the resumption of the shelling include a number of both foreign policy and domestic political objectives. Mao's decision to shell the offshore islands was made ostensibly because China wanted both to express its support for the Arab struggle against imperialist aggression and also because it hoped the bombardment would divert American attention from the Middle East. However, it has also been suggested there were other reasons for the bombardment. One was that Mao wanted to instigate a conflict to serve the goal of domestic reform, the Great Leap Forward, which he had launched in early 1958. Other reasons were that he also wanted to test American resolve, waste US resources, and

---

[36] Yan 1998, 606–607.   [37] Nanjing Ed. Committee 1994, 518–519; Yan 1998, 672–675.
[38] CKSD June 22, 1957.
[39] On the 1958 Taiwan Strait crisis, see also: Garver 1997, 133–139; Tucker 2012, 142–158; Jian 2001, 163–204; Qiang 1994, 178–207.

weaken US–Taiwan ties by triggering conflicting expectations and demonstrating Taiwan's total and embarrassing dependence on the United States.[40]

While all these reasons may have contributed to Mao's decision, another important but unspoken reason was that the PLA needed a preemptive shelling of the KMT-held isles along China's southeastern coast to ensure the smooth introduction and build-up of its Air Force in Fujian. A successful reinforcement of Communist air power in the Fujian military region, including jet planes, missiles, and other military infrastructure, would allow Communist China to gain vital air dominance along its southeastern coastal borders.[41] No matter what the reasons were for Mao's decision, he nevertheless gave a green light to the bombardment plan. But before the shelling started, Mao summoned Cao Juren to Beijing, and told him to leak the news of the upcoming bombardment through the *Nanyang Business Daily,* a Singaporean newspaper run by Cao himself.[42] In Washington, on hearing about the renewed crisis in the Taiwan Strait, President Eisenhower complained to his colleagues that although Chiang had ignored his advice to reduce his forces on the offshore islands, the Generalissimo now once again came "whining to us." But publicly, as in the past, Ike did not hesitate to declare that US forces would be used for the protection of Quemoy. To the amazement and consternation of America's allies worldwide, the president even claimed that he could not rule out the option of atomic weapons.[43]

On September 4, in an effort to prevent US naval vessels from approaching Quemoy, Beijing announced the establishment of its territorial waters at twelve nautical miles and declared that no foreign aircraft or vessels would be allowed to cross that boundary. Washington responded two days later by issuing a statement emphasizing that the protection of Quemoy and Matsu had become related to the defense of Taiwan, which the United States was bound by treaty obligation to defend. In the same statement, however, Washington also indicated its willingness to resume the ambassadorial talks which Mao had broken off in early 1958 after the American representative, U. Alexis Johnson, was reassigned and not subsequently replaced. Zhou Enlai responded the next day by expressing Beijing's intention to sit down at the negotiation table with the Americans to discuss the elimination of tension in the Taiwan Strait. Perhaps under heavy pressure from the Kremlin, whose leaders were annoyed at not being informed of the shelling in advance and who were by no means willing to

---

[40] Tucker 2012, 140–141; Huei 2019, 187–196.
[41] Fei 1988, 653–655; Nanjing Ed. Committee 1994, 502–503; Qiming and Yaguang 1997, 210–214.
[42] Xiaopeng 1996, 275. Apparently Chiang did not take this news coverage too seriously, as there was no way he and his staff could predict exactly when a genuine armed conflict would take place. Hundreds were killed in Quemoy after the shelling started on that evening, including three of Chiang's high-ranking generals and two American advisers.
[43] Kaufman 2001, 133–135; Taylor 2009, 493–494.

be dragged into a nuclear war over the offshore islands, Mao and his close confidants began to revise their stance.[44]

The policy shift over the crisis on the part of the Chinese Communists was not only directed toward the Americans but also aimed at the Nationalists. On September 10, five days before Beijing and Washington reopened the Warsaw ambassadorial talks, Zhou Enlai called Cao Juren to Beijing again for another urgent meeting. The premier wanted Cao to convey fresh messages to Taipei, which Cao dutifully did through his private letters, all dated September 25, sent to Chiang Ching-kuo, Defense Minister Yu Dawei, and Huang Shaogu, now newly appointed as Chiang's foreign minister.[45] Cao notified Taipei that if Chiang Kai-shek agreed to abandon his "reliance" on US military protection and the "self-conceit" that he had registered over his special relations with the Americans, then Beijing promised it would not attack Taiwan. Cao also guaranteed that, starting from October 6, the PLA would stop the siege of Quemoy as long as the Americans stopped providing protection for Nationalist ships. Most significantly, he conveyed Mao's secret message that Beijing actually "concurred with Chiang" that the KMT should continue to hold the offshore islands, adding that top CCP leaders now harbored no intention of destroying Chiang's forces on these islands. In addition, Cao indicated that Mao proposed the evacuation of Nationalist troops from the offshore islands so as to create a "demilitarized" Quemoy and Matsu and then to transform these two island groups into free economic zones across the Strait. It was Mao's wish, Cao further noted, that direct port-to-port shipping lines between Taiwan and the mainland could be opened in the near future.[46] Beijing's shift of stance fully demonstrated a paradoxical feature of the offshore island crisis; the occupation of Quemoy and Matsu might serve the PRC's military-strategic purposes in the eventual "liberation" of Taiwan. And yet the possible US intervention of the crisis and the resultant cutoff of ties between Taiwan and the offshore islands would lead to a permanent "two-China" scenario that would be detrimental to Beijing's legitimacy.

Jay Taylor's 2009 book makes the claim that, based on a private account given by a very senior CCP official in 1994, during the 1958 offshore island crisis Chiang sent a message to Zhou Enlai via a secret messenger to the effect that if the PLA did not stop its shelling, he would have "to do what the Americans wanted" – withdraw from the offshore islands – and, as a result, over time this move would threaten the indivisibility of China.[47] Whether this is true or not, it is intriguing that on September 27, 1958, two days after Cao

---

[44] Zhai 1994, 187–189; Jian 2001, 185–188.
[45] KMT Central Committee 1959, 2:508; Chunying 2004, 667–669.
[46] US Central Intelligence Agency 1958b; CKSD September 30, 1958; CCKD October 25, 1958; ROC Institute 1959, 6:1525.
[47] Taylor 2009, 501, 686.

sent his letters to Taipei, Chiang confided in his personal diary the following rambling thoughts: "[O]nly the Chinese [ourselves] truly understand the way we do business; this is particularly true when it comes to [our] understanding of the Chinese Communist activities and their mentality."[48] It is possible that Cao's three private letters to Taipei might have served as Beijing's response to Chiang's secret threat to withdraw from the islands. To be sure, more archival evidence is needed before one can solve this historical puzzle.

One thing is certain, as Beijing and Washington resumed bilateral talks in Warsaw, President Eisenhower did begin thinking about pressuring Chiang for a serious reconsideration of evacuating the offshore islands, or at least for a reduction of the level of Nationalist troop strength on these islands. Chiang, of course, refused to follow suit. His refusal to comply with what Eisenhower wished coincided with Beijing's announcement in the early hours of October 6 that it would halt the shelling for seven days, a move which Chiang had known from Cao from the previous week. Initially not entirely confident about the authenticity of Cao's messages, Chiang was rather surprised that leaders in Beijing had really kept their promise of stopping the shelling.[49]

Meanwhile, it became obvious that the Eisenhower administration was seeking Beijing's commitment for a nonmilitary policy in dealing with the Taiwan issue. In turn, Washington offered to push Chiang to withdraw from the offshore islands and give up his plan for the military recovery of the mainland. The Americans understood the withdrawal, if taking place, would damage the morale of the government and people on Taiwan. But to top decision-makers in Washington, to avoid an all-out confrontation with the PRC over these offshore islands was their top priority. Seeing such a design of "trading Quemoy and Matsu for Taiwan and the Pescadores" as a dangerous formalization of the separation between Taiwan and China, Communist leaders in Beijing shifted their stance once again and moved closer to the position of their Nationalist adversary. On October 13, Cao hurriedly flew to Beijing again, and this time Mao asked him to make it known to Taipei that Mao was resolved to leave the offshore islands in Chiang's hands, thereby maintaining a mainland connection with Nationalist-ruled Taiwan and avoiding a de facto "two-China" situation. Instead of requesting the withdrawal of Chiang's forces from Quemoy and Matsu, as suggested in Cao's September 25th letters, Mao now unequivocally favored a continued Nationalist military presence on these isles.[50] Coincidentally, Chiang Kai-she's top aides were also working on a statement exemplifying why the Nationalists could not abandon the offshore islands. And the CCP peace overtures became one critical element Taipei sought to include to convince the Americans that a spontaneous withdrawal

---

[48] CKSD September 27, 1958.   [49] CKSD October 6, 1958.
[50] Party Research Center of the CCP 1997, 181–182; Jian 2001, 199–202.

from Quemoy or Matsu was dangerous.⁵¹ In hindsight, the crisis on Quemoy started as a military confrontation between the KMT and the CCP at tactical level. As the crisis evolved into a possible redefinition of what "China" really was, top leaders across the Strait might begin to harbor very different thoughts as to how to go off the stage.

Beijing's secret proposal arrived at the very moment when Washington was ready to apply more pressure on Chiang Kai-shek over the island issue. When John Foster Dulles's motorcade drove through the grimy city of Taipei on October 20, the PLA temporarily resumed its shelling of Quemoy as a gesture of protest. But the purpose of the Secretary of State's visit to Taipei was not to boost Taiwan's morale to continue its fight against the Communists as had been perceived world-wide. Rather, Dulles criticized the KMT as militaristic and apt to precipitate a world war, as well as having only "a limited life expectancy." He then gave the Generalissimo a list of things Taipei had to do if it wished to prevent itself from being liquidated. These included seeking an "armistice" with the Chinese mainland, avoiding commando raids and "alike provocations," and accepting any solution to the offshore islands problem as long as the civilian population on Taiwan would not be turned over to the Communists.⁵²

While Chiang Kai-shek was faced with Dulles's startling criticism and list of demands in Taipei, Mao proffered his arch rival yet another option: an immediate cross-Strait agreement engineered to push back against American pressure. On October 23, Beijing informed Taipei through the Cao Juren channel that Mao's decision to restart the shelling was in fact a "blessing in disguise," as such a move would "scare" the Americans and reinforce Chiang's bargaining position vis-à-vis Dulles, allowing Taipei to "extort" more military and economic aid from Washington. Cao reiterated Mao's willingness to allow the offshore islands to remain in Chiang's possession, and conveyed Mao's suggestion that CCP-KMT bilateral meetings be held in Hong Kong without delay so as to pave a way for a peaceful reunification.⁵³ Cao further stipulated that issues to be discussed might include the election of Taiwan's future leadership and the maintenance of Taiwan's autonomous status, the transformation of offshore islands as a pivot for cross-Strait economic exchange, and the dispatch of a KMT military delegation to inspect the Chinese mainland as a first step toward reducing mutual hostility.⁵⁴ To show that he was really serious, Mao sent Zhang Shijao (a respected revolutionary under Sun Yat-sen who had also participated in the 1949 KMT-CCP peace negotiations) to Hong Kong to await the arrival of Chiang's envoy. Fully authorized by Mao on the negotiation table,

---

[51] CCKD October 25, 26, 27 and 31, 1958.
[52] US Office of the Historian 1996a, 415–416; CKSD October 20 and 21, 1958.
[53] CCKD October 25 and 26, 1958; US Central Intelligence Agency 1958b.
[54] Zong 1963, 6:1679.

Zhang went so far as to inform a KMT contact in Hong Kong that Beijing was ready to return to Taiwan the Upper and Lower Dachen islands that Chiang had evacuated in early 1955, as long as Chiang chose to cool his relationship with the United States.[55]

During the last week of October 1958, Chiang Kai-shek seemed caught in the dilemma of having to choose between engaging in secret dialogues with the Chinese Communists or enduring the difficult relationship in his alliance with an overbearing American patron. One irony is that America was eager to end the military conflict over the offshore islands so as to protect Taiwan from being attacked by the PRC, even though this would weaken Chiang Kai-shek's political myth of using the offshore islands as a stepping stone to the promised counterattack of the mainland. On the other hand, Chiang might actually want to prolong the confrontation with the PRC through the offshore islands crisis for purposes of his own, although a continued military standoff might damage the stability of his rule in Taiwan. But if such a "dilemma" did exist, it was ephemeral; before leaving Taipei on October 24, Dulles made Chiang bend to his will by agreeing to renounce publicly the use of military means to restore Nationalist rule to the Chinese mainland. A euphemism of Dulles's "strong recommendation" in this regard was rephrased in the joint communiqué to read "the principal means" for restoring freedom to the Chinese people on the mainland would be "implementation of Sun Yat-sen's Three Principles of the People," and that "the foundation of this mission resides in the hearts and minds of the Chinese people and not in the use of force."[56] In essence, the communiqué would transform the nature of Chiang's policy toward the mainland from a crucial "incentive" to spark anti-communist revolution to a "response" in the event of such a revolution. This formulation also implied that the most effective way for the KMT to make progress was to focus on implementing the Three Principles in the area they controlled, namely, Taiwan. Beijing reacted by announcing the next day that the shelling would continue only on alternate days, thus permitting Chiang's forces to be resupplied and the islands to remain in Nationalist hands. The second offshore islands crisis thus virtually came to an end.[57]

11.4 Toward the End of an Issue

The signing of the Chiang-Dulles communiqué renouncing a military recovery of the mainland, followed by a cluster of political gestures to dismiss the

---

[55] CCKD October 25, 1958; KMT Central Committee 1959, 2:508; US Central Intelligence Agency 1958a.
[56] The final text of the Chiang-Dulles joint communiqué of October 1958 can be found at US Office of the Historian 1996a, 442–443.
[57] Jian 2001, 199–202.

rumored secret dealings across the Strait, all reinforced the impression that Chiang Kai-shek had to comply with US wishes regarding the troubled offshore islands, and that he had no other recourse than to adhere to his American patrons. This may be true, but the Chinese Communists also decided that a continued Nationalist presence on the offshore islands would best serve their interests. It would demonstrate to the world that the unfinished CCP-KMT conflict remained a domestic issue, and both entities across the Strait were interconnected under the large fabric of "one China."

Although such a "tacit consensus" (i.e., keeping the islands in Chiang's hands so as to avoid a "two Chinas" situation) did not wholly rule out cross-Strait tensions in the years to come, it did marginalize the offshore islands and prevent them from becoming a major source of potential military confrontation between Washington, Beijing, and Taipei. In April 1960, Chiang Kai-shek was annoyed by a US intelligence report that Mao might renew the shelling of Quemoy and Matsu as a way to "congratulate" Chiang on his reelection as the ROC president.[58] It took a timely, secret letter from Cao Juren to assure the Chiangs, father and son, that no military actions were imminent in the foreseeable future and that Beijing's stance toward the islands remained unchanged.[59] Indeed, nothing precipitous would happen that spring.

When President Eisenhower visited Taiwan on June 18, 1960, the PLA resumed its massive bombardment of Quemoy as way of protest.[60] The resumed shelling quickly led to a new round of policy reexamination within the State Department. The focal point was whether Washington should bring up with Chiang the old subject of evacuating the offshore islands or whether the United States should decide which of the islands was to be defended (excluding a few relatively sizable, isolated isles separate from the Quemoy and Matsu groups which Taipei was determined to defend).[61] It took the State Department almost two months to conclude, on August 5, that it was contrary to American interests to induce Taipei to abandon the offshore islands.[62] But before that, in July, Zhou Enlai had secretly reassured Taipei via Hong Kong channels that Beijing did not intend to reverse its current stance and to occupy the islands.[63]

While the "tacit consensus" over the status of KMT-held offshore islands remained effective across the Strait, issues surrounding these islands continued to dominate America's domestic politics. During the 1960 presidential campaign, the Democratic candidate John F. Kennedy openly stated that the United

---

[58] This piece of intelligence was conveyed to Ching-kuo by Ray S. Cline. See CKSD April 16, 23, and May 5, 1960; CCKD April 11 and May 2, 1960.
[59] Li 1993, 368–369; US Central Intelligence Agency 1971, 23–24.
[60] US Department of State 2001, reel 1, no. 793.00/6–1760; US Department of State 2001, reel 1, no. 793.00/6–1960.
[61] US Department of State 2001, reel 2, no. 793.00/6–2060; US Department of State 2001, reel 11, no. 793.5/7–1460.
[62] US Department of State 1960, reel 11.   [63] Tong 1996, 276.

States should not defend Quemoy and Matsu simply because they were "symbols of freedom," whereas the Republican candidate Richard Nixon had argued for US protection of the islands as part of the fight against communism. Chiang rebuffed the Kennedy line by repeating that his government would fight to the death for Quemoy and Matsu. "Naïve," "near-sightedness," and "impractical" were some of the terms Chiang used privately to characterize the young Democratic presidential candidate in his diary.[64]

Policy debates over the offshore islands went on to become one of the new Democratic administration's key tasks immediately after Kennedy took office. As the youngest president ever elected in American history, Kennedy promised the American people a "New Frontier," a new approach to government policy initiatives. Under such a political aura, Kennedy's foreign policy and national security advisors saw an opportunity to implement a new China policy, one that sought to establish a new basis for US–Taiwan relations under which Washington would be willing to support Chiang's government in Taiwan, but not his mainland ambitions. Among the new proposals put forward by the State Department was one to persuade Chiang to evacuate the offshore islands as an inducement for Washington's allies to share the commitment to defend Taiwan. If successful in getting Chiang to abandon the islands, Kennedy's aides saw the liquidation of a potentially dangerous confrontation and a means whereby the China-Taiwan conflict might be turned into "a period of a de facto peace, with a hundred miles of blue water between the contestants, in which the needed free-world consensus about Taiwan's right to a separate future might grow."[65]

By July 1961, a draft proposal entitled "Contingency Planning for Possible Renewed Chinese Communist Attack on the Offshore Islands" was carefully discussed and debated among White House and State Department staff. It concluded by clearly defining that US national interests lay in the withdrawal of Nationalist forces from the islands.[66] Ultimately, no concrete action was undertaken on the part of Washington to force Chiang to change the status quo of the offshore islands, especially as the US military establishment still argued for the importance of keeping the islands in Nationalist hands.[67]

More significant from a historical point of view, policy debates and discussions over the Nationalist-held offshore islands in the early months of the Kennedy administration turned out to be the last serious involvement in the issue by the US government except for a brief interlude in the summer of 1962. Beijing's loss of interest in taking control of the islands was certainly the direct consequence of a much quieter offshore situation. The rationale behind the Chinese Communists was probably multifaceted, such as a growing confidence

---

[64] Taylor 2009, 509–510; CKSD October 17 and 28, 1960.
[65] US Office of the Historian 1996b, 27–28, 48–49.
[66] US Office of the Historian 1996b, 93–94.   [67] McGhee 1961, reel 1.

in PRC military technology allowing the PLA to launch a direct attack on Taiwan while bypassing the offshore islands, and the fear that any military movement against the islands in the south would generate an adverse impact on China's northern defenses vis-à-vis the increasingly hostile Soviet Unions.[68] And, of course, the secret cross-Strait communications and the KMT-CCP tacit understanding, generated during the 1958 crisis, certainly played a role in reducing the importance of the issue so that it ceased to be a critical factor in the triangular relationship.

What does the story of the offshore island crises in the 1950s inform observers of contemporary cross-Taiwan Strait issues? It might be reasonable to argue that the relationship between China and Taiwan will be peaceful when both sides have a general consensus about what "China" really means, or at least when both sides agree to disagree as in the so-called 1992 Consensus. Tensions will become inevitable, when the definition of "China" is faced with a fundamental shift. The shift which China most fears is one in which Taiwan moves openly toward de facto or de jure independence. Such concerns mirror what was revealed in our analysis of the earlier Straits crises: that the CCP feared above all outcomes such as an abandonment of the islands that would suggest a two-China reality. In that regard, the underlying concerns of the two sides remain surprisingly constant even if the larger context has shifted. The situation is likely to become even worse when such a change involves superpowers like the United States. Given the different background of time and space, the stories discussed in this chapter might bear little resemblance of what is happening today in the Taiwan Strait area. But one should never forget that sometimes the nature and essence of a tension or conflict will never change.

---

[68] Cao Juren first conveyed such a rationale to Nationalist Chinese high officials in the spring of 1960. See Li 1993, 368–369; US Central Intelligence Agency 1971, 23–24.

12 Alliances, State-Building, and Development in Asia

James Lee

After the Korean War, the United States sought to contain the spread of Communism by concluding alliance treaties in Asia, which formed a "hub-and-spokes" system of bilateral alliances with the United States at the center.[1] It might seem that this system, which has often been contrasted with the multilateral alliance system in Europe, gave the United States preponderant influence.[2] But the reality was more complex, because US allies were able to exploit their strategic importance, the United States' perceptions of their vulnerability, and the United States' overriding concern with the containment of Communism to exert leverage over the United States. At times there were open arguments in which the United States was forced to accept compromises; but more often there were partnerships in which US allies were able to direct foreign aid, as well as other US resources, to advance their own interests. In an argument that resonates with Robert Keohane's observation about the "big influence of small allies," Taehyun Kim and Chang Jae Baik have characterized South Korea's policy as "taming and tamed by the United States."[3]

This chapter shifts the standard lens on the alliances to examine how the United States became involved in state-building and economic development as part of its strategy for containing Communism in Asia. US alliances did not only involve treaties and the forward deployment of US forces but also vast programs of economic assistance, overseen by a bureaucratic machinery staffed with American advisors, that became the vehicle for institutional reform. Much of the literature on this topic has focused on US relations with

---

[1] Much of the archival evidence for this chapter draws on the author's dissertation research, which was supported by a grant from the Lynde and Harry Bradley Foundation.
[2] On the contrast with multilateralism with Europe, see Hemmer and Katzenstein 2002. Victor Cha (2016) advances an explanation for US alliances in Asia that emphasizes the United States' desire to restrain irredentism in Taiwan and South Korea.
[3] Keohane 1971; Kim and Baik 2011.

individual countries.[4] This chapter takes a broader perspective by examining the role of these programs in the United States' regional strategy as well as the development strategies that US allies actually pursued. It also identifies the limits and opportunities for US influence and shows how allies knew how to turn a weak hand into a hard bargain. The countries considered to be under the greatest threat from the Chinese Communists received a high level of development assistance, but that same condition of vulnerability also shielded them from US pressure, leading the United States to focus on development strategy as an area where meaningful bargains could be made. By highlighting the interdependence of national security and political economy, this chapter shows how alliances in Asia were maintained through both military and economic commitments. As a result of those commitments, development strategy became a way for the United States to defend its geopolitical interests and for US allies to secure their domestic political interests, shaping the creation of the developmental state and the economic divergence between Northeast and Southeast Asia.

12.1 Alliances and State-Building

The United States created the hub-and-spokes alliance system in Asia in response to the Korean War, which marked a dramatic escalation in the threat posed by the international Communist movement.[5] President Truman stated on June 27, 1950, that "the attack upon Korea makes it plain beyond all doubt that Communism has passed beyond the use of subversion to conquer independent nations and will now use armed invasion and war."[6] An explicit commitment by the United States to take action in response to armed attack was now deemed necessary. NSC 48/5 defined a strategic objective of maintaining the "off-shore defense line" extending from Japan to New Zealand and, separately, upholding the security of Taiwan and South Korea. Pursuant to that end, the United States defined a role in regional security that, in a remarkable five-year period, would coalesce into the hub-and-spokes system of bilateral alliances.[7] Washington made a credible threat to Communist countries that attempting to repeat the invasion of June 1950 would trigger another US response.

Yet there were still fears that attempts at subversion would continue. The fact that Communist countries had openly employed new instruments of aggression

---

[4] Cullather 1996; Dower 1999; Brazinsky 2007.
[5] The international Communist movement was perceived to be monolithic at the time. For example, an intelligence estimate produced in the State Department on June 25, 1950, stated that "the North Korean Government is completely under Kremlin control and there is no possibility that the North Koreans acted without prior instruction from Moscow. The move against South Korea must therefore be considered a Soviet move" (Estimates Group 1976).
[6] Truman 1976.   [7] Lay 1977.

did not mean that they had abandoned old ones. Even though the Soviet leadership declared a policy of "peaceful coexistence" after the death of Stalin in 1953, Beijing's subsequent decision to initiate a crisis over Quemoy and Matsu dispelled any notion of its willingness to adhere to the status quo. US officials feared that the Chinese Communists would seek to undermine US allies by employing tactics below the threshold that would trigger US retaliation.[8] The United States could deter the use of military force, but how would it deter the use of subversion, coercion, or economic and psychological warfare?

The question was how to build what is now called resilience. Addressing these kinds of nontraditional security threats involved identifying sources of domestic discontent that could spiral out of control if they continued to fester. Under that scenario, allies facing domestic pressure would distance themselves from the United States, and drift closer to Communism; or their governments would be undermined from within. As late as 1960, US officials warned in NSC 6008/1 that the Socialist Party in Japan was "dominated by extreme left-wing elements advocating a Communist-oriented neutralism" and that "if Japan's trade relationship with the United States significantly deteriorated, the Japanese leadership would consider a shift toward reliance on the Communist bloc to be the only alternative."[9]

The challenge was developing a long-term, self-sustaining response to the vulnerabilities that US allies faced. The United States did not consider Australia and New Zealand to be under a significant threat, and its efforts to uphold their security were limited to defense cooperation under the aegis of ANZUS.[10] But in Northeast and Southeast Asia, US interventions exhibited much greater variation, as threat assessments varied. In the Philippines, the United States saw the threat not as subversion but as an armed insurgency, which it believed (wrongly) had evaporated as early as 1952; this belief led the United States to abandon many of the ambitious proposals it had originally developed to promote Philippine development.[11] Among allies that faced the most acute nontraditional security threats, the United States took an active role in state-building to promote economic development and improve the quality of governance. It failed in South Vietnam, but succeeded in Japan, South Korea, and Taiwan, helping to lay the foundations for what scholars would later call the "developmental state."

For allies that faced particularly acute security threats, it was not enough for the United States to "deliver" a certain level of economic or military aid, or to

---

[8] See Dulles 1986b and Rostow 1985, 14–16.   [9] National Security Council 1994.
[10] On the perceived lack of a significant Communist subversive threat in Australia, see US Department of State 1976; on the perceived lack of a significant Communist subversive threat in New Zealand, see US Department of State 1977.
[11] Lee 2020b. On the history of Communism in the Philippines, see Kunio 1994, 157–160.

help its allies to achieve a certain level of growth. Direct assistance was costly, and the United States could not afford (literally) to underwrite the stability of the region. Washington came under pressure to develop a long-term response to the threat of subversion, economic coercion, and psychological warfare that would not involve indefinite commitments of US aid. Externally, this meant sponsoring economic and political cooperation among US allies, which ironically led to an ever-widening set of US commitments and an ever-growing set of "dominoes," as Michael Schaller and Andrew Rotter have shown. In particular, the United States sought to create markets for Japan in Southeast Asia that would obviate the need for US assistance over the long term.[12]

Internally, US interventions involved helping to create institutions that would deliver a level of economic growth and a quality of governance that, if far from democratic, would not prove to be so insufferable as to provoke rebellion or defection. Richard Doner, Bryan Ritchie, and Dan Slater have argued that the developmental states of East Asia responded to a domestic need to deliver side payments to potentially "restive popular sectors" among countries that were also externally vulnerable.[13] Supplementing their argument from the perspective of US strategy (whose significance is arguably underappreciated in their theory), these developmental states also served the United States' interest in helping its allies to respond to nontraditional security threats. Accordingly, the United States played a significant role in the creation of the developmental states in East Asia, as I have argued elsewhere, belying the notion that the "Washington Consensus" of laissez-faire economics has been a hallmark of US foreign policy.[14] Then, as now, the United States has proven more willing and able to support industrial policies during times of vulnerability and acute strategic competition.[15]

Developmental states did not arise across the region. The Philippines and South Vietnam present a striking contrast with US allies in Northeast Asia in terms of their long-term economic development. Although proposals for state-led industrialization were floated and tested in Southeast Asia as well, the United States proved less willing (in the case of the Philippines) or less able (in the case of South Vietnam) to invest the necessary resources for turning those proposals into a reality. Yet all of these cases show that state-led industrialization was a strategic option for the United States to defend its allies and partners in Asia, regardless of whether or not it decided to exercise that option or how effectively it did so.

---

[12] Rotter 1987; Schaller 1997.   [13] Doner, Ritchie, and Slater 2005.
[14] Lee 2020b. Richard Stubbs also discusses the United States' support for state-led development in East Asia in the context of the Cold War, though he places more emphasis on the impact of the Korean War and the Vietnam War (Stubbs 2005).
[15] On current US support for industrial policy, see Atlantic Council 2021.

12.2 Strategic Competition with the Chinese Communists

To form a more comprehensive picture of US strategy, it is necessary to consider the principal challenge the United States faced in Asia during the first half of the Cold War. The United States' involvement in the security and development of Asia was an outgrowth of its strategic competition with the Chinese Communists. Although the Soviet Union was the United States' principal adversary in the Cold War, the People's Republic of China was still a formidable adversary. NSC 166/1 stated that "the primary problem of U.S. foreign policy in the Far East is to cope with the altered structure of power which arises from the existence of a strong and hostile Communist China, and from the alliance of Communist China with the USSR."[16] With the United States' sphere of influence extending along China's periphery, Washington's strategy centered on both deterrence and resilience: deterring Beijing from a military venture, especially in the Taiwan Strait; and strengthening the ability of US allies to resist Beijing's efforts at economic coercion, psychological warfare, and subversion.

The hub-and-spokes system helped the United States to achieve its first objective. It was, in effect, an encirclement of China to prevent further Communist expansion in Asia.[17] But alliances were not enough. As much as the hub-and-spokes system rested on the United States' network of forward-deployed forces, US officials also considered the security of Asian allies to be dependent on perceptions. Not only was there the risk of subversion but there was also the risk that US allies might disengage from the alliance system altogether in favor of a posture of neutrality. On the first day of the Korean War, an intelligence estimate produced in the State Department warned that "failure of the United States to take any action in Korea would strengthen existing widespread desire for neutrality" in Japan; that "the tendency for flight or defection to the Communists would increase, military morale and governmental efficiency would deteriorate, and prospects for a Communist take-over would greatly improve" in Taiwan; and that Communist subversion would spread in Southeast Asia because of the belief in a "Communist destiny." Even though the vital question of the hour on June 25, 1950, was US military intervention in the Korean Peninsula, the implications of that decision hinged on subjective factors like "feelings of vulnerability," "confidence," "morale," and the "general will to resist."[18] The United States' formal commitment to its allies' security may have provided a significant degree of assurance, but whether or not those allies saw that commitment as still being in their interest remained an open question. US officials were determined to limit the appeal of

---

[16] National Security Council 1985a. [17] See National Security Council 1985a.
[18] Estimates Group 1976.

the "outside option," whether in the form of a declaration of neutrality or outright defection to Communism.

State-building and economic development became a prominent feature of US strategy in Asia, for both material and nonmaterial reasons. The material reason was that economic stability was an important adjunct to political stability and military readiness, enabling US allies to balance against the threat of Communism. NSC 166/2, a statement of US policy toward Taiwan from 1953, concluded that "some economic aid will probably be required so long as the present military programs are continued." The United States did not want to maintain economic stability through disbursements of US aid indefinitely, however.[19] NSC 166/2 also stated that over the long term, one of the goals of US policy should be to "assist the Chinese National Government to develop a well-balanced foreign trade which will meet the needs of the Formosan economy after the termination of U.S. economic assistance."[20] Hence, state-building and economic development served the material objective of enabling US allies to provide for their own security.

But there was also a nonmaterial reason for these interventions. Conditions of prosperity, especially those that were self-sustaining, could bolster allies' legitimacy, morale, and will to resist. NSC 5503 stated that a "constructive social and economic program" in Taiwan would help to enable the Nationalists "to deserve the support and allegiance of the people of Formosa and to serve as the focal point of the free Chinese alternative to Communism."[21] Stated in negative terms, there was a risk that economic instability would lead to subversion, a causal belief that Ethan Kapstein has called "grievance theory."[22] An interagency working group on South Korea warned in 1955 that "should this economic situation deteriorate substantially, or should a chaotic political situation develop, the Communists might be able to exploit their potential assets for subversion."[23] Economic growth was not only a way of financing military expenditures but also an indicator of performance and legitimacy.

At a more fundamental level of strategy, the United States' involvement in state-building and economic development in Asia was a corollary of its decision to contain the PRC, rather than seek a posture of either accommodation or outright hostility. In the spring of 1950, the Truman administration had contemplated recognition of the Chinese Communists; during the Korean War, there had been some exploratory studies and contingency planning for supporting a Nationalist offensive against the Chinese mainland so as to draw PLA

---

[19] Haggard and Zheng 2013, 440. [20] National Security Council 1985b.
[21] National Security Council 1986. [22] Kapstein 2017.
[23] Interdepartmental Working Group 1993.

forces away from Korea.²⁴ But by 1953, the Eisenhower administration had decided against any of these extremes. NSC 166/1 listed three policies that were "currently unacceptable to the United States": they included "the overthrow or replacement of the Chinese Communist regime by the use of U.S. armed force," "support with U.S. forces of an attempt by the Chinese Government on Formosa forcibly to overthrow the Chinese regime," and "concessions to Communist China designed to overcome the regime's basic hostility to the West." Opting for a strategy of containment, NSC 166/1 concluded that US policy should "reduce the relative power position of Communist China in Asia: primarily by developing the political, economic and military strength of non-Communist Asian countries."²⁵ The prominence of state-building and development in US strategy was a direct consequence of the fact that US officials believed that the United States could not neutralize its strategic competitor with military force. This was an important reason why US strategy in Asia was different from US strategy in Latin America and Africa, in which military interventions and covert operations featured much more prominently.²⁶

The United States ultimately proved to have a mixed track record in this area. In Northeast Asia, US aid programs played a significant role in the creation of developmental states. US efforts to supervise development planning – often with a view to circumventing corruption in allied governments – enhanced the autonomy of economic bureaucracies and provided them with policy instruments for steering resources toward strategic industries, whether they were state-owned enterprises or private enterprises that were state-favored. In Southeast Asia, US programs were far less successful, either because American officials considered development to be less important for US interests or because the political obstacles were too great. In the Philippines, there was initially an ambitious plan for creating a developmental state at the time when the Huk Rebellion seemed to pose its greatest threat; but after the defeat of the Huks in 1954, the United States scaled back its programs in favor of maintaining a minimal level of stability. In South Vietnam, the United States also sought to promote state-led economic development under the guidance of an economic planning agency, but failed because of insuperable obstacles. As the historian Andrew Gawthorpe writes, "there was ultimately only so far the GVN [Government of Viet Nam] could be pushed."²⁷

Yet the same could be said of all US allies, though some allies were more receptive to US advice and had greater institutional capacity for implementing that advice. The relative success of the United States' programs in Northeast

---

²⁴ On the debate about recognizing the Chinese Communists, see Christensen 1996, 77–137. On the United States' contingency planning for supporting a Nationalist counteroffensive, see Lin 2016, 196–215.
²⁵ National Security Council 1985a.   ²⁶ Lee 2020b, 741–746.   ²⁷ Gawthorpe 2018, 187.

Asia did not evince a lack of agency on the part of the governments of Japan, South Korea, and Taiwan; nor did the United States evince a consistent grasp of the "best" policies for its allies' development. The creation of the developmental states of Northeast Asia involved adaptation and bargaining, with Washington often forced to back down when its desired policies infringed on its allies' conceptions of their vital interests. The United States could deter its allies from certain actions, but they too could deter the United States, channeling American power down a course that ultimately led toward planned capitalism.

12.3 State-Building, Development, and US Strategy in Asia

In both Northeast Asia and Southeast Asia, there were US plans to support state-led development under the guidance of economic planning agencies.[28] Though this may seem anathema to the notion of the "Washington Consensus" of the 1980s, it proceeded from an attempt to secure US interests. At the start of the Cold War, US allies needed an emergency infusion of foreign exchange in the form of US aid. To ensure that its aid was being used effectively, the United States required its allies to integrate aid spending into a national development plan; and that requirement naturally led to the additional requirement that its allies develop and maintain planning agencies. For example, in December 1948, the United States presented a statement to the Far Eastern Commission that outlined the actions it was undertaking in Japan: the Occupation authorities would "assure rigorous limitation of credit extension to projects contributing to economic recovery of Japan"; "improve the effectiveness of the present allocation and rationing system, particularly to the end of maximizing exports"; and "tighten existing foreign exchange controls, to the extent that such measures can be appropriately be delegated to Japanese agencies."[29] By 1952, those controls became, in Chalmers Johnson's words, "the single most important instrument of guidance and industrial control that MITI ever possessed."[30] Similar policies unfolded in Taiwan and South Korea, where US aid helped to create autonomous bureaucracies, such as the Council on US Aid (in Taiwan) and the Ministry of Reconstruction (in South Korea), that coordinated with US aid agencies.[31] Comparable plans also existed for the Philippines and South Vietnam, though they were never implemented as effectively as the plans in Northeast Asia.[32]

---

[28] See also Stubbs 2005.   [29] United States Government 1974.
[30] Johnson 1982, 194–195; see also Lee 2020b, 746.
[31] Haggard, Kim, and Moon 1991, 855; Lee 2020a, 472–473.
[32] On plans for state-led development in the Philippines, see United States Economic Survey Mission to the Philippines 1950, 66–69. On plans for South Vietnam, see Joint Development Group 1969, 152–153.

The United States' support for economic planning also had a long-term objective: enable its allies to substitute export revenue for US aid as a source of foreign exchange. Much of the planning centered on how dollars would be spent, and the United States needed to ensure that its allies would be able to earn their own dollars after the end of the US programs, or else its allies would suffer an economic collapse that could trigger Communist subversion. When NSC 166/2 stated that one of the goals of US policy should be to "assist the Chinese National Government to develop a well-balanced foreign trade which will meet the needs of the Formosan economy after the termination of U.S. economic assistance," it was referring to foreign exchange.[33] Broadly speaking, US support for planned capitalism was a policy of rationing foreign exchange and overseeing a developmental transition that would obviate the need for direct US economic assistance. While previous studies have raised the connection between the United States' support for export-led growth and its interest in reducing the level of aid, they have presented these policies as a response to exigencies (such as problems with the balance of payments or a change of administration in the United States) in the period from the mid-1950s to the early 1960s.[34] But, as shown in NSC 166/2, a statement of policy from 1953, having export revenue eventually replace US aid as a source of foreign exchange had been an objective of US strategy from an early point in the Cold War.

The question remains as to how much leverage the United States exerted over its allies, and how much agency US allies were able to exercise themselves. The answer to this question necessarily varies, and it can be broken down into three categories of allies: cases in which the United States ultimately succeeded in helping to create highly successful models of state-led industrialization (Japan, South Korea, and Taiwan); the case in which the United States saw an opportunity to promote state-led industrialization but decided not to (the Philippines); and the case in which the United States attempted to promote state-led industrialization but ultimately failed (South Vietnam). For the developmental states of Northeast Asia, the United States exercised considerable leverage, but within limits. When one considers the fact that Japan was formally under occupation – the fact that the United States financed almost the entirety of Taiwan's current account deficit between 1951 and 1962, and the fact that 75 percent of South Korea's fixed capital formation was a direct consequence of US aid – it may come as a surprise that these allies exercised much agency at all.[35] Yet the material facts of these relationships do not serve as a reliable measure of power. For all of these cases, the United States was

---

[33] National Security Council 1985b.
[34] Haggard and Zheng 2013, 440; Haggard 1990, 98; Haggard, Kim, and Moon 1991, 850–851.
[35] Haggard 1990, 84.

dependent on its allies for implementing the policies it desired. In Japan, for example, Sheldon Garon writes that "the Americans undeniably set the broad policy outlines," but that Japanese bureaucrats were responsible for putting those policies into practice; and the Occupation actually strengthened the Ministry of Labor and MITI by weakening rival centers of power, such as the military.[36] And it may be said for all of the developmental states of Northeast Asia that there was not an imposition of the United States' favored policies from the outside, but rather a convergence between the United States' preferences and established traditions of mercantilism.

Further insight into the relative weight of American hegemony and allied agency may be found by considering historical episodes in which overtly conflicting preferences were brought to the fore. In the case of South Korea, these episodes appeared periodically during the presidency of Syngman Rhee, and during the early years of the junta that gave rise to the presidency of Park Chung Hee. A vivid example of the tension between US and South Korean officials during this period can be found in a 1956 letter from Paik Too Chin (the Economic Coordinator for South Korea) to Tyler Wood (the Economic Coordinator for the United Nations Command). Referring to Wood's criticism of South Korea's administration of PL 480 procurements, Paik complained that Wood's "letter seems to me to be so provocative and unfriendly in tone" and said that Wood's accusation of Paik "hurts me deeply." In conclusion, Paik stated that "the main object of this letter is to make it quite clear that your friendly cooperation is welcome and deeply appreciated; but, to be quite frank with you, carping criticism is not."[37] Despite its dependence on US aid, the Rhee government did not yield to US pressure to develop closer economic relations with Japan. The United States did succeed in fostering economic planning through the creation of the Combined Economic Board; but the South Korean economic bureaucracy was not autonomous from the political system, in which clientelism was endemic.[38] Assessing the Rhee era as a whole, Gregg Brazinsky writes that "until his regime was overthrown in 1960, Rhee managed to utilize the ROK's vital strategic position to ignore American advice."[39]

After Park Chung Hee came to power, there was greater consistency between US and South Korean objectives in the area of state-building and economic development. But that consistency only cohered after an initial period of turmoil in the bilateral relationship, which showed both the opportunities and the limits of US leverage. After the coup in May 1961, the United States exerted pressure on the junta to agree on a timetable for restoring civilian rule. When

---

[36] Johnson 1982, 157–197; Garon 1984, 447.   [37] Too-Chin 1956.
[38] Combined Economic Board 1953; Haggard, Kim, and Moon 1991, 852, 855.
[39] Brazinsky 2005, 85.

the Kennedy administration discovered in March 1963 that Park planned to hold a referendum for continuing martial law for another four years, it delivered a formal protest, and the junta backed down.[40] In economic policy, as well, the United States was able to deter the junta from adopting extreme courses of action. When the junta attempted to extract funds for state-owned enterprises by nationalizing citizens' savings in 1962, US officials denounced the plan as "the greatest financial coup in Korean history" and issued "strong representations on our part as to its economic effects."[41] After the United States threatened to cut off aid, Park shelved the plan.[42] Contrary to the prevalent view that Park wished to pursue export-led growth under a capitalist model from the beginning (a view that John Lie has called a "retrospective construct"), the model enshrined in the Second Five-Year Plan developed over time.[43] It reflected a considerable degree of US pressure, as well as US assistance. Joel Bernstein, who was appointed director of the USAID mission in South Korea in 1964, later summarized US aid policy as including the following provisions: "improvement in economic policies and in economic planning"; "realistic exchange rates coupled with removal of trade controls"; "heavy stress on development of exports as lead sector for economic growth"; and a "modernized structure for economic planning, budgeting, and monetary management."[44] When Robert Nathan, a consultant for USAID, had an opportunity to observe the program in South Korea firsthand, he remarked that the economic bureaucracy was "a kind of joint venture" between Washington and Seoul.[45]

US influence should not be overstated, however. The United States did not pressure South Korea into adopting a development model it did not want, but channeled it toward a model that was acceptable to both parties. As Atul Kohli reminds us, this model of state-led development was not simply created in the early Cold War, but established on the basis of a deeper historical legacy from the period of Japanese colonial rule.[46] Considered together, the Rhee and Park eras in South Korea suggest that the extent of US hegemony and allied agency can be summarized in the following terms: the United States could influence the tactics that its ally used to pursue its ally's interests, but the United States could not change how its ally defined those interests. For all of the pressure emanating from Washington, the United States could not fundamentally change the patrimonial character of the South Korean state during the Rhee era. The fact that South Korea began pursuing an export-led growth strategy during the 1960s was not only because of a fundamental shift in US policy but also because of a change of regime within South Korea that saw development

[40] Kim and Baik 2011, 71–72.   [41] "US Relations with the Korean Military Junta," 1963.
[42] Kim 2011, 103.   [43] Lie 1998, 55–56.
[44] "Memorandum on DAC Comments on Program Evaluation," 1968.
[45] Quoted in Brazinsky 2005, 90.   [46] Kohli 2004.

become an integral element of national security.[47] Once the junta was in power, the United States succeeded in exerting pressure over the means, not the end, of pursuing development.

A similar pattern developed in the case of United States' relations with Taiwan. As with other allies and security partners, the United States planned to gradually phase out aid as Taiwan earned foreign exchange from export revenue. Pursuant to that end, Washington used the bureaucratic machinery of the US aid program to enhance economic planning in Taiwan's government (such as the Council on US Aid and the Economic Stabilization Board).[48] But it faced an obstacle: the Nationalists' paramount objective was the counteroffensive against the Chinese Communists, and that objective assumed such an overriding importance that Taipei would not make long-range plans for development.[49] Applying pressure or leverage would not have succeeded in changing the Nationalists' minds, if US assessments were correct. Ever since the Korean War, US officials had been concerned about the risk of the Nationalists defecting to the Chinese Communists if there was a collapse of morale in Taiwan. Starting in 1955, this concern became more prominent among US officials when Allen Dulles, the Director of Central Intelligence, warned of the risk of subversion in a memorandum to Secretary of State John Foster Dulles. Observing that "since 1949 the hope for a 'return to the mainland' has been an important cohesive factor among the Chinese Nationalists," Dulles listed pessimism about the likelihood of a successful counteroffensive as a factor that would raise the risk of subversion. Dulles believed that this was true both for the mainlanders who had fled to Taiwan with the Nationalists and for the local Taiwanese who had been there before.[50] According to this reasoning, if the United States pressured the Nationalists to give up on the hope of returning to the mainland, it would have led to the loss of Taiwan to the Chinese Communists. As I have argued elsewhere, the United States' policy for resolving this dilemma was to persuade the Nationalists to think of the notion of a "counteroffensive" as an ideological competition rather than a military campaign. By showcasing economic prosperity in Taiwan, the Nationalists could compete with the Chinese Communists for legitimacy and achieve self-reliance.[51] Compared to US relations with South Korea, US relations with Taiwan exhibited less conflict and coercion.[52]

---

[47] On the role of modernization in Park's ideology and conception of national security, see Moon and Jun 2011.
[48] Haggard 1990, 86–87.
[49] An analysis of the Nationalists' strategic objectives and their implications for economic policy can be found in Sturm 1959.
[50] Dulles (1986a [16 March 1955, Document 159]). See also Garver 1997, 126–127.
[51] Lee 2020a. [52] Haggard 1990, 84.

Alliances, State-Building, and Development in Asia 237

There were still limits to the United States' influence on Taiwan. In October 1958 (in the context of the Second Taiwan Strait Crisis), the Eisenhower administration attempted to convince the KMT to tone down its rhetoric about a counteroffensive. After John Foster Dulles delivered his talking points to Chiang Kai-shek, Huang Shao-Ku, the ROC Foreign Minister, retorted that "the suggestion advanced by Secretary Dulles appears to be of such a nature as almost to shake the foundation of the Republic of China," and that "any suggestion by this Government which suggests its contentment with its present status of exile" would be "suicidal."[53] Ultimately, the October 23 Joint Communiqué stated that ideological competition (Sun Yat-sen's "Three Principles of the People," which included economic development) would be the Nationalists' "principal means" for the "restoration of freedom to its people on the mainland," rather than the use of force.[54] In saying that it would rely primarily – but not exclusively – on ideological competition to achieve its interests, Taipei conceded to Washington on tactics and points of emphasis but not on fundamental interests. Washington, on the other hand, secured a statement from Taipei that downplayed the use of force against the PRC, which Washington was not willing to support. As with the case of South Korea, this episode shows that the United States had leverage over Taiwan, but that Taiwan also exercised agency. The combination of US pressure and Nationalist opposition resulted in a compromise that enabled both Washington and Taipei to pursue their interests through state-building and economic development.[55]

These cases were not typical. If the United States helped its Northeast Asian allies to achieve high rapid economic development, the United States' pursuit of self-interest elsewhere in Asia was decidedly less enlightened. Washington's consistent support for economic development in Japan, South Korea, and Taiwan was predicated on the belief that those allies faced long-term security threats, especially in the form of economic coercion, psychological warfare, and subversion. In the Philippines, by contrast, US officials believed that the Communist insurgency known as the Huk Rebellion was not particularly serious. An assessment by the Joint Chiefs of Staff in September 1950 stated that "the ultimate objective of the 'Peoples [sic] Liberation Army' undoubtedly is the overthrow of the Philippine Republic and the substitution of

---

[53] Department of State 1996a.
[54] Department of State 1996b. Jay Taylor interprets the reference to "principal means" to mean that Dulles "totally capitulated" on pressuring Chiang to renounce the use of force (Taylor 2011, 500). But this seems to be an overstatement. The language of the Joint Communiqué was not as explicit as the language of Dulles' initial talking points; but in the record of his conversations with Chiang Kai-shek and his cable to President Eisenhower, Dulles appeared to believe that he had secured a real concession. See section 8 of Dulles 1996a; Department of State 1996c; and Dulles 1996b.
[55] Jacoby 1966.

a Communist regime. On the basis of military factors alone, the Huks lack the capability to achieve this objective."[56] By August 1952, NSC 152/3 confidently concluded that "the Communist Hukbalahap movement in the Philippines was broken during the past year and is no longer considered to be a major threat to the stability of the government."[57] US estimates in the early 1950s concluded that the Communist threat had passed.[58]

This threat assessment had a significant impact on the United States' interest in supporting development in the Philippines. As I have argued elsewhere, the United States' support for industrialization and land reform declined significantly over the course of the 1950s. It refrained from exercising the kind of pressure and skillful diplomacy that contributed to state-led industrialization in South Korea and Taiwan.[59] Nick Cullather concludes that "U.S. policies made crony capitalism possible, but could also threaten it." This prompted a response on the Filipino side "to prevent those policies from interfering with their plans, to use the strategic value of their country as leverage, to create room for autonomous action."[60] It was conspicuous that the United States was not making a determined effort to promote development: US aid officials gave their Philippine counterparts a veto over the allocation of aid; that aid was given to government officials rather than private enterprise; and the funds were siphoned off as patronage.[61] They decided not to make the kinds of interventions that proved to be successful elsewhere, because they concluded that it was not in their interest to do so.

US policies sometimes became blatantly cynical. In September 1952 (just after the National Security Council reported its assessment of the Huk threat in NSC 152/3), US Ambassador Raymond Spruance sent a letter to Secretary of State Dean Acheson arguing that it was not in the United States' interest to support industrialization in the Philippines. In a chain of reasoning with colonial overtones, Spruance stated:

> To be kept out of the Communist camp, Japan must be able to trade with the free nations and obtain the materials and the markets needed to support her ever increasing population ... if all of the free countries of the Far East industrialized to the limit of their capacities and failed to increase their capacity for the production of food and raw materials, the result might be the forcing of Japan into the arms of the Communists ... it follows that our major effort should go to clearing up the basic land problems and not to pushing the industrialization of the Philippines.[62]

Besides the acknowledgment of receipt of the letter – which referred to "very active consideration" of the proposal at the interagency level and stated that the Bureau of Far Eastern Affairs was "much impressed" by Spruance's argument – there is no record of an official response from Dean Acheson or the State

[56] Johnson 1976. [57] Harriman 1983. [58] Kunio 1994, 157–160. [59] Lee 2020b, 752–756. [60] Cullather 1994, 3–4. [61] Cullather 1994, 92. [62] Spruance 1987.

Department.[63] There is, however, a suggestive note in the original copy of the letter at the National Archives. On a routing slip dated September 15, 1952, that was used to forward the letter from the State Department to the Mutual Security Agency, someone (identified only by the initial "L.") noted: "Very interesting – esp. on Japan."[64] Two months after Spruance sent his letter, the Mutual Security Agency issued a set of guidelines for the US aid program that were consistent with his recommendations: supporting production of food and raw materials.[65] Owing to the absence of an urgent Communist security threat, the United States had relegated the Philippines to the periphery, with Japan as the industrial core.

In the case of South Vietnam, the United States attempted to support state-led industrialization but never succeeded in creating a viable developmental state. Shortly after the Johnson administration began expanding the American military presence in Vietnam, Washington and Saigon established the Joint Development Group to formulate policy recommendations. Although it was unofficial, the fact that members of the group went on to hold senior positions in the South Vietnamese government suggests that it had considerable influence. For example, in 1968, Vu Quoc Thuc became minister of state and continued to hold a supervisory position in the Joint Development Group.[66] In 1969, the group published its recommendation for the creation of an Institute of Planning and Development, with features that are instantly recognizable to observers of the developmental state:

-First, it should be a permanent group, one that would not exist at the pleasure of a particular official or by virtue of a particular and not necessarily enduring policy.

-Second, as a corollary to the above, it should be an apolitical body, so that it can preserve some independence in its approach to problems and give judgments and advice unaffected by political expediency.

-Third, it should be a thoroughly professional body of technical and economic personnel, with sufficient incentives of all kinds to its staff to persuade men of the highest qualifications and competence to make a career of development planning and implementation.

-Fourth, while it should be linked somewhat closely to decision-making in the government, and particularly to the National Planning Council, it should not be so closely linked that it would be in the position of having to undertake task order assignments to provide justification for decisions which have already been taken.

These criteria can be summarized by saying that the proposed group should be permanent, professional, and <u>reasonably</u> independent.[67]

To use Chalmers Johnson's terminology, this institute was to serve as an autonomous agency within the South Vietnamese government that would be

---

[63] Johnson 1987.   [64] Spruance 1952.   [65] Mutual Security Agency 1952.
[66] Joint Development Group 1969, x–xi.   [67] Joint Development Group 1969, 153.

insulated from political manipulation, and it would have the necessary incentives for attracting the best and brightest to serve as its personnel.

Yet the United States never succeeded in helping to create a developmental state in South Vietnam, and the proposal of the Joint Development Group ultimately proved to only be an aspiration. A comprehensive account of the failures of US policy in South Vietnam is beyond the scope of this chapter; but it is worth observing, in broad terms, that a compelling interest was not sufficient for ensuring the success of US strategy. The United States' relative success in Japan, South Korea, and Taiwan was conditioned by historical legacies that lay beyond the scope of any American policy, decision, or program; and when they became part of the United States' sphere of influence during the Cold War, their institutional endowments were more propitious than those that South Vietnam possessed. Although France also had a history of achieving state-led industrialization, its tendency to impose that model on colonial Indochina was much more limited compared to Japan's imposition of its state-led model on colonial Korea. For example, even though the colonial authorities created the Hanoi École de Droit d'Administration to train civil servants, the Hanoi École had only limited ties with the Parisian École Nationale d'Administration and did not attempt to replicate French *dirigisme* in Vietnam. Moreover, when the United States attempted to improve public administration in South Vietnam by applying modernization theory to the training of civil servants, its efforts were hampered by US officials' lack of understanding of South Vietnam's politics and history.[68] As such, the case of South Vietnam not only lends support to Atul Kohli's argument about the significance of Japanese colonialism for South Korea's developmental state but also demonstrates the limits of the United States' influence on its Cold War allies.[69]

12.4 Conclusion

This chapter has examined the political economy of the hub-and-spokes system, examining how long-term security threats led to US involvement in state-building and industrialization, while allies that did not face major threats received considerably less US support (often for decidedly cynical reasons). Assessing the relative impact of US hegemony and allies' agency, this chapter has argued that the United States could affect its allies' choice of strategy, but not how they defined their interests. Although political questions remained outside the scope of US influence, economic development proved to be an area where bargains could be made: There were often disagreements about how best to achieve development, but the goal of development was shared. This chapter

[68] Elkind 2016, 59–65.   [69] Atul Kohli 2004.

has also argued that the United States did not always exercise as much influence as it could have, refraining from productive interventions when they were not perceived to be in its interest. This chapter has also suggested that the postwar development of East Asia should be seen in light of the strategic competition between the United States and the Chinese Communists. The consolidation of the developmental state reflected the United States' efforts at shoring up weak points along the periphery of China: weak in the sense that they were believed to be vulnerable to a range of security threats, both military and nonmilitary in nature. The United States succeeded in Japan, South Korea, and Taiwan, but ultimately failed in South Vietnam, and it didn't even try in the Philippines.

Both the actual and the potential range of US interventions show that state-led development was a strategic option, and that the United States viewed economic planning to be consonant with capitalism. This ideological flexibility reflected the urgency of containing Communism, but it also shows that even the United States did not always adhere to the "Washington Consensus." US aversion to industrial policy was a feature of a historical era, one that had not come into being at the beginning of the Cold War and that today is beginning to fade amid the pressure of renewed strategic competition with the PRC.[70] The successes and failures of US foreign policy during the Cold War are still relevant to contemporary international relations, not only in the field of development but also in the field of strategy. Decisions made half a century ago shaped long-term trends, such as the economic divergence between Northeast and Southeast Asia, that US officials did not anticipate at the time.

[70] Atlantic Council 2021.

13 Credibility and the US Intervention in Vietnam in the Era of Incomplete US Hegemony

Yuen Foong Khong

13.1 Credibility and the Vietnam War in the Era of Incomplete US Hegemony

> But George, wouldn't all these countries say that Uncle Sam was a paper tiger, wouldn't we lose credibility breaking the word of three presidents, if we did as you have proposed? It would seem to be an irreparable blow.

–President Lyndon Johnson's response to Undersecretary of State George Ball's proposal against US military intervention in south Vietnam, July 21, 1965.

George Ball's answer to Johnson was, "No sir. The worse blow would be that the mightiest power on earth is unable to defeat a handful of guerrillas" (Meeting on Vietnam, July 21, 1965, LBJ Library; also cited in Khong 1992, 126). That Ball's prescient counsel against intervention and his prediction about greater loss of US credibility if the United States intervened and failed to "save" south Vietnam were disregarded by the principals can be taken as indication of how strongly President Johnson and his senior advisers held to the belief that US prestige and credibility were at stake in Vietnam. Most archive-based scholarly accounts of the Johnson administration's decision to intervene in Vietnam in 1965 also give pride of place to concerns about the loss of US prestige and credibility if south Vietnam were to fall to communism.

Yet the premium that US decision-makers placed on prestige and credibility has always puzzled, as well as confounded, many scholars and practitioners: How was it that the fate of south Vietnam – "a strategically insignificant entity of the US's making eight thousand miles away" – became such an important test of US resolve and credibility? This chapter will attempt to provide an answer to this question. Consistent with this volume's motif of seeking new insights about the "logic and empirical consequences of [hierarchical] regional systems," I argue that America's position in the hierarchy of nations – its hegemonic status – in Asia in the 1950s and 1960s can shed light on this emphasis on prestige and credibility. More specifically, I argue that because US hegemony in Asia was "incomplete" – both in terms of its reach and acceptance – US policymakers became fixated on maintaining America's international prestige and the credibility of its power. Incomplete hegemony gave rise to a heightened sense of the need to protect US prestige and credibility, and Vietnam became the focus of these concerns in the 1960s. Had the reach and buy in of America's leadership in Asia been wider or greater, policymakers would have had more room to relegate Vietnam to the nonvital (to US prestige and credibility) category of international dilemmas.

The argument will proceed as follows. Section 13.1 will provide working definitions of prestige, credibility, and hegemony, followed by an assessment of the nature of US hegemony in Asia. Taking a leaf from Michael Mastanduno's (2003) insight that America's hegemony in Asia was "incomplete" in the 1990s, I suggest that US hegemony was *even more incomplete in the 1950s and 1960s* – the age of bipolarity – when the Vietnam dilemma presented itself, when even fewer countries accepted America's leadership or its vision for order in the region, given the competition of a Soviet–Chinese-inspired regional order.

Having established the incompleteness of US hegemony during its unipolar moment in Section 13.2, Section 13.3 will examine the role of prestige and credibility concerns in US decision-making during the First Indochina War (1946–54) or French–Vietminh War. Prestige and credibility concerns were invoked by those in favor of US intervention to "save" the French, but those concerns were trumped by President Eisenhower's insistence on the need for joint action with US allies. When joint action was not forthcoming, Eisenhower decided against using US air power in Vietnam.

Section 13.4 will focus on the Second Indochina War (1965–75) or "the Vietnam War," as it is commonly known in the United States. It will examine how prestige and credibility concerns played a crucial role in the lead up to the deployment of 100,000 combat troops to south Vietnam. Having "lost" north Vietnam to the Vietminh in 1954 because of Eisenhower's decision against intervention, the Johnson administration felt that US prestige and credibility would suffer an irreparable blow if, by abstaining from military intervention, south Vietnam fell to communism. Of special interest are new accounts of National Security Adviser McGeorge Bundy's take on prestige and credibility that elevate the importance of those considerations to the extent of discounting whether the United States could win in Vietnam. Section 13.5 will examine plausible alternative explanations or objects to the argument presented in this chapter. Section 13.6, the conclusion, will sketch out the implications of the argument and speculate about its general relevance.

13.2 Definitions

"Prestige," according to former Secretary of State Dean Acheson, is "the shadow cast by power" (1969, 405). Robert Gilpin, a major theorist of how struggles over the hierarchy of prestige bring about change in world politics, agrees with Acheson and elaborates: "Prestige is the reputation for power and military power in particular. ... In the language of contemporary strategic theory, prestige involves the credibility of a state's power and willingness to deter or compel other states in order to achieve its objectives" (Gilpin 1981, 31).

The reason great powers place a premium on prestige is because:

> Prestige, rather than power, is the everyday currency of international relations, much as authority is the central ordering feature of domestic society ... prestige is "enormously important" because *"if your strength* [credibility of your power] *is recognized, you can generally achieve your aims without having to use it."* It is for this reason that in the conduct of diplomacy and the resolution of conflicts ... there is actually relatively little use of overt force or, for that matter explicit threats. Rather, the bargaining among states and the outcomes of negotiations are determined principally by the relative prestige of the parties involved. (Gilpin 1981, 31)

Prestige and credibility are so closely related that strategic theorists like Gilpin and policymakers like Henry Kissinger tend to deploy the two terms together or interchangeably. One's "reputation for military power" or "the shadow cast by [one's] power" may be thought of as the perception by others, of one's power credibility, namely the confidence that others have in one's aptitude and willingness to use that power. Henry Kissinger's argument about why the United States could not just walk away from Vietnam concretizes this notion by emphasizing both [US] credibility and prestige as the lynchpin of global and regional stability:

> However fashionable it is to ridicule the terms "credibility" or "prestige," they are not empty phrases; other nationas can gear their actions to ours only if they can count on our steadiness .... In many parts of the world the Middle East, Europe, Latin American, and even Japan – stability depends on confidence in America's promise. (Kissinger, *White House Years*)

The "confidence in America's promise" – or what US-Vietnam decision-makers called "our reputation as guarantor" – takes on a special importance in the nuclear age: The success of nuclear deterrence and extended deterrence was premised on the adversary's belief that one had the will to use nuclear weapons in defense of one's vital interests. At the strategic level, therefore, "resolve" becomes important for both conventional and nuclear deterrence. Gilpin's and Kissinger's analyses of what prestige does for great powers also tells us why prestige and credibility are so highly prized: Once established, they enable the great power to obtain its objectives without having to use force (or explicit threats) most of the time. Prestige and credibility will thus prove especially invaluable to the hegemon's task of convincing others to accept its leadership and its vision of regional/global order.

That the United States emerged as the predominant global power in the post-World War II era is beyond dispute (Leffler 1993). The United States has also been widely seen as exercising hegemony over the Western hemisphere, Western Europe, the Middle East, and East Asia (Katzenstein 2005; Layne 2006, 3). Hegemony in IR parlance means more than economic-military predominance; it must also entail the acceptance, by the relevant regional powers, of the predominant power's leadership and special prerogatives in providing order (Ikenberry 2004, 356–358; Kang 2010, 22; Goh 2015, 5–6; Mastanduno 2019, 481). Michael Mastanduno summarizes the IR notion of hegemony well:

A unipolar distribution of power, by itself, is not sufficient to establish hegemony. There must also be some meaningful degree of acquiescence on the part of other major states in the region. In a hegemonic order, the leader must have followers, and the more these followers are willing to recognize the hegemonic order as legitimate and share its values and purposes, the more durable the order will be. (Mastanduno 2002, 183)

Of even greater interest for the purposes of our argument is Mastanduno's assessment of US hegemony in post-Cold War Asia as being "incomplete." For Mastanduno:

[T]he U.S. hegemonic order [in Asia in the 1990s] is incomplete. One regional power, Japan, has embraced the U.S.-centered order and found its security in the maintenance of that order. A second regional power, China, is considerably more ambivalent, despite the fact that the United States has made it a foreign policy priority to integrate China into the existing order. A third major player, India, is similarly ambivalent about U.S. hegemony, and the United States has only recently begun any serious attempt to integrate India. (Mastanduno 2003, 186)

Mastanduno's characterization of America's incomplete hegemony is a much-needed corrective to existing understandings of US hegemony in Asia that blithely and implicitly assume that it was universally accepted in Asia (Cf. Layne 2006 and Katzenstein 2005). In fact, Mastanduno's analysis of post-Cold War Asia understates that incompleteness: It leaves out North Korea, a key actor whose nuclear ambitions and antics tantamount to an in-your-face rejection of US visions of regional order. It is for this reason that US administrations have taken to labeling North Korea as a "rogue" state that is part of the "axis of evil." Also excluded are ASEAN countries such as Indonesia and Malaysia that, though generally supportive of a strong US economic-military presence in the region, are also ambivalent about singular US leadership. ASEAN's creation of regional institutions such as the ASEAN

Regional Forum (1994), the East Asian Summit (2005), and the ASEAN Defense Ministers Meeting (2006) that draw in the great powers but with ASEAN "at the driver's seat" demonstrate ASEAN's interest in having a role in shaping Asia's security architecture instead of leaving it to the United States or China.

A different take on America's incomplete hegemony can be adduced from David Sylvan and Stephen Majeski's "patron-client" model of how America relates to the rest of the world. Designating the United States as the patron-in-chief, Sylvan and Majeski define clients as those who receive substantial US economic and military aid, provide bases or places for the US military to project its power, and generally receptive to US leadership (Sylvan and Majeski 2009, 29, 259, fn 56). Especially suggestive are their quantitative assessments of the proportion of US clients – based on the above-mentioned criteria – in each of the regions of the world. In the year 2005, the proportion of US clients was as follows: Western hemisphere – 97 percent; Middle East/North Africa – 55 percent; Europe – 43 percent; East Asia/Oceania – 43 percent; Caucasus, Central and South Asia – 13 percent; and Africa – 7 percent (Sylvan and Majeski 2009, 33–37).

These findings reinforce the argument about the incompleteness of US hegemony in the 1990s and 2000s by placing a number on the proportion of countries that are United States' clients in Europe, the Middle East, and East Asia. These are regions traditionally seen by the United States as operating under or receptive to US hegemony, where the United States has a "vital interest" in preventing the "rise of a hostile hegemon." Yet the proportion of US "clients" in these three regions hover around 45–55 percent. Even allowing room for some slippage between "clients" and "countries accepting of US hegemony," it is manifest that US hegemony was incomplete in the three regions during America's unipolar moment. The only region where US hegemony was nearly complete (97 percent) was the Western hemisphere. Sylvan and Majeski's analysis thus provides some idea of what "complete" hegemony consists in, while showing how incomplete US hegemony in East Asia was in the 1990s.

If America's hegemony in East Asia was incomplete during its unipolar moment, what are we to make of it in the 1960s? American hegemony in the 1960s was more incomplete in terms of hegemonic reach and legitimacy, the Sylvan and Majeski study suggests. The latter classified thirteen countries in East Asia and Oceania as "clients" (in 2005) of the United States.[1] Of the thirteen, it can be argued that ten (thirteen minus Indonesia, Malaysia, and

---

[1] Sylvan and Majeski's classification of clients and nonclients of the United States in East Asia and Oceania (in 2005) is as follows: Clients – Australia, Indonesia, Japan, Malaysia, Marshall Islands, Micronesia, New Zealand, Palau, Philippines, Singapore, South Korea, Taiwan, and Thailand. Nonclients – Brunei, Burma, Cambodia, China, (East Timor), Fiji, Kiribati, Laos,

Singapore) were also clients of the United States in the mid-1950s and up to mid-1960s (the relevant time span for our analysis of US–Vietnam decision-making). Adding Indonesia, Malaysia, and Singapore to the other seventeen "Nonclients" (see footnote 1) results in a 10–20, or 1:2 clients to nonclients ratio. The main hold outs – those denying and rejecting US leadership and its vision for regional order – were like those of the 1990s. North Korea attempted a forced "unification" with the South in 1950 and made the United States fight its first Asian land war to save South Korea. China was not only a holdout, it also contested US hegemony explicitly. On turning communist, it allied with the Soviet Union to advocate "wars of national liberation" and a socialist utopia as alternatives to the US capitalist-democratic path to development and progress. Burma, Laos, and Cambodia were socialist or communist-prone, while the governments of Malaya, Singapore, and Indonesia were preoccupied with fighting domestic communist insurgencies – the outcomes of those struggles would only be known in the mid- and late 1960s. The dissident that posed the longest and costliest challenge to US hegemony in the 1950s and 1960s, however, was Vietnam, first in 1954, and then in 1965.

13.3 Prestige, Credibility, and the First Indochina War (1946–1954)

The First Indochina War was fought between a France determined to reinstate its colonial rule in Vietnam in the aftermath of World War II, and the Vietminh, or Vietnamese communists (under Ho Chi Minh's leadership), who wanted to be free of their colonial masters. Despite post-World War II US rhetoric in favor of decolonization in the developing world, the onset of the Cold War meant that it required the cooperation of Western European countries to counter the Soviet threat in Europe. France played the Cold War card adroitly and impressed upon US policymakers the necessity of helping it to prevail against the Vietminh in Vietnam, not only to prevent the spread of communism in Southeast Asia but also to ensure the survival of the government in Paris and its willingness to participate in the European Defense Community (EDC). Beginning in 1951, the United States provided financial support to France. By 1952, the United States was financing 30 percent of the cost of France's war against the Vietminh, by 1953–54, it was underwriting 80 percent of the cost (Herring: 222; Gelb and Betts: 46).

Despite the United States' heavy financial commitment to the French cause, it did not translate into military action when the French implored the United States to intervene in the decisive France–Vietminh battle at Dien Bien Phu in the spring of 1954. The French request was for the United States to use air

Mongolia, Nauru, North Korea, Papau New Guinea, Samoa, Solomon Islands, Tonga, Vanuatu, and Vietnam.

power to attack the Vietminh positions surrounding the garrison. The Eisenhower administration seriously considered acceding to the French request but pulled back from the brink of intervention at the last minute. Without US intervention, the French were doomed, and the Vietminh would succeed in driving the French out of Vietnam. This rejection of the French request needs to be explained because it also occurred during the era of incomplete hegemony, where prestige and credibility concerns should have mattered greatly.

Interestingly, concerns about US prestige and credibility did not feature prominently in President Eisenhower or his advisers' assessment of the stakes in Vietnam. It is reasonable to assume that the United States had recently demonstrated resolve by fighting in Korea: The credibility of its power and the willingness to use it to enforce its preferred vision of regional order in East Asia were manifest. At great cost to itself, the United States succeeded in restoring the status quo ante in Korea. In other words, the temporal proximity of having demonstrated the credibility of American power in Korea made it less of an issue when confronted with the challenge in Dien Bien Phu.

The Korean War also taught Eisenhower another lesson: the costliness – in reputation, men, and money – of fighting alone. Eisenhower hewed closer to viewpoint of the Congressional leaders whose John Foster Dulles consulted and whose concurrence he sought for an air strike against the Vietminh: "we want no more Koreas with the United States furnishing 90% of the manpower" (*FRUS*, 1952–1954, 13:1224). The Congressional leaders were against the unilateral use of force by the United States because they feared the United States would end up fighting China "alone," as in Korea. The Eisenhower administration had estimated that there was an even chance that the Chinese would intervene in the face of an impending Vietminh defeat (Kahin 1986, 46). Still, Eisenhower and the Congressional leaders were willing to go along with Dulles' air strike if the United States could get Britain and other allies to join in the fight.

That was the context in which President Eisenhower wrote to British Prime Minister Winston Churchill, asking the latter to join the United States in using air power to attack the Vietminh positions in Dien Bien Phu. Eisenhower assessed the strategic loss of north Vietnam in balance of power terms: "[If] Indochina passes into the hands of the Communists the ultimate effect of our and your global strategic position with the consequent shift in the power ration throughout Asia and the Pacific could be disastrous and, I know, unacceptable to you and me" (*FRUS* 1952–54, 40). Churchill was dubious about "united action" with the United States to save the French garrison at Dien Bien Phu; his unwillingness to commit his nation gave Eisenhower pause about intervening in 1954. In this episode, Eisenhower seemed to have put a premium on "united action" (with the British) above all else. In response to the entreaties of those like Chairman of the Joint Chiefs of Staff Admiral Arthur Radford and Vice

President Richard Nixon to intervene with or without the British, Eisenhower retorted that for him, "the concept of leadership implied associates. Without allies and associates the leader is just an adventurer like Genghis Khan" (*FRUS* 1952–1954, 13, 1440).

The Vietminh's victory and ejection of the French from Vietnam meant that the United States would have to live with the shift in the power equation (in China's favor, according to American perceptions) in Asia, however "disastrous and unacceptable" to the United States that may be. US leadership of the region was stalled or suffered a serious setback with the conclusion of the First Indochina War. As an NSC document put it in the aftermath of the French defeat in 1954:

French reverses there [north Vietnam] had damaged American prestige and raised "doubts in Asia concerning U.S. leadership and the ability of the U.S. to check the further expansion of Communism in Asia." It was imperative . . . that the United States "protect its position and restore its prestige in the Far East by a new initiative in Southeast Asia, where the situation must be stabilized . . . to prevent further losses to Communism." (cited in Anderson 1988, 129)

In the next decade, successive administrations would take the NSC advice – on the need to preserve American prestige and leadership – to heart, culminating in the Johnson administration's decision to fight the Second Indochina War to "prevent further losses to Communism."

13.4 Partial Hegemony and Credibility Concerns

What the Vietnam War (or Second Indochina War) was about depends on whose perspective we are viewing it from. For Ho Chi Minh, the Vietminh, and the Vietminh's southern counterpart, the National Liberation Front (NLF), it was about the reunification of north and south Vietnam, which had been provided for by the Final Declaration of the 1954 Geneva Agreement. The cochair of the Geneva Conference, British Foreign Secretary Anthony Eden had observed that "[w]ithout the firm and explicit assurance of national elections [to be held in 1956] aimed at reunifying the country, the Vietminh would never have agreed to the armistice" (cited in Kahin 1986, 61). For George McT. Kahin, author of the most detailed study of the 1965 decision, the promise of elections was "the heart of the Geneva Agreements" (Kahin 1986, 61). The Vietminh's interest in the 1956 elections is easy to fathom: They expected to win handsomely.

President Dwight Eisenhower wrote in his memoirs: "I have never talked or corresponded with a person knowledgeable in Indochinese affairs who did not agree that had elections been held as of the time of fighting, possibly 80 percent of the population would have voted for communist Ho Chi Minh as their leader" (1963, 372). US Undersecretary of State Bedell Smith predicted the same 80 percent margin for a communist electoral victory in 1956 in his briefing to Congress on the Geneva Conference (*FRUS* 1952–1954, 13, 1732). For the same reason, it is easy to understand why south Vietnam, led by Ngo Dinh Diem, a Catholic and staunch anti-communist, was against holding the election. With the Cold War and the US policy of containment in full throttle, the imperative was of building a viable noncommunist south Vietnam led by the United States to acquiesced in Diem's decision not to hold the 1956 elections. From the late 1950s to the early 1960s, the Diem government sought to consolidate its rule over the south, often via repressive methods; it also incarcerated and killed many northerners who had remained in the south to work toward reunification. Diem's policies caused serious domestic turmoil, including shocking episodes of Buddhist monks immolating themselves in protest against the Diem regime. In December 1960, Ho Chi Minh and his Politburo decided to "step up the armed struggle" and created the NLF to overthrow the Diem government, which it described as the "disguised colonial regime of the U.S. imperialists" (cited in Kahin 1986, 115). Over the next few years, Diem's singular error was not so much his repressive policies (which the United States could turn a blind eye toward, given the imperative of containing the communists), but his inability to win the war in the south against the NLF guerillas. A frustrated United States sanctioned a military coup to depose Diem in November 1963, which ended in his assassination. US policymakers who hoped for political stability in (post-Diem) south Vietnam so that it can focus on fighting the NLF were disappointed. Infighting and competition for power among the generals involved in the coup led to six changes in the top leadership in the next one and a half years. It was not until June 1965 that Nguyen van Thieu became president, a position he would hold until the collapse of south Vietnam in 1975. It was hardly surprising that the post-Diem political instability made the south's position increasingly precarious as the NLF continued to make substantial battlefield gains. By late 1964, the United States found itself in a position (akin to that in 1954 on north Vietnam) of having to decide whether to intervene militarily to "save" south Vietnam.

As far as the United States was concerned, the Vietnam War was about its response to the attempted military takeover of southern Vietnam by North Vietnam. North Vietnam was perceived to be acting at the behest of, or in concert with, Mao Zedong's China to expand communism's power and influence in Southeast Asia. The US response – taking the fight to Vietnam via aerial bombardment of North Vietnam in early 1965 and deploying 100,000 combat troops in July 1965 – is traditionally viewed as an instance of America's Cold War containment policy in which it sought to prevent the expansion of Soviet and Chinese power through their proxies.

The flip side of stopping communist expansionism was about establishing or consolidating US leadership, that is, hegemony, in the region. That the United States saw the war and insurgencies (in the other Southeast Asian nations) as challenges to its leadership in East Asia and beyond can be inferred from the constant refrain that it was vital for US interests and world peace to maintain US credibility: If the Vietnamese communists, for example, were allowed to take over south Vietnam by force, US prestige and credibility would be lost, and with that world respect for US leadership. A world where US leadership was not taken seriously would be a world imperiled.

This line of reasoning is evident in the Johnson-Ball exchange cited at the beginning of this chapter. At the same July 21 National Security Council meeting, US Secretary of State Dean Rusk argued against Ball's (his deputy) withdrawal proposal: "If the Communist world finds out we will not pursue our commitments to the end, I don't know where they will stay their hand" (Meeting on Vietnam, July 21, 1965, LBJ Library; also cited in Khong 1992, 128). Secretary of Defense Robert McNamara chipped in by adding that Ball "understated the cost of cutting our losses"; he "agreed with Mr. Rusk on the international effect [of withdrawing] (Meeting on Vietnam, July 21, 1965, LBJ Library; also cited in Khong 1992, 124–125).[2]

The importance of pursuing "our commitments to the end" also resonated strongly in the Defense Department, with Secretary of Defense Robert McNamara's "whiz kids" resorting to quantitative reasoning to assess why the United States should fight in Vietnam. John McNaughton, Assistant Secretary of Defense and one of McNamara's closest advisers, argued in an (in)famous memo that the United States was in Vietnam: "70% – To avoid a humiliating U.S. defeat (to our reputation as a guarantor)," 20% – To keep SVN [South Vietnam] (and the adjacent) territory from Chinese hands, and "10% – To permit the people of SVN to enjoy a better, freer way of life" (cited in Kahin: 313). Avoiding "a humiliating defeat" and preserving "our reputation as a guarantor" are different ways of saying maintaining US prestige and credibility.

The case for preserving America's reputation as a guarantor was most systematically articulated by National Security Adviser (to Presidents Kennedy and Johnson) McGeorge Bundy. For Bundy, the issue in 1965 was less about winning and more about showing the world that the United States

---

[2] The focus on prestige and commitments can be explained in part by the "lessons of history" that informed some of the key policymakers. For President Johnson and Dean Rusk, the 1930s and Munich showed that appeasement whet the appetite of dictatorial aggressors and merely postpone the day of reckoning (World War II); Chamberlain's appeasement of Hitler devastated Britain's prestige and standing as the world hegemon and hastened its decline. The US intervention in Korea in 1950 and eventual success in beating back North Korea's aggression, on the other hand, demonstrated US resolve and enhanced US credibility as well as its vision of security order in East Asia (see Khong 1992).

made the effort and did all it could to stop communist expansionism. Gordon Goldstein, author of the most authoritative account of McGeorge Bundy's Vietnam decision-making, summarized Bundy's notes to himself in March 1965 as follows: "[I]t would be better ... to deploy one hundred thousand combat forces to South Vietnam and lose rather than send no troops at all" (Goldstein 2008, 183). Elaborating on the latter, Goldstein wrote:

> The "cardinal" principle for the United States in Vietnam is "not to be a Paper Tiger" ... Bundy was *fixated not on prevailing militarily but on maintaining America's credibility in the Cold War*. The American combat troop commitment did not have to advance a compelling military strategy or have a real prospect of success. It simply needed to dramatize the proposition that the United States was prepared to pay a real cost in blood and treasure to maintain its position of global leadership. (Goldstein 2008, 221, emphasis added)

For Bundy, the United States must be seen by others to have done its part (in Vietnam), and even if it lost, it would be worth it because the United States would have demonstrated resolve, and the relevant audiences would have faith in the United States, appreciate its power, and be acceptant of US leadership.

Who were these intended audiences? The world at large to be sure, but audiences that one finds repeatedly in the archival record are the United States itself, and friends and foes in Europe and East Asia. In debates about whether to intervene in Vietnam, US decision-makers showed great concern, on the one hand, about whether friends like France, Italy, Japan, Thailand, Malaya, and Indonesia would take the United States' words and commitments seriously if it did not fight in south Vietnam; and on the other hand, about whether adversaries like China and the Soviet Union would "stay their hand" if they and their proxies were not stopped in Vietnam (Meeting on Vietnam, July 21, 1965, LBJ Library; also cited in Khong 1992, 124–133).

Policymakers worried frequently and consistently about the loss of US prestige and credibility if the United States failed to "save" south Vietnam. Those – like French President Charles De Gaulle, Senators Mike Mansfield and William Fulbright, and Undersecretary of State George Ball – who argued that Vietnam was a "rotten country" and "losing" and that it would not impact on US credibility were in the minority. The majority – from President Johnson and his senior national security advisers – felt that US leadership of the region, and for that matter the free world, would suffer an irrecoverable setback to US prestige and credibility if south Vietnam were to fall to communism.

That this fixation on prestige and credibility can be explained by America's partial hegemony in East Asia is intuitively and empirically plausible, but the argument is based on correlation, that is, the correlation between incomplete US hegemony in the 1960s and the prominence of credibility concerns in Vietnam decision-making. The argument will command greater credence if we could show (a) how incomplete hegemony is implicated or expressed in the decision-makers discussions of credibility; and (b) that rival explanations do less well than the one provided in this chapter.

How might worries about incomplete hegemony manifest themselves in the decision-makers' discussions? One answer is to examine what the decision-makers thought US allies and friends would do in the event the United States refrained from intervention and south Vietnam went communist. At the abstract or theoretical level, the "domino theory," which informed the thinking of most of the principals, envisaged that the fall of south Vietnam would lead to the rest of Southeast Asia toppling, like a row of dominos, into the communist sphere. The crude version foresaw a repeat of the communist strategy in south Vietnam, where Chinese-sponsored guerrillas would mount successful insurgencies to topple the governments of Thailand, Malaysia, Singapore, and so on. The sophisticated version of the theory was premised less on externally sponsored communist insurrections and more on how the fall of south Vietnam would create strong pressures for noncommunist Southeast Asia to accommodate China politically and fall eventually into its orbit. In a 1964 oral history about French President Charles de Gaulle, former US President Dwight, Eisenhower – who was the first to use the domino metaphor – criticized de Gaulle for not appreciating the stakes in Vietnam:

[If] we let the thing [Southeast Asia] go, not only Indonesia, but ... India would become totally isolated. I think that really the defense of Southeast Asia today ... is the defense of India, and if that whole sub-continent of some 400 million people ... falls to the communists or breaks with the West ... I'll tell you, then we become more and more isolated in this world. (Transcript of Meeting with General Dwight Eisenhower 1964)

If US hegemony had been more complete, if more of Southeast Asia (and India?) had been steadfast followers of the United States, aligned solidly with it (like the Western hemisphere), the United States would have had more confidence in its ability to convince Southeast Asia to stick with it. The domino theory's impact on Vietnam decision-making would not have been as great.

But the decision-makers went beyond the domino theory in their deliberations on whether to intervene in Vietnam. They asked questions about specific countries and identified those most in danger of falling into the communist orbit. In the July 21 meeting, President Johnson raised his usual question about whether the United States could win in Vietnam. George Ball said no, likening intervention in Vietnam to "giving cobalt treatment to a terminal cancer case [south Vietnam]" (Meeting on Vietnam, July 21, 1965, LBJ Library; also cited in Khong 1992, 126–127). Anticipating questions on the strategic consequences of a US withdrawal, Ball acknowledged that south Vietnam "would soon come under Hanoi control." Thailand, a good but never a staunch ally, would be "our main problem" although "if we wanted to make a stand in Thailand, we might be able to make it." South Korea, Taiwan, Indonesia, and Malaysia would also be problems. Japan was less of a problem; in fact it took the view that the United States was "propping up a lifeless government" (in south Vietnam) and felt that the it should cut its losses instead of getting into a protracted war. Western Europe also took Japan's position: "they look upon us as if we got ourselves into an imprudent situation." Although Ball did not elaborate what he meant by the countries that would be "problems," the context of the discussion suggests that he saw them as places that would encounter communist pressures to accommodate or succumb. Hence the suggestion about Thailand (instead of south Vietnam) as the place to make a stand: even Ball had to concede that the United States would have to take a stand somewhere in Southeast Asia – given his superiors' concerns about maintaining US credibility – to quell the doubts that South Korea, Taiwan, Malaysia, and Indonesia would have about US resolve if south Vietnam fell (Ball quotes above from Meeting on Vietnam, July 21, 1965, LBJ Library; also cited in Khong 1992, 126–127).

In his discussion with his military advisers the next day, President Johnson took up Ball's idea of making the United States stand in Thailand instead of south Vietnam (Meeting on Vietnam, July 22, 1965, LBJ Library; also cited in Khong 1992, 132).

PRESIDENT: Suppose we told Ky [south Vietnamese Prime Minister] of requirements we need – he turns them down – and we have to get out and make our stand in Thailand.
BROWN [SECRETARY OF US AIR FORCE]: The Thais will go with the winner.
PRESIDENT: If we didn't stop in Thailand, where would we stop?
MCNAMARA: Laos, Cambodia, Thailand, Burma, surely affect Malaysia. In 2–3 years communist domination would stop there, but ripple effect would be great in Japan, India. We would have to give up some bases. Ayub [Khan, head of Pakistan government] would move closer to China. Greece, Turkey would move to neutralist positions. Communist agitation would increase in Africa.

McNamara's filling in the specifics of the sophisticated version of the domino theory is instructive because it implicitly assumes that the countries mentioned will not hitch their economic and political fortunes with the United States, the erstwhile hegemon. The "buy in" from these countries on US leadership of the region was so tenuous and limited that the United States needed to demonstrate its resolve in Vietnam to convince them of its hegemonic credentials.

13.5 Alternative Explanations and Historical Puzzles

At this juncture in our analysis, it is useful to consider two plausible alternative explanations to the incomplete hegemony-heightened credibility explanation articulated in this chapter. The latter would command greater credence if the alternative explanations are judged to be less persuasive than the one provided here. The first alternative explanation focuses on domestic instead of international credibility, that is, President Lyndon Johnson's desire to protect his domestic prestige and credibility vis-à-vis his political opponents and detractors from both the Republican and Democratic parties. If south Vietnam were to be "lost" under his watch, his domestic credibility would be so severely damaged that he would not be able to get legislation passed on the Great Society programs that was to be his legacy to America (Berman 1982). In Johnson's view, "Harry Truman ... lost his effectiveness from the day the Communists took over in China" (cited in Kearns: 252). This explanation is undoubtedly part of the story, even though the documentation is much sparser than the international credibility explanation. Perhaps for good reasons, few politicians would want to leave a paper trail revealing the domestic calculus – focusing on protecting one's personal prestige and credibility – behind a war decision. Both domestic and international credibility arguments can explain why Johnson chose war, but given the paucity of documentary evidence for the former, it is safer to treat the domestic argument as a plausible but unproven explanation compared to the international credibility explanation. For unless we can show that the principal policymakers were prevaricating or did not believe that the credibility of US power was at stake, and yet continue to emphasize it in successive memos and NSC meetings (to make them look good for posterity), the international credibility argument is the better documented, and hence more convincing argument.

The second is less an alternative explanation and more a historical puzzle that might weaken the argument presented here if true. The puzzle is raised by Wen-qing Ngoei in Chapter 14, which argues that by the "mid-1960s" most of Southeast Asia had fallen into America's orbit. Objectively, therefore, there should not be any worries by the Johnson administration about the credibility and prestige of US power, since the "facts on the ground" were that much of Southeast Asia was spoken for (they were with America). As Ngoei put it in the elegant final sentence of his chapter: "It is thus no small irony and tragic that, right when U.S. combat forces were being deployed to Vietnam to supposedly inoculate the region against communism, Southeast Asia was already substantially titled toward the United States" (Chapter 14).

Yet this chapter has argued that President Johnson and his advisers were preoccupied with losing prestige and credibility if the United States did not fight in Vietnam. Were they misperceiving, or were they delusional? I believe they were neither misperceiving nor delusional in July of 1965. The key point here is that in *July 1965* – when the administration was making the fateful decision to fight in Vietnam – the "facts on the ground" suggest that only two Southeast Asian countries – formal treaty allies Thailand the Philippines – may be confidently assessed as aligned with the United States. Malaysia and Singapore were going through the throes of separation, and while their leadership tended to be pro-British, whether they would gravitate to the United States remained unclear. Indonesia's President Sukarno lauded the breakup as the natural consequence of "inauthentic" neo-colonial formations imposed on the region by their former colonial master. For Sukarno, the breakup meant that the alignments of Malaysia and Singapore would be up for grabs. And Indonesia, the largest and most consequential nation in Southeast Asia, was undoubtedly aligned with China in July 1965. In fact, Indonesia was seen as a leader of the Beijing–Hanoi–Pyongyang–Phnom Penh–Jakarta axis detested by the United States. In the US perspective, these were the countries in East Asia that rejected US leadership and were working at the behest of China to spread communism in the region. The critical fact is that the coup against Sukarno – by officers of the Indonesia military who felt that he was too close to Beijing – did not happen until October 1965, more than two months after the United States dispatched troops to south Vietnam. Sukarno himself only handed power over to Suharto in January 1966. In other words, when the Johnson administration was assessing the state of Southeast Asia in July (in relation to their Vietnam decision-making), they correctly assumed that Indonesia was aligned with China. As McGeorge Bundy would observe a few decades later, Indonesia "fell firmly the other way – against the Communists – late in 1965" (Goldstein: 222), implying that he and his colleagues could not have known that in July 1965 and that their assumption of Indonesia as being pro-China then was reasonable. Finally, we also need to factor in the Indochinese states of Cambodia, Laos, Burma, and Vietnam: they were ideological brethrens and political allies of China, not the United States, back in the summer of 1965. Objectively and subjectively (in the US view), therefore, *the majority* in Southeast Asia were more closely aligned with China than they were with the United States. US hegemony in East and Southeast Asia was very incomplete and this helps explain US anxieties about its prestige and credibility and the need to demonstrate resolve in the region.

13.6 Conclusion

Historians and political scientists have tended to portray the First and Second Indochina Wars as wars of decolonization that were inevitably caught up in Cold War dynamics, resulting in both the United States and China–Soviet Union having strong vested interests in their outcomes. Much of the scholarship in English focus on the two wars as instances of (the US policy) containment. These interpretations accord with the historical evidence, but they are also partial. Adopting a longer historical perspective and with an eye on the United States' hegemonic status in Asia, I have argued that the First and Second

Indochina Wars (and the Korean War before that) should also be viewed as challenges to US hegemony or leadership in the region. The challenger was China, who, according to the United States, was working in tandem with the Soviets in instigating and supporting the Vietnamese communists in defiance of American power and leadership. And this challenge evoked America's deepest concerns about its prestige and credibility precisely because its leadership position or the reach/legitimacy of its hegemony was so partial.

A major implication of the our analysis is that although the United States, like all great powers, guards its prestige and credibility jealously, its case in Vietnam suggests that the impact of these factors on policy varies with the hegemon's position in the regional or international system. The surprising and inordinate influence of prestige and credibility concerns in Vietnam's decision-making in 1965, I have argued, may be explained by America's incomplete hegemony in East Asia. That incompleteness gave rise to a lack of strategic confidence, in itself and its allies, that prompted the United States to make Vietnam – however unpromising it seemed to many – a test case of its resolve and credibility. The implicit counterfactual to this claim is that a more complete US hegemony would have been less prone to viewing challenges in the periphery as crucial tests of its international prestige and credibility. President George W. Bush's restrained response to the 2001 EP3 incident with China in the South China Sea and President Barack Obama's inaction after Syria crossed his "red line" of using chemical weapons are two instances where US prestige and credibility were at stake, but in both cases, the United States did not allow these concerns to dictate policy. According to Jeffrey Goldberg, Obama believed that the US foreign policy establishment "makes a fetish of credibility – particularly the sort of credibility purchased with force." As President, Obama was not going to drop bombs on "someone to prove that you're willing to drop bombs on someone is just about the worst reason to use force" (Goldberg 2016).

In the conclusion to his seminal account of how the United States became involved in the Second Indochina War, the historian George Herring summarized his findings this way:

The United States intervened in Vietnam to block the apparent march of a Soviet-directed Communism across Asia, enlarged its commitment to halt a presumably expansionist Communist China, and eventually made Vietnam a test of its determination to uphold world order .... It elevated into a major international conflict what might have remained a localized struggle. *By raising the stakes into a test of its own credibility*, it perilously narrowed its options. A policy so flawed in its premises cannot help but fail, and in this case the results were disastrous. (Herring: 270, emphasis added)

As Herring's summary and the work of many others indicate, maintaining US credibility is a key explanation of the Johnson administration's decision to fight the Second Indochina War. It follows that the novelty of this chapter lies less its retelling of the prestige and credibility story, and more in linking them to America's incomplete hegemony in Asia. That linkage, I argue, helps solve the puzzle of why even "the best and the brightest" ended up "raising the stakes [in Vietnam] into a test of its [America's] own credibility." Prestige and credibility are indeed "variables" – their impact on US decision-making varies with the extent and depth of US hegemony. The more incomplete one's hegemony, the greater the obsession with proving and maintaining one's international credibility. McGeorge Bundy's willingness to wage war in Vietnam – even if the United States could not win – to avoid being a "paper tiger" demonstrates the extreme value that he and President Lyndon Johnson, also a believer in the "paper tiger" metaphor, placed on being the "real thing", the ferocious superpower with the inclination and will to subdue all those with the temerity to challenge its leadership and its vision of regional order.

We began this chapter with George Ball's counsel against intervention. Having heard his share of how the United States must avoid being perceived as a "paper tiger," Ball made a different play on the metaphor as it became increasingly obvious that President Johnson was inclined to take the advice of the Bundy, Rusk, and McNamara. In one of his final memos on Vietnam to the president, Ball argued: "Once on the tiger's back, we cannot be sure of picking the place to dismount." It was Ball's way of warning the president against the treacherous and uncontrollable path, with unforeseen consequences, that he would be taking the United States by intervening in the Second Indochina War. But Johnson did mount the tiger. He plunged America into an unwinnable war, one that would eventually lead to 58,000 American (combat) deaths, over 300,000 injured, and cost $150 billion dollars. Reunifying their country against US objections cost the Vietnamese communists close to a million deaths. Half a million South Vietnamese troops were also wounded, while over 200,000 died defending the south (Turley, 195–96).

Failure to win in Vietnam also derailed Johnson's chances for reelection. He chose not to run in 1968. Senator William Fulbright, Chairman of the Senate Foreign Relations Committee, a good friend of Johnson but also one of the most vocal critics of America's war in Vietnam surmised: "It is a curiosity of human nature that lack of self-assurance seems to breed an exaggerated sense of power and mission. When a nation is very powerful but lacking in self-confidence, it is likely to behave in a manner dangerous to itself and to others" (cited in Kimball 1990, 116). Fulbright was only half right. The lack of US "self-assurance" and "self-confidence" – expressed in terms of not losing prestige and credibility and not wanting to be a paper tiger – was not just about the psyche of Johnson and his advisers, they also had material and ideational roots. Incomplete hegemony reinforced the fear of falling dominos in Southeast Asia and beyond, making it difficult for the decision-makers to possess the kind of self-assurance described by Fulbright. President Johnson and his advisers worried incessantly about how inaction in Vietnam would lead the other Southeast Asian countries to accommodate and align with China and the Soviet Union. Yet, fighting the Second Indochina War and losing would do great damage not only to US self-confidence but also to the confidence that others would have in the United States. Another critic of the war, George Kennan, had argued that "there is more respect to be won in the opinion of the world by a resolute and courageous liquidation of unsound positions than in the most stubborn pursuit of extravagant or unpromising objectives" (Hearings Before the Committee on Foreign Relations, 1966). George Ball would agree, for he had warned his superiors before they plunged America fully into war, that "[t]he worse blow [to US prestige and credibility] would be that the mightiest power on earth is unable to defeat a handful of guerrillas" (Meeting on Vietnam, July 21, 1965, LBJ Library; also cited in Khong 1992, 127).

14 Nationalism and Anglo-American Neo-colonialism in Southeast Asia, 1945–1965

Wen-Qing Ngoei

In 1965, Indonesian leader Sukarno lamented in his memoir that "colonialism wasn't retreating in [his] backyard, just changing shape."[1] His views might seem, at first glance, out of step with the reality. The colonial powers appeared to be in full retreat from Southeast Asia after World War II: America had granted the Philippines independence in 1946; the Netherlands had exited Indonesia in 1949 after failing to recolonize the archipelago; French forces met a similar fate at the hands of Indochina's nationalists a few short years later; and Britain, supposedly gleaning from contemporary examples that resistance was futile, relinquished its control over Burma, Malaya, and Singapore between the late 1940s and early 1960s (Table 14.1). In this vein, President Lyndon Johnson's decision to Americanize the Vietnam War in 1964 looked like the desperate, final gasp of a moribund imperial system. Historians have certainly described Washington's ensuing military debacle in Vietnam as the end of the United States' "short-lived empire" in Southeast Asia, a failure emblematic of the decisive, region-wide triumph of indigenous nationalism over Western colonialism after 1945.[2]

Yet, Sukarno's remarks were not aimed at formal colonial rule. His claim was that new embodiments of colonialism had emerged in postwar Southeast Asia, and that conservative nationalists had not ejected their colonial rulers after independence but colluded with them to preserve, rebrand, and even hide their now informal empires. He described the compact between colonizer and formerly colonized with the portmanteau, *nekolim*, a fairly obvious combination of neo-colonialism and neo-imperialism.[3] And, his particular beef was with the rise of Malaysia in 1963, a new federation of one-time British colonies: Malaya (known to be pro-British and anti-communist), Singapore (host to Britain's most important military bases in Asia), and the British Borneo territories of Sabah and Sarawak.[4] Sukarno had insisted for

---

[1] Soekarno 1965, 302–304. [2] McMahon 1999, 221–222. Also see Hunt and Levine 2012.
[3] Legge 1972, 343; Ngoei 2019a, 135.
[4] To clarify the change in names from Malaya to Malaysia: The Federation of Malaya, which gained independence from Britain in 1957, refers only to the states of the Malay Peninsula. In 1963, Malaya merged with Singapore as well as Britain's Borneo territories, Sabah and Sarawak,

Table 14.1 *Southeast Asia decolonization timeline, 1946–1965**

Year of Independence	Countries	Colonizer/Other
1946	Republic of the Philippines	The United States
1948	Union of Burma/Myanmar	Britain
1949	Republic of Indonesia	The Netherlands
1953	Kingdom of Laos	France
1953	Kingdom of Cambodia	
1954	Democratic Republic of Vietnam (North) Republic of Vietnam (South)	
1957	Federation of Malaya (Malay Peninsula only)	Britain
1963	Federation of Malaysia (Malaya, Singapore, Sabah, Sarawak)	Britain
1965	Republic of Singapore	Separation from Malaysia

* The Kingdom of Thailand (formerly Siam) was not formally colonized by the Euro-American powers (see Chapter 3, this volume).

years before Malaysia's creation that the federation was a "British neo-colonial plot" to extend the life of London's imperial power in the region as well as imperil Indonesia. Attempting to cripple British neo-colonialism, Sukarno launched *Konfrontasi* (the Confrontation, 1963–66), a military, ideological, and economic campaign by Indonesia to fracture Malaysia – it was a decision he made while egged on by senior Chinese leaders and inspired by Beijing's revolutionary antagonism against the Western powers (though he never personally embraced communism).

14.1 Argument

Sukarno's wordplay, if somewhat banal, did contain kernels of truth. As this chapter shows, Anglo-American neo-colonial projects melded easily with the anti-communist nationalism of Southeast Asia's conservative elites. At base, London and Washington's neo-colonial designs centered on maintaining strategic assets in Southeast Asia such as their military bases, enabling their projection of power into the region; on cultivating intimate ties with indigenous leaders to sustain political influence over former colonies; and on ensuring Southeast Asia's economies – their natural resources and markets – remained open to Britain and the United States. And, most of Southeast Asia's conservative elites were broadly sympathetic to these Anglo-American objectives. They

to form the Federation of Malaysia. In 1965, Singapore separated from the federation, though Malaysia would retain its name.

saw in the continuity of London's and Washington's influence in Southeast Asia the promise of forging beneficial links to the prosperous West, paths to rapid economic development, and security guarantees against communist threats at home and abroad. Crucially, race played into the equation. The Cold War goals of Kuala Lumpur, London, and Washington intermingled on account of their shared antipathy toward communist-led China and Chinese-influenced left-wing movements in Southeast Asia (Table 14.2); their nearly identical fears that the millions-strong Chinese diaspora in the region would serve the expansionist agenda of the Chinese Communist Party (CCP); and their common desire that British and/or US power remain strong in Southeast Asia to contain all these perceived threats.[5]

Table 14.2 *Selected left-wing movements of Southeast Asia, 1945–1965*

Countries	Movement	Brief Description	Conclusion
The Philippines	Hukbalahap (Huk)	Peasant rebellion (1947–54) with links to the Communist Party of the Philippines and legitimate grouses against Philippine elite's long-standing monopoly of political power and resources	The Philippine government defeated Huks with US backing in the form of military equipment, assistance in psychological warfare, and counterinsurgency operations
Malaya	Malayan Communist Party (MCP)	Guerrilla faction of the MCP launched an anti-British insurrection in 1948 to win independence for Malaya and Singapore	British, Commonwealth, and Malayan forces crippled the MCP by the mid-1950s, killing thousands of MCP guerrillas
Indonesia	Indonesian Communist Party (PKI)	The PKI, the third-largest communist party in the world with ties to Beijing, became by the early 1960s the bedrock of political support of the left-leaning President Sukarno. In 1965, the PKI launched a coup to preempt an anticipated move by conservative military officials to seize power	Conservative military officials responded to PKI actions with a countercoup. With US assistance, the conservative, right-wing military orchestrated a massacre of the PKI and installed an anti-communist, pro-US dictatorship

[5] Ngoei 2019a, 5.

In fact, British neo-colonialism in Malaya was unexceptional. By the end of 1965, when nearly 200,000 US forces had deployed to Vietnam, Thailand and the Philippines had been allies of the United States for years; Malaysia and Singapore were pro-British but would lean increasingly toward Washington; and Indonesia's new anti-communist military leaders, about to conclude their brutal purge of the republic's communists, gradually set about ensconcing their nation within the US orbit. From this broad, regional view, anti-communist regimes in Southeast Asia connected to, and augmented by, Anglo-American military and economic networks presided over the most resource-rich, prosperous, and populous countries of the region (Table 14.3). The persistence of Western imperialism in Southeast Asia was therefore more characteristic of the region's postwar developments than the end of formal colonialism. Indeed, Washington's fiasco in Vietnam is the anomaly which proves the rule. When Britain's military finally retreated from its Southeast Asian bases in the late 1960s, Malaysia and Singapore would cast their lot with the United States, making the region's overall pro-US trajectory more rather

Table 14.3 *Cold War alignments of Southeast Asian states, 1940s–1960s (selected)*

Countries	Declared or Formal Arrangements	Cold War Alignments
The Philippines	Ally of the United States from independence in 1946	Anti-communist and pro-US
Thailand	Ally of the United States from 1950	Anti-communist and pro-US
Malaya/ Malaysia	Ally of Britain from independence in 1957	Anti-communist and pro-British from independence in 1957, increasingly pro-US thereafter
Singapore	Declared itself neutral and nonaligned	Anti-communist and pro-British from the late 1950s, increasingly pro-US from mid-1960s
Indonesia	Declared itself neutral and nonaligned	1950s: Favored the USSR and China but open to US courting Early 1960s: Leaned increasingly toward China, belligerent toward the United States and Britain, and their regional partners Mid-1960s onward: Gradually aligned with United States following right-wing coup in 1965

than less pronounced.[6] Colonialism in Southeast Asia had indeed changed its shape, as Sukarno believed, transitioning into US hegemony by the 1970s.

To illustrate this, the chapter focuses first on the case study of Malaya as an example of a general pattern of developments across postwar Southeast Asia. It explores how anti-Chinese prejudice undergirded the common anti-communist cause of Malaya's conservative elites and their former colonial rulers. Following, it clarifies that Sukarno's complaint about British neo-colonialism in Malaya was not without substance, noting how this British–Malayan anti-communist collaboration also isolated and destabilized Sukarno's pro-China regime by 1965, paving the way for the Indonesian army's right-wing (and US-assisted) coup against him. The Malaya case study serves to highlight how conservative nationalists across the region – in Thailand from the 1950s and Indonesia from the mid-1960s – were similarly wary of China and how its presumably loyal diasporic networks might enable Beijing to seize control of Southeast Asia. Equally, it reveals how anti-communist nationalists were thus motivated to build or reinforce ties with the United States, itself a former colonial power that like Britain intended its imperial presence in the region to endure.

As other chapters in this book underscore, race featured prominently in this neo-colonial saga. Racial thinking about China and its diaspora, rejuvenated and updated in Southeast Asian anti-communism, became the connective tissue for Anglo-American neo-colonialism and nationalism.[7]

This chapter concludes with a brief discussion of the irony surrounding America's decision to escalate the Vietnam conflict in the mid-1960s, how its ill-fated intervention to save the wider region from communism occurred when most Southeast Asian states had already crushed their local communist rivals with US or British support and aligned themselves with the United States.

14.2 British Neo-colonialism and Anti-Chinese Anti-communism in Malaya

British leaders quickly recognized after World War II that the Euro-American colonial order could not return to business as usual in Southeast Asia. Japan's early victories over the Western powers during the war, and its cultivation of pro-independence movements in the territories it had briefly controlled, had made the rising tide of Southeast Asian nationalism seem irreversible. There was ready proof of this new reality in France and the Netherlands' faltering efforts to impose the status quo antebellum upon their colonies. If Britain wished to retain its status as a world power, to keep more than a toehold in its colonial possessions, it must seek bargains with suitable collaborators

---

[6] Ngoei 2017, 903–932. [7] Ngoei 2021; Ngoei 2022.

among the nationalists who clamored for the decolonization of Malaya.[8] After all, British investments in Malaya's rubber industry were vitally important to the empire, weakened as it was by World War II. Malaya was the "world's largest rubber supplier ... Britain's biggest dollar earner, and kept the United States its most important customer." Britain's economic reconstruction simply could not succeed if Malaya's formal independence veered off in an anti-British direction.[9]

As such, British officials aimed to grant Malaya formal independence while ensuring their former colony's new leaders chose to anchor their state firmly within Britain's sphere, allowing British businesses in Malaya to maintain their valuable influence and continue to flourish. Historians have used the term "nation-building colonialism" to describe this process, wherein an empire pursues power through the "cultivation, sponsorship, and ordering of other peoples' nations."[10] Certainly, the word "neo-colonial" applies here, too. London sought not the dissolution of its empire but its evolution into a less obtrusive yet still potent form.

Ironically, it would be the anti-British nationalists of Malaya who gifted London with a compelling premise to enlist Malaya's conservative nationalists as collaborators for Britain's neo-colonial cause. In 1948, the guerrilla fighters of the Malayan Communist Party (MCP) – formed in 1930 with support from the USSR, the CCP, and a certain Ho Chi Minh – kicked off their armed revolt against British colonial authorities. London declared the crisis an emergency and strove to destroy the guerrillas, who had briefly been their partners, though expediently, against Imperial Japan. The MCP's postwar insurrection involved, among other things, assassinating European rubber plantation owners, British officials, and Britain's local informants, along with sabotaging Malaya's economic infrastructure. The Malayan Emergency, as London termed it, stretched till 1960.

Predictably, Britain brought its imperial counterinsurgency repertoire – refined by years of suppression programs elsewhere in the empire – to bear on the MCP.[11] But the anti-MCP campaign was not merely a shooting war. It was also a struggle for Malayan hearts and minds to ensure a pro-British state arose in the colony's place. Here, a fact that proved most useful to Britain was the MCP's membership being 95 percent ethnic Chinese; some recently arrived, others local-born, many from impoverished backgrounds. Why? Because anti-Chinese sentiment had long existed in Southeast Asia and might be marshaled for Britain's purposes. These sentiments coursed powerfully through indigenous communities across the region, having arisen from a history of bitterness against Chinese merchants (itinerant or based in Southeast Asia) who had allegedly prospered at the expense of locals; from exaggerated suspicions that regional Chinese might be agents of the Qing

---

[8] Ngoei 2019a, 49–50. See also Kratoska 2003, 3–22.   [9] Ngoei 2019a, 46–49.
[10] Kramer 2011, 1366.   [11] French 2012; Hack 2021.

Dynasty; and from crude xenophobia that deemed diasporic Chinese hateful interlopers. Furthermore, colonial authorities in Southeast Asia had over the centuries occasionally stoked this anti-Chinese prejudice to deflect local animosity away from themselves, a practice that sometimes escalated into indigenous violence against, and even massacres of, Southeast Asia's Chinese. Indeed, regional ill will against diasporic Chinese may have burned somewhat brighter in the early Cold War, thanks to the CCP's conspicuous wooing of Southeast Asia's Chinese; its infiltrating of the region's Chinese cultural organizations and middle schools, pouring into them copious amounts of communist propaganda; and its courting of indigenous communist factions in the region. The MCP's ideological materials (anthems, propaganda, and more) also inadvertently did Britain a favor by crowing about its links to the CCP, situating their "war of liberation of the Malayan people" within the worldwide Marxist–Leninist revolution, the vanguard of which was China, which the MCP called a "friend and brother."[12]

Thus, Britain's anti-MCP propaganda from the late 1940s through 1950s gamely conflated the MCP's mostly Chinese composition with the Cold War bogeyman of revolutionary communism, emphasizing that communism was at once barbaric and fundamentally foreign. British messaging along these subtle racialized themes met the receptive ears of the indigenous Malays who comprised nearly half the country's population. At any rate, most non-Chinese in Malaya, not just the Malays but also Indians and communities of mixed European and Asian heritage, already distrusted the MCP, wary that so few of its members hailed from outside of the Chinese community. This state of affairs made the MCP's somewhat bloodless drive to recruit non-Chinese even more anemic. Worse, following Japan's surrender in 1945, the MCP had conducted a spree of deadly reprisals against Malays for allegedly collaborating with Japanese occupying forces. For most Malays, then, sympathy for the MCP's anti-colonial, pro-independence movement was dead on arrival.

British officials and Malay conservative elites (including members of the Malay aristocracy) thus came together easily via an intertwining of enduring anti-Chinese hatred, anti-MCP grievances and security concerns, and racialized anti-communism. Malay elites found it made good sense to ally themselves with Britain, the most convenient party on hand with the security tools to protect them from both MCP violence and the possibility that China might intervene in Malaya through local communists. Likewise, Britain knew well that a firm partnership with the majority ethnic group and non-Chinese in Malaya served their neo-colonial aims.[13]

---

[12] Ngoei 2019, 51–52; Ngoei 2021, 246.
[13] Ngoei 2019a, Ch. 2. For more on British relations with the Malay community and its elites in the immediate wake of World War II, see Lau 1991.

But if winning Malays over to racialized anti-communism seemed easy, bringing Malaya's Chinese on board Britain's anti-MCP campaign promised to be more challenging. At minimum, British officials had to persuade Malaya's Chinese elites to turn their community against an organization made almost entirely of Chinese and to support the brutal suppression of those who might be kith or kin. Moreover, the MCP for a time after 1945 enjoyed high regard among scores of Malayan Chinese. MCP fighters had, like the Vietminh in Indochina, been the backbone of a resistance movement against the Japanese. And many of Malaya's Chinese (even the non-communists) genuinely entertained sympathies for the CCP, and cheered that the communists had driven Chiang Kai Shek's corrupt KMT (Kuomintang, or Guomindang) to Taiwan. To be sure, other Chinese in Malaya maintained vague but emotionally resonant affiliations with Taipei, judging that the KMT remained more representative of Chinese culture and history than the CCP. Britain would need to redirect all such Chinese alignments, whether to Beijing or Taipei, toward a future Malayan nation-state, one in which ethnic Chinese could coexist peacefully with other ethnicities who had traditionally treated them with hostility. In short, Britain could not simply cut the Chinese out of their plans since they comprised nearly 40 percent of Malaya's population.

Britain's task proved less onerous than expected, though. Many of Malaya's Chinese elites ultimately sided with Britain. After all, a fair number of them had accumulated significant wealth under British rule; some of their families had been resident in Malaya for centuries, and were thoroughly Anglicized (many Christianized, too) after generations in the empire. Importantly, most of these elites anticipated that the MCP would treat thriving capitalists like them as class enemies, a chilling thought shared also by the Malay elites who were part of the aristocracy. Thus, like their Malay counterparts, local Chinese elites reached for British security guarantees.

Particularly important in this regard was a well-known, successful Malayan Chinese businessman named Tan Cheng Lock. Tan was the kind of conservative nationalist that Britain sought among Malayan Chinese. He was pro-British and also commanded the deep respect of Malayan Chinese in and beyond elite circles. Britain hoped he would convince Malayan Chinese to unite with the Malays in support of both the anti-MCP campaign and the creation of an independent, multiracial, and anti-communist Malaya. Tan responded positively to these exhortations by senior British officials and helped sway Malaya's Chinese community toward Britain.

In 1949, Tan founded the Malayan Chinese Association (MCA), pushing for the rapid establishment of MCA chapters all over the country. With these chapters as nodes to spread his message, he urged Malayan Chinese to "Wake up and Unite" with the Malays and other ethnic communities of the country. He urged the pursuit of "inter-communal understanding" with Malays especially, to thereby create "one nationality" for Malaya to someday become independent. He was also adept at prodding the MCA's wealthiest members to invest in uplifting the poor within the Chinese community, stating in public that these moves would make Malayan Chinese "Communist-proof," would dampen the "siren voice of Communism." Crucially, he and British officials labored to compel Malayan Chinese to participate in the anti-MCP effort. Tan believed that the "best man" to subdue the ethnic Chinese "Communist rebel or agent" in Malaya is the Chinese "detective or soldier." In fact, many Malayan Chinese were sufficiently moved by Tan and British officials to be informants (at great risk to their lives), to serve in the Malayan Special Constabulary and as interpreters in the jungle fighting squads, and more besides. The MCP, finding that more and more Malayan Chinese had become part of the anti-Chinese anti-communist campaign, could only circulate propaganda materials that blasted all ethnic Chinese who joined Malaya's auxiliary force. In the words of a US diplomat extoling Britain's ostensible success with turning Malayan Chinese against the MCP: "it is time we learnt the trick of ... having Asians fight Asian battles ... where necessary, yellow men will be killed by yellow men rather than by white men alone."[14]

Clearly, Tan's impact on Malayan politics was profound. By the early 1950s, Malay royals thought Tan so popular that they began fretting over the prospect of him leading a movement to abolish the Malay monarchy and become the president of a Malayan republic. The overwrought anxieties of aristocrats aside, British officials did express irritation at Tan's "monopoly" over the Chinese community's dealings with colonial authorities. Nevertheless, they appreciated that the very existence of the MCA and Tan's messaging had soothed Sino-Malay tensions, increasing the potential of a multiracial Malayan coalition that would aid Britain against the communists. The MCP, too, absorbed that Tan's efforts could endanger their cause, attempting (and failing) to kill him in a grenade attack. Going after the much beloved Tan was but one of the MCP's self-defeating moves, the list of which included intimidating and brutalizing Chinese villagers throughout Malaya to acquire funding, food, and medical supplies. As the MCP's revolt wore on, the admiration that it once enjoyed among Malayan Chinese took a serious hit.[15]

The MCP's grenade attack on Tan only convinced him that he was on the right side of history. In 1952, he had the MCA reach across the political aisle to the dominant Malay nationalist party, UMNO (United Malays National Organization), forming the Alliance coalition. (That same year, Tan was knighted for his services to the British Empire.) By then, UMNO's leader, the future Malayan Prime Minister Tunku Abdul Rahman[16] (1957–70), was also ready to combine forces with the MCA, reasoning that it was a necessary and

[14] Ngoei 2019a, 46, 56, 61–66. [15] Ngoei 2019a, 56–57, 64.
[16] "Tunku" is the Malay word for prince. In British, Malayan, and Singaporean records, Prince Abdul Rahman was typically referred to as "the Tunku." US diplomatic records followed suit from the early 1960s onward. This chapter does the same.

pragmatic bargain for Malaya to secure a peaceful future as an independent nation. At any rate, British leaders had also impressed on all local political elites that London simply would not grant Malaya independence until its major ethnic communities – Chinese, Malay, and Indian – came to a "durable accord." Naturally, both Tan and the Tunku were eager to persuade London that this accord was already manifest, with the Alliance drawing into its fold the Malayan Indian Congress (a party for ethnic Indians, just as the MCA was for ethnic Chinese). Furthermore, both men calculated that when Britain eventually organized national elections in Malaya, the multiracial Alliance would surely score thumping wins. For each major ethnic community would be able to project their hopes upon the party representing their ethnicity within the Alliance coalition. In the 1955 national elections, the Alliance did win all but one of the political seats available.[17]

Just two years later, Britain granted formal independence to Malaya, confident in the pro-British, anti-communist collaborators who sat in its government. In effect, British colonialism in Malaya had morphed via the consent and collaboration of indigenous nationalists into an informal mode, its neo-colonial substance barely veiled by London's official handover of power to local, pro-West leaders. By 1960, when Malaya's government declared the emergency at an end, the MCP had already been decimated and iced out of Malayan politics.

Malaya's path to independence suggests that Sukarno's charges of British *nekolim* were broadly accurate. In fact, Britain remained almost entirely responsible for Malaysia's (including Singapore's) national defense into the late 1960s, due not only to agreements with willing Malayan and Singaporean leaders but also to the vast military installations that Britain still controlled in Singapore (plus several in the Malay peninsula). Some 30,000 British servicemen were stationed in Singapore alone, a deployment second in size to only the 50,000 troops that London had committed to NATO. The Tunku, for his part, once openly admitted that his nation's defense arrangements with London made it "treaty-bound" to support Britain's military response against any aggressors and connected Malaya intimately with the US-led SEATO, of which Britain was a member, even though Malaya (and Malaysia afterward) never joined the pact. To boot, Britain's maintenance of its Singapore bases contributed to 20 percent of Singapore's national income (approximately US$200 million at the time), and in small and large ways fed the livelihoods of nearly a tenth of the country's population for years after the republic's independence.[18]

All that said, Sukarno's bad blood with Malaya and Britain ran even deeper. After Malaya gained independence in 1957, it would assist Britain and the

---

[17] Ngoei 2019a, 62, 69, 71–72.
[18] Ngoei 2019a, 117–118, 138. "Tunku" is the Malay word for prince. In British, Malayan, and Singaporean records, Prince Abdul Rahman was typically referred to as "the Tunku." U.S. diplomatic records followed suit from the early 1960s onward. This chapter does the same.

United States in an abortive operation to remove the left-leaning Sukarno from power. The Tunku enabled arms purchased in Singapore to be smuggled through Malaya to Indonesian rebels, allowed these rebels to promote their cause in Malaya, and more. And though the Tunku and Sukarno would publicly declare that bygones were bygones in 1959, the Malayan leader readily supported operations against Indonesia during *Konfrontasi*. The Tunku would also make plain before *Konfrontasi* even commenced that the formation of Malaysia was to ensure that communists had "no opportunity to work against Britain and the Americans," that Malaysia was inherently "anti-communist," signaling therefore an underlying antagonism toward Indonesia, then home to the third-largest communist party in world.[19]

As Sukarno had foreseen, the creation of Malaysia did pose a threat to Indonesia, though it must be said that Sukarno's assertiveness was partly galvanized by Beijing's repeated promises to back him in a conflict against Britain and Malaysia. But whereas China was a no-show in the actual confrontations that ensued, Britain, Commonwealth forces, and the Tunku's government collaborated easily to destabilize Sukarno's regime. Britain and Malaysia covertly aided secessionist movements in Indonesia and launched clandestine raids into Indonesian Borneo that kept pushing Indonesia's military onto the backfoot.[20]

Even Singapore, part of Malaysia until August 1965, played a substantial role in diplomatically isolating Indonesia. Singapore Prime Minister Lee Kuan Yew, on whirlwind tours of Afro-Asian states in 1962 and 1964, successfully persuaded major nonaligned nations (India, Yugoslavia, Burma, Egypt, and others) that Sukarno was the unreasonable aggressor, that Malaysia was an innocent victim with just recourse to British military protection. Per this line of reasoning, Britain's Singapore bases were not evidence of neo-colonialism but indispensable facilities for Malaysia's defense against Indonesia. In early 1965, Lee's diplomacy bore yet more fruit when the United Nations Security Council (UNSC) welcomed Malaysia as a nonpermanent member, endorsed by the nonaligned nations in the UNSC that Lee had visited. Needless to say, Lee and the Malaysian diplomats accompanying him on these visits never revealed to their hosts any information about the secret British–Malaysian attacks on Indonesian Borneo. Playing the victim made this mandatory.[21] Sukarno, frustrated that he could not block Malaysia's entry into the UNSC, had Indonesia's delegates withdraw from the United Nations altogether, sending his nation further into isolation. Anti-communist army officers would soon seize power and shunt Sukarno from authority.

---

[19] Ngoei 2019a, 128, 138–144. For detailed information about Beijing's promises to support Sukarno's *Konfrontasi*, see Zhou 2015.
[20] Zhou 2015; Ngoei 2019a, 128, 138–144.   [21] Ngoei 2019a, 138–144.

Despite carrying the day against Sukarno, albeit indirectly, British leaders acknowledged during *Konfrontasi* that clinging to power in Southeast Asia – maintaining its military installations in Singapore, in particular – had finally become too expensive. From the late 1960s, London began to withdraw its military from Singapore and the region altogether, a turn of events that saw Malaysia's and Singapore's pro-British alignment gradually transform into a pro-US tilt.

14.3 Southeast Asia's Pro-US Trajectory after 1945: Comparing Malaya, Indonesia, and Thailand

Developments in Malaya were not unique, and to a fair degree mirrored the pro-US trajectory of most Southeast Asian nations, bar the states that once comprised French Indochina. Prevailing indigenous prejudice against local Chinese populations also simmered in countries like Indonesia and Thailand, an animus entangled with suspicions that China would seek hegemony in the region with the aid of its diaspora. Just like in Malaya, this indigenous antagonism in Indonesia and Thailand factored significantly in both states' adoption of an anti-communist position and determination to buttress US neo-colonialism in Southeast Asia.

Even so, it is worth briefly looking beyond the similarities to note some differences between Malaya's example and developments in Indonesia and Thailand. For one, British neo-colonialism unfolded in the context of a colonized territory (Malaya) gaining formal independence but remaining closely linked economically, militarily, and ideologically to its former foreign ruler. In contrast, Indonesia and Thailand had not been colonies of the United States; as Sawasdipakdi outlines in Chapter 3 in this volume, Thailand had never been formally colonized.

Nevertheless, US neo-colonialism in the Cold War – operationalized in its policy of containment against the USSR and China – ran on much the same logic as Britain's endeavor to maintain influence in its former colonies. More parallels exist between Washington's and London's strategies for Southeast Asia than not. Both the United States and Britain sought to quash revolutionary communist factions in the region, believing that communist predominance would wall Southeast Asia off to Western influence as well as scotch new opportunities to develop beneficial economic and politico-security ties. Washington in particular sought to integrate Southeast Asian states into a postwar liberal international order, making the region one component of the many US-led economic and security networks that spanned much of the world. However, US and British leaders both shared the conviction that, after World War II, Southeast Asian nationalism could not be snuffed out, that nationalists must be enticed and cajoled into collaborating with the West. Thus, Britain and the United States attempted to fashion neo-colonial relationships with regional actors to replace the outmoded, formal colonialism of the nineteenth century. Where Britain cultivated conservative Malay and Chinese nationalists with the guarantees of safety from the mostly-Chinese MCP, the United States likewise offered economic and military aid to win over the conservative elites of Indonesia and Thailand (as well as other states of the region), promising to help rout domestic left-wing threats and stem the influence of Moscow and, above all, Beijing. As it turned out, the Western powers and their partners in Indonesia and Thailand were united by fears that Beijing would weaponize its diaspora and turn it into a fifth column for asserting control over the region.[22]

Of course, the US-Indonesian relationship in the early Cold War when compared to that of Britain and Malaya was more fraught. Though the United States had helpfully pressured the Netherlands to end its recolonization campaign in Indonesia, US leaders proffering economic and military aid to Sukarno through the 1950s could neither pry him from his connections to the Indonesian communists (despite not being a communist himself) nor dampen his admiration of the radical anti-imperialism he perceived in Chinese communism.[23] Ultimately, the United States switched tack after failing to overthrow Sukarno in the late 1950s, choosing instead to nurture collaborators within the Indonesian army, providing its officers training, equipment, and funding. With this move, Washington hit the jackpot, finding ardent anti-communists in the Indonesian Army officers who vehemently objected to both Sukarno's pro-China tendencies and the apparent sway that the Indonesian Communist Party (PKI) held over him. By the mid-1960s, US courting of Indonesia's army had produced what one historian has dubbed a conservative, right-wing "government-in-waiting," primed to wrest control of the republic when a suitable moment arrived.[24]

It would be the PKI that like the MCP in Malaya inadvertently manufactured precisely such a moment, kicking open the door to its own destruction. High-ranking members of the PKI had surmised correctly that members of the Indonesian Army were plotting a coup and shared with Chinese leaders in Beijing (including Mao Zedong) their plan to team up with pro-Sukarno air force officers, sequester and protect Sukarno, and then establish a revolutionary military committee to take control of the country and solidify Indonesia's pro-China leanings. In October 1965, when a small band of PKI leaders actually made their move, they not only caught Beijing off guard but also played into the hands of the right-wing segments of the Indonesia Army.[25]

Major General Suharto of the army, a fervent anti-communist, rapidly seized the initiative. With a powerful misinformation campaign that benefited from

---

[22] Ngoei 2019, 47–49. Also see Ngoei 2014. [23] Guan 2018, 85, 87–88.
[24] Roosa 2006, Ch. 6. [25] See Zhou 2014.

US assistance and equipment (rendered opportunistically by the US embassy in Jakarta), Suharto and his army officers disingenuously alleged that the PKI was working *against* Sukarno; that the PKI was a puppet of the CCP; and that ethnic Chinese Indonesians were empowering China's encroachments in Indonesia. At base, Suharto and US officials (though not directly in concert) had expediently capitalized on the popular antipathy which non-Chinese Indonesians felt toward ethnic Chinese and China, spurring ordinary Indonesians and the armed forces to perpetrate a massive and bloody anti-Chinese, anti-communist purge. The Indonesian massacre extinguished upward of half a million lives within a few months, thousands of them ethnic Chinese, some communists, but certainly not all. The army would also coerce Indonesian Chinese to leave the country altogether, causing an estimated 200,000 Chinese, including those whose families had long settled in Indonesia, to flee to China. This savage racialized anti-communism enabled the new regime (which Suharto came to dominate) to eclipse and oust Sukarno. Indonesia would break diplomatic relations with China in 1967, send Chinese ambassadorial staff packing, and align itself firmly with the United States.[26]

The anti-Chinese violence in Indonesia in 1965 was not unique in the country's history (like in Malaya, it tapped into a history of racial and ethnic antagonism). As recently as 1963, Sukarno himself had passed discriminatory laws against Chinese residents in Indonesia, permitting officials to evict Indonesian Chinese from their homes on the premise that they posed threats to national security. Only a decade prior, he had affirmed the anti-Chinese hatred swirling in Indonesian society by restricting the economic activities of Indonesian Chinese, which saw about 100,000 ethnic Chinese leave the republic to avoid other extreme forms of persecution. In the early twentieth century, too, Indonesian nationalists fueled local antagonism toward, and attacks on, the local Chinese communities, derogating them as "capitalists, infidels ... aliens, and as collaborators of the hated" Dutch.[27] In Indonesia, as in Malaya, indigenous anti-Chinese prejudice, its vicious predilections stimulated and channeled by conservative elites and Western powers into anti-communist violence, had enabled Southeast Asian nationalism and Anglo-American neo-colonialism to intertwine, becoming mutually constitutive.

Thailand's switch from a purported neutrality in foreign relations to firm US ally, member of SEATO, and host to US forces resembled developments in Malaya's and Indonesia's early Cold War history, as did its tradition of anti-Chinese sentiments. When nationalists in Siam began in the 1930s to construct a national identity based on the Thai ethnicity, they fed popular prejudices against the Chinese communities in the kingdom, dialing up Thai resentment

[26] Roosa 2006, Ch. 6; Zhou 2015, 209, 219–220, 224.
[27] Kuhn 2008, 271, 287–289, 296–297; Amrith 2012, 95, 124; Zhou 2015, 219.

that ethnic Chinese dominated the economy. The nationalists clearly intended to consolidate the meaning of a pure Thai by designating ethnic Chinese as the "other." In this period, Thai Prime Minister Lieutenant-Colonel Plaek Phibunsongkhram, known to Western leaders as Phibun, would introduce a "Thai-ification" program, forcing Chinese out of major labor and industrial sectors and replacing them with ethnic Thai. (Sukarno executed a similar scheme two decades later, as did the Philippine government, in fact.) The Phibun government of the 1930s also targeted KMT activists in Thailand for arrest and deportation, concerned that these activists might draw Thai Chinese loyalties and resources toward mainland China (which the KMT still controlled at the time).[28]

With the CCP's 1949 victory in the mainland, however, Thai nationalism's animosity toward domestic Chinese and KMT-led China intersected with the Cold War anti-communism of the United States. The new communist government of China had begun to excoriate Phibun in its newspapers, condemning his prejudicial treatment of Thai Chinese in the 1930s, and declaring that China would back its diaspora.[29] Indeed, the CCP came to decide by 1950 that it would "redouble efforts to utilize overseas Chinese groups" for the "strengthening and expanding [of] Communist influence in Southeast Asia." US intelligence soon discovered, too, that CCP agents in Thailand had been working with the "alien minority" of Thai Chinese, through Chinese language schools and cultural activities, building the "largest alien Communist Party" in Southeast Asia besides the MCP in Malaya.[30]

Phibun, perceiving that China and the overseas Chinese in Thailand now represented a possible threat, resolved in 1950 to acquire military and economic aid from the United States, to use these resources to suppress local Chinese and leftist rivals as well as guard against China's apparent expansionist ambitions. This fateful decision, animated by anti-Chinese and anti-China fears, produced what one historian has called a "foreign policy revolution" in Thai history, setting Thailand on a direct path into the US orbit.[31]

The United States was happy to meet Phibun halfway. After all, Thailand was located strategically in the center of mainland Southeast Asia, surrounded by Burma, Malaya, and Indochina, all of which faced the armed revolts of local communist factions in the late 1940s and early 1950s. For US containment policy to make progress in this sector of Southeast Asia, American decision-makers accepted they must shake hands with Phibun. In doing so, they looked past Phibun's sordid record of supporting Japan during World War II, past even the fact that, after resigning in 1945 when the Allies won, he barged back into power via

---

[28] Kuhn 2008, 271, 287–289, 296–297.   [29] Ngoei, forthcoming. Also see Fineman 2009.
[30] Ngoei 2021, 245–247.   [31] Fineman 2009.

a military coup in 1947, undermining Thailand's democratically elected postwar government.[32]

Phibun, desperate to prove to the United States that he was a suitable collaborator, wanted to seal the deal. Thus, he supported US policy toward Vietnam by officially recognizing former Annamese emperor Bao Dai as Vietnamese leader, a figurehead who France had cynically installed in 1949 to placate Vietnamese nationalists. Phibun knew that Bao Dai had little to no stock with the Vietnamese people, that Ho Chi Minh was far more popular, but hoped his actions would win over the Americans. His gambit paid off. US leaders definitely saw in Phibun's conservative, military-dominated regime a choice ally against the radical, left-wing movements of the region. Generous amounts of US aid began to flow toward Phibun's government, raising his prestige in the military, empowering him to crush his political rivals.[33]

In July 1950, Phibun would take another pro-US action by sending Thai expeditionary forces to support the American-led UN coalition in the Korean War. He and the Thai military anticipated (accurately) that such a decision would elicit further rewards from Washington in the form of military equipment, and brazenly stamped on civilian opposition in parliament to the deployment of Thai forces. The civilian wing of the Thai parliament, hobbled, continued to stubbornly insist that Thailand nurture good relations on both sides of the Cold War divide, not just with the United States. This became their undoing. Phibun and the military elites labeled them dissidents, throwing into this same category all activists and journalists who chose to quibble with the pro-US turn in Thai policy. A government crackdown swiftly followed and turned Thailand into something of a police state by 1953. US leaders, keen on the supposed stability guaranteed by a conservative, anti-communist strongman, stuck by Phibun, as well as embraced and supported the subsequent authoritarian military leaders of Thailand who mounted coups to fill his shoes. Throughout, Thailand remained a loyal Cold War ally, joining SEATO in 1954, offering Bangkok to serve as the organization's headquarters, as well as Thai air and naval bases for US military campaigns against North Vietnam. By the late 1960s, US officials judged that Thailand's military regime had absorbed so much aid from the United States over the decades, and set itself so decisively against China (during the wars in Korea and Vietnam), that Thai leaders had little leeway to try an alternate superpower patron.[34]

---

[32] Fineman 1997, Ch. 1–3.   [33] Fineman 2009.   [34] Fineman 2009; Fineman 1997, Ch. 9–10.

14.4 Conclusion: US Hegemony in Southeast Asia and the Question of Vietnam

Comparing the aims and actions of Phibun with those of Suharto and the Tunku reveals patterns more characteristic of Southeast Asia's Cold War history than the facile binary of Euro-American colonialism versus local self-determination. Southeast Asian nationalists were not bent on a narrow program for independence, on the expulsion of every vestige of Western colonialism. For conservative Southeast Asian nationalists looking to preserve or upgrade the status and privileges that they had enjoyed in the colonial era, reinvigorated and new connections to the appropriate Western powers promised to shield them from a range of threats. The region's conservative nationalists believed one such threat emanated from Beijing, and perceived that threat in the CCP's vigorous efforts to expand its influence through its Southeast Asian diaspora; in China's military intervention in the Korean War; and in its willingness to encourage the aggression of left-wing leaders like Sukarno. From the 1940s through 1960s, therefore, the pro-US trajectories of Thailand and Indonesia, as well as Malaya's alignment with Britain and the United States, all occurred because a rejuvenated local hostility toward China and Southeast Asian Chinese had converged with the goals of Anglo-American neo-colonialism.

For their part, Britain and the United States' post-1945 imperial projects in the region proved relatively more dynamic than those of the French and Dutch – they did not fixate on restoring a colonial system already broken by the war against Japan. Instead, the Anglo-American allies strove to incorporate formally independent states into a US-led international order of economic and security networks, an informal empire of nation-states that of their own volition had acquiesced to American predominance. These key developments, in combination with the Philippines being a traditional US ally, the Indonesian Army's anti-communist coup tilting the republic away from Beijing, and Singapore eventually leaning toward Washington, meant that much of Southeast Asia was firmly anti-communist by late 1965, inherently upholding de facto US hegemony in the region.[35]

The suggestion that the United States enjoyed such influence in Southeast Asia, wider than often thought, sits uneasily with Washington's anxiety about the region's dominoes falling to communism and Khong's arguments in this volume about the sources of American commitments to Vietnam. Had US leaders completely misread regional developments? Why Americanize the Vietnam conflict when Southeast Asia was largely won over? Why, when the containment of Vietnam's revolution and China's (presumed) regional ambitions was more or less accomplished, did the US still commit to the fight?

---

[35] Ngoei 2019b, 301–312.

The past has more than enough room to accommodate the conflicting US assessments of Southeast Asia, for Washington to simultaneously discern its burgeoning informal empire while still convinced that its regional allies quaked under the shadow of communist expansionism. US decision-makers did glimpse in the rise of Malaysia the creation of a "wide-anticommunist arc" in Southeast Asia, believing the new federation completed a geostrategic crescent through the region, connecting anti-communist Thailand on one end and pro-US Philippines on the other. In this grand US vision, the arc "enclose[ed] the entire South China Sea" – Washington did indeed behold its substantial advantage over its Soviet and Chinese competitors. In 1963, President John F. Kennedy would even describe Malaysia as "the best hope" for regional security.[36]

But American optimism and strategic insight about Southeast Asia was also tenuous, inconsistent. US leaders often despaired, unsure if the various twists and turns of Southeast Asian affairs truly favored US aims. This certainly was the case with Indonesia, the most populous of Southeast Asian nations, which US officials had deemed a "far greater prize than Vietnam" from the early Cold War. Until 1967, Washington was never fully confident of what Suharto's right-wing coup augured for the republic; it kept holding out for confirmations of the new regime's alignment, delaying the decision to count Indonesia in America's corner.[37] Thus, it is no surprise that US officials were frequently pessimistic when it came to South Vietnam in the early 1960s, where the local communist faction was clearly growing in popularity and strength, and the Saigon government remained unstable despite decades of US economic and military aid. Add to the bleak US assessments of Vietnam the profound insecurity of President Lyndon Johnson, a leader that archival records show was so obsessed with his credibility and image that he chose to stake his reputation on the fate of Vietnam (against the counsel of his advisors and allies), and America ended up plunging headlong into a disastrous land war in Asia.[38] Here, then, we are left with the profound irony of Southeast Asia's Cold War – that Lyndon Johnson's tragic decision occurred just as most of the region was tilting toward Washington, when a nascent US hegemony had begun to take hold in Southeast Asia.

[36] Ngoei 2019a, 114–115. [37] Lawrence 2022. [38] Logevall 1999.

15 Mandates, Trusteeship, and Decolonization in the North Pacific: Balancing Self-Determination, Development, and Security

Joanne Wallis and Jack Corbett

15.1 Introduction

Both colonization and decolonization are ongoing processes rather than singular events.[1] While we can point to specific moments when legal authority was claimed or transferred, or when flags were raised and taken down, an undue focus on these events risks missing the threads that tie eras and regimes together. It also tends to create hard, conceptual distinctions – colonized and independent, for example – that provide a degree of analytic clarity, but come at the expense of both empirical accuracy and a broader theoretical appreciation of diversity and its importance to international order.[2] The fluidity of the continuum between colonization and sovereignty is particularly evident in the case in small islands generally and Pacific Island states specifically. Colonialism arrived late to much of the Pacific and was thus short-lived compared to other regions. Imperial powers also struggled to extend control beyond their administrative capitals. Yet newly independent states remain enmeshed in relations of dependence with metropolitan countries. Pacific countries receive some of the highest levels of Official Development Assistance per capita in the world, for example.[3] Indeed, while many island communities opted for sovereign independence between the 1960s and 1990s, a significant number retained forms of "non-sovereignty" or "free association" with states such as the United States, UK, France, and New Zealand in a belief that close links with metropolitan powers would lead to improved development outcomes. For our purposes the key point is that these alternative forms of sovereignty reflect a century-long process of experimentation with political forms for island communities and demonstrate historical legacies and the ambiguity of sovereignty itself.

---

[1] Banivanua-Mar 2016.   [2] Phillips and Sharman 2015.   [3] Dornan and Pryke 2017.

To substantiate this claim, this chapter traces the history of the ways island communities in the North Pacific have been governed over more than a century. The islands that constitute the North Pacific are today referred to as the Commonwealth of Northern Mariana Islands, the Federated States of Micronesia, Guam, Kiribati, Nauru, the Republic of Marshall Islands, and the Republic of Palau. To explain how these political units emerged, we argue that the diversity of sovereign forms reflects an attempt to balance the legitimation and then gradual delegitimation of imperialism, calls for greater self-determination by island communities, the developmental benefits of constitutional relationships with metropolitan powers, and the strategic interests of those powers. In doing so, we decenter the dominant Westphalian narrative about the form and function of states.[4] We consider how the differing forms and levels of sovereignty have created both opportunities and risks for Micronesians. Sovereignty brings with it the power to negotiate – and balance – diplomatic relations, but also vulnerability to coercion. Contingent sovereignty, in the form of compacts of free association, can have developmental and defence benefits, but can also leave states dependent on the United States, in particular. And remaining as US colonies brings economic opportunities and places territories within the US security umbrella, but leaves territories vulnerable to militarization and other forms of exploitation. The diversity of political forms in Micronesia also generates dilemmas for the United States, particularly the dilemma inherent to coloniality in a liberal international order: how to safeguard US interests without enforcing outcomes.

To flesh this out we begin by describing European, and later, Japanese colonization of the North Pacific. We then focus on the League of Nation's mandate system, which saw Japan granted the "South Seas Mandate" over former German territories north of the equator after World War I, including the Mariana Islands minus Guam, which the United States occupied in 1898 following Spain's defeat in the Spanish–American War, and the Caroline Islands. Australia, New Zealand, and Britain acquired a Class C mandate over Nauru and Britain one over the Gilbert Islands (now Kiribati). After World War II, in which some of the bloodiest battles were fought in the North Pacific, the mandate system was replaced by the trusteeship system, with the United States acquiring Japan's territories under the "strategic" Trust Territory of the Pacific Islands. We conclude by evaluating how the independence of this uniquely "strategic" Trust Territory, which was the last to decolonize, was negotiated in "free association" with the United States.

---

[4] Shilliam 2006; Adler-Nissen and Gammeltoft-Hansen 2008; Kayaoglu 2010; Hobson 2012; Adler-Nissen and Gad 2013.

15.2 Colonization and Mandates

The Pacific region was settled in waves of migration, from east to west, over a 50,000-year period.[5] Our focus is relatively contemporary by comparison, but it is important to note the obvious point from the outset that a myriad of political forms and practices pre-date the arrival of Europeans and shaped the way colonial administrators governed.[6] The districts that made up the US Trust Territory of the Pacific Islands map roughly on to existing language groups, for example. Much of the scholarship on these "traditional" political systems has been undertaken by anthropologists.[7] There is also a more recent attempt to recover our understanding of precolonial forms of diplomacy and consider how this might be shaping the present, too.[8] These studies highlight that while linguistic and cultural diversity led to a view that most societies in the Pacific existed in isolation from each other, complex patterns of exchange nevertheless linked islands sometimes thousands of kilometers apart.[9] The importance of interisland linkages also underpins recent understandings of modern statehood – Pacific countries increasingly present themselves to the world as "Large Ocean States,"[10] which is meant to "subvert narratives that focus on their 'smallness' and 'vulnerability' and to instead promote one that emphasises their resilience and potential," as well as their long-standing interconnectedness.[11] The retelling of this history has become a crucial means by which Pacific Islanders have sought to cultivate collaboration amidst diversity in a bid to counter and adapt to coloniality.[12] Reflecting the audience for this edited volume and the general neglect of the Pacific region by mainstream IR, our focus is more legal and institutional than these other studies. But we nevertheless take inspiration from them in our attempt to explain what the recent political forms are and summarize narratives of how they came to be.

The Spanish were the first Europeans to arrive in the Pacific. Spain claimed Guam in 1565 as a waypoint for galleons travelling to its colonies in the Philippines and Mexico. It took over the administration of the island in 1668. The Spanish conquest of Guam and the other Mariana Islands (contemporary Commonwealth of Northern Mariana Islands), and the length of their rule, partly explains the divergent political status of these islands compared to the rest of Micronesia, where the Spanish presence was much more limited until the late nineteenth century. As elsewhere, an enduring legacy of this period is the presence of Catholicism in much of the region.

---

[5] D'Arcy 2006.   [6] Puas 2021.
[7] Sahlins 1963; Thomas 1989; Lawson 2013; Kabutaulaka 2015.
[8] Nanau 2021; Naupa 2022; Waqavakatoga 2023.
[9] D'Arcy 2006, 146–147, cf. Hau'ofa 1994; Puas 2021, 43.   [10] Pacific Islands Forum 2012.
[11] Strating and Wallis 2022.   [12] Fry 2019.

However, Spain's colonization ended in the late nineteenth century. During the 1898 Spanish–American War, the United States seized Guam. Spain then sold the rest of its claim to the Micronesian subregion (indigenous inhabitants were not consulted and most were unaware) to Germany. During this period the United States also formally took Hawaii (where it had first arrived in the 1840s), the Philippines, and numerous uninhabited islands. It then acquired American Samoa in 1899. Germany had been expanding its influence through the region for some time. Germany negotiated with local chiefs to annex what has become the contemporary Republic of Marshall Islands in 1886 and then forcibly seized Nauru two years later. The main commercial interests for German colonists were copra, a source of coconut oil, and phosphate mining on Nauru and Angaur (Palau).[13]

German colonization was short-lived; shortly after the outbreak of World War I its territories were seized. After the war, the German territories were divided up by the victors, who saw annexation as compensation for their war losses. The Treaty of Versailles recognized Japan's occupation of the Micronesian islands, Australia's occupation of New Guinea and Nauru, and New Zealand's occupation of Western Samoa. However, the United States opposed Japanese annexation of the Micronesian islands because it was concerned that Japan could use them to cut off its access to the Philippines, and potentially as launching points from which to threaten Hawaii and Guam.[14] The compromise was the "South Seas Mandate" (contemporary Commonwealth of Northern Mariana Islands, Federated States of Micronesia, Palau, and the Republic of Marshall Islands).[15] This compromise reflected a broader one "between partisans of imperial annexation and those who wanted all colonies placed under international control."[16] Indeed, the Mandates system was "the only defence against a charge of simple annexation."[17]

Notably, the populations of the islands subject to League of Nations Mandates had no say in these decisions. According to Article 22 of the League Covenant, these peoples were assumed to be "not yet able to stand by themselves under the strenuous conditions of the modern world." Based on this assumption, the Mandate system supposedly "applied the principle that the well-being and development of such peoples form a sacred trust of civilization." For League members, the "best method of giving practical effect to this principle" was that "the tutelage of such people should be entrusted to advanced nations." A permanent Commission was established to "receive and examine the annual reports of the Mandatories and to advice the [League] Council on all matters relating to the observance of the mandates."

---

[13] See Firth 1997a.   [14] Hanlon 2014, 43.   [15] Hanlon 2014, 43.   [16] Susan 2015, 2.
[17] Susan 2015, 32.

Article 22 of the League Covenant provided that the perceived "stage of development of the people" determined the character of the Mandate to which they were subject. Pacific Island territories, "owing to the sparseness of their population, or their small size, or their remoteness from centres of civilization, or their geographic contiguity to the territory of the Mandatory," were seen as being "best administered under the laws of the Mandatory as integral portions of its territory" under what was known as a Class C Mandate. This meant that Nauru effectively reentered Australian colonial control, and the territories falling under the South Seas Mandate came under Japanese colonial control.

While the League of Nations Covenant stated that the populations of its Mandates should be subject to "safeguards . . . in the interests of the indigenous population," in practice this meant very little. Oversight by the Mandates Commission was weak, and "mandated territories were not better governed than colonies across the board."[18] It meant even less for the people of the Micronesian subregion after Japan withdrew from the League in the mid-1930s and was therefore no longer bound by the Covenant. Indeed, Japan had used its effective colonization of the territories subject to the South Sea Mandate as an opportunity to engage in an extension program of immigration into the region during the 1920s and 1930s, a consequence of which were estimates that indigenous inhabitants were outnumbered by 1935.[19]

Japan violated the requirements of the League Covenant from the beginning of its Mandate. Rather than safeguarding the interests of the indigenous populations, Japan designated Micronesians as a "third-class people"[20] and implemented a system of direct rule, whereby "colonial authorities appointed agents but gave them little or no responsibility to act on their own initiative."[21] This approach reflected the intensity of Japanese colonial rule; while the British or Australian governments sent only tens of colonial officials, the Japanese sent hundreds. The majority of the early migrants were men and intermarriage was relatively common (the first president of the Federated States of Micronesia, Tosiwo Nakayama, had a Japanese father).

Japanese colonization was also short-lived. Several islands in Micronesia became sites from which, and later upon which, the bloodiest battles of the Pacific War were fought. As the United States had feared, Japan used its territories in Micronesia to mount assaults on US bases in Hawaii, and later Guam, with its December 1941 attack on the US naval base at Pearl Harbour in Honolulu precipitating the formal entry of the United States into the war. As the war progressed, Japan then used its territories as bases from which to attack other US and Australian territories in the Pacific, including New Guinea and Solomon Islands.

---

[18] Susan 2015, 4.   [19] Susan 2015, 46.   [20] Firth 1997a, 263.   [21] Firth 1997a, 274.

By May 1942, Japan's Greater East Asia Co-Prosperity Sphere included most of Southeast Asia, the Gilbert Islands (part of contemporary Kiribati), Solomon Islands, New Guinea, and parts of Papua. Japan's expansion was only halted by the Battles of the Coral Sea and Midway, in which the Americans and Australians repelled the Japanese advance. From January 1944, the Americans and Australians reclaimed their territories and took Japanese islands, beginning with Majuro Atoll in the Marshalls, and gradually extending to the entirety of Japanese Micronesia.[22]

15.3 "Strategic" Trusteeship

At the end of World War II, the US Department of Defense wanted to address its strategic vulnerabilities through the Micronesian region, which had become evident during World War II.[23] To that end, it sought, and the US government acquired, Japan's territories in Micronesia under the United Nations trusteeship model. Like the Mandate system, the Trusteeship model was justified on the grounds of "native welfare," but differed by introducing emerging international norms about improving political development.[24] Article 76 of the United Nations Charter therefore specified that the "basic objectives" of the trusteeship system included promoting "the political, economic, social, and educational advancement of the inhabitants of trust territories, and their progressive development towards self-government or independence"; encouraging "respect for human rights and for fundamental freedoms"; and ensuring "equal treatment in social, economic, and commercial matters," and "in the administration of justice." There were eleven Trust Territories, including four in the Pacific region: Papua New Guinea (Australia), Nauru (Australia), Western Samoa (New Zealand), and the Trust Territory of the Pacific Islands (the United States).

The Trust Territory of the Pacific Islands, which consisted of islands that would become the contemporary Federated States of Micronesia, Republic of Marshall Islands, Palau, and the Commonwealth of the Northern Mariana Islands, was formally approved by the UN in 1947 (Table 15.1).[25] It was designated as a "strategic area" under Article 82 of the United Nations Charter,[26] given the American lives lost fighting for the islands during the war, and its proximity to US bases on Hawaii and Guam.[27] This meant that

---

[22] Firth 1997b.
[23] The sections on "Strategic Trusteeship" and "Free Association" have been rewritten for this chapter based on material collected for Corbett 2023. Some phrases and the use of some quotes may recur.
[24] Fry 2019, 66; cf, Roff 1991, Chapter 1.
[25] The US Trust Territory period has attracted considerable scholarship. See, for example, Gale 1979; McHenry 1975; Nufer 1978.
[26] United Nations Security Council 1947.   [27] McHenry 1975.

Table 15.1 Transitions between colonization and sovereignty in the North Pacific

Country	Colonization	Trusteeship	Current status
Commonwealth of Northern Mariana Islands	Initially claimed by Spain in 1521 (as part of Spanish East Indies) Sold to Germany under the German–Spanish Treaty of 1899	Occupied by Japan in 1914 League of Nations Mandate held by Japan from 1919 as part of the South Seas Mandate Occupied by the United States in 1944 Administered by the United States as part of the United Nations Trust Territory of the Pacific Islands from 1947	Commonwealth of the United States since 1986 (having rejected integration with Guam and approved commonwealth status in a 1975 referendum)
Federated States of Micronesia	Claimed by Spain in 1528, although Europeans did not visit again until 1696. Spanish founded a settlement in 1887 (as part of Spanish East Indies) Sold to Germany in 1899 after the 1898 Spanish–American War	Captured by Japan in 1914 League of Nations Mandate awarded to Japan in 1919 as part of the South Seas Mandate Administered by the United States under the Trust Territory of the Pacific Islands from 1947	Compact of Free Association with the United States from 1986
Guam	Initially claimed by Spain in 1521 (part of the Marianas archipelago) as part of the Spanish East Indies Ceded to the United States in 1899 after the 1898 Spanish–American War	Invaded by Japan in 1941 Reoccupied by the United States in 1944	Unincorporated territory of the United States
Kiribati	British protectorate (as the Gilbert and Ellice Islands) from 1886 under the Anglo-German Agreement	British Crown colony from 1916 Occupied by Japan from 1941 to 1943 Reoccupied by the British in 1943	Independent state since 1979 (Tuvalu becomes a separate state in 1978)

Nauru	Annexed by Germany in 1888 under the 1886 Anglo-German Agreement and incorporated into the Marshall Islands Protectorate	Occupied by Australia in 1914 League of Nations Mandate held by Australia, New Zealand, and the United Kingdom from 1923 Occupied by Japan from 1942 to 1945 United Nations Trusteeship held by Australia, New Zealand, and the United Kingdom from 1947	Independent state from 1968
Republic of Marshall Islands	Formally claimed by Spain in 1874 as part of the Spanish East Indies	Occupied by Japan in 1914 League of Nations Mandate held by Japan from 1919 as part of the South Seas Mandate Occupied by the United States in 1944 Administered by the United States as part of the United Nations Trust Territory of the Pacific Islands from 1947	Compact of Free Association with the United States from 1986
Republic of Palau	Made part of the Spanish East Indies in 1885 Sold to Germany in 1899 after the 1898 Spanish–American War	Occupied by Japan in 1914 League of Nations Mandate held by Japan from 1919 as part of the South Seas Mandate Occupied by the United States from 1944 Administered by the United States as part of the United Nations Trust Territory of the Pacific Islands from 1947	Compact of Free Association with the United States from 1994

oversight of the Trust Territory was exercised by the United Nations Security Council, rather than the General Assembly, as was the case for the other ten trusteeships. Consequently, the United States was not obliged to report to the Trusteeship Council, and for decades the islands were essentially shut off from the world. It also meant that the United States was entitled to establish military bases and station armed forces in the Trust Territory, as well as to enlist the local population.

Occupation by the United States brought some benefits to the local populations. Indigenous Chamorros from Guam and American Samoans enjoyed free access to the United States from 1950 and 1951, respectively. Reflecting the militarization of these US territories, many Chamorros and American Samoans joined the US military.[28] But while the extensive militarization of Guam generated an economic boom, it also led to significant in-migration, first by Palauans, later by Federated States of Micronesia citizens, and later still by Filipinos and others from mainland Asia who arrived as teachers and medical professionals, as well as semiskilled laborers. This meant that the Chamorros became a minority in Guam.[29]

Nuclear testing in the Marshall Islands in the late 1940s and early 1950s left whole islands uninhabitable and brought severe health effects from radiation poisoning to local populations. This legacy reflects a common US attitude, captured in this quote by Henry Kissinger in the late 1960s when discussing the possibility of exercising eminent domain provisions to cease land for military purposes in Micronesia: "There are only 90,000 people out there. Who gives a damn?"[30] The political battle for compensation to the victims of the US nuclear legacy in the Pacific is ongoing and linked to a broader regional consensus on denuclearization enshrined in the *South Pacific Nuclear Free Zone Treaty* signed in 1985, which prohibited the use (or threat of use), testing, and stationing of nuclear weapons in the Pacific Islands,[31] and which the United States has not joined. More recently, several Pacific states have been at the vanguard of efforts to secure implementation of the 2020 *Treaty on the Prohibition of Nuclear Weapons*.

For critics, the US administration of the Trust Territory of the Pacific Islands amounted to de facto annexation in a bid to balance the military importance of the islands against the United States' and UN's opposition to colonialism.[32] The nature of US administration slowly began to shift during the 1960s. One reason is that, despite its unique status, the US Trust Territory was not immune to the growing strength of international norms about what constituted legitimate self-determination.[33] District-level advisory bodies, whose boundaries had

---

[28] Shigematsu and Camacho 2010. [29] Nero 1997a.
[30] This is widely quoted. For a recent example, see Kuper 2022. [31] Power 1986.
[32] Power 1986; cf, Roff 1991, 57. [33] United Nations Department of Political Affairs 1993.

a basis in the remnants of the Micronesian traditional system of political organization, were established early on as part of the Trust Territory administrative architecture.[34] A territory-wide representative body – the Congress of Micronesia – was authorized in 1964 to represent each district.[35] It created a Future Political Status Commission in 1967 to negotiate the end of the Trusteeship.[36] Micronesian criticism of American rule described it as a "zoo philosophy" in that administrators saw no reason for Micronesians to modernize.[37] Indeed, the region was colloquially known as the "Rust Territory" due to the pervasive sense of neglect.[38] But the Future Political Status Commission was also concerned that the pursuit of decolonial dignity had to be balanced against the need for development. Marshallese intellectual Carl Heine reflected:

> As Micronesia continues in its quest for a political future, it must be kept in mind that there are those who will sacrifice everything in the name of "Micronesian dignity." Whatever the choice may be, it must be remembered that there can be no dignity if there is poverty; there can be no dignity of the human life if there is hunger; there can be no dignity of the mind if there is ignorance; there can be no dignity if the body is sick; and there can be no dignity if the soul is without hope. Also, there can be no dignity if these outer islands people have no sense of belonging to their own government simply because that government does not care or will not extend its hand that far.[39]

Micronesian and international pressure to decolonize was balanced against shifting US security imperatives. From the late 1960s, the Nixon Doctrine moved the American defence perimeter from Japan, Okinawa, and the Philippines to Guam and the Trust Territory. This increased the strategic importance of the islands right at the historical moment when decolonization was gathering pace across the globe. In this context, the United States had to find a new way to legitimize their presence in the region. This intent is captured in the 1963 Solomon Report, commissioned by the US Government to draft recommendations for its future policy toward Micronesia. The report argued that increased development aid and intensive education and public awareness about the benefits of US rule were the best way to ensure local agreement to a strong presence.[40] That report has since been described by critics as a "America's ruthless blueprint for the assimilation of Micronesia."[41] Ironically, in practice it could be said to have had the opposite effect, with increased education of Micronesian elites generating growing decolonial awareness that were in turn reflected in later negotiations about political status.[42]

---

[34] Heine 1970, 197.
[35] Secretary of Interior Order No. 2882, September 28, 1964, cited in Roff 1991, 65.
[36] Heine 1970, 201.   [37] Heine 1970, 88.   [38] Heine 1970, 88.   [39] Heine 1970, 88.
[40] McHenry 1975.   [41] Solomon 1963.   [42] McHenry 1975, 10.

15.4 Free Association

The decade after the establishment of the Political Status Commission involved intense negotiations to find a de jure status that Micronesians found tolerable, conformed with international ideas about self-determination, and continued to guarantee US security interests in the region.[43] Ultimately, the solution was a unique form of independence in "free association" with the United States. This solution was created specifically for small island territories that desired greater autonomy over domestic policy but were deemed too small in terms of population and resources to be viable states. Notions of what constituted "viability" were vague, but the core idea was that these territories would struggle to generate enough revenue via their domestic economy to become self-sufficient.[44] Free association was pioneered by Cook Islands in 1965 (and later Niue) as a means of obtaining independence from New Zealand. The formula distinguished between domestic and foreign policy, with the metropolitan power responsible for the latter.[45] The Cook Islands model was then adapted to islands in the Eastern Caribbean in 1967, albeit the British version was more restrictive, and by 1983 six of the seven associated states had become fully independent.[46]

A key principle of the free association formula, as exemplified by earlier Pacific and Caribbean precedents, was the right of either party to unilaterally terminate the agreement.[47] But unilateral termination threatened US security interests. The United States initially offered "Commonwealth" status to the whole group, except Guam, which it retained as "unincorporated territory" due to its military significance. Commonwealth status is analogous to that of Puerto Rico, in that the islands would become part of the United States, would enjoy considerable autonomy, but would not be states.[48] Micronesian negotiators rejected this option. They preferred associated statehood but held out the possibility that if the terms were unacceptable, they would opt for full independence. This created tension between the Trust Territory districts. The result was that the leaders of the Mariana Islands, who had experienced a much longer association with the US Naval Administration than the rest of Micronesia,[49] unilaterally pursued the Commonwealth option. They told the United Nations Trusteeship Council in 1967 that any attempt to block their remaining part of the United States was another form of colonialism.[50] They even threatened the use of force if their desired status was approved by the United Nations.[51] Ultimately, in 1976, they won. Under the "covenant" the Commonwealth of

---

[43] Gale 1979, 203. [44] Doumenge 1983. [45] See e.g. McHenry 1975, 119.
[46] Gilmore 1978, 489. The Seventh, Montserrat, remains a BOT as does Anguilla which seceded from the Associated State of St Kitts-Nevis-Anguilla.
[47] Gale 1979, 218. [48] See Quimby 2016 for a summary. [49] Nufer 1978, 49, 87.
[50] Quimby 2016, 207. [51] Hanlon 2014, 125–126.

the Northern Mariana Islands does not have voting rights in the US Congress, but since 2009 they have been represented in the House of Representatives by a nonvoting delegate.

Disagreements between the districts did not stop with the secession of the Commonwealth of the Northern Mariana Islands. The American preference was that the islands continued to be governed as a group. But after negotiations stalled in 1975, the United States reluctantly accepted that it had no option but to accept further fragmentation.[52] Each of the remaining Trust Territories favored a form of free association with the United States. But the Marshall Islands and Palau did not want to be joined with the rest of Micronesia.[53] Indeed, as Dwight Heine, the first Speaker of the Congress of Micronesia, bluntly stated: "We hate each other more than we hate the Americans."[54] The key reason was the two districts felt that they had greater development potential on their own. Kwajalein (in the Republic of Marshall Islands), Babeldoab (in Palau), and Malakal (in Palau) were the main sites of interest to the US military in the 1970s. In particular, the US base on the former had increased revenues to the Marshall Islands who were reluctant to redistribute it to the other districts on the grounds that they also had to bear the brunt of the military presence.[55] Palau has not housed a base of the same magnitude as Kwajalein, but the overall assessment that each had greater development potential on their own, despite the fact that they would be much smaller, has been proven correct, with the World Bank estimating GDP per capita in 2021 to be around $3,500 for the Federated States of Micronesia, $6,000 for the Republic of Marshall Islands, and $12,000 for Palau.[56]

The Federated States of Micronesia and the Republic of Marshall Islands became independent in free association with the United States in 1986. While Palau became largely self-governing in 1981, when it declared itself the Republic of Palau, but the US trusteeship continued, as Palau's 1980 Constitution prohibited nuclear vessels or aircraft entry into their territory.[57] This was at odds with the compact, which explicitly allowed the free movement of the US military, and meant that ratification of the compact would be unconstitutional in Palau. The United States wanted to keep the option of a military presence in Palau open, and to limit the potential for the Soviets to attempt to establish a foothold there.[58] The US desire for strategic denial had been heightened by Kiribati signing a fishing agreement with the Soviet Union in 1985 that allowed Soviet vessels to fish in its waters.[59] The United States was

---

[52] Nero 1997b. [53] Kiste 1986, 132. [54] Cited in Heine 1974, 110.
[55] Boneparth and Wilkinson 1995; Veenendaal 2017. [56] World Bank 2023.
[57] Hinck 1990. Successive referenda saw increased support for the United States but the 75 percent threshold needed to change the Palauan constitution was only reached after the Cold War ended; see Crocombe 2001, 395–396.
[58] Branigin 1985. [59] Dorrance 1990; Hegarty 1991.

concerned that the Soviets could use fishing as a cover for their surveillance of US military activities at Kwajalein in the Marshall Islands.[60] But Palauan critics were concerned about the impact of potential US military basing; as antinuclear activist, Roman Bedor, observed: "If the US military is going to protect the people of Palau from the Russians, then who is going to protect us from the U.S. military?"[61] The United States and pro-US Palauans tried to force the issue during successive referenda amidst considerable political upheaval, including the assassination of the first president of Palau, Haruo Remeliik, who was a vocal critic of the compact, in 1985. Palauans only amended their constitution and became a freely associated state with the United States in 1994.[62]

The complexities of agreeing de jure American control did not end there, however. The uniquely strategic Trust Territory was also among the last to decolonize because of controversy over the extent of the states' sovereignty and the nature of their engagement in international affairs. The Trust Territory states had drafted their own constitutions and under the compacts would control all their territory. But the United States was to be responsible for their defence, Micronesians would serve in the US military and enjoy freedom of movement to and from the United States, and the United States would provide financial assistance in return for the negotiated use of specific islands by its military.[63] There were concerns that the compacts therefore did not provide genuine independence[64] and that the USSR would veto the free association formula at the United Nations. The US solution was to terminate the trusteeship unilaterally rather than seeking the approval of the United Nations Trusteeship Council, as had been the convention for the other ten territories. For critics, these and other aspects of the formula effectively mean that the island remain under the de facto control of the US despite the veneer of self-determination.[65] This perception can also explain why the Republic of Marshall Islands and the Federated States of Micronesia did not become UN member states until 1991, after the Cold War had ended.[66] There was also considerable tension between the United States and compact states about how they would engage in international affairs, including whether they would represent themselves at the United Nations. Ultimately, this was decided in favor of the Republic of Marshall Islands and the Federated States of Micronesia.

While critics argue that the free association formula is colonization by another name, many Marshallese and Micronesians rejected claims that their

---

[60] Danby 1987. [61] Quoted in Branigin 1985. [62] Nero 1997b.
[63] See Hanlon 2014, 123–124. [64] Prince 1989.
[65] See e.g. Clark 1980; Green 1974; Macdonald 1981; Prince 1989; Bergsman 1976; Roff 1991.
[66] Nero 1997b.

political status had been forced on them. As the second president of the Federated States of Micronesia, John Haglelgam, observed:

"Was the Federation "forced" on the FSM [Federated States of Micronesia]? Was 'Free Association" truly "Free?" These questions arise again and again, and mostly from outsiders ...
The short answers, of course, are "No" and "Yes." The Federation was not forced upon us and Free Association was truly free. This is not to say that there have not been and will not always be differences with the United States, but it is to say that our form of government is adapted to our own circumstances ...
The Government of the FSM is an invention designed to foster a sense of political unity among the states of the FSM. It is not simply a product of American cultural imperialism or political domination.[67]

For our purposes, the point is that the formula reflected a balance of interests that reveal the past experiences of island communities with imported political forms, their desire for development, international norms about self-determination, and US strategic interests, each of which have their genesis in the previous eras of colonization. It is also important to note that in some cases the balance outlined for the peoples of Palau, the Republic of Marshall Islands, and the Federated States of Micronesia could not be struck: the Commonwealth of the Northern Mariana Islands opted against independence, and given its value as a US military base, Guam was given no choice. Both became self-governing unincorporated territories of the United States.

The diversity of state and territory forms in Micronesia also has consequences for self-determination and development in the region. The US territories, Guam, and the Commonwealth of the Northern Mariana Islands have higher levels of development than their independent Micronesian neighbors.[68] But formal development statistics obscure inequality between the indigenous populations and American citizens, particularly in Guam. And the economic support provided by the United States comes at a cost for the self-determination of the indigenous populations, again, particularly in Guam, where more than one-third of the territory is occupied by US military installations.[69]

15.5 Conclusion: Navigating the Continuum between Colonization and Sovereignty

International controversy over the compact of free association model died down in the decades after the compacts were established. But while the three compact states accepted the ongoing use of the islands – as required – by the US military in exchange for substantial economic support, a desire to reduce financial dependence on the United States solidified. Consequently, when the

---

[67] Haglelgam 1991, 7; cf, Puas 2021. [68] Need stats. [69] Burrows 2017.

Republic of Marshall Islands and the Federated States of Micronesia renewed their compacts with the United States in 2003 (known as "Compact II"), Compact Trust Funds were established for each with the goal of reducing their dependence on the United States by providing them with an ongoing source of revenue after 2023, when Compact II was due to expire. A similar Compact Trust Fund had been created for Palau in 1995, with the same intent, although the Palau second compact was not due to expire until 2024.[70]

While the Republic of Marshall Islands and the Federated States of Micronesia, in particular, hoped to move toward greater self-reliance from the United States after the Compact II expired in 2023, it became clear that their Compact Trust Funds were insufficient to lead to the economic self-reliance of their governments. Indeed, in 2022, the United States provided approximately one-third of the Republic of Marshall Islands, the Federated States of Micronesia, and Palau's annual budgets.[71] Concern about their future financial capacity underpinned negotiations on the third compacts in 2022 and 2023. These negotiations were also shaped by US interests in Micronesia, with the subregion increasingly seen as a potential front line in US strategic competition with China, given its geographic location. As Palau President Tommy Remengesau observed in a 2019 opinion piece on an American website popular in Washington: "[I]n many ways, Palau's and our neighbours' strategic importance is the same as it was during World War II." He went on to remind the United States of the strategic value of the compact states, including proposing that the United States established "a larger U.S. armed forces and law enforcement presence."[72] In 2020, Remengesau then formally invited the United States to build a military base in Palau, proposing in a letter to the then US defense secretary Mark Esper that "[w]e should use the mechanisms of the compact to establish a regular US military presence in Palau."[73]

Remengesau's efforts to emphasize the strategic significance – and military potential – of Palau illustrate how islands, even those with constrained sovereignty, can instrumentalize broader geopolitical competition for their benefit. Indeed, what differentiated the negotiations on the third compacts was the presence of a third party that offered an alternative source of development to the compact states: the United States' strategic competitor, China. While the compact negotiations had languished under several earlier administrations, recognizing that they required concerted attention, the Biden administration appointed a Presidential Envoy for Compact Negotiations, Joseph Yun, in March 2022. After a year of intense negotiations, in May 2023, the United States signed the third compact agreement with the Federated States of Micronesia and Palau. Although the compact agreements have not yet been

---

[70] US Department of the Interior, n.d.   [71] US Government Accountability Office 2022.
[72] Remengesau Jr. 2019.   [73] Quoted in Carreon and Doherty 2020.

published, comments by the leaders of both compact states indicated that they include significant funding pledges – US$6.5 billion over twenty years[74] – with Palauan President Surangel Whipps Jr observing that Palau had negotiated double the amount of funding that the US negotiators initially offered, including a pledge of US$100 million to Palau's Compact Trust Fund.[75]

The funding pledged to the Republic of Marshall Islands is similarly generous, reportedly US$700 billion of new support over four years, which Foreign Minister Kitlang Kabua commented was "because of China. We're not naïve."[76] Even Yun admitted that "[i]t's not secret – China is a factor."[77] But, by mid-2023, the third compact with Marshall Islands had not been signed, primarily because of Marshallese concern about the legacy of massive US nuclear testing in the country from 1946 to 1958. Those tests gave rise to generations of health consequences and significant environmental damage. Although the United States argued that it had settled claims relating to this legacy under previous compact agreements, activists in Marshall Islands and beyond continued to push for a formal apology and greater restitution, while the US government said that it was considering its options.[78] This exemplified the ambivalences of the relationship between the compact states and the United States – geopolitical competition provided opportunities for the compact states to negotiate more generous development support, but the legacy of nuclear testing served as a reminder that this assistance comes at a cost.

Indeed, a tension emerged during the compact negotiations between how the United States sees it role in Micronesia which in crucial respects, including both strategic and development imperatives, remains unchanged since 1947, and the Micronesian view of free association as a form of strategic rent.[79] This led to tensions about the allocation and oversight of compact funds, in particular, with US policymakers seeking greater controls to guard against misappropriation and corruption. Many Micronesians argued that this paternalism was at odds with the partnership implied in the idea of a rental agreement. The dilemma for Micronesians remains, in many ways, the same today as it was when they were first occupied by external powers:

[O]ne of the greatest threats to their continued survival on their islands – i.e. their strategic location – has also proved to be the source of their most substantial form of revenue, American transfer payments as recompense for the US' right of 'strategic denial' in the region.[80]

---

[74] Dziedzic 2023. [75] Quoted in *RNZ Pacific* 2023. [76] Quoted in McKenzie 2023.
[77] Quoted in McKenzie 2023. [78] Martina and Brunnstrom 2022. [79] Puas 2021.
[80] Petersen 1998, 186, cf. Pöllath 2018. Strategic denial was also a key reason why the British annexed the Gilbert and Ellice Islands; see Munro and Firth 1986.

This dilemma also shapes domestic politics. Secessionist movements have been ubiquitous in the Federated States of Micronesia in particular, despite the compacts providing each state with considerable devolved powers. Indeed, some commentators have argued that the level of devolution in the Federated States of Micronesia constitution has created a unitary state characterized by "all checks and no balances."[81] One explanation is that this structure was designed with two competing imperatives in mind: a belief that strong national government would be better placed to protect the Federated States of Micronesia against US interference, but at the same time a desire to mitigate against the risk that the compact would enable the United States to co-opt the national government. If this occurred, the United States would still struggle to interfere in local affairs.[82] Another is that the powers granted to the states enabled the smaller three to mitigate against the threat of domination by Chuuk state (the largest).[83] Successive constitutional conventions have failed to resolve this, with some citizens favoring further devolution, others centralization, and others still the status quo. A proportion of those who have served in the US military favor becoming the fifty-first state of the United States on the grounds that it would improve material well-being.[84] The politics of these issues are further complicated by the significant number of Micronesians that now reside in the United States. But putting this heterogeneity aside, the core point is that the nature of the Federated States of Micronesia's multilevel institutions, and its ongoing relationship with the United States, reflect an attempt to balance and adapt to the "problem space" of coloniality.[85]

This highlights the fluidity of the continuum between colonization and sovereignty – the decolonization of the Micronesian subregion is incomplete and unlikely to ever be achieved for Guam or the Commonwealth of the Northern Mariana Islands, given their military significance to the United States and the demographic changes that colonization has brought. While the compact states can assert their sovereignty, they do so with the knowledge that they are also unlikely to ever be able to unilaterally exercise full control over their foreign and defense affairs, again given their strategic importance to the United States. However, they need to maintain a balance between autonomy and dependence on the United States to continue to extract the funding required to ensure their viability.[86] In the alternative, while Kiribati and Nauru are fully sovereign, they lack the ongoing financial support provided to other Micronesian states and territories by the United States. While Kiribati and Nauru have used their sovereignty to extract some financial benefits from China and Australia, respectively (particularly in the context of Nauru hosting

---

[81] See Meller and Meller 1969; Meller 1980; Meller 1990; Underwood 2006.
[82] Petersen 1993, 13.　[83] Underwood 2006.　[84] Puas 2021, 192.
[85] Scott 2004; Getachew 2019.　[86] Petersen 1998, 199–200.

Australian refugee processing facilities), their development levels remain significantly lower than their Micronesian neighbors. The disparity between levels of GDP per capita among sovereign and nonsovereign territories, with the former lower than the latter, suggests that there is indeed a trade-off between autonomy on the one hand and development on the other.[87]

---

[87] Bertram 2015.

Part V

Conclusion

16 Conclusion: A Newly Dynamic East Asian International Order

Andrew J. Coe and Scott Wolford

In the previous volume of this project (Coe and Wolford (2020), we argued that the fundamental principle of international relations in East Asia from antiquity into the nineteenth century – which we referred to as "Historical East Asia" – was that China's preponderance of power in the region engendered stability. China's rulers used its overwhelming size and might to establish and maintain a hierarchical order that reinforced its dominance and ensured order would be quickly restored in the rare moments when political upheaval temporarily weakened China. The events described in the current volume, occurring during a period from the end of the nineteenth century through to the early Cold War that we call "Transitional East Asia," seem to us to demonstrate the converse: that China's fall from dominance encouraged instability. As China declined, the traditional order was contested and eventually overthrown, and a cohort of rising powers competed to fill the vacuum.

In this conclusion, we outline a political economy of Transitional East Asia that we believe sheds light on the diverse conflicts the region faced during this period. We trace the end of China's hegemony, and the instability that attended it, to the different policies the region's states chose toward commerce, development, and reform – collectively, their choices over what we will call modernization. States that pursued modernization gained wealth and power relative to those that did not, or that did so less thoroughly. These choices had fateful consequences for the balance of power within the region and generated strong incentives for modernized upstarts to overthrow the traditional order. Once this was done, a more dynamic order arose as great powers competed to impose a new hegemony, or at least a new stability, forming coalitions with the region's other states and offering new ideologies to legitimize their rule.

In the sections to follow, we use recent theories of comparative politics and international relations to help explain this period of East Asia's history, though we also identify some important gaps in explanation that merit further investigation. In Section 16.1, we draw on theories of the politics of economic development to explain why some states modernized, while others refrained. Next, in Section 16.2, we apply theories of economic interdependence and war to understand why these different choices led to new clashes over the regional order. In Section 16.3, we synthesize these two theoretical perspectives to offer an analytical narrative of the evolution from the stable equilibrium of Historical East Asia to the unstable dynamism of Transitional East Asia.

Sections 16.4–16.6 explore important consequences of the new order. Section 16.4 these examines the competition among the great powers and the clashes that resulted from attempts to supplant China as hegemon. Next, Section 16.5 considers the shifting relationships between the great powers and the region's less powerful states into the Cold War era. Finally, Section 16.6 discusses how opposing coalitions attempted to legitimate their bids for hegemony.

16.1 Modernization

Reading the chapters in this volume, one cannot help but ponder how different the history of East Asia would have been had China pursued modernization when Japan did, or had Japan delayed modernization for as long as China did. Looking back from the end of this volume's temporal coverage, why was Japan's modernization so early and successful, and China's too little and too late? Why was the question of modernization seemingly the source of civil conflict in China and Japan, but not in Thailand?

These are specific examples of a central question in the modern study of comparative politics: Why many states remain economically underdeveloped? Puzzlingly, governments often choose policies that clearly impede development. Of course, changing policies to be more favorable to development would inevitably create domestic winners – those who would benefit from the new policies – and losers – those who would suffer under them. But the rise in overall prosperity that attends development should enable the winners to compensate the losers by enough to win their support for changing policy. The puzzle deepens for underdeveloped states that inhabit a dangerous international environment: for such states, development offers not only a rise in prosperity but also an improvement in their ability to resist external threats. Why then do states persist with policies that simultaneously retard development and endanger their security?

Acemoglu and Robinson (2006) advance a compelling answer to this question: Development influences not only the distribution of income but also the balance of power between domestic interests, and thereby creates a commitment problem. Development's winners can translate their increased income into greater power in domestic politics, relative to its losers. This can render the winners unable to commit to compensating the losers from the gains from development: Once their power has increased, the winners have little reason to follow through on paying any promised compensation. Prospective losers may thus oppose policies favorable to development and external power because these would lead to the loss of their own wealth and internal power. In effect, ruling elites face a trade-off between political stability and economic development.

Whether a commitment problem exists and how it will be resolved depend on how severe this trade-off is. How much prosperity and security are sacrificed, and how much political stability is gained, under policies that preserve the domestic balance of power ("stable" policies, for short), compared to those that would maximize economic growth and external power ("growth" policies)? This determines the magnitude of the conflict of interest between the winners and losers from growth policies, which in turn determines what policies will be chosen, and whether it will result from peaceful accommodation or conflict. We can use this theory to understand the variation in the choices East Asia's states made toward modernization, which played such a crucial role in the events of this volume.

When a state resides in a politically benign and economically stagnant region with relatively modest scope for commerce or growth – like Historical East Asia before large-scale European contact – then the difference in prosperity and security between stable and growth policies is also modest, so the impact on political stability weighs heavier in the regime's choice of policies. When the incumbent elite is well-entrenched in power, it should be more tolerant of commerce and innovation, even if it still wishes to exert some control over them. But when its rule is less established, it should opt for more restrictive policies that minimize the potential for political instability. The potential winners from growth policies have little cause to oppose the latter choice, since it doesn't make much difference for the economy or external security in such a setting. This fits the pattern observed in China's policies toward commerce in Historical East Asia (HEA). When a dynasty's rule was secure, it tended to tolerate more trade, whereas policies were often tightened when a new dynasty came to power (Coe and Wolford 2020, 272–273).

If the gap between stability and prosperity grows – if the returns from reform rise – the supporters of growth policies may become restive. Supporters of stable policies will have to either repress or co-opt them to maintain the status quo. In Historical East Asia, the increasing opportunities for commerce presented by Europeans led to renewed efforts to suppress and constrict commerce, including repression of local merchants (the Qing branding merchant ships as "pirates") and co-optation in the form of allowing only state-approved merchants or ports to engage in commerce (e.g., the Canton system in China or restriction of European commerce to Dejima in Japan).

Eventually, the gap may become large enough that repression and co-optation are not sufficient to placate supporters of growth policies. Then civil conflict may occur, as a pro-development, modernizing or reform coalition contests the policies of the pro-stability, traditional coalition. Such conflicts occurred repeatedly in East Asia, in both China (the Taiping Rebellion, the 1911 Revolution and its chaotic aftermath; see Chapter 7) and Japan (Nobunaga's war of unification, the Meiji Restoration and Boshin War), as traditional elites failed to successfully repress or co-opt those who anticipated benefiting from modernization under a different policy regime. Some of these conflicts clearly derived in part from a perceived drastic increase in the danger of sticking with status quo policies, relative to keeping up with external threats through modernization. China's loss of the First Opium War was a powerful incitement to the Taiping rebels, while Japan's observation of the results of the Opium Wars and its own humiliation at the hands of the United States motivated the Meiji reformers. But the remarkable increase in prosperity Japan enjoyed soon after pursuing modernization demonstrates the immense economic gains that were also at stake.

Finally, the gap may be so large that even the would-be losers from optimal policies nonetheless agree to them. This occurs when the gains from switching to optimal policies are so large that even the "losers" from those policies still gain prosperity in absolute terms, even after domestic power shifts to the winners from optimal policies. This is likeliest to occur in those places that face dire external threats and expect a dramatic rise in prosperity from modernization, such as Thailand in the nineteenth century. Sandwiched between colonies of Britain and France, and for that reason exposed both to potentially massive gains from trade with and existential threats from the two, Thailand managed a successful transition to modernizing policies under its incumbent ruler (Chapter 3).

Of course, states do not always have the luxury of choosing their modernization policies free of outside influence. Acemoglu and Robinson's theory allows for the severity of an external threat to affect a regime's trade-off between stable and optimal policies but does not consider the possibility that a foreign power might act to directly influence a regime's choice of policies. Transitional East Asia offers many examples of such influence, leading Haggard and Kang in the Introduction to call for a revival in political science of research on imperialism.

We can offer some conjectures based on extending Acemoglu and Robinson's theory. For external powers, too, a state's choice over policies presents a trade-off. If a state selects growth-optimal policies, this can create gains for external powers, who benefit from commerce with the more prosperous developing state. If the state in question is friendly to the external powers, there is little downside for them from its modernization. Thailand sought to reach accommodations with Britain and France as it modernized. Britain and France subsequently enjoyed friendly relations and commerce with a useful buffer between their colonial possessions; Thailand maintained its independence and developed economically (Chapter 3). Similarly, the United States encouraged modernization and reform coalitions in allies like South Korea and Taiwan in the Cold War period.

However, if the modernizing state would be hostile, then external powers will also suffer a shift in the balance of power in favor of the modernizing state, which might then act to lessen the gains from commerce they would otherwise enjoy. Though the United States reaped considerable commercial gains from Perry's expedition to open Japan, modernization eventually transformed Japan into a major power that posed a serious challenge to American interests in China and later the whole region. It is not hard to imagine that a similar outcome might have resulted had the Taiping Rebellion succeeded, or the Kuomintang unified the mainland, given what has followed the adoption of modernizing policies both on Taiwan and by the CCP after the events covered in this volume.

If an external power has enough strength, it might be able to coerce a nonmodernizing regime into adopting favorable policies, such as openness to commerce with the external power, while averting the rise of a potentially hostile modernizing coalition.[1] This strategy preserves stability and also the external power's influence over the regime, while still gaining some of the benefits of modernization. If the policies favored by the external power exploit the subject state, however, they may undermine the domestic legitimacy of the nonmodernizing regime and paradoxically increase its dependence on the external power even as it is being coerced. That increase in dependence creates additional leverage for the external power, enabling it to extract further policy changes from the subject state, which in turn loses more domestic support. The coerced regime becomes a puppet state, requiring ever more support from the external power to avoid domestic overthrow. The Qing entered this relationship with Britain after the Opium Wars, and it lasted exactly as long as Britain and the other imperial powers could maintain their supremacy (Chapter 7). Similarly, governments in East Germany and other Warsaw Pact states had the same relationship with the Soviet Union, and just like the Qing were quickly overthrown foreign when support for their puppet regimes ended.

16.2 Interdependence and War

The events described in this volume make clear that East Asian states' economic policies were a source of severe conflicts of interest between those states

---

[1] In Chapter 1 Haggard and Kang address this possibility in their treatment of imperialism.

and outside powers like Britain and the United States, and also among East Asian states themselves. The Opium Wars and Perry's coercive expedition were clearly oriented toward forcing China and Japan to alter their restrictive policies toward commerce, and the subsequent Sino-Japanese Wars were about whether China or Japan would exercise control over the economies of Korea and Manchuria. In the former, relative closure to trade led to war, but in the latter, Korea, China, and Japan were already engaged in growing commerce, and yet war still occurred. Why did opening to commerce satisfy Britain and the United States, but not Japan subsequently?

The relationship between commerce and conflict has long been studied in IR theory. Of the many strands of this literature, Copeland (2015) develops a theory that seems the most readily applicable to Transitional East Asia. In this theory, great powers must seek commerce as a means of enriching and thereby empowering themselves relative to other states and may use force if this seems likely to increase their access to commerce. Because greater reliance on commerce also implies increased vulnerability if trade were to be curtailed, great powers are also more likely to use force to the extent that they believe it is necessary to preserve access to commerce in the future. Thus, when a great power enjoys commercial access and expects it to continue, there is no cause for belligerence, but when its "trade expectations" (as Copeland calls them) decline, it is more likely to resort to war.

As Copeland himself argues, this theory fits well with much of the behavior of the European great powers, Japan, and the United States in Transitional East Asia. Britain and the United States and later other great powers used force against Qing China and Tokugawa Japan to overcome their resistance to commerce, but not against Thailand with its quick opening to commerce. Russia and Japan (Chapter 4), and then China and Japan (Chapter 8), and then the Soviet Union and Japan, waged war over Manchuria in part because each expected that the other would attempt to exclude it from economic access to its valuable resources.[2] Japan invaded Southeast Asia in order to guarantee its access to resources that the European powers and the United States controlled (Chapter 9), but only after they had been denied to Japan, and the United States fought to reverse the invasion. After World War II, wars in Korea (Chapter 10) and Southeast Asia (Chapter 13) were driven in part by US fears that if these countries (and perhaps others in the region thereafter) fell

---

[2] Copeland (2015) argues that his theory does not explain China's willingness to go to war with Japan in 1937. But King in Chapter 8 shows that in fact China saw Japan's attempt to monopolize Manchuria's resources, as well as other Japanese policies toward China, as predatory and a serious impediment to China's economic development. Japan's negative reactions to China's efforts to gain economic autonomy undermined China's expectations for growth and commerce with Japan and rendered China more willing to go to war.

under Communist rule, their economies would be closed to the United States and its now-ally Japan.

Yet this theory cannot explain why Qing China and Tokugawa Japan were relatively closed to commerce in the first place, much less why either would violently resist European efforts to expand commerce with them. How and why could the region have maintained an order, prior to large-scale European contact, in which trade was sometimes seriously constrained, and states like China occasionally resorted to violence to enforce those constraints?

In Copeland's theory, such states are simply irrational, as the imperative to empower themselves relative to other states through trade should otherwise have led them to oppose the tributary order's restrictions. This implication only arises from the realist premise – upon which Copeland's theory is explicitly based – that great powers' policies must rationally be dictated by external threats. Plainly, this was not so for China for much of its history, as we discussed in the previous section. East Asia thus offers fertile ground on which to generalize Copeland's theory to a setting in which internal threats may be more pressing than external ones and can be ameliorated with less rather than more commerce.

We can offer some conjectures, based on the crucial idea present in Copeland's theory that a state's choice of policy toward commerce can create economic and political externalities for other states. As Copeland observes, a state's open policies create economic benefits for other states by increasing the latter's commercial access, while restrictive policies deny those benefits. However, open policies may also generate political *costs* for other states, by enriching and empowering participants in commerce *within* those states relative to their ruling elites. If a state's ruling elites are not heavily involved in commerce and have chosen restrictive policies toward commerce in order to minimize internal political threats, these political costs might outweigh the economic benefits. If so, the state's rulers would actually prefer that other states *also* imposed restrictions on commerce. Conceivably, a state might then resort to war to force another state to *restrict* commerce, in order to ensure its own domestic political stability.

This argument implies that a regional order in which the most economically important states are ruled by noncommercial elites, and adopt similar restrictive commercial policies, can be relatively stable. Each state's policy creates positive externalities for other governments, reinforcing their domestic hold on power by suppressing the rise of commerce-oriented challengers. The general reduction in regional commerce that results also lessens the economic costs for any one state of adopting restrictive policies, and thus the incentive for its government or a challenger to it to open to commerce. By restricting commerce, states also suppress a source of shifts in the balance of power, contributing to the order's stability and ensuring that power is determined primarily by a state's population.

By contrast, if the governments of the most economically important states adopt contrasting policies – some encouraging commerce, others restricting it – then the order is bound to become unstable. Trading states will empower commercial participants within nontrading states and amplify their incentives to contest ruling elites' restrictive policies, threatening the latter's hold on power. The balance of wealth and power will shift toward trading states that will have an increasingly strong interest in causing other states to adopt open policies. The durability of this kind of mixed order will depend on whether the nontrading states possess, and retain as the balance shifts, enough power to avoid being coerced into relaxing their policies. If they do not, then their own move to open policies will cause further shifts in the balance of power, contributing new instability to the regional order.

16.3   Origins of Instability in Transitional East Asia

We have seen that theories from comparative politics can help us to explain the varying choices East Asia's states made toward modernization, and IR theory can illuminate why different choices led to conflicts among the powers involved in the region. But why did the previously durable order of Historical East Asia unravel in the first place, and why did the resulting instability persist for the entire period of Transitional East Asia? Why did this instability play out in the way we observe in this volume, in which outright conflict occurs repeatedly?

Here, we sketch an analytic narrative of this period based on the arguments presented in the previous sections. First we briefly describe the sources of the tributary order's durability, drawing in part on our conclusion from the previous volume (Coe and Wolford 2020). Then we account for the initial rise of instability and explain how the resulting changes in the region's order led to a continuing stream of new shocks, so that instability persisted.

Until well into the nineteenth century, China enjoyed a durable preponderance of power over all other states involved in the region, owing largely to the fact that it was so much more populous and wealthier. China established and maintained an international order based on the tributary system, whose norms legitimized China's dominance as well as the subordinate positions of the other states. Acceptance by regional governments of China's hegemony was rewarded with investiture and protection from China. This reinforced the stability of those governments by deterring domestic challengers, and thereby rendered these states loyal to the broader order, cementing China's position. This order was most likely to be disturbed in the rare instances of political upheaval in China, which created windows of opportunity for other states to contest their position in the regional hierarchy.

In the region's most important states, political economies relied heavily on land rents, with interstate commerce less central to domestic elites. These elites tolerated or curtailed trade in response to the varying threat it posed to their domestic power. In times of greater internal threat, such as when new dynasties were being entrenched, commerce was either tightly controlled by the region's monarchies through the tribute system or was criminalized and took the form of smuggling.

Of the region's states, China's stupendous size meant that it had the least to fear from external threats, so that suppressing internal threats weighed heavily in the trade-off China's rulers faced and led them to exert control over trade. So long as China could protect rulers in other states, it could ensure that they also faced less severe external threats, tilting their rulers' own trade-off in favor of controlling trade. By conditioning its support for these rulers on whether they obeyed the tribute system, including in their policies toward trade, China could tip the scale yet further in favor of restraining trade.

Moreover, this equilibrium was self-reinforcing. When the most important states in the region strictly controlled trade, the potential external gains to any state allowing unfettered commerce were relatively modest, lessening that state's incentive to deviate from the norm. If some state did so anyway, it would create two negative externalities for the other states. First, smuggling would increase and potentially generate internal threats in other states as smugglers sought changes in policies toward trade. Second, the free-trading state would experience increased power relative to the other states and face incentives to coerce them into allowing more commerce in order to access their markets, creating an external threat. These externalities ensured that controlled trade states had strong reasons to support China's enforcement of the tributary system against any deviant free-trading state, which in turn would make it easier for China to do so successfully.

The self-reinforcing nature of this restricted trade order initially enabled it to manage the arrival of seaborne Europeans. The new opportunities for gains from trade these Europeans brought raised the incentives for states to deviate by allowing more commerce, creating a new threat to the order. However, the most important states in the region imposed restrictions on trade with Europeans analogous to those of the tributary system that were effective in suppressing this threat. By controlling where, how, and how much the Europeans could trade in China and Japan, rulers upheld the order by ensuring that some of the new wealth created by European commerce was captured by agrarian elites, and that the commercial elites did not grow so rich or powerful or independent as to be able and willing to contest agrarian rule.

European states, residing within a very different regional order of intense competition based on commerce, had strong incentives to undermine the East Asian order from the start. Asian states' restrictions on trade reduced Europeans' access to their markets and denied them the wealth that would have resulted from unfettered contact. Given the size of their markets and the availability of valuable goods, China's and Japan's restrictions imposed the largest loss on European traders, and their restrictions would be the most important to overcome. However, European states initially lacked the power to coerce China or Japan to change those policies.

The problem for the tributary order was that European states were not subject to similar controls elsewhere. China and Japan could control trade (to a certain extent) within East Asia, but they could not constrain European commerce with Africa, the Americas, South Asia, or within Europe itself. Relatively free trade with or colonization of much of the rest of the world massively enriched Europe and its offshoot in the United States, and this new wealth was eventually translated into military power sufficient to match even the strongest states of East Asia. Newly empowered, the United Kingdom and the United States forced greater openness on China and Japan through the Opium Wars and the Perry expedition.

It seems crucial to observe that while these events led quickly to the destruction of the tributary order, they were only the most proximate cause. The seeds of its demise were laid, not by opium merchants or new warships, but by the successes of European merchants and conquerors elsewhere in the world. If the Europeans had faced a hegemon like China in each of the other regions, they might well have suffered the same commercial restrictions everywhere. This in turn would have drastically reduced the increase in wealth and concomitant power they realized from overseas commerce, delaying perhaps indefinitely the time when a state as small as Britain could develop the radically disproportionate power it needed to effectively coerce a state as immense as China.

This change in the balance of power between Europe and East Asia had swift, dramatic consequences for the stability of the traditional order. The unmistakably growing threat posed by the European states, and the rapid rise in commerce resulting from their "opening" of China and Japan, meant that the trade-off East Asian states faced toward commerce now tilted in favor of allowing more. Weaker, smaller states like Thailand faced the greatest external threat and also had the most economically to gain from increased commerce, and so moved quickly toward modernization (Chapter 3). Stronger states like China and Japan were better able to resist, granting just enough openness to placate the Europeans. However, as commerce grew, so did the wealth and power of the domestic elites and regions that were most exposed to trade, generating new internal threats. Less than two decades after China and Japan were "opened," coalitions supporting social, political, and economic reform attempted to overthrow traditional rule in the Taiping Rebellion and Meiji Restoration.[3] Victorious in Japan, these elites initiated a regime that pursued modernization to achieve the prosperity and power needed to fend off the European threat. The incumbent Qing in China held on to power and engaged only in delayed, half-hearted attempts at modernization as they continued to restrict commerce.

Over time, these differential responses to increased commerce changed the balance of power *within* East Asia, undermining the old hierarchy and contributing new sources of instability. Because opening up and modernizing risked being overthrown, the Qing elected to meet the increased external threat by relinquishing ever more control over Chinese commerce and governance to the Europeans, especially the British, in exchange for their support (Chapter 7). Although the Qing suffered a decline in domestic popularity and China weakened relative to Japan, the British helped the Qing to stay in power (intervening in the later part of the Taiping Rebellion) and shielded China from outright foreign conquest. In effect, the Qing became the "sick man" of East Asia, kept on life support by the British even as China fell further behind. By contrast, Japan under the new Meiji regime underwent major reforms and experienced massive commercial expansion and rapid economic growth, which it translated into burgeoning military power.

The rise of a powerful, trade-fueled regime in Japan created a new challenge to a tributary order already on its deathbed. Japan's new prosperity and power were heavily dependent on commerce, and if it wished to continue growing, it needed greater access to its neighbors' markets. It turned first to the closest such markets, in Korea and Manchuria, but with ambitions mirroring those of the Europeans: to eventually open the rest of China, the region's largest market by far. Accepting Japan's demands for unrestricted access would lead to commerce that would undermine Korea's and China's traditional governments, so Korea resisted with China's support. But tolerating Korea's and China's restrictions would constrain Japan's growth and ability to resist European coercion, which Japan could not accept. Thus, any compromise would render peace costly for one or both sides. Japan went to war to avoid these costs.

Remarkably, *none of this was novel in East Asian experience.* The same circumstances had arisen 300 years earlier in the Imjin War, with Toyotomi Hideyoshi's unification of Japan at the head of a commerce-oriented domestic

---

[3] It is unclear whether the Taiping rebels, had they succeeded in overthrowing the Qing, would have pursued modernization akin to the Meiji regime. On the one hand, the origins and ideological core of the movement lay in religious radicalism and ethnic nationalism. On the other hand, the movement evinced more openness to commerce than the Qing, and one of its most important elites penned a treatise with a program for modernization to be implemented once the Taipings had gained power. See Platt 2012.

coalition and subsequent invasion of the mainland to gain access (through conquest, or failing that, an opening of trade) to Korea and China. Then, Japan was defeated, and the Hideyoshi regime overthrown by a less commercially dependent coalition that was accepted back into a preserved tributary order. But this time, a Japan strengthened by modernization and extensive contact with the West overcame a China weakened by dependency, winning the misleadingly named First Sino-Japanese War, and began to assert control over Korea.

Japan's decisive victory over China overthrew the traditional hierarchy of the tributary order. Now that its stoutest defender had been unmistakably humbled, observers within and without the region understood that the way was open for commerce and colonization. Russia and Japan competed to exploit China's revealed weakness in Korea and Manchuria, with Japan again emerging victorious and colonizing Korea. Facing a far more severe external threat, with Britain increasingly preoccupied elsewhere, the balance in China finally tipped. The Qing were overthrown, and though the decay of central authority in their final years and interference by Japan and the Soviet Union resulted in a long civil conflict (Chapter 7), a commerce-oriented faction under the Kuomintang eventually consolidated rule in Nanjing, and China belatedly undertook modernization.

With increased commerce came increased vulnerability to external shocks. The Great Depression, and the protectionist reactions to it by Japan's major commercial partners, hit Japan especially hard. Once again, China and Japan confronted a costly peace: Japan could redress its economic (and thereby security) vulnerability and reduce the costs of adjusting to the global contraction if it gained greater control over crucial resources in China and elsewhere in the region, but this could only come at the cost of China's own unification and modernization (Chapter 8). The Second Sino-Japanese War resulted, but only exacerbated Japan's difficulties when the United States responded harshly to Japan's aggression, leading to war between the two nations (Chapter 9).

To a remarkable degree, East Asian history proceeded to repeat itself. Just as it had after the Opium War and Perry expedition, power in the region shifted drastically in favor of external states after World War II, and similar consequences followed. China was devastated during the war and partly occupied by a great power from outside the region – the USSR in Manchuria this time, rather than Britain in Canton – and Japan conceded to the United States. Paralleling the Taiping Rebellion, civil conflict intensified in China, and once again the faction that favored restrictions on commerce emerged victorious. Just as the Qing did, the Communist government in China chose to rely on the great power's support and protection, and the resulting reduction in external threat tipped the balance back in favor of a focus on internal threats – this time from the exiled Kuomintang in Taiwan and other social forces within China itself – and strict control of trade (Chapter 11). China again suffered a period of economic decline relative to other states in the region. In an echo of the Meiji Restoration, Japan again experienced regime change, the new government again pursued commerce and modernization, its economy again experienced remarkable commercial expansion and growth, and Japan once again rose to join the ranks of the advanced industrial states.

Riven once again between one set of states, led by China, that imposed strict control over commerce and an opposing set that did not, similar conflicts of interest arose.[4] Just as in the late nineteenth century, China's relative closure as well as those of other aligned states created serious impediments to the economic development of Japan and other commerce-oriented states, while the latter group's expansion of relatively free commerce threatened the domestic stability of the closed states. This time, the United States led the commerce-oriented coalition, and the possession of nuclear weapons by the Soviet Union deterred any attempt to open China by force. Instead, a series of proxy conflicts in the region pitted China and the USSR against the United States and its allies over the loyalties of the region's other governments (Chapter 14). This crucial difference makes it all the more notable that, just as it had at the turn of the century, the underlying conflict of interest over commercial control led first to war over Korea, with China supporting the side in favor of closure and Japan supporting the side more oriented toward commerce (Chapter 10).

Obviously the contest after World War II between communism and capitalism was different in many ways from the previous struggle between traditional agrarian rule and modernizing forces. But an important commonality is that each was characterized by opposite responses to the political risks and economic opportunities created by free enterprise generally and commerce specifically: one ideology focused on minimizing political risks, the other on maximizing economic opportunities. The twentieth century's version of this divide would persist until after the events of this volume, when a new modernizing coalition arose in China.

Instability persisted even after the initial shift in power toward the West in the nineteenth century in large part because the region's two most important states did not coordinate their pursuit or abandonment of modernization and commerce. They faced different trade-offs between prosperity and external security on the one hand, and internal stability on the other, and so chose different policies at different times. The concomitant shifts in the balance of power amplified conflicts of interest over policy, and wars that resulted from

---

[4] Of course, the United States and its allies imposed comprehensive sanctions on China and other Communist-ruled states, but this was partly in response to the latter states' unwillingness to allow free enterprise.

these choices drove much of the dynamism we observe in Transitional East Asia.

In the rest of this chapter, we turn to examining the competition among great powers this new dynamism incited.

16.4 Great Power Competition

In contrast to Historical East Asia, great power competition in Transitional East Asia was both more frequent and more intense. Where Europe was animated over much of the period by the question of what to do *with* a powerful Germany, the slow collapse of the Qing posed the question of what to do *without* a powerful China. Yet, beyond common accounts focused on declining–rising power relations or the politics of retrenchment, IR theory rarely discusses the politics of great power competition in the shadow of another's decline. Transitional East Asia (TEA) is useful for theory-building in that regard because it gives us decades of observations on a declining, declined, and then recovering empire in a system that hadn't previously been a site of significant great power competition.

Hegemonic interregna weren't new in the region, but the decline of the tributary system meant that the new competitors for dominance – Japan, Britain, France, Russia, and the United States – lacked HEA's common conjecture that some power would unite China and claim the mandate of heaven. The de jure anarchy and de facto hierarchy of the Westphalian system had supplanted the de jure hierarchy and de facto anarchy of the "Eastphalia" (Park, S. Y. 2020). The new system didn't rule out the establishment of a regional hegemony, nor did it demand one. In fact, the Westphalian system had arguably developed rules that tried to prevent the kinds of hegemony China had enjoyed under the tributary system (see Waltz 1979; Wagner 2007). What made this ideational change possible was the entry of multiple new great powers competing for influence if not dominance for the first time in (many) centuries. A system of legal hierarchy was easy to maintain when there was no plausible balancing coalition among weaker and geographically isolated states (Coe and Wolford 2020), but it collapsed under the weight of industrialization and military development in Europe, the Americas, and, closer to the erstwhile hegemonic center, Japan.

In early TEA, Qing decline prompted a series of wars over dominance in the areas outside its shrinking military reach (see Wolford 2023), including the First Sino-Japanese War (Park, S. H. 2020), Boxer, and Russo-Japanese Wars (Chapter 4). As hierarchies weaken – for example, as the credibility of China's commitment to protect Korea declined – we see both increasing risks of civil conflict (McCormack 2018), like Korea's Donghak Rebellion, and interstate war (McDonald 2015), sometimes as the result of those domestic conflicts; the

First Sino-Japanese War, for example, was prompted by the Donghak Rebellion. Recognizing the risks of an intensified competition, like the ongoing Scramble for Africa, that might follow a Qing collapse, the great powers effectively settled on the American "Open Door" policy, under which purely exclusive zones of influence were ruled out. They collectively intervened to suppress the Boxer Rebellion in 1900. The Qing would survive, propped up by imperial powers that claimed exclusive rights of trade and extraterritoriality, collected Qing customs revenues, and even continued colonizing erstwhile tributary states.[5]

This arrangement, accepted de facto if not de jure by the other imperial powers, wasn't unlike the one that oversaw and exploited the decline of the Ottoman empire, but IR theory has few tools to understand the collective management of a great power's decline. China and the Ottoman empire survived on great power life support, punctuated by periods of interstate war, yet Russia's decline from the Soviet period to early Putinism saw no great powers fighting each other on its territory; they were, in fact, generous in subsidizing the withdrawal of the Red Army from East Germany (Sarotte 2009) and slow-walking NATO expansion through the 1990s. Yet like Qing and Republican China, Russia waged a series of civil wars along its now-contracted (but still imperial) periphery. Post-Soviet Russia had nuclear weapons, of course, but the case shows that coordination in managing a great power's decline isn't unusual. Returning to TEA, one possibility is to think of the Open Door as an attempt at a coordinating device proposed by a new imperial power. Under the Open Door the great powers would collectively draw lines around what constituted acceptable exploitation of the declining power, the violation of which would reveal the aggressive intentions of the violators and prompt intervention from the others (see Wolford 2019a). Although the American proposal did not succeed in generating support at the time, it ultimately did carry over into the multilateral aspirations of the postwar period.

The IR theory is on firmer ground explaining the series of great power wars that began in 1839 and ended only in 1953. With Republican China beset by warlordism after toppling the Qing (Chapter 7), the question of who, if anyone, was to dominate continental East Asia would be answered only once there was widespread agreement over which coalitions would form to block any such move toward hegemony (see Wagner 1993). Japan's invasion of Manchuria in 1931, designed to seize a sphere of influence before the Kuomintang could win the Chinese Civil War, heralded the end of any pretense to an Open Door.[6] Other great powers recognized this bid for hegemony for what it was, precisely

---

[5] And in 1921, Soviet Russia occupied and then recognized the independence of Mongolia, creating a new client state, while stripping Republican China of territory.
[6] Even if Japan wouldn't announce as much until 1937.

because of Japan's willingness to risk conflict by invading China; if its aims weren't expansive, it wouldn't have tolerated a risk of general war. Yet Japan (correctly) doubted that other great powers would cooperate to stop it, and continued uncertainty over the makeup of potential balancing coalitions enabled the invasion of the rest of China in 1937, Russo-Japanese fighting in 1938–39, the dramatic expansion of empire building (Chapter 9) into Southeast Asia and the Pacific that provoked war with the British and Americans in 1941 (Monteiro and Debs 2020), and North Korea's invasion of South Korea in 1950, with Chinese and Soviet backing. Not until the end of the Korean War (Chapter 10) and the Taiwan Strait Crises (Chapter 11) establish (a) the American commitment to the regional status quo, embodied in a network of defense pacts (Chapter 12), and (b) China's re-emergence as a military counterweight did great power competition switch from direct confrontation to contention over the loyalty of middle and minor powers (Chapter 13; Chapter 14). Anchored by great powers (Wolford 2017) and facing sufficiently powerful enemies (Phillips and Wolford 2021), each coalition mostly maintained its internal coherence and, therefore, the preservation of the post-Korea status quo often identified with the "San Francisco System" (but see Chapter 2). Border conflicts between China and the Soviet Union are a notable exception, but (fortunately for the authors) they occurred only after 1965, when our temporal scope ends.

Finally, and returning to the contrast between the German and Chinese questions of the period under study, it's notable that a Germany in relative decline launched a general war in the early twentieth century (see Wolford 2019b, Chapter 4), yet a more rapidly declining China was a victim not the aggressor. It's hard to disentangle several different causes, though: (a) persistent domestic unrest, like the Boxer Rebellion, the 1911 Revolution, and the descent into warlordism, making foreign war impracticable, (b) a relatively lower starting point of military-industrial development, and (c) potential targets of preventive war being outside China's military reach. Germany's bids to secure its place between rival great powers didn't occur in the context of significant domestic unrest – the *Kaiserreich* wasn't unpopular, and the Nazis had already crushed effective opposition to fascism by the mid-1930s – and its rivals were close by. China, by contrast, was beset by civil war and revolution, and while it couldn't reach its rivals militarily, *they* could reach *it*, which may go some way to explaining why Chinese, like Ottoman, decline led to a great power being carved up, and why the collapsing Soviet Union, both near its rivals and possessed of a substantial nuclear deterrent, didn't suffer direct predation. All these issues are potentially interesting avenues for the future development of IR theory.

16.5 Varieties of Hierarchy

We can see in TEA patterns consistent with other recent work on hierarchy and conflict, with hierarchs and their subordinate states sharing ideological preferences if not political institutions, as well as alliance commitments and side-taking in international conflicts (Lake 2009; McDonald 2015; Gunitsky 2017). Yet the era is also useful for demonstrating wide variation in hierarchical relationships, as the tributary system – itself more flexible in practice than its strictures dictated in principle – was followed by several competing modes of hierarchy, most inspired by the Westphalian-imperial model but all of which shared key ideas with the tributary system of investiture, deference, and protection against threats from outside the hierarchy. The key differences, we argue, are that (a) the single hierarchy of HEA was replaced by a system with multiple, competing hierarchies, and (b) the types of hierarchical relationships we observe depend on changes in relative power between China, Japan, their rivals, and their partners.

Early imperial encroachments into the tributary system involved indirect control over China itself, like the establishment of treaty ports, extraterritoriality, and the cession of sovereign functions (like customs collection) to outside powers.[7] And as Qing influence waned still further, other powers became strong enough to exercise forms of direct control, establishing colonies – for example, Korea and Taiwan for Japan, Hong Kong and Singapore for Britain, Indochina for France, the Philippines for the United States, and a smattering of Pacific Islands for Germany – or engaging in outright conquest, like Japan in the Ryukyus (see Dudden 2005).[8] After the world wars delegitimized (the rhetorical admission of) colonialism, indirect control took on a variety of new forms, from mandates and trusteeships for the League and the UN, respectively, to the conditional sovereignties and special legal statuses, like free association, that characterize the postwar North Pacific (Chapter 15).

Yet one key aspect of hierarchical politics remained constant from HEA to TEA: alliance commitments. Under the tributary system, China committed itself to the governments it invested, whether against internal threats, like the Ho's usurpation of the Tran in the early fifteenth century Vietnam (Anderson 2020) or foreign invasion, like Hideyoshi's attempted conquest of Korea in the late sixteenth century (Swope 2009). Yet the fall of the Qing and the entry of other great powers into the region meant that the latter often had to compete over which subordinate states they'd protect (from the others), leading to a set

---

[7] Again, this wasn't unlike the dominant response to Ottoman decline.
[8] Whether conquest-cum-annexation constitutes imperialism isn't always clear – not least because of the strategic use of the term in political rhetoric – but if the annexed units still have less freedom relative to the center than others, i.e. as long as we see "heterogeneous contracting" between a strong center and subordinate units (McConaughey, Musgrave, and Nexon 2018; 195), then we can say that even formal annexation produces imperial relations.

of concerns that had been largely irrelevant to a one-hierarch system. Where Kang and Huang (2022) can describe tributary relations as mainly about the prevention of domestic conflict, that may be because Imperial China's tributaries were few and (literally) far between. The Imjin War of 1592–98, in which China came to Korea's defense, is the exception that proves the rule; Korea wasn't in a position to invade Japan, nor was any other main tributary in a position to find itself at war with Vietnam. Yet, with multiple regional great powers competing for influence in the decades after Qing collapse, alliance politics took on a different character, concerned with not only the political survival of favored governing factions but also (a) the prevention of great power war and (b) inter-hierarchy balances of power, both almost unthinkable in HEA.

The rival coalitions that stalemated on the Korean peninsula and the Taiwan Strait in the 1950s formed two very different, yet essentially stable, hierarchies. The American alliance network, which was primarily maritime, included defense commitments to Japan, South Korea, Taiwan, the Philippines, Australia, and New Zealand. Yet these alliances performed multiple *interstate* functions, not just deterring invasions of South Korea and Taiwan but also (a) reassuring other allies about the consequences of Japan's rearmament and (b) restraining the leaderships in South Korea and Taiwan from provoking conflicts that might entrap the United States in unwanted wars (Cha 2016). Benson (2012), for example, shows that ambiguities built into the American commitment to Taiwan reflected the fact that proximity to China, in the form of Taiwan's continued control over Kinmen and Matsu, made it difficult to gauge who shot first. The choice of potential great power patrons, especially in Southeast Asia (Chapter 13; Chapter 14), also likely made great powers more tolerant of deviations from their own ideal domestic policies in securing subordinates' loyalties, in contrast to the strict requirements for investiture in previous centuries. The United States, for example, allied with autocratic governments that it might otherwise find detestable outside the context of great power competition, yet in HEA China had much greater choice over and sway within those regimes it invested.

The communist coalition, by contrast, was primarily land-based and characterized by increasingly intense competition for political influence between its principals: Communist China and Soviet Russia. Entrapment was a clear concern, as North Korea only won its backers' assent for invading the South in 1950 once the communists had won the Chinese Civil War and Stalin was optimistic enough that China would bear the brunt of the response if the United States intervened (Stueck 2004; Wada 2013). But as the approach of nuclear parity moved the Soviet Union toward a policy of "peaceful coexistence" with the West, China presented itself as more committed to global revolution, setting the stage for fights over the right to "invest" regimes in other communist states, including Cambodia and Vietnam.[9] So while the maritime coalition was concerned with containing the continental coalition, the continental coalition was increasingly concerned over its own leadership, because (a) it had two competitors for the top spot in the hierarchy and (b) there was, rhetoric aside, little chance that the rival maritime coalition would pose a serious threat to the continent. Indeed, the United States worked hard to ensure that its commitments to South Korea and Taiwan were purely defensive (see, again, Benson 2012). Communist China and Soviet Russia competed for influence over Vietnam as its conflict with the French and then the United States continued through the period of interest, culminating in China's 1979 invasion of Vietnam to (a) pull the latter's forces off China's Cambodian clients and (b) prove that accepting investiture from an alternative source, like the Russians, wasn't worth Beijing's disapproval. The logic of the tributary system survived, if not as a universalizing concept, then as the rationale of competition between multiple potential hierarchs.

16.6 Legitimating International Order

Transitional East Asia was also the site of an intense ideological competition that had been largely absent from HEA, as a new set of great powers sought to build support for their own imperial projects by legitimating them in the eyes of domestic and foreign audiences. TEA gave middle and minor powers new choices – some more feasible than others – over which hierarchy to join, with Siam choosing early to cast its lot with outside powers (Chapter 3), Japan pushing to join the Westphalian system as an imperial equal (Chapter 6) before embarking on a more revisionist quest for empire (Chapter 9), and Southeast Asian states choosing between rival coalitions during the Cold War (Chapter 13; Chapter 14). In this section, we argue that even as the tributary system ceded ground to alternatives, the process of building and maintaining legitimacy was similar across HEA and TEA, differing only in the sense that the ideological processes obviated by the tributary system's lack of competitors were dragged out into the open with the introduction of powerful, attractive competitors.

Like any successful ideology, the tributary system justified itself to its adherents by

- Defining identities and social roles, like "relations of super- and subordination" (Waltz 1979, 81).

---

[9] The Third International was nothing if not a screen for investiture and coercive policy dissemination.

- Prescribing and proscribing behaviors, including both how to comply and how to respond to noncompliance, establishing shared expectations about one's own and others' behavior.
- Explaining why compliance worked for each actor *internally*, that is, the consequences for themselves (and possibly others) if they don't comply, where compliance means not just following the rules but also enforcing the rules on others.
- Explaining why compliance worked for each actor *externally*, that is, in comparison to other systems by which politics might be organized.

In game-theoretic terms, ideologies do not only describe why adhering to a set of social roles, beliefs, and strategies are better than provoking punishment by deviating from prescribed behavior. They also explain why the equilibrium entailed by those social roles, beliefs, and strategies is better than *other* equilibria defined by other sets of social roles, beliefs, and strategies – that is, by other ideologies. In other words, a theory of ideological competition is a theory of competition between equilibria; a successful ideology represents (a) one idea among many of how to organize politics and (b) survives by convincing its adherents that other equilibria aren't as attractive, whether by suppressing comparisons or outlasting others.

The IR context also adds a dimension missing from more common models of ideological competition that assume a stable (often domestic) political system. For Izzo et al. (2023), ideologies exist in essentially free and fair competition: voters can select an underlying theory about the world that then informs their preferences over policies in electoral competition. This is reasonable when parties compete in fair electoral systems, but in many cases – like international relations – competition is endogenously unfair. Great powers compete for audiences, and victory often means an ideological monopoly that denies actors alternative lenses through which to view not just their own experiences but those of others as well; they also work domestically to suppress or compete with information about alternatives.

Therefore, ideologies, like the patterns of social and international organization described by the tributary system, survive not only when they seem to "work" but also when evidence of successful competitors is limited. The dramatic shifts in the distribution of power associated with European encroachment in the nineteenth century created opportunities for elites in TEA to compare their own domestic and international equilibria with alternative arrangements, some of which offered a chance to seize greater political power in states that were otherwise committed (or resigned) to the tributary system.

Japan's adoption of European ideas of trade and international organization marked the most important such local shift in TEA, pivoting from making compromises with the maritime empires to competing on more or less level ground with them. This alternative model, which held out the prospect of rapid industrialization and enhancements in military power – to say nothing of a measure of independence from the Europeans – opened many local eyes to the possibility that the domestic and international structures of the tributary system might have attractive, viable alternatives. Japan used its new ideological model to appeal to factions in Korea ahead of the First Sino-Japanese War, and its victory in the Russo-Japanese War awakened foreign publics to alternatives not just to the tributary system but also to imperial domination by Europeans. Indeed, its mid-century project of a "Greater East-Asian Co-Prosperity Sphere" used the language of Pan-Asianism to veil its own vision of racial superiority (Chapter 9). Yet, even then, the story was that it was better to be dominated by Japan than by Europeans. After all, even the Americans had passed the Chinese Exclusion Acts and stood with the British in firmly rejecting Japan's proposal for a racial equality clause in the League Covenant after World War I (Chapter 6). Japan's rush to modernization also influenced the Kuomintang in its push to topple the Qing and reorder China (Chapter 7).

By the time of the early Cold War, the period that ends this volume, ideological competition was in more or less full swing, though in contrast to Europe's (mostly) two-system competition, there were at least three major ideological competitors in TEA. The American-led open-economy system accommodated developmentalist states that departed from liberal norms (Chapter 12). But the main contenders were the two strains of closed-economy (Communist) systems, one Russian and one Chinese, with the latter two differing in large part over who would exercise sway over the other closed-economy systems. The Sino-Soviet split wouldn't break out fully into the open until the end of the period studied in this volume. But competition for the loyalty of communist governments in Southeast Asia was nascent in the wake of the Korean War and France's ejection from Indochina. And though the language of competition between the two biggest communist powers was couched in terms of global revolution – in particular whether Khrushchev had abandoned Stalin's cause – it ultimately took the form of competition over whether Beijing or Moscow would recognize and invest new communist regimes. The Cold War underscored how ideological competition is also violent, with great powers waging costly wars for demonstrative reasons, like the United States in Vietnam, but it also showed how ideological competition could alter patterns of violence, with China and Taiwan using the backdrop of the Taiwan Strait Crises of the 1950s to reach accommodations out of the view of their ideological patrons (Chapter 11).

What can IR theory take from this view of TEA? First, power and ideas work together (see Morrow 2014), with changes in the nature of ideological competition occurring alongside changes in the distribution of power. Such competition isn't mere window-dressing: to the extent that foreign and domestic audiences accept a particular ideology, the more cooperative they're likely to be when the chips are down and the great powers countenance war. Second, and inconsistent with many an ideology's teleological structure, there's nothing inevitable about any given ideology's success. The tributary system, with its relatively closed economies and autocratic politics, dominated HEA for centuries, *and* competitors were mostly absent. Its victory, to its adherents, seemed almost total. Yet changes in the distribution of power and economic interests spawned changes in the distribution of ideas, with first Japan and then others adopting new organizing ideologies for international and domestic politics. Finally, this view of ideology offers a useful way of thinking about politics as a competition in the creation of common knowledge, especially when it comes to beliefs about ideological alternatives, both foreign and domestic. Ideologies help make equilibria not only self-enforcing but also competitive, making rhetoric and even the pursuit of prestige not mere window-dressing but the very ideational stuff that, along with power, supports or alternatively undermines systems of international relations.

Bibliography

Accinelli, Robert. 1996. *Crisis and Commitment: United States Policy toward Taiwan, 1950–1955*. Chapel Hill: The University of North Carolina Press.
Acemoglu, Daron and James A. Robinson. 2006. "Economic Backwardness in Political Perspective." *American Political Science Review* 100 (1): 115–131.
Acharya, Amitav. 2022. "Race and Racism in the Founding of the Modern World Order." *International Affairs* 98 (1): 23–43.
Acharya, Amitav, and Barry Buzan. 2007. "Preface: Why Is There No Non-Western IR Theory: Reflections on and from Asia." *International Relations of the Asia-Pacific* 7 (3)(September): 285–286.
Acheson, Dean. 1969. *Present at Creation: My Years in the State Department*. New York: W. W. Norton.
Adler-Nissen, Rebecca, and Thomas Gammeltoft-Hansen. 2008. *Sovereignty Games: Instrumentalizing State Sovereignty in Europe and Beyond*. New York: Springer.
Adler-Nissen, Rebecca, and Ulrick Pram Gad, ed. 2013. *European Integration and Postcolonial Sovereignty Games*. New York: Routledge.
Allan, Bentley B., Srdjan Vucetic, and Ted Hopf. 2018. "The Distribution of Identity and the Future of International Order: China's Hegemonic Prospects." *International Organization* 72 (4): 839–869.
Amdrade, Tonio. 2020. "The Zheng State and the Fall of Dutch Formosa, 1662." In *East Asia in the World: Twelve Events Shaped the Modern International Order*, edited by Stephan Haggard, and David C. Kang, 149–163. Cambridge: Cambridge University Press.
Amrith, Sunil. 2012. *Migration and Diaspora in Modern Asia*. London: Cambridge University Press.
Anderson, David L. 1988. "J. Lawton Collins, John Foster Dulles, and the Eisenhower Administration's 'Point of No Return' in Vietnam." *Diplomatic History* 2 (12): 127–147.
Anderson, James A. 2020. "The Ming Invasion of Vietnam, 1407–1427." In *East Asia in the World: Twelve Events that Shaped the Modern International Order*, edited by David C. Kang, and Stephan Haggard, 97–107. New York: Cambridge University Press.
Ang, Guan Cheng. 2018. *Southeast Asia's Cold War: An Interpretative History*. Honolulu: University of Hawai'i Press.
Arima, Manabu. 2002. *Teikoku no Shōwa*. Tokyo: Kōdansha.

Asada, Sadao. 2006a. "Between the Old Diplomacy and the New, 1918–1922: The Washington System and the Origins of Japanese – American Rapprochement." *Diplomatic History* 30 (2): 211–230.

Asada, Sadao. 2006b. *From Mahan to Pearl Harbor: The Imperial Japanese Navy and the United States*. Annapolis: Naval Institute Press.

Atlantic Council. 2021. "The Biden White House Plan for a New US Industrial Policy." *Atlantic Council*, June 23. www.atlanticcouncil.org/commentary/transcript/the-biden-white-house-plan-for-a-new-us-industrial-policy/.

Aung, Wei Yan. 2019. "The Day Japan Signed War Reparations for Myanmar." *The Irrawaddy*, November 5, 2019. www.irrawaddy.com/specials/on-this-day/day-japan-signed-war-reparations-myanmar.html.

Aydin, Cemil. 2007. *The Politics of Anti-Westernism in Asia: Visions of World Order in Pan-Islamic and Pan-Asian Thought*. New York: Columbia University Press.

Baker, Christopher John, and Pasuk Phongpaichit. 2022. *A History of Thailand*. 4th ed. New York: Cambridge University Press.

Banivanua-Mar, Tracey. 2016. *Decolonisation and the Pacific: Indigenous Globalization and the Ends of Empire*. Cambridge: Cambridge University Press.

Baran, Paul, and Paul Sweezy. 1966. *Monopoly Capital: An Essay on the American Economic and Social Order*. New York: Monthly Review Press.

Barder, Alexander D. 2021. *Global Race War: International Politics and Racial Hierarchy*. Oxford: Oxford University Press.

Barnhart, Michael A. 1987. *Japan Prepares for Total War: The Search for Economic Security, 1919–1941*. Ithaca: Cornell University Press.

Bas, Muhammet A. and Andrew J. Coe. 2016. "A Dynamic Theory of Nuclear Proliferation and Preventive War." *International Organization* 70 (4): 655–685.

Bass, Gary. 2023. *Judgment at Tokyo: World War II on Trial and the Making of Modern Asia*. New York: Knopf.

Bastin, John, and Harry J. Benda. 1986. *A History of Modern Southeast Asia: Colonialism, Nationalism, and Decolonization*. Translated by Cheunjit Ampaipan and Pranee Kanjanutthiti. 2nd ed. Bangkok: Thammasat University Press.

Beard, Steven Matthew. 2019. "Fighting, Bargaining, and War Termination." PhD thesis, University of Colorado at Boulder.

Beasley, William G. 1987. *Japanese Imperialism, 1894–1945*. Oxford: Clarendon Press.

Bell, Duncan. 2014. "Before the Democratic Peace: Racial Utopianism, Empire and the Abolition of War." European Journal of International Relations 20 (3): 647–670.

Benson, Brett V. 2012. *Constructing International Security: Alliances, Deterrence, and Moral Hazard*. New York: Cambridge University Press.

Berger, Thomas. 2012. *War, Guilt, and World Politics after World War II*. New York: Cambridge University Press.

Bergsman, P eter. 1976. "The Marianas, the United States, and the United Nations: The Uncertain Status of the New American Commonwealth." *California Western International Law Journal* 6 (2): 382–412.

Berman, Larry. 1982. *Planning a Tragedy: The Americanization of the War in Vietnam*. New York: W.W. Norton.

Bernstein, Joel. 1968. "Memorandum on DAC Comments on Program Evaluation." August 15, Box 3, Chronological Files 7/1/66–12/31/68, Joel Bernstein Papers, Hoover Institution Archives.

Bertram, Geoffrey. 2015. "Is Independence Good or Bad for Development in Small Island Economies? A Long-Run Analysis." *Region et Development* 42 (1): 31–54.

Bethencourt, Francisco. 2013. *Racisms: From the Crusades to the Twentieth Century.* Princeton: Princeton University Press.

Bhabha, Homi K. 2012. *The Location of Culture.* London: Routledge.

Bickers, Robert. 2011. *The Scramble for China: Foreign Devils in the Qing Empire, 1832–1914.* London: Allen Lane.

Bickers, Robert, and R. G. Tiedemann, eds. 2007. *The Boxers, China, and the World.* Lanham Maryland: Rowman & Littlefield.

Blanken, Leo J. 2012. *Rational Empires: Institutional Incentives and Imperial Expansion.* Chicago: Chicago University Press.

Boecking, Felix. 2017. *No Great Wall: Trade, Tariffs, and Nationalism in Republican China, 1927–1945.* Cambridge, MA: Harvard University Press.

Boneparth, Ellen, and M. James Wilkinson. 1995. "Terminating Trusteeship for the Federated States of Micronesia and the Republic of the Marshall Islands." *Pacific Studies* 18 (2): 61–77.

Boone, Ilsley. 1910. *The Conquering Christ.* Boston: Bible Study.

Boorman, Howard, L. and Richard C. Howard. 1967–1979. *Biographical Dictionary of Republican China*, Vol. 2. New York: Columbia University Press.

Bourgon, Jerome. 2003. "Abolishing 'Cruel Punishments': A Reappraisal of the Chinese Roots and Long-Term Efficiency of the Xinzheng Legal Reforms." *Modern Asian Studies* 37 (4): 851–862.

Bowers, Faubion. 1967. "The Late General Macarthur, Warts and All." *Esquire*, January 1.

Boyce, Robert. 2009. *The Great Interwar Crisis and the Collapse of Globalization.* London: Palgrave Macmillan.

Branigin, William. 1985. "Killing of Leader Baffles Palau." *The Washington Post*, August 18. www.washingtonpost.com/archive/politics/1985/08/18/killing-of-leader-baffles-palau/32d65ec3-1ca5-4e97-a13d-b167b1ed2066/.

Brazinsky, Gregg. 2005. "From Pupil to Model: South Korea and American Development Policy during the Early Park Chung Hee Era." *Diplomatic History* 29 (1)(January): 85–115.

Brazinsky, Gregg. 2007. *Nation Building in South Korea: Koreans, Americans, and the Making of a Democracy.* Chapel Hill: University of North Carolina Press.

Breuer, Adam, and Alastair Iain Johnston. 2019. "Memes, Narratives, and the Emergent US-China Security Dilemma." *Cambridge Review of International Affairs* 32 (4): 429–455.

Brooks, Sydney. 1905. "Some Results of the War." *The North American Review* 181 (587): 588–596.

Brown, Owen. 2024. "The Underside of Order: Race in the Constitution of International Order." *International Organization* 78(Winter): 38–66.

Buck, Pearl. 1994. "Our 25,000,000 Forgotten Allies of Korea." *The Free Korea* (Korean Student Federation of North America), February 1944.

Buckley, Roger. 1992. *US-Japan Alliance Diplomacy 1945–1990*. Cambridge: Cambridge University Press.
Bukovansky, Mlada, and Edward Keene. 2023. "Modernity and Granularity in History and International Relations." In *The Oxford Handbook of History and International Relations*, edited by Mlada Bukovansky, Edward Keene, Christian Reus-Smit, and Maja Spanu, 3–18. Oxford: Oxford University Press.
Burrows, Ian. 2017. "Guam: America's Military Base in the Western Pacific." *ABC News*, August 9. www.abc.net.au/news/2017-08-09/where-is-guam-and-how-many-us-troops-are-there/8788566.
Bush, Richard C. 2004. *At Cross Purposes: U.S.-Taiwan Relations since 1942*. New York: Routledge.
Buszynski, Leszek. 2011. "The San Francisco System: Contemporary Meaning and Challenges." *Asian Perspective* 35 (3): 315–335.
Buzan, Barry and Evelyn Goh. 2020. *Rethinking Sino-Japanese Alienation: History Problems and Historical Opportunities*. Oxford: Oxford University Press.
Buzan, Barry, and George Lawson. 2015. *The Global Transformation: History, Modernity and the Making of International Relations*. Cambridge: Cambridge University Press.
Búzás, Zoltán I. 2021. "Racism and Antiracism in the Liberal International Order." *International Organization* 75 (2): 440–463.
Calder, Kent E. 2004. "Securing Security through Prosperity: The San Francisco System in Comparative Perspective." *The Pacific Review* 17 (1): 135–157.
Callahan, William A. 2005. "Nationalism, Civilization and Transnational Relations: The Discourse of Greater China." *Journal of Contemporary China* 14 (43): 269–289.
Carnegie, Andrew. 1905. "An Anglo-French-American Understanding." *The North American Review* 181 (587): 510–517.
Carreon, Bernadette, and Ben Doherty. 2020. "Pacific Nation of Palau Invites US to Build a Military Base to Counter China." *The Guardian*, September 4. www.theguardian.com/world/2020/sep/04/pacific-nation-of-palau-invites-us-to-build-a-military-base-to-counter-china.
Carroll, John M. 2010. "The Canton System: Conflict and Accommodation in the Contact Zone." *Journal of the Royal Asiatic Society Hong Kong Branch* 50: 51–66.
Cavalier, Jacqueline M. 2005. "Immigration's Impact." In *The Industrial Revolution in America: Iron and Steel*, edited by Kevin Hillstrom, and Laurie Collier Hillstrom, 183–209. Santa Barbara: ABC-CLIO.
Cha, Victor D. 2016. *Powerplay: The Origins of the American Alliance System in Asia*. Princeton: Princeton University Press.
Chadefaux, Thomas. 2011. "Bargaining over Power: When Do Shifts in Power Lead to War?" *International Theory* 3 (2): 228–253.
Chang, Gordon. 1990. *Friends and Enemies: The United States, China, and the Soviet Union, 1948–1972*. Stanford: Stanford University Press.
Chang, Gordon H. 2019. *Ghosts of Gold Mountain: The Epic Story of the Chinese Who Built the Transcontinental Railroad*. Boston: Mariner Books.
Chakrabarty, Dipesh. 2000. *Provincializing Europe: Postcolonial Thought and Historical Difference*. Princeton: Princeton University Press.
Chen, Hurng Yu. 2014. "Territorial Disputes in the South China Sea under the San Francisco Peace Treaty." *Issues & Studies* 50 (3)(September): 169–196. https://core.ac.uk/download/pdf/225236036.pdf.

Chen, Jian. 2001. *Mao's China and the Cold War*. Chapel Hill: The University of North Carolina Press.

Chiang, Kai-shek (CKSD). 1954–1955. Diary Entries for Various Dates, 1954–1955. Chiang Kai-shek Diaries, Hoover Institution Archives, Stanford University, box 51.

Chiang, Ching-kuo (CCKD). 1956. Diary Entries for Various Dates, 1956. Chiang Ching-kuo Diaries, Hoover Institution Archives, Stanford University, box 8.

Christensen, Thomas J. 1996. *Useful Adversaries: Grand Strategy, Domestic Mobilization, and Sino-American Conflict, 1947–1958*. Princeton: Princeton University Press.

Christensen, Thomas J. 2011. *Worse than a Monolith: Alliance Politics and Problems of Coercive Diplomacy in Asia*. Princeton: Princeton University Press.

Clark, Christopher. 2012. *The Sleepwalkers: How Europe Went to War in 1914*. New York: HarperCollins.

Clark, Roger S. 1980. "Self-Determination and Free Association-Should the United Nations Terminate the Pacific Islands Trust." *Harvard International Law Journal* 21 (1): 1–86.

Coble, Parks M. 1991. *Facing Japan: Chinese Politics and Japanese Imperialism, 1931–1937*. Cambridge, MA: Harvard University Press.

Coble, Parks M. 2003. *Chinese Capitalists in Japan's New Order: The Occupied Lower Yangzi, 1937–1945*. Berkeley: University of California Press.

Coe, Andrew J. 2011. "Costly Peace: A New Rationalist Explanation for War." Typescript Los Angeles: University of Southern California.

Coe, Andrew J., and Scott Wolford. 2020. "East Asian History and International Relations." In *East Asia in the World: Twelve Events that Shaped the Modern International Order*, edited by Stephan Haggard, and David C. Kang, 263–281. Cambridge: Cambridge University Press.

Coe, Andrew J. and Scott Wolford. 2020. "East Asian History and International Relations." In *East Asia in the World: Twelve Events that Shaped the Modern International Order*, edited by David C. Kang, and Stephan Haggard, 263–281. New York: Cambridge University Press.

Cohen, Paul A. 1997. *History in Three Keys: The Boxers as Event, Experience, and Myth*. New York: Colombia University Press.

Collins, Sandra. 2008. *The 1940 Tokyo Games: The Missing Olympics*. London: Routledge.

Combined Economic Board. 1953. "Combined Economic Board Agreement for a Program of Economic Reconstruction and Financial Stabilization." File 225, Syngman Rhee Papers, Institute for Modern Korea Studies, Yonsei University.

Connaughton, Richard. 2004. *Rising Sun and Tumbling Bear: Russia's War with Japan*. London: Cassell.

Conrad, Sebastian. 2003. "Entangled Memories: Versions of the Past in Germany and Japan, 1945–2000." *Journal of Contemporary History* 38 (1): 85–99.

Copeland, Dale. 2015. *Economic Interdependence and War*. Princeton: Princeton University Press.

Corbett, Jack. 2023. *Statehood à la Carte in the Caribbean and the Pacific: Secession, Regionalism, and Postcolonial Politics*. Oxford: Oxford University Press.

Crider, John H. 1945. "Prophecy of Peace: President Hopeful for Future, Thinks Arms Cuts May Come Later Hails Yalta Plans but Says Some of These Are Secret Now." *New York Times*, March 1.
Crocombe, Ron. 2001. *The South Pacific*. Suva: University of the South Pacific.
Crowley, James B. 1966. *Japan's Quest for Autonomy: National Security and Foreign Policy, 1930–1938*. Princeton: Princeton University Press.
Cullather, Nick. 1994. *Illusions of Influence: The Political Economy of United States-Philippines Relations, 1952–1960*. Stanford: Stanford University Press.
Cullather, Nick. 1996. "'Fuel for the Good Dragon': The United States and Industrial Policy in Taiwan, 1950–1965." *Diplomatic History* 20 (1): 1–25. https://doi.org/10.1111/j.1467-7709.1996.tb00250.x.
Cumings, Bruce. 2005. *Korea's Place in the Sun: A Modern History, 199–200*. New York: W. W. Norton.
Cumings, Bruce. 2010. *The Korean War*. New York: Modern Library.
D'Arcy, Paul. 2006. *The People of the Sea: Environment, Identity, and History in Oceania*. Honolulu: University of Hawaii Press.
Danby, Michael. 1987. "Moscow's South Pacific Push." *IPA Review* 40 (4): 49–52.
Debs, Alexandre and Nuno P. Monteiro. 2014. "Known Unknowns: Power Shifts, Uncertainty, and War." *International Organization* 68 (1): 1–31.
Department of General Political Warfare, ROC Ministry of National Defense. 1956. "The CCP War Guidelines and Strategies for Peace." Contemporary Taiwan Collection, Library of the Institute of Oriental Culture, University of Tokyo, no. C125: 437.
Department of State. 1945. "Scholarship Opportunities Open to Students from Korea." *The Department of State Bulletin* 12 (June): 1059.
Department of State. 1976. "Department of State Policy Statement [21 April 1950, Document 96]." In *Foreign Relations of the United States, 1950*, Volume 6, edited by Neal H. Petersen, William Z. Slany, Charles S. Sampson, John P. Glennon, and David W. Mabon. Washington, DC: U.S. Government Printing Office. https://history.state.gov/historicaldocuments/frus1950v06/d96.
Department of State. 1977. "Department of State Policy Statement for New Zealand [30 July 1951, Document 1]." In *Foreign Relations of the United States, 1951*, Volume 6, Part 2, edited by Paul Claussen, John P. Glennon, David W. Mabon, Neal H. Petersen, and Carl N. Raether. Washington, DC: U.S. Government Printing Office. https://history.state.gov/historicaldocuments/frus1951v06p2/d1.
Department of State. 1996. "Memorandum of Conversation [22 October 1958, Document 203]." In *Foreign Relations of the United States, 1958–1960*, Volume 19, edited by Harriet Dashiell Schwar. Washington, DC: U.S. Government Printing Office. https://history.state.gov/historicaldocuments/frus1958-60v19/d203.
Department of State. 1996. "Joint Communiqué [23 October 1958, Document 209]." In *Foreign Relations of the United States, 1958–1960*, Volume 19, edited by Harriet Dashiell Schwar. Washington, DC: U.S. Government Printing Office. https://history.state.gov/historicaldocuments/frus1958-60v19/d209.
Department of State. 1996. "Memorandum of Conversation [23 October 1958, Document 207]." In *Foreign Relations of the United States, 1958–1960*, Volume 19, edited by Harriet Dashiell Schwar. Washington, DC: U.S. Government Printing Office. https://history.state.gov/historicaldocuments/frus1958-60v19/d207.

Dickinson, Frederick R. 2013. *World War I and the Triumph of a New Japan.* Cambridge: Cambridge University Press.

Dickinson, Frederick R. "Tragic War, Lasting Peace: Japan and the Construction of Global Peace, 1919–1930." In *Beyond Versailles: The 1919 Moment and a New Order in East Asia*, edited by Tosh Minohara and Evan Dawley, 247–270. Lanham MD: Lexington Books.

Dincecco, Mark, and Yuhua Wang. 2018. "Violence Conflict and Political Development over the Long Run: China versus Europe." *Annual Review of Political Science* 21: 341–358.

Division of Far Eastern Affairs, Memo, December 10, 1941, 895.01/60-11/26. In 대한민국임시정부자료집 [Materials of the Korean Provisional Government]. National Institute of Korean History, 2007, 20: 146.

Dominguez, Jorge I. 1979. "Responses to Occupations by the United States: Caliban's Dilemma." Pacific Historical Review 48 (4)(November): 591–605.

Doner, Richard F., Bryan K. Ritchie, and Dan Slater. 2005. "Systemic Vulnerability and the Origins of Developmental States: Northeast Asia and Southeast Asia in Comparative Perspective." *International Organization* 59 (2)(Spring): 327–361. https://doi.org/10.1017/S0020818305050113.

Dornan, Matthew, and Jonathan Pryke. 2017. "Foreign Aid to the Pacific: Trends and Developments in the Twenty-First Century." *Asia & the Pacific Policy Studies* 4 (3): 386–404.

Dorrance, John C. 1990. "The Soviet Union and the Pacific Islands: A Current Assessment." *Asian Survey* 30 (9): 908–925.

Doumenge, François. 1983. *Viability of Small Island States: A Descriptive Study.* Geneva: United Nations Conference on Trade and Development.

Dower, John. 1999. *Embracing Defeat: Japan in the Wake of World War II.* New York: W.W. Norton.

Dower, John W. 1986. *War without Mercy: Race and Power in the Pacific War.* New York: Pantheon Books.

Dower, John W. 2014. "The San Francisco System: Past, Present, Future in U.S.-Japan-China Relations." *Asia-Pacific Journal* 12 (8)(February): 1–41.

Dower, John W. 2015. "The San Francisco System: Past, Present, Future." In *The San Francisco System and Its Legacies: Continuation, Transformation and Historical Reconciliation in the Asia-Pacific*, edited by Kimie Hara, 213–251. London: Routledge.

Doyle, Michael. 1986. *Empires.* Ithaca: Cornell University Press.

Du Bois, W. E. B. 2014. The Problem of the Color Line at the Turn of the Twentieth Century. New York: Fordham University Press.

Du Bois, W. E. B. 2015 (1903). *The Souls of Black Folk.* New Haven: Yale University Press.

Du Bois, W. E. B. and Nahum Dimitri Chandler. 2014. *The Problem of the Color Line at the Turn of the Century: The Essential Early Essays.* New York: Fordham University Press.

Duara, Prasenjit. 2007. "The Imperialism of 'Free Nations': Japan, Manchukuo, and the History of the Present." In *Imperial Formations*, edited by Ann Stoler, Carole McGranahan, and Peter Perdue, 211–239. Santa Fe: SAR Press.

Dudden, Alexis. 2005. "Japanese Colonial Control in International Terms." *Japanese Studies* 25 (1): 1–20.

Dudden, Alexis. 2008. *Troubled Apologies among Japan, Korea, and the United States*. New York: Columbia University Press.

Dudden, Alexis. 2020. "Matthew Perry in Japan, 1852–1854." In *East Asia in the World: Twelve Events Shaped the Modern International Order*, edited by Stephan Haggard and David C. Kang, 188–205. Cambridge: Cambridge University Press.

Dulles, Allen. 1986a. "Memorandum from the Director of Central Intelligence (Dulles) to the Secretary of State (Dulles) [16 March 1955, Document 1959]." In *Foreign Relations of the United States, 1955–1957*, Vol. 2, edited by Harriet D. Schwar. Washington, DC: U.S. Government Printing Office. https://history.state.gov/historicaldocuments/frus1955-57v02/d159.

Dulles, Allen. 1986b. "National Intelligence Estimate [5 January 1956, Document 126]." In *Foreign Relations of the United States, 1958–1960*, Vol. 3, edited by Harriet D. Schwar, and Louis J. Smith. Washington, DC: U.S. Government Printing Office. https://history.state.gov/historicaldocuments/frus1955-57v03/d126.

Dulles, John Foster. 1996a. "Talking Paper Prepared by Secretary of State Dulles [21 October 1958, Document 196]." In *Foreign Relations of the United States, 1958–1960*, Vol. 19, edited by Harriet Dashiell Schwar. Washington, DC: U.S. Government Printing Office. https://history.state.gov/historicaldocuments/frus1958-60v19/d196.

Dulles, John Foster. 1996b. "Telegram from Secretary of State Dulles to the Department of State [23 October 1958, Document 210]." In *Foreign Relations of the United States, 1958–1960*, Vol. 19, edited by Harriet Dashiell Schwar. Washington, DC: U.S. Government Printing Office. https://history.state.gov/historicaldocuments/frus1958-60v19/d210.

Dutt, Vidya Prakash. 1968. "The First Week of Revolution: The Wuchang Uprising." In *China in Revolution: The First Phase, 1900–1913*, edited by Mary Clabaugh Wright, 383–416. New Haven: Yale University Press.

Duus, Peter. 1996. "Imperialism without Colonies: The Vision of a Greater East Asia Co-Prosperity Sphere." *Diplomacy and Statecraft* 7 (1): 54–72.

Dziedzic, Stephen. 2023. "United States and Federated States of Micronesia Renew Strategic Pact in Bid to Counter China." *ABC News*, May 16. www.abc.net.au/news/2023-05-16/us-federated-states-of-micronesia-palau-china-pact/102350178.

Easton, David. 1985. "Political Science in the United States: Past and Present." *International Political Science Review* 6 (1): 133–152.

Editorial Committee of the Biography of Su Yu. 2000. *Su Yu Zhuan (The biography of Su Yu)*. Beijing: Dangdai Zhongguo chubanshe.

Edwards, Willard. 1945a. "Charges Reds Silence Korea's Freedom Plea." *Chicago Daily Tribune*, May 5.

Edwards, Willard. 1945b. "Snub to Korea Laid to Secret Deal at Yalta." *Chicago Daily Tribune*, May 7.

Eisenhower, Dwight. 1963. *Mandate for Change*. New York: Doubleday.

Eisenhower, Dwight. 1964. "Transcript of Meeting with General Dwight E. Eisenhower." August 25, Gettysburg, Pennsylvania. Eisenhower Library. www.eisenhowerlibrary.gov/sites/default/files/research/online-documents/post-presidential/162-001.pdf.

Elkind, Jessica. 2016. *Aid under Fire: Nation Building and the Vietnam War*. Lexington: University Press of Kentucky.

Elkins, Caroline. 2023. *Legacy of Violence: A History of the British Empire*. New York: Knopf Doubleday.
Elleman, Bruce. 2002. *Wilson and China: A Revised History of the Shandong Question*. Armonk: Taylor & Francis.
Emmers, Ralf. 2009. *Geopolitics and Maritime Territorial Disputes in East Asia*. London: Routledge.
Esherick, Joseph. 1976. *Reform and Revolution in China: The 1911 Revolution in Hunan and Hubei*. Berkeley: University of California Press.
Esherick, Joseph W. 1988. *The Origins of the Boxer Uprising*. California: University of California Press.
Esherick, Joseph W. 1994. "Founding a Republic, Electing a President: How Sun Ya-sen Became Guofu." In *China's Republican Revolution*, edited by Eto Shinkichi, and Harold Z. Schiffrin. Tokyo: University of Tokyo Press.
Esherick, Joseph W. 2012. "Reconsidering 1911: Lessons of a Sudden Revolution." *Journal of Modern Chinese History* 6 (1): 1–14.
Estimates Group. 1976. "Intelligence Estimate Prepared by the Estimates Group, Office of Intelligence Research, Department of State [25 June 1950, Document 82]." In *Foreign Relations of the United States, 1950*, Vol. 7, edited by John P. Glennon. Washington, DC: U.S. Government Printing Office. https://history.state.gov/historicaldocuments/frus1950v07/d82.
Fanon, Franz. 1965. *The Wretched of the Earth*. New York: Grove Press.
Fanon, Franz. 1967. *Black Skin, White Masks*. New York: Grove Press.
Farrell, Brian P., ed. 2018. *Empire in Asia: A New Global History*, Vol. 2, The Long Nineteenth Century. London: Bloomsbury Academic.
Farrell, Henry, and Abraham L. Newman. 2019. "Weaponized Interdependence: How Global Economic Networks Shape State Coercion." *International Security* 44 (1): 42–79.
Fearon, James D. 1995. "Rationalist Explanations for War." *International Organization* 49 (3): 379–414.
Fields, David. 2017. "Syngman Rhee: Socialist." Cold War International History Project Working Paper 82 (June). Fields: Done, see 9 comments
Fields, David P. 2019. *Foreign Friends: Syngman Rhee, American Exceptionalism, and the Division of Korea*. Lexington: University Press of Kentucky.
Filson, Darren and Suzanne Werner. 2002. "A Bargaining Model of War and Peace: Anticipating the Onset, Duration, and Outcome of War." *American Journal of Political Science* 46 (2): 819–837.
Fineman, Daniel. 1997. *A Special Relationship: The United States and Military Government in Thailand, 1947–1958*. Honolulu: University of Hawaii Press.
Fineman, Daniel. 2009. "Phibun, the Cold War and Thailand's Foreign Policy Revolution of 1950." In *Connecting Histories: Decolonization and the Cold War in Southeast Asia, 1945–1962*, edited by Christopher Goscha, and Christian Ostermann, 275–300. Stanford: Stanford University Press.
Firth, Stewart. 1997a. "Colonial Administration and the Invention of the Native." In *The Cambridge History of the Pacific Islanders*, edited by Donald Denoon, Malama Meleisea, Stewart Firth, Jocelyn Linnekin, and Karen Nero, 253–288. Cambridge: Cambridge University Press.

Firth, Stewart. 1997b. "The War in the Pacific." In *The Cambridge History of the Pacific Islanders*, edited by Donald Denoon, Malama Meleisea, Stewart Firth, Jocelyn Linnekin, and Karen Nero, 291–323. Cambridge: Cambridge University Press.

Fischer, Fritz. 1967. *Germany's Aims in the First World War*. New York: W.W. Norton.

Foot, Rosemary. 1995. *The Practice of Power: US Relations with China since 1949*. Oxford: Oxford University Press.

Foot, Rosemary, and Evelyn Goh. 2018. "The International Relations of East Asia: A New Research Prospectus." *International Studies Review* 21 (3): 398–423.

Foreign Relations of the United States, 1952–1954, Indochina, Volume 13, Part 2, Page 1440.

Foster, Anne. 2010. *Projections of Power: The United States and Europe in Colonial Southeast Asia, 1919–1941*. Durham: Duke University Press.

Forrestal, Michael V. 1963. Memorandum to President Kennedy on U.S. Relations with the Military Junta. Box 127A, Korea General 8/62–3/63, National Security Files, Papers of President Kennedy, John F. Kennedy Presidential Library.

Freeman, Bianca, Daegyeong G. Kim, and David A. Lake. 2022. "Race in International Relations: Beyond the 'Norm against Noticing'." *Annual Review of Political Science* 25: 175–196.

French, David. 2012. *The British Way in Counterinsurgency, 1945–1957*. Oxford: Oxford University Press.

Frieden, Jeffrey. 1994. "International Investment and Colonial Control: A New Interpretation." *International Organization* 48 (4)(Autumn): 559–593.

Friend, Theodore. 1965. *Between Two Empires: The Ordeal of the Philippines, 1929–1946*. New Haven: Yale University Press.

Fry, Greg. 2019. *Framing the Islands: Power and Diplomatic Agency in Pacific Regionalism*. Canberra: Australian National University Press.

Fujitani, Takashi. 2013. *Race for Empire: Koreans as Japanese and Japanese as Americans during World War II*. Berkeley: University of California Press.

Fukuda, Madoka. 2023. "New Strategies of China Regarding the 'One-China' Principle." *The Sasakawa Peace Foundation*, March 16. www.spf.org/japan-us-taiwan-research/en/article/fukuda_01.html.

Fukuyama, Francis. 2018. *Identity: The Demand for Dignity and the Politics of Resentment*. London: Farrar, Straus and Giroux.

Furukawa, Takahisa. 2015. *Konoe Fumimaro*. Tokyo: Yoshikawa Kōbunkan.

Gale, James Scarth. 1909. *Korea in Transition*. New York: Young People's Missionary Movement of the United States and Canada.

Gale, Roger W. 1979. *The Americanization of Micronesia: A Study of the Consolidation of US Rule in the Pacific*. Lanham MD: University Press of America.

Gallicchio, Marc. 2000. *The African American Encounter with Japan & China: Black Internationalism in Asia, 1895–1945*. Chapel Hill NC: University of North Carolina Press.

Gao, Bai. 1997. *Economic Ideology and Japanese Industrial Policy: Developmentalism from 1931 to 1965*. Cambridge: Cambridge University Press.

Garon, Sheldon. 1984. "The Imperial Bureaucracy and Labor Policy in Postwar Japan." *Journal of Asian Studies* 43 (3)(May): 441–457. https://doi.org/10.2307/2055757.

Gartner, Scott Sigmund and Randolph M. Siverson. 1996. "War Expansion and War Outcome." *Journal of Conflict Resolution* 40 (1): 4–15.

Gartzke, Erik. 1999. "War Is in the Error Term." *International Organization* 53 (3): 567–587.

Gartzke, Erik, and Jiakun J. Zhang. 2015. "Trade and War." In *The Oxford Handbook of the Political Economy of International Trade*, edited by Lisa L. Martin, 419–438. Oxford: Oxford University Press.

Gartzke, Erik, and Yonatan Lupu. 2012. "Trading on Preconceptions: Why World War I Was Not a Failure of Economic Interdependence." *International Security* 36 (4): 115–150.

Garver, John W. 1997. *The Sino-American Alliance: Nationalist China and American Cold War Strategy in Asia*. Armonk: M. E. Sharpe.

Gasster, Michael. 1980. "The Republican Revolutionary Movement." In *The Cambridge History of China, Volume 11: Late Ch'ing 1800–1911, Part 2*, edited by John K. Fairbank, and Kwang-Ching Liu, 493–654. Cambridge: Cambridge University Press.

Gawthorpe, Andrew J. 2018. *To Build as Well as Destroy: American Nation Building in South Vietnam*. Ithaca: Cornell University Press.

General Headquarters Supreme Commander for the Allied Powers. 1945. "Summation No. 1: Non-military Activities in Japan and Korea for the Months of September–October 1945." (October), 175.

George C. McGhee to McGeorge Bundy, Memo, August 25, 1961. "The Offshore Island: Alternative Courses and Probable Consequences." In *John F. Kennedy National Security Files 1961–1963*. Microfilm, reel 1.

Gerth, Karl. 2003. *China Made: Consumer Culture and the Creation of the Nation*. Cambridge, MA: Harvard University Press.

Getachew, Adom. 2018. *Worldmaking after Empire: The Rise and Fall of Self-Determination*. Princeton: Princeton University Press.

Getachew, Adom. 2019. *Worldmaking after Empire*. Princeton: Princeton University Press.

Gilmore, William C. 1978. "Legal Perspectives on Associated Statehood in the Eastern Caribbean." *Virginia Journal of International Law* 19: 311–328.

Gilpin, Robert. 1981. *War and Change in World Politics*. Cambridge: Cambridge University Press.

Goemans, Hein. 2000. *War and Punishment: The Causes of War Termination and the First World War*. Princeton: Princeton University Press.

Goh, Evelyn. 2007. "Great Powers and Hierarchical Order in Southeast Asia: Analyzing Regional Security Strategies." *International Security* 32 (3): 113–157. www.jstor.org/stable/30130520.

Goh, Evelyn. 2013a. "Making Headway on the 'Economic-Security Nexus': Contributions from South East Asia." *The Asan Forum* 1 (3): 1–8.

Goh, Evelyn. 2013b. *The Struggle for Order: Hegemony, Hierarchy and Transition in Post-Cold War East Asia*. Oxford: Oxford University Press.

Goh, Evelyn. 2014. "East Asia as Regional International Society: The Problem of Great Power Management." In *Contesting International Society in East Asia*, edited by Barry Buzan, and Yongjin Zhang, 167–187. Cambridge: Cambridge University Press.

Goh, Evelyn. 2019. "Conceptualizing the Economic-Security-Identity Nexus in East Asia's Regional Order." In *Japan and Asia's Contested Order: The Interplay of*

Security, Economics, and Identity, edited by Yul Sohn, and T. J. Pempel, 17–37. Singapore: Palgrave MacMillan.

Goldberg, Jeffrey. 2016. "The Obama Doctrine." *The Atlantic*, April 15. www.theatlantic.com/magazine/archive/2016/04/the-obama-doctrine/471525/.

Goldstein, Gordon M. 2008. *Lessons in Disaster: McGeorge Bundy and the Path to War in Vietnam*. New York: Holt Paperbacks.

Gong, Gerrit W. 1984. *The Standard of "Civilization" in International Society*. Oxford: Clarendon Press.

Gourevitch, Peter. 1978. "The Second Image Reversed: The International Sources of Domestic Politics." *International Organization* 32 (4)(Autumn): 881–912.

Green, D. Michael. 1974. "Termination of the U.S. Pacific Islands Trusteeship." *Texas International Law Journal* 9 (2)(Summer): 175–204.

Green, D. Michael. 2017. *By More than Providence: Grand Strategy and American Power in the Asia Pacific since 1783*. New York: Columbia University Press.

Grew, Joseph. 1945. "Review of Policy Regarding Korea." *The Department of State Bulletin* 12(June): 1058–1059.

Gries, Peter Hayes. 2004. *China's New Nationalism: Pride, Politics, and Diplomacy*. Berkeley: University of California Press.

Gripentrog, John. 2021. *Prelude to Pearl Harbor: Ideology and Culture in US-Japan Relations, 1919–1941*. New York: Rowman & Littlefield.

Gunitsky, Seva. 2017. *Aftershocks: Great Powers and Domestic Reforms in the Twentieth Century*. Princeton: Princeton University Press.

Hack, Karl. 2021. *The Malayan Emergency: Revolution and Counterinsurgency at the End of Empire*. New York: Cambridge University Press.

Haggard, Stephan. 1990. *Pathways from the Periphery: The Politics of Growth in the Newly Industrializing Countries*. Ithaca: Cornell University Press.

Haggard, Stephan. 2018. *Developmental States*. New York: Cambridge University Press.

Haggard, Stephan, and David C. Kang, eds. 2020. *East Asia in the World: Twelve Events Shaped the Modern International Order*. Cambridge: Cambridge University Press.

Haggard, Stephan, and Yu Zheng. 2013. "Institutional Innovation and Investment in Taiwan: The Micro-foundations of the Developmental State." *Business and Politics* 15 (4) (December): 435–466. https://doi.org/10.1515/bap-2012-0010.

Haggard, Stephan, Byung-kook Kim, and Chung-in Moon. 1991. "The Transition to Export-led Growth in South Korea: 1954–1966." *Journal of Asian Studies* 50 (4) (November): 850–873. https://doi.org/10.2307/2058544.

Haglelgam, John. 1991. "Problems of National Unity and Economic Development in the Federated States of Micronesia." Lecture, Micronesian Area Research Center, University of Guam, Mangilao, April 4, 1991.

Hall, Daniel G. E. 1979. *A History of South-East Asia*. Translated by Warunayupa Sanitwong Na Aytthaya, Wilaswong Pongsaboot, Chusiri Chamornman, Pensri Duke, Petchari Sumitra, Tamsook Noomnont, Rossukon Itsarasena, and Srisook Tawichaprasit. Bangkok: The Foundation for the Promotion of Social Sciences and Humanities Textbooks Projects.

Halsey, Stephen R. 2015. *Quest for Power: European Imperialism and the Making of Chinese Statecraft*. Cambridge MA: Harvard University Press.

Han, Enze. 2022. "Racialised Threat Perception within International Society: From Japan to China." *The Chinese Journal of International Politics* 15 (3)(September): 272–288.
Hanlon, David L. 2014. *Making Micronesia: A Political Biography of Tosiwo Nakayama*. Honolulu: University of Hawaii Press.
Hara, Kimie. 2001. "50 Years from San Francisco: Re-examining the Peace Treaty and Japan's Territorial Problems." *Pacific Affairs* 74 (3)(Autumn): 361–382.
Hara, Kimie. 2006. "Cold War Frontiers in the Asia-Pacific: The Troubling Legacy of the San Francisco Treaty." *The Asia-Pacific Journal* 4 (9)(September): 2–7.
Hara, Kimie. 2007. *Cold War Frontiers in the Asia-Pacific: Divided Territories in the San Francisco System*. New York: Routledge.
Harper, Tim. 2020. *Underground Asia: Global Revolutionaries and the Assault on Empire*. Cambridge MA: Belknap.
Harriman, Averell. 1983. "Report Prepared by the Office of the Director of Mutual Security [18 August 1952, Document 162]." In *Foreign Relations of the United States, 1952–1954*, Vol. 1, Pt. 1, edited by David M. Baehler, Herbert A. Fine, Ralph R. Goodwin, et al., 639–684. Washington, DC: U.S. Government Printing Office. https://history.state.gov/historicaldocuments/frus1952-54v01p1/d162.
Harrison, Rachel. 2010. "Introduction: The Allure of Ambiguity: The 'West' and the Making of Thai Identities." In *The Ambiguous Allure of the West: Traces of the Colonial in Thailand*, edited by Rachel Harrison, and Peter A. Jackson, 1–36. Hong Kong: Hong Kong University Press.
Hart-Landsberg, Martin. 1998. *Korea: Division, Reunification, & U.S. Foreign Policy*. New York: Monthly Review Press.
Hartman, Carl. 1943. "Freedom, Coming for Korea." *Wisconsin State Journal* (December 6).
Hastings, Max. 2013. *Catastrophe 1914: Europe Goes to War*. New York: Knopf.
Hatano, Sumio. 1995. "Senji Nihon no Wilsonianism to sono kokunaiteki bunmyaku." *Tsukuba hōsei* 18 (2): 69–98.
Hatano, Sumio. 1996. *Taiheyō Sensō to Ajia gaikō*. Tokyo: Tokyo Daigaku Shuppankai.
Hattori, Ryūji. 2001. *Higashi Ajia kokusai kankyō no hendō to Nihon gaikō 1918–1931*. Tokyo: Yūhikaku.
Hau'ofa, Epeli. 1994. "Our Sea of Islands." *The Contemporary Pacific* 6 (1): 148–161.
Hayton, Bill. 2014. *The South China Sea: The Struggle for Power in Asia*. New Haven: Yale University Press.
He, Dongfang. 2000. *Zhang Aiping Zhuan (The Biography of Zhang Aiping)*, Vol. 2. Beijing: Renmin chubanshe.
Hegarty, David. 1991. "The External Powers in the South Pacific." In *South Pacific Security: Issues and Perspectives*, edited by Stephen Henningham, and Desmond Ball, 90–108. Canberra: Australian National University.
Heine, Carl. 1970. "Micronesia: Unification and the Coming of Self-Government." In *Politics of Melanesia*, edited by Marion Ward, 193–206. Port Moresby: Research School of Pacific Studies and the University of Papua New Guinea.
Heine, Carl. 1974. *Micronesia at the Crossroads: A Reappraisal of the Micronesian Political Dilemma*. Canberra: Australian National University Press.
Hemmer, Christopher, and Peter J. Katzenstein. 2002. "Why Is There No NATO in Asia? Collective Identity, Regionalism, and the Origins of Multilateralism."

International Organization 56 (3)(Summer): 575–607. https://doi.org/10.1162/002081802760199890.

Henry, Iain D. 2022. *Reliability and Alliance Interdependence: The United States and Its Allies in Asia, 1949–1969*. Ithaca: Cornell University Press.

Hinck, Jon. 1990. "The Republic of Palau and the United States: Self-Determination Becomes the Price of Free Association." *California Law Review* 78 (4) 915–971.

Hobson, John. 2004. *The Eastern Origins of Western Civilization*. New York: Cambridge University Press.

Hobson, John. 2012. *The Eurocentric Conception of World Politics: Western International Theory, 1760–2010*. New York: Cambridge University Press.

Hobson, John M. 2012. *The Eurocentric Conception of World Politics: Western International Theory, 1760–2010*. New York: Cambridge University Press.

Holsti, Kalevi J. 1991. *Peace and War: Armed Conflicts and International Order, 1648–1989*. New York: Cambridge University Press.

Hoopes, Townsend. 1973. *The Devil and John Foster Dulles*. Boston: Little, Brown.

Hori, Kazuo. 2009. *Higashi Ajia shihonshugi shiron*, Vol. 1. Tokyo: Minerva Shobō.

Horowitz, Richard S. 2008. "The Ambiguities of an Imperial Institution: Crisis and Transition in the Chinese Maritime Customs, 1899–1911." *Journal of Imperial and Commonwealth History* 36: 275–294.

Horowitz, Richard S. 2020. "The Opium. Wars of 1839–1860." In *East Asia in the World: Twelve Events Shaped the Modern International Order*, edited by Stephan Haggard, and David C. Kang, 164–187. Cambridge: Cambridge University Press.

Hosoya, Chihiro and Makoto Saitō, eds. 1978. *Washinton taisei to Nichi-Bei kankei*. Tokyo: Daigaku Shuppankai.

Hsu, Immanuel C. Y. 1980. "Late Ch'ing Foreign Relations, 1866–1905." In *The Cambridge History of China, Volume 11: Late Ch'ing 1800–1911*, Pt. 2, edited by John K. Fairbank, and Kwang-Ching Liu, 70–141. Cambridge: Cambridge University Press.

Huang, Chin-Hao, and David C. Kang. 2022. *State Formation through Emulation: The East Asian Model*. New York: Cambridge University Press.

Huei, Pang Yang. 2019. *Strait Rituals: China, Taiwan, and the United States in the Taiwan Strait Crises, 1954–1958*. Hong Kong: Hong Kong University Press.

Huff, Greg. 2020. *World War II and Southeast Asia: Economy and Society under Japanese Occupation*. Cambridge: Cambridge University Press.

Hulbert, Homer B. 1906. *The Passing of Korea*. New York: Doubleday, Page.

Hunt, Michael H. and Steven I. Levine. 2012. *Arc of Empire: America's Wars in Asia from the Philippines to Vietnam*. Chapel Hill: University of North Carolina Press.

Ichiko, Chuzo. 1980. "Political and Institutional Reform 1901–1911." In *The Cambridge History of China, Volume 11: Late Ch'ing 1800–1911*, Pt. 2, edited by John K. Fairbank, and Kwang-Ching Liu, 589–647. Cambridge: Cambridge University Press.

Ikenberry, G. John. 2004. "American Hegemony and East Asian Order." *Australian Journal of International Affairs* 58: 353–367.

Immigration and Ethnic History Society. "Page Law (1875)." Immigration History. https://immigrationhistory.org/item/page-act/.

Inoue, Toshikazu. 1994. *Kiki no naka no kyōchō gaikō: Nit-Chū sensō ni itaru taigai seisaku no keisei to tenkai*. Tokyo: Yamakawa Shuppansha.
Interdepartmental Working Group. 1993. "Staff Study Prepared by an Interdepartmental Working Group for the Operations Coordinating Board [16 November 1955, Document 99]." In *Foreign Relations of the United States, 1955–1957*, Vol. 23, Pt. 2, edited by Louis J. Smith. Washington, DC: U.S. Government Printing Office. https://history.state.gov/historicaldocuments/frus1955-57v23p2/d99.
Iriye, Akira. 1965. *After Imperialism: The Search for a New Order in the Far East, 1921–1931*. Cambridge, MA: Harvard University Press.
Iriye, Akira. 1974. "The Failure of Economic Expansionism." In *Japan in Crisis: Essays on Taishō Democracy*, edited by Bernard S. Silberman and Harvey D. Harootunian, 180–197. Princeton: Princeton University Press.
Iriye, Akira. 1981. *Power and Culture: The Japanese – American War, 1941–1945*. Cambridge, MA: Harvard University Press.
Iriye, Akira. 2013 (1987). *The Origins of the Second World War in Asia and the Pacific*. New York: Routledge.
Isaac, Benjamin. 2004. *The Invention of Racism in Classical Antiquity*. Princeton: Princeton University Press.
Ishihara, Yusuke. 2023. "Renegotiating Japan's Postwar Bargains: The Transformation of Japanese Foreign Policy and the Pluralisation of the U.S. Hegemonic Order in the 1970s." PhD Thesis, The Australian National University.
Izzo, Federica, Gregory J. Martin, and Steven Callender. 2023. "Ideological Competition." *American Journal of Political Science* 67 (3): 687–700.
Jacob, Frank. 2017. *The Russo-Japanese War and Its Shaping of the Twentieth Century*. London: Routledge.
Jacoby, Neil. 1966. *U.S. Aid to Taiwan: A Study of Foreign Aid, Self-Help and Development*. New York: Frederick A. Praeger.
Japan, Navy Ministry. 1942. "Gaikō kondankai (Taiheiyō kenshō seitei ni tsuite)" [Concerning the Establishment of a Pacific Charter], September 26, in *Shōwa shakai keizai shiryō shūsei* Vol. 17, edited by Ōkubo Tatsumasa, Nagata Motoya, Maegawa Kunio, and Hyōdō Tōru, and Doi Akira (editorial supervisor). Tokyo: Daitō Bunka Daigaku Tōyō Kenkyūjo, 1985.
Jeong, Byeong-jun, ed. 1996. 이승만관계서한자료집 *[Correspondence and Materials Related to Syngman Rhee]*, Vol. 1. Seoul: National Institute of Korean History.
Jeshurun, Chandran. 1970. "The Anglo-French Declaration of January 1896 and the Independence of Siam." *Journal of the Siam Society* LVIII part 2, 58: 105–126.
Jiang, Keyi. 2023. "Clashing Asianisms: Li Dazhao and Yoshino Sakuzō in China–Japan Relations" (PhD dissertation, The Chinese University of Hong Kong,), Ch. 5.
Johnson, Chalmers. 1982. *MITI and the Japanese Miracle: The Growth of Industrial Policy, 1925–1975*. Stanford: Stanford University Press.
Johnson, Louis. 1976. "Memorandum by the Secretary of Defense (Johnson) to the Executive Secretary of the National Security Council (Lay) [14 September 1950, Document 837]." In *Foreign Relations of the United States, 1950*, Vol. 6, edited by Neal H. Petersen, William Z. Slany, Charles S. Sampson, John P. Glennon, and David W. Mabon. Washington, DC: U.S. Government Printing Office. https://history.state.gov/historicaldocuments/frus1950v06/d837.

Johnson, Ural Alexis. 1987. "The Acting Assistant Secretary of State for Far Eastern Affairs (Johnson) to the Ambassador in the Philippines [13 November 1952, Document 318]." In *Foreign Relations of the United States, 1952–1954*, Vol. 12, Pt. 2, edited by Carl N. Raether and Harriet D. Schwar. Washington, DC: U.S. Government Printing Office. https://history.state.gov/historicaldocuments/frus1952-54v12p2/d318.

Johnson, Ural Alexis. 1987. "The Acting Assistant Secretary of State for Far Eastern Affairs to the Ambassador in the Philippines [13 November 1952, Document 318]." In *Foreign Relations of the United States, 1952–1954*, Vol. 12, Pt. 2, edited by Carl N. Raether, and Harriet D. Schwar. Washington, DC: U.S. Government Printing Office. https://history.state.gov/historicaldocuments/frus1952-54v12p2/d318.

Johnston, Alastair Iain. 2023. "Racism and Security Dilemmas." *International Politics*, 61 (2): 1–14.

Johnston, Richard J. H. 1945. "Korean Red Group Assailed by Rhee." *New York Times*, November 22.

Joint Development Group. 1969. *The Postwar Development of the Republic of Vietnam: Policies and Programs*, Vol. 1. New York and Saigon: Joint Development Group. https://pdf.usaid.gov/pdf_docs/PNABJ230.pdf.

Kabutaulaka, Tarcisius. 2015. "Re-presenting Melanesia: Ignoble Savages and Melanesian Alter-Natives." *The Contemporary Pacific* 27 (1): 110–145.

Kahin, George McT. 1986. *Intervention: How America Became Involved in Vietnam*. New York: Alfred Knopf.

Kanagawa, Nadia. 2020. "East Asia's First World War." In *East Asia in the World: Twelve Events Shaped the Modern International Order*, edited by Stephan Haggard, and David C. Kang, 67–80. Cambridge: Cambridge University Press.

Kang, David C. 2010. *East Asia before the West: Five Centuries of Trade and Tribute*. Contemporary Asia in the World. New York: Columbia University Press.

Kang, David C. 2013. "International Relations Theory and East Asian History." *Journal of East Asian Studies* 13 (2)(May): 181–205.

Kang, David C. 2020. "International Order in Historical East Asia: Tribute and Hierarchy Beyond Sinocentrism and Eurocentrism." *International Organization* 74 (1): 65–93. https://doi.org/10.1017/S0020818319000274.

Kang, David C., and Alex Yu-Ting Lin. 2019. "U.S. Bias in the Study of International Relations: Using Europe to study Asia." *Journal of Global Security Studies* 4 (3) (July): 393–401.

Kang, David C., and Kenneth Swope. 2020. "East Asian International Relations over the Longue Duree." In *East Asia in the World: Twelve Events Shaped the Modern International Order*, edited by Stephan Haggard, and David C. Kang, 22–43. Cambridge: Cambridge University Press.

Kang, David C., and Xinru Ma. 2018. "Power Transitions: Thucydides Didn't Live in East Asia." *The Washington Quarterly* 41, (1)(March): 137–145.

Kang, David C., Ronan Tse-min Fu, and Meredith Shaw. 2016. "Measuring War in Early Modern East Asia: Introducing Chinese and Korean Language Sources." *International Studies Quarterly* 60 (4)(December): 766–777.

Kapstein, Ethan. 2017. *Seeds of Stability: Land Reform and US Foreign Policy*. Cambridge: Cambridge University Press.

Katō, Yōko. 2005. *Sensō no ronri: Nichi-Ro Sensō kara Taiheiyō Sensō made.* Tokyo: Keisō Shobō.
Katō, Yōko. 2007. "What Caused the Russo-Japanese War – Korea or Manchuria?" *Social Science Japan Journal* 10 (1): 95–103.
Katō, Yōko. 2009. *Soredemo, Nihonjin wa "sensō" o eranda.* Tokyo: Asahi Shuppansha.
Katzenstein, Peter. 2005. *A World of Regions: Asia and Europe in the American Imperium.* Ithaca: Cornell University Press.
Kaufman, Victor S. 2001. *Confronting Communism: U.S. and British Policies toward China.* Columbia: University of Missouri Press.
Kawanishi, Kōsuke. 2016. *Dai Tōa Kyōeiken: Teikoku Nihon no Nanpō taiken.* Tokyo: Kōdansha.
Kayaoglu, Turan. 2010. "Westphalian Eurocentrism in International Relations Theory." *International Studies Review* 12 (2): 193–217.
Kearns, Doris. 1976. *Lyndon Johnson and the American Dream.* New York: Harper and Row.
Kei, Nemoto. 2010. *Teikō to kyōryoku no hazama: kindai Birumashi no naka no Igirisu to Nihon.* Tokyo: Iwanami Shoten.
Kelly, Jason M. 2021. *Market Maoists: The Communist Origins of China's Capitalist Ascent.* Cambridge, MA: Harvard University Press.
Kennedy, Dane. 2013. "Postcolonialism and History." In *The Oxford Handbook of Postcolonial Studies*, edited by Graham Huggan, 467–488. Oxford University Press.
Keohane, Robert O. 1971. "The Big Influence of Small Allies." *Foreign Policy* (2) (Spring): 161–182. https://doi.org/10.2307/1147864.
Khong, Yuen Foong. 1992. *Analogies at War: Korea, Munich, Dien Bien Phu, and the Vietnam Decisions of 1965.* Princeton: Princeton University Press.
Kim, D. G. 2024. "Anti-Asian Racism and the Rise of Hawkish Mass Opinion in China." *Political Science Quarterly* 139 (2): 177–199.
Kim, Ho-dong. 2004. *Holy War in China: The Muslim Rebellion and State in Chinese Central Asia, 1864–1877.* Stanford: Stanford University Press.
Kim, Hyung-A. 2011. "State Building: The Military Junta's Path to Modernity through Administrative Reforms." In *The Park Chung Hee Era: The Transformation of South Korea*, edited by Byung-kook Kim, and Ezra Vogel, 85–111. Cambridge, MA: Harvard University Press.
Kim, Key-Hiuk. 1980. *The Last Phase of the East Asian World Order: Korea, Japan, and the Chinese Empire: 1830–1882.* Berkeley: University of California Press.
Kim, Taehyun, and Chang Jae Baik. 2011. "Taming and Tamed by the United States." In *The Park Chung Hee Era: The Transformation of South Korea*, edited by Byung-kook Kim, and Ezra Vogel, 58–84. Cambridge, MA: Harvard University Press.
Kimball, Jeffrey P., ed. (1990). *To Reason Why: The Debate about the Causes of the U.S. Involvement in the Vietnam War.* New York: McGraw-Hill.
Kimura, Kan. 2019. *The Burden of the Past: Problems of Historical Perception in Japan–Korea Relations.* Ann Arbor: University of Michigan Press.
King, Amy. 2016a. "'Reconstructing China': Japanese Technicians and Industrialization in the Early People's Republic of China." *Modern Asian Studies* 50 (1): 141–174.

King, Amy. 2016b. *China–Japan Relations after World War Two: Empire, Industry and War, 1949–1971*. Cambridge: Cambridge University Press. https://doi.org/10.1017/CBO9781316443439.
King, Amy. 2018. "Economics and Security." In *New Directions in Strategic Thinking 2.0*, edited by Russell W. Glenn, 23–35. Acton: ANU Press.
King, Amy. 2022. "China's External Economic Relations during the Mao Years." In *The Cambridge Economic History of China*, Vol. 2, edited by Richard von Glahn, and Debin Ma, 685–721. Cambridge: Cambridge University Press. King: Done, see 1 comment.
Kinmonth, Earl. 1999. "The Mouse That Roared: Saitō Takao, Conservative Critic of Japan's 'Holy War' in China." *Journal of Japanese Studies* 25 (2)(Summer): 331–360.
Kirby, William C. 1997. "The Internationalization of China: Foreign Relations at Home and Abroad in the Republican Era." *China Quarterly* 150(June): 433–458.
Kisaka, Jun'ichirō. "'Dai Nihon Teikoku' no hōkai." In *Kōza Nihon rekishi 10 (Kindai 4)*, edited by Rekishigaku Kenkyūkai and Nihonshi Kenkyūkai, 289–341. Tokyo: Tokyo Daigaku Shuppankai.
Kissinger, Henry. 1979. *White House Years*. London: Little, Brown.
Kiste, Robert C. 1986. "Termination of the US Trusteeship in Micronesia." *Journal of Pacific History* 21 (3): 127–138.
Kittiarsa, Pattana. 2010. "An Ambiguous Intimacy: Farang as Siamese Occidentalism." In *The Ambiguous Allure of the West: Traces of the Colonial in Thailand*, edited by Rachel Harrison, and Peter A. Jackson, 57–74. Hong Kong: Hong Kong University Press.
KMT Central Committee. 1959. "A Bloody Lesson: A History of CCP United Front and Plot for Peace Negotiations." Contemporary Taiwan Collection, Library of the Institute of Oriental Culture, University of Tokyo, no. CD2:508.
Kobayashi, Hideo. 2007. *Nitchū Sensō: senmetsusen kara shōmōsen e*. Tokyo: Kōdansha Gendai Shinsho.
Kobayashi, Michihiko. 2020. *Kindai Nihon to gunbu, 1868–1945*. Tokyo: Kodansha Gendai Shinsho.
Koda, Yoji. 2005. "The Russo-Japanese War: Primary Causes of Japanese Success." *Naval War College Review* 58 (2): 10–44.
Kohli, Atul. 2004. *State-Directed Development: Political Power and Industrialization in the Global Periphery*. Princeton: Princeton University Press.
Kohli, Atul. 2019. *Imperialism and the Developing World: How Britain and the United States Shaped the Global Periphery*. Oxford: Oxford University Press.
Koji, Hirata. 2013. "Britain's Men on the Spot in China: John Jordan, Yuan Shikai, and the Reorganization Loan, 1912–1914." *Modern Asian Studies* 47 (3): 895–934.
Kokobun, Ryosei, Yoshihide Soeya, Akio Takahara, and Shin Kawashima. 2017. *Japan–China Relations in the Modern Era*. Translated by Keith Krulak. Abingdon: Routledge.
Korea Information Bureau. 1919. *"Mansei", Little Martyrs of Korea*. Philadelphia: Korea Information Bureau.
Konoe, Fumimaro. 1918. "Ei-Bei hon'i no heiwashugi o haisu," *Nihon oyobi Nihonjin*. December 15: 23–26.
Kowner, Rotem, ed. 2006. *The Impact of the Russo-Japanese War*. New York: Routledge.

Krairiksh, Piriya. 2018. "'Rao mai dai rian cha pen farang ...' phra ratchadamrat ratchakan tee ha gap kan 'pen khon Thai roo samer farang'" [We do not study to be westerner ... "Rama V's speech and how to be a Thai with knowledge on par with westerners.]." *Silpa Wattanatham*, November 17. www.silpa-mag.com/history/article_12765.

Kramer, Paul. 2011. "Power and Connection: Imperial Histories of the United States in the World." *American Historical Review* 116 (5): 1348–1391.

Kratoska, Paul H. 2003. "Dimensions of Decolonization." In *Transformation of Southeast Asia: International Perspectives on Decolonization*, edited by Marc Frey, Ronald Pruessen, and Tan Tai Yong, 83–104. Armonk: M.E. Sharpe.

Kuhn, Philip. 2008. *Chinese among Others: Emigration in Modern Times*. New York: Rowman & Littlefield.

Kuik, Cheng-Chwee. 2008. "The Essence of Hedging: Malaysia and Singapore's Response to a Rising China." *Contemporary Southeast Asia: A Journal of International and Strategic Affairs* 30 (2): 159–185. muse.jhu.edu/article/256501.

Kunio, Yoshihara. 1994. *The Nation and Economic Growth: The Philippines and Thailand*. Oxford: Oxford University Press.

Kuper, Kenneth Gofigan. 2022. "How Are Islands Imagined?" *The Pacific Islands Times*, April 8. www.pacificislandtimes.com/post/how-are-islands-imagined.

Kurosawa, Fumitaka. 1985. "Tanaka gaikō to rikugun." *Gunji shigaku* 21 (3): 17–34.

Lake, David A. 2009. *Hierarchy in International Relations*. Ithaca: Cornell University Press.

Lake, David A. 2024. *Indirect Rule: The Making of US International Hierarchy*. Ithaca: Cornell University Press.

Lake, Marilyn, and Henry Reynolds. 2008. *Drawing the Global Colour Line: White Men's Countries and the International Challenge of Racial Equality*. Cambridge: Cambridge University Press.

Langer, William. 1945. "The State Department." *Congressional Record* 79 (1)(July): 6580–6581.

Langer, William L. 1935. *The Diplomacy of Imperialism, 1890–1902*, 2 Vols. New York: Alfred A. Knopf.

Larsen, Kirk W. 2008. *Tradition, Treaties, and Trade: Qing Imperialism and Chosŏn Korea, 1850–1910*. Cambridge MA: Harvard University Asia Center.

Larson, Jane Leung. 2007. "The 1905 Anti-American Boycott as a Transnational Chinese Movement." *Chinese America, History and Perspectives*, The Free Library. Retrieved July 2, 2023 from www.thefreelibrary.com/The+1905+anti-American+boycott+as+a+transnational+Chinese+movement.-a0161127972.

Lau, Albert. 1991. *The Malayan Union Controversy, 1942–1948*. New York: Oxford University Press.

Lauren, Paul Gordon. 1978. "Human Rights in History: Diplomacy and Racial Equality at the Paris Peace Conference." *Diplomatic History* 2 (3): 257–278.

Lauren, Paul Gordon. 1988. *Power and Prejudice: The Politics and Diplomacy or Racial Discrimination*. Boulder CO: Westview Press.

Lawrence, Ken. 1998. "U.S. Stamps That Went to War: The Overrun Countries Stamps of 1943 and 1944." *American Philatelist* (January) 112 (1): 48–74.

Lawrence, Mark Atwood. 2005. *Assuming the Burden: Europe and the American Commitment to War in Vietnam*. Berkeley: University of California Press.

Lawrence, Mark Atwood. 2022. "A Far Greater Prize than Vietnam: The United States, Indonesia, and the Vietnam War." In *The Vietnam War in the Pacific World*, edited by Brian Cuddy, and Fredrik Logevall, 69–86. Chapel Hill: University of North Carolina Press.

Lawson, Stephanie. 2013. "'Melanesia' the History and Politics of an Idea." *The Journal of Pacific History* 48 (1): 1–22.

Lay, James. 1977. "Report to the National Security Council by the Executive Secretary [17 May 1951, Document 12]." In *Foreign Relations of the United States, 1951*, Vol. 6, Pt. 1, edited by Paul Claussen, John P. Glennon, David W. Mabon, Neal H. Petersen, and Carl N. Raether. Washington, DC: U.S. Government Printing Office. https://history.state.gov/historicaldocuments/frus1951v06p1/d12.

Layne, Christopher. 2006. *The Peace of Illusions: American Grand Strategy from 1940 to the Present*. Ithaca: Cornell University Press.

Lee, Christopher J., ed. 2010. *Making a World after Empire: The Bandung Moment and Its Political Afterlives*. Athens: Ohio University Press.

Lee, Erika. 2003. *At America's Gates: Chinese Immigration during the Exclusion Era, 1882–1943*. Chapel Hill: The University of North Carolina Press.

Lee, Erika. 2015. *The Making of Asian America: A History*. New York: Simon & Schuster Papers.

Lee, James. 2020a. "American Diplomacy and Export-Oriented Industrialization on Taiwan." *Journal of East Asian Studies* 20 (November): 472–473. https://doi.org/10.1017/jea.2020.9.

Lee, James. 2020b. "US Grand Strategy and the Origins of the Developmental State." *Journal of Strategic Studies* 43 (5): 737–761.

Lee, Ji-Young. 2016. *China's Hegemony: Four Hundred Years of East Asian Domination*. Colombia: Columbia University Press.

Lee, Ji-Young. 2020. "The Founding of the Korean Chosŏn Dynasty, 1392." In *East Asia in the World: Twelve Events Shaped the Modern International Order*, edited by Stephan Haggard, and David C. Kang, 81–96. Cambridge: Cambridge University Press.

Lee, Seokwoo. 2002. "The 1951 San Francisco Peace Treaty with Japan and the Territorial Disputes in East Asia." *Pacific Rim Law & Policy Journal* 1 (11): 63–146.

Lee, Seokwoo, and Jon M. Van Dyke. 2010. "The 1951 San Francisco Peace Treaty and Its Relevance to the Sovereignty of Dokdo." *Chinese Journal of International Law* 9 (4)(December): 741–762.

Leffler, Melvyn. 1993. *A Preponderance of Power: National Security, the Truman Administration, and the Cold War*. Stanford: Stanford University Press.

Legge, John D. 1972. *Sukarno: A Political Biography*. New York: Praeger.

Lei, Mao and Xiaofang Fan. 1996. Guogong Liangdang Tanpan Tongshi (A General History of the KMT-CCP Negotiations). Lanzhou: Lanzhou Daxue chubanshe.

Lester, Robert E., ed. 1990. *President Dwight D. Eisenhower's Office Files, 1953–1961*, part 2. Bethesda: University Publications of America. Microfilm, reel 6.

Leventoğlu, Bahar and Branislav Slantchev. 2007. "The Armed Peace: A Punctuated Equilibrium Theory of War." *American Journal of Political Science* 51 (4): 755–771.

Levy, Jack S. 1990/1. "Preferences, Constraints, and Choices in July 1914." *International Security* 15 (3): 151–186.

Levy, Jack S. and John A. Vasquez, eds. 2014. *The Outbreak of the First World War: Structure, Politics, and Decision-Making*. Cambridge: Cambridge University Press.
Levy, Jack S. and William Mulligan. 2021. "Why 1914 but Not before? A Comparative Study of the July Crisis and Its Precursors." *Security Studies* 30 (2): 213–244.
Lew-Williams, Beth. 2018. *The Chinese Must Go: Violence, Exclusion, and the Making of the Alien in America*. Cambridge, MA: Harvard University Press.
Li, Wei. 1993. *Cao Juren zhuan*. Jiangsu sheng xin hua shu dian fa xing.
Liang-lin, Hsiao. 1974. *China's Foreign Trade Statistics, 1864–1949*. Cambridge, MA: Harvard University Press.
Liang, Qichao. 1936. "Mieguo xinfa" [New Rules for Destroying Countries]. In *Yinbingshi heji, wenji*, Vol. 3. Shanghai: Shanghai Zhonghua Shuju.
Lie, John. 1998. *Han Unbound: The Political Economy of South Korea*. Stanford: Stanford University Press.
Liff, Adam, and Dalto Lin. 2022. "The 'One China' Framework at 50 (1972–2022): The Myth of 'Consensus' and Its Evolving Policy Significance." *The China Quarterly* 252: 977–1000.
Liff, Adam P. 2023. "Kishida the Accelerator: Japan's Defense Evolution after Abe." *The Washington Quarterly* 46 (1): 63–83.
Lin, Hsiao-ting. 2016. *Accidental State: Chiang Kai-Shek, the United States, and the Making of Taiwan*. Cambridge, MA: Harvard University Press. Lin: Done, see 7 comments.
Lind, Jennifer M. 2010. *Sorry States: Apologies in International Politics*. Ithaca: Cornell University Press.
Link, Arthur. (1967–1994). S. ed. Papers of Woodrow Wilson (PWW). Princeton: Princeton University Press.
Linklater, Andrew. 2016. "The 'Standard of Civilisation' in World Politics." *Human Figurations* 5 (2)(July): 1–17. http://hdl.handle.net/2027/spo.11217607.0005.205.
Liu, Lydia. 2004. *The Clash of Empires: The Invention of China in Modern World Making*. Cambridge, MA: Harvard University Press.
Liu, Xiaoyuan. 1996. *A Partnership for Disorder: China, the United States, and Their Policies for the Postwar Disposition of the Japanese Empire, 1941–1945*. New York: Cambridge University Press.
Logevall, Fredrik. 1999. *Choosing War: The Lost Chance for Peace and the Escalation of the War in Vietnam*. Berkeley: University of California Press.
Loos, Tamara. 2010. "Competitive Colonialisms: Siam and the Malay Muslim South." In *The Ambiguous Allure of the West: Traces of the Colonial in Thailand*, edited by Rachel Harrison, and Peter A. Jackson. Hong Kong: Hong Kong University Press.
Loos, Tamara Lynn. 2016. *Bones around My Neck: The Life and Exile of a Prince Provocateur*. Ithaca: Cornell University Press.
Ma, Yinchu. 1940. "Zhongguo zhi guoji maoyi" [China's International Trade]. *Xinan Shiye Tongxun [Southwest Industrial News]* 1 (4).
Ma, Yinchu. 1947. "DuiRi maoyi kaifang yu sunhai peichang wenti" [Opening up Trade with Japan and the Issue of Damage Compensation]. *Daxue Yuekan [University Monthly]* 6 (3–4).
Macauley, Melissa. 2021. *Distant Shores: Colonial Encounters on China's Maritime Frontier*. Princeton: Princeton University Press.

Macdonald, Ross J. 1981. "Termination of the Strategic Trusteeship: Free Association, the United Nations and International Law." *Brooklyn Journal of International Law* 7 (2): 235–282.

Manela, Erez. 2009. *The Wilsonian Moment: Self-Determination and the International Origins of Anticolonial Nationalism*. Oxford: Oxford University Press.

Manela, Erez. 2020. "International Society as a Historical Subject." *Diplomatic History* 44 (2): 184–209.

Mao, Haijian. 2016. *The Qing Empire and the Opium War: The Collapse of the Heavenly Dynasty*. New York: Cambridge University Press.

Mark, Ethan. 2018. *Japan's Occupation of Java in the Second World War: A Transnational History*. London: Bloomsbury.

Martina, Michael, and David Brunnstrom. 2022. "U.S. Aims for 'Top Line' Deal on Aid to Three Pacific Island Countries." *Reuters*, December 9. www.reuters.com/world/us-aims-top-line-deal-aid-three-pacific-island-countries-2022-12-09/.

Mastanduno, Michael. 2002. "Incomplete Hegemony: The US and Security Order in Asia." In *America Unrivaled: The Future of the Balance of Power*, edited by John G. Ikenberry, 181–210. Ithaca: Cornell University Press.

Mastanduno, Michael. 2019. "Partner Politics: Russia, China, and the Challenge of Extending US Hegemony after the Cold War." *Security Studies* 28 (3): 479–504. https://doi.org/10.1080/09636412.2019.1604984.

Mastanduno, Michael. 2003. "Incomplete Hegemony: The United States and Security Order in Asia." In *Asian Security Order: Instrumental and Normative Features*, edited by Muthiah Alagappa, 141–170. Stanford: Stanford University Press.

Matray, James I. 1981. "Captive of the Cold War: The Decision to Divide Korea at the 38th Parallel." *Pacific Historical Review* 50 (2)(May): 145–168. https://doi.org/10.2307/3638724.

Matsui, Masato. 1972. "The Russo-Japanese Agreement of 1907: Its Causes and the Progress of Negotiations." *Modern Asian Studies* 6 (1): 33–48.

Matsusaka, Yoshihisa Tak. 2001. *The Making of Japanese Manchuria, 1904–1932*. Cambridge: Harvard University Asia Center.

Mazower, Mark. 2012. *Governing the World: The History of an Idea*. London: Penguin Press.

Mcconaughey M., P. Musgrave, and D. H. Nexon. 2018. "Beyond Anarchy: Logics of Political Organization, Hierarchy, and International Structure." *International Theory* 10 (2): 181–218. doi:10.1017/S1752971918000040.

McCord, Edward A. 1993. *The Power of the Gun: The Emergence of Modern Chinese Warlordism*. Berkeley: University of California Press.

McCormack, Daniel. 2018. *Great Powers and International Hierarchy*. New York: Springer.

McCormick, Thomas. 1967. *China Market: America's Quest for Informal Empire, 1893–1901*. Chicago: Quadrangle Books.

McDonald, Patrick J. 2015. Great Powers, Hierarchy, and Endogenous Regimes: Rethinking the Domestic Causes of Peace. *International Organization* 69 (3): 557–588.

McHenry, Donald F. 1975. *Micronesia, Trust Betrayed: Altruism vs Self Interest in American Foreign Policy*. Washington, D.C.: Carnegie Endowment for International Peace.

McKee, Delber L. 1986. "The Chinese Boycott of 1905–1906 Reconsidered: The Role of Chinese Americans." *Pacific Historical Review* 55 (2): 165–191.

McKenzie, Francine. 2017. "Race, Empire, and World Order: Robert Borden and Racial Equality at the Paris Peace Conference of 1919." In *Dominion of Race: Rethinking Canada's International History*, edited by Laura Madokoro, David Meren and Francine McKenzie, 73–93. Vancouver: University of British Columbia Press.

McKenzie, Pete. 2023. "Marshall Islands Enjoys Newfound Leverage with U.S." *Washington Post*, January 29. www.postguam.com/news/pacific/marshall-islands-enjoys-new-leverage/article_19c4d8f4-9e9e-11ed-8fbd-fbd86dfedbe2.html.

McKeown, Adam. 1999. "Conceptualizing Chinese Diasporas, 1842 to 1949." *The Journal of Asian Studies* 58 (2): 306–337.

McLean, Roderick R. 2007. *Royalty and Diplomacy in Europe, 1890–1914*. Cambridge: Cambridge University Press.

McMahon, Robert J. 1999. *Limits of Empire: The United States in Southeast Asia after World War II*. New York: Columbia University Press.

McNamee, Lachlan. 2023. *Settling for Less: Why States Colonize and Why They Stop*. Princeton: Princeton University Press.

Mead, Kullada Kesboonchoo. 2004. *The Rise and Decline of Thai Absolutism*. 1st ed. Vol. 22 of *RoutledgeCurzon Studies in the Modern History of Asia*. London: RoutledgeCurzon.

Meeting on Vietnam, July 21, 1965, notes (by Jack Valenti), Meeting Notes File, Lyndon Baines Johnson Library, Austin, Texas.

Meienberger, Norbert. 1980. *The Emergence of Constitutional Government in China (1905–1908): The Concept Sanctioned by the Empress Dowager Tz'u-Hsi*. Bern: P. Lang.

Meller, Norman. 1980. "On Matters Constitutional in Micronesia." *The Journal of Pacific History* 15 (2): 83–92.

Meller, Norman. 1990. "The Micronesian Executive: The Federated States of Micronesia, Kiribati, and the Marshall Islands." *Pacific Studies* 14: 55–72.

Meller, Norman, and Terza Meller. 1969. *The Congress of Micronesia: Development of the Legislative Process in the Trust Territory of the Pacific Islands*. Honolulu: University of Hawai'i Press.

Merida, Tarik. 2023. *Japanese Racial Identities within US-Japan Relations, 1853–1919*. Edinburgh: Edinburgh University Press.

Miller, David Hunter. 1928. *The Drafting of the Covenant*. New York: G.P. Putnam's Sons.

Miller, Edward S. 2005. "Japan's Other Victory: Overseas Financing of the Russo-Japanese War." In *The Russo-Japanese War in Global Perspective: World War Zero*, edited by John Steinberg, Bruce Menning, David Schimmelpenninck van der Oye, David Wolff, and Shinji Yokote, 465–483. Leiden: Brill.

Miller, Manjari Chatterjee. 2013. *Wronged by Empire: Post-Imperial Ideology and Foreign Policy in India and China*. Stanford: Stanford University Press.

Miller, Stuart Creighton. 1982. *"Benevolent Assimilation": The American Conquest of the Philippines, 1899–1903*. New Haven: Yale University Press.

Mimura, Janis. 2011. *Planning for Empire: Reform Bureaucrats and the Japanese Wartime State*. Ithaca: Cornell University Press.

Minohara, Tosh. 2020. "The Elusive Equality: Versailles as a Turning Point in U.S.-Japan Race Relations." In *Beyond Versailles: The 1919 Moment and a New Order in East Asia*, edited by Tosh Minohara, and Evan Dawley, 129. Lexington Books.

Mishra, Pankaj. 2012. *From the Ruins of Empire: The Revolt against the West and the Remaking of Asia*. London: Allen Lane.

Miskovic, Natasa, Harald Fischer-Tiné, and Nada Boskovska, eds. 2014. *The Non-aligned Movement and the Cold War: Delhi, Bandung, Belgrade*. New York: Routledge.

Mitter, Rana. 2013. *China's War with Japan, 1937–1945: The Struggle for Survival*. London: Allen Lane.

Moazzin, Ghassan. 2022. *Foreign Banks and Global Finance in Modern China: Banking on the Chinese Frontier, 1870–1919*. New ed. New York: Cambridge University Press.

Monteiro, Nuno P. and Alexandre Debs. 2020. "An Economic Theory of War." *Journal of Politics* 82 (1): 255–268.

Moon, Chung-in, and Byung-joon Jun. 2011. "Modernization Strategy: Ideas and Influences." In *The Park Chung Hee Era: The Transformation of South Korea*, edited by Byung-kook Kim, and Ezra Vogel, 115–139. Cambridge, MA: Harvard University Press.

Morrow, James D. 2014. *Order within Anarchy: The Laws of War as an International Institution*. New York: Cambridge University Press.

Mori, Yasuo. 2020. "*Kokka sōdōin*" *no jidai: hikaku no shiza kara*. Nagoya: Nagoya Daigaku Shuppankai.

Morse, Wayne L. 1945. "Remarks." *Congressional Record* 79 (1)(July): 8159–8162.

Moselle Eubanks to Harry S. Truman, 22 May 1945, 895.01/5-2245. 1995. In 美國務省韓國關係文書 *[Internal affairs of Korea, 1945–1949]*, Vol. 8. Seoul: Areum Press, 297–298.

Mulder, Nicholas. 2022. *The Economic Weapon: The Rise of Sanctions as a Tool of Modern War*. New Haven: Yale University Press.

Munro, Doug and Stewart Firth. 1986. "Towards Colonial Protectorates: The Case of the Gilbert and Ellice Islands." *Australian Journal of Politics & History* 32: 63–71.

Musgrave, Paul, and Daniel H. Nexon. 2018. "Defending Hierarchy from the Moon to the Indian Ocean." *International Organization* 72 (3): 591–626.

Mutual Security Agency. 1952. "Mutual Security Agency Priority Objectives [15 November 1952]." Box 4323, Decimal File 796.5-MAP/1-1250 – 796.5-MSP/12-2452, RG 59, National Archives and Records Administration.

Myerson, Roger. 1992. "On the Value of Game Theory in Social Science." *Rationality and Society* 4 (1): 62–73.

Nakano, Satoshi. 2019. *Japan's Colonial Moment in Southeast Asia, 1942–1945: The Occupiers Experience*. Milton Park, Abingdon: Routledge.

Nakatani, Tadashi. 2016. *Tsuyoi Amerika to yowai Amerika no hazama de: Dai-ichiji sekaitaisengo no Higashi Ajia chitsujo o meguru Nichi-Bei-Ei kankei*. Tokyo: Chikura Shobō.

Naksuk, Panchawach. 2022. "Meau 'farang' chai sue ploi jom tee Siam wang kad kwang ror ha nai kan sadet prapat Europe pee 2440 [When the West propagated rumors against Siam, in the hope to obstruct Chulalongkorn's trip to Europea in 1987]." *Silpawattanatham*, March 2. www.silpa-mag.com/history/article_34538.

Nanau, Gordon Leau. 2021. "Oceanic Diplomacy: Popo and Supu Diplomacy in the Modern State of Solomon Islands: In Brief 2021/28." Canberra: Department of Pacific Affairs, Australian National University.

Nanjing Military Region Editorial Committee of the Biography of Nie Fengzhi (Nanjing Ed. Committee). 1994. *Jiechu Jiangling Nie Fengzhi (Nie Fengzhi: An Excellent General)*. Nanjing: Jiangsu renmin chubanshe.

Nathan, Andrew J. 1976. *Peking Politics, 1918–1923*. Berkeley: University of California Press.

National Graduate Institute for Policy Studies (GRIPS). 1951. "Security Treaty between Japan and the United States of America." September 8. Institute for Advanced Studies on Asia (IASA). The University of Tokyo. https://worldjpn.net/documents/texts/docs/19510908.T2E.html.

National Security Council. 1985a. "Statement of Policy by the National Security Council [6 November 1953, Document 149]." In *Foreign Relations of the United States, 1952–1954*, Vol. 14, Pt. 1, edited by David W. Mabon, and Harriet D. Schwar. Washington, DC: U.S. Government Printing Office. https://history.state.gov/historicaldocuments/frus1952-54v14p1/d149.

National Security Council. 1985b. "Statement of Policy by the National Security Council [6 November 1953, Document 150]." In *Foreign Relations of the United States, 1952–1954*, Vol. 14, Pt. 1, edited by David W. Mabon, and Harriet D. Schwar. Washington, DC: U.S. Government Printing Office. https://history.state.gov/historicaldocuments/frus1952-54v14p1/d150.

National Security Council. 1985c. "Statement of Policy by the National Security Council [6 November 1953, Document 150]." In *Foreign Relations of the United States, 1952–1954*, Vol. 13, Pt. 1, edited by David W. Mabon, and Harriet D. Schwar. Washington, DC: U.S. Government Printing Office. https://history.state.gov/historicaldocuments/frus1952-54v14p1/d150.

National Security Council. 1986. "National Security Council Report [15 January 1955, Document 12]." In *Foreign Relations of the United States, 1955–1957*, Vol. 2, edited by Harriet D. Schwar. Washington, DC: U.S. Government Printing Office. https://history.state.gov/historicaldocuments/frus1955-57v02/d12.

National Security Council. 1994. "National Security Council Report [11 June 1960, Document 175]." In *Foreign Relations of the United States, 1958–1960*, Vol. 18, edited by Madeline Chi, and Louis J. Smith. Washington, DC: U.S. Government Printing Office. https://history.state.gov/historicaldocuments/frus1958-60v18/d175.

Naupa, Anna. 2022. "Sealed with Kava and Betel Nut: Lessons in Oceanic Diplomacy from the Mota Lava Treaty: In Brief 2022/11." Canberra: Department of Pacific Affairs, Australian National University.

Nero, Karen. 1997a. "The End of Insularity." In *The Cambridge History of the Pacific Islanders*, edited by Donald Denoon, Malama Meleisea, Stewart Firth, Jocelyn Linnekin, and Karen Nero, 439–467. Cambridge: Cambridge University Press.

Nero, Karen. 1997b. "The Material World Remade." In *The Cambridge History of the Pacific Islanders*, edited by Donald Denoon, Malama Meleisea, Stewart Firth, Jocelyn Linnekin, and Karen Nero, 359–396. Cambridge: Cambridge University Press.

New York Times. 1922. "Koreans Publish Appeal to Conference; Ask Independence as Guarantee of Peace." January 1.
New York Times. 1943. "V. Hope for Korea." December 2.
New York Times. 1945a. "Churchill Bars Yalta Disclosure: Refusing Labor's Demands, He Says All Secret Accords Have Been Revealed." June 8.
New York Times. 1945b. "Grew Denies Allies Pledged Korea to Russia at Yalta: Grew Denies Big 3 Gave Russia Korea." June 9.
Ngai, Mae. 2021. *The Chinese Question: The Gold Rushes and Global Politics*. New York: W. W. Norton.
Ngoei, Wen-Qing. 2014. "The Domino Logic of the Darkest Moment: The Fall of Singapore, the Atlantic Echo Chamber, and 'Chinese Penetration' in US Cold War Policy toward Southeast Asia." *Journal of American-East Asian Relations* 21 (3): 215–245.
Ngoei, Wen-Qing. 2017. "A Wide Anticommunist Arc: Britain, ASEAN, and Nixon's Triangular Diplomacy." *Diplomatic History* 41 (5): 903–932.
Ngoei, Wen-Qing. 2019a. *Arc of Containment: Britain, the United States, and Anticommunism in Southeast Asia*. Ithaca: Cornell University Press.
Ngoei, Wen-Qing. 2019b. "There and Back Again: What the Cold War for Southeast Asia Can Teach us about Sino-U.S. Competition in the Region Today." *International Journal: Canada's Journal of Global Policy Analysis* 74 (2): 301–312.
Ngoei, Wen-Qing. 2021. "The United States and the 'Chinese Problem' of Southeast Asia." *Diplomatic History* 45 (2)(June): 240–252.
Ngoei, Wen-Qing. 2022. "The Deeper Roots of a Potential New Cold War with China." *Washington Post*, April 5.
Ngoei, Wen-Qing. 2025. "The Vietnam War and the Regional Context." In *Cambridge History of the Vietnam War*, Vol. 3, edited by Pierre Asselin, and Lien Hang Nguyen, 163–188. New York: Cambridge University Press.
Nield, Robert. 2015. *China's Foreign Places: The Foreign Presence in China in the Treaty Port Era, 1840–1943*. Hong Kong: Hong Kong University Press.
Nish, Ian. 1985. *The Origins of the Russo-Japanese War*. Reading: Addison Wesley Longman Limited.
Nufer, Harold F. 1978. *Micronesia under American Rule: An Evaluation of the Strategic Trusteeship (1947–77)*. Hicksville: Exposition Press.
Omi, Michael, and Howard Winant. 2014. *Racial Formation in the United States*. 3rd ed. Milton Park, Abingdon: Routledge.
Ono, Shinji. 1994. "A Deliberate Rumor: National Anxiety in China on the Eve of the Xinhai Revolution." In *China's Republican Revolution*, edited by Eto Shinkichi, and Harold Z. Schiffrin, 25–40. Tokyo: University of Tokyo Press.
Organksi, Abramo Fimo Kenneth. and Jacek Kugler. 1977. "The Costs of Major Wars: The Phoenix Factor." *American Political Science Review* 71 (4): 1347–1366.
Osiander, Andreas. 1994. *The States System of Europe, 1640–1990: Peacemaking and the Conditions of International Stability*. Oxford: Clarendon.
Pacific Islands Forum. 2012. "43rd Pacific Islands Forum opens in the Cook Islands." Pacific Islands Forum Secretariat, Fiji. www.forumsec.org/2012/08/29/43rd-pacific-islands-forum-opens-in-the-cook-islands/.
Paine, Sarah C.M. 1996. *Imperial Rivals: China, Russia, and Their Disputed Frontier*. Armonk: M.E. Sharpe.

Paine, Sarah C.M. 2003. *The Sino-Japanese War of 1894–1895: Preceptions, Power, and Primacy*. Cambridge: Cambridge University Press.
Paine, Sarah C.M. 2014. *The Wars for Asia*. Cambridge: Cambridge University Press.
Paine, Sarah C.M. 2017. *The Japanese Empire: Grand Strategy from the Meiji Restoration to the Pacific War*. Cambridge: Cambridge University Press.
Paik, Too-Chin. 1956. "Paik to Wood [6 March 1956]." File 222, Syngman Rhee Papers, Institute for Modern Korea Studies, Yonsei University.
Park, Saeyoung. 2020. "The Death of Eastphalia, 1874." In *East Asia in the World: Twelve Events Shaped the Modern International Order*, edited by Stephan Haggard, and David C. Kang, 239–260. Cambridge: Cambridge University Press.
Park, Seo-Hyun. 2013. "Changing Definitions of Sovereignty in Nineteenth-Century East Asia: Japan and Korea between China and the West." *Journal of East Asian Studies* 13 (2): 281–307.
Park, Seo-Hyun. 2017. *Sovereignty and Status in East Asian International Relations*. Cambridge: Cambridge University Press.
Park, Seo-Hyun. 2020. "The Sino-Japanese War, 1894–1895." In *East Asia in the World: Twelve Events Shaped the Modern International Order*, edited by Stephan Haggard, and David C. Kang, 224–238. Cambridge: Cambridge University Press.
Party Research Center of the CCP Central Committee, ed. 1997. *Zhou Enlai Nianpu, 1949–1976 (Chronology of Zhou Enlai, 1949–1976)*, Vol. 1 and 2. Beijing: Zhongyang Wenxian chubanshe.
Paullin, Charles Oscar. 1910. "The Opening of Korea by Commodore Shufeldt," *Political Science Quarterly* 25 (3): 470–499. https://doi.org/10.2307/2141171.
Pederson, Susan. 2015. *The Guardians: The League of Nations and the Crisis of Europe*. Oxford: Oxford University Press.
Petersen, Glenn. 1993. *Ethnicity and Interests at the 1990 Federated States of Micronesia Constitutional Convention*. Canberra: Dept. of Political and Social Change, Research School of Pacific Studies, Australian National University.
Petersen, Glenn. 1998. "Strategic Location and Sovereignty: Modern Micronesia in the Historical Context of American Expansionism." *Space and Polity* 2 (2): 179–205. https://doi.org/10.1080/13562579808721779.
Pfaelzer, Jean. 2007. *Driven Out: The Forgotten War against Chinese Americans*. New York: Random House Inc.
Phillips, Andrew, and Jason Campbell Sharman. 2015. *International Order in Diversity: War, Trade and Rule in the Indian Ocean*, Vol. 137. Cambridge: Cambridge University Press.
Phillips, Julianne, and Scott Wolford. 2021. "Collective Deterrence in the Shadow of Shifting Power." *International Studies Quarterly* 65 (1): 136–145.
Phiramontri, Rom. 2016. "Phra Sahai Kap Ekarat Siam [The King's Friend and Siam's Independence]." *Journal of Russian Studies* 7 (1): 1–36.
Platt, Stephen R. 2012. *Autumn in the Heavenly Kingdom: China, the West, and the Epic Story of the Taiping Civil War*. New York: Knopf.
Player, Cyril Arthur. 1921. "They Love Peace, But-." *Detroit News*. September 4.
Pöllath, Moritz. 2018. "Revisiting Island Decolonization: The Pursuit of Self-Government in Pacific Island Polities under US Hegemony." *Island Studies Journal* 1: 235–250.

Posrithong, Natanaree. 2009–2010. "The Russo-Siamese Relations: The Reign of King Chulalongkorn." *Silpakorn University International Journal* 9–10: 87–115.
Powell, Robert. 1999. *In the Shadow of Power: States and Strategies in International Relations*. Princeton: Princeton University Press.
Powell, Robert. 2006. "War as a Commitment Problem." *International Organization* 60 (1): 169–203.
Power, Paul F. 1986. "The South Pacific Nuclear-Weapon-Free-Zone." *Pacific Affairs* 59 (3): 455–475.
Prince, H. G. 1989. "The United States, the United Nations, and Micronesia: Questions of Procedure, Substance, and Faith." *Michigan Journal of International Law* 11 (1): 11–89.
Pruit, Sarah. 2018. "Why are North and South Korea Divided?" History. Updated June 25, 2021. www.history.com/news/north-south-korea-divided-reasons-facts.
Puas, Gonzaga. 2021. *The Federated States of Micronesia's Engagement with the outside World: Control, Self-Preservation and Continuity*. Canberra: Australian National University Press.
Pyle, Kenneth B. 2006. "Profound Forces in the Making of Modern Japan." *Journal of Japanese Studies* 32 (2)(Summer): 393–418.
Pyle, Kenneth B. 2007. *Japan Rising: The Resurgence of Japanese Power and Purpose*. New York: PublicAffairs.
Qin, Yucheng. 2009. *The Diplomacy of Nationalism: The Six Companies and China's Policy toward Exclusion*. Honolulu: University of Hawai'i Press.
Quimby, Frank. 2016. "Northern Mariana Islands." In *In Pacific Ways: Government and Politics in the Pacific Islands*, edited by Stephen Levine, 211–227. Melbourne: Victoria University Press.
Rajchagool, Chaiyan. 1994. *The Rise and Fall of the Thai Absolute Monarchy: Foundations of the Modern Thai State from Feudalism to Peripheral Capitalism*. 1st ed. Vol. 2 of Studies in Contemporary Thailand. Bangkok: White Lotus.
Rankin, Mary Backus. 2002. "Nationalistic Contestation and Mobilization Politics: Practice and Rhetoric of Railway-Rights Recovery at the End of the Qing." *Modern China* 28 (3): 315–361.
Ravina, Mark. 2017. *To Stand with the Nations of the World: Japan's Meiji Restoration in World History*. Oxford: Oxford University Press.
Reiter, Dan. 2009. *How Wars End*. Princeton: Princeton University Press.
Remengesau Jr, Tommy. 2019. "Pacific Defense Pact Renewal Vital to the US amid Rising Tension with China." *The Hill*, May 17. https://thehill.com/blogs/congress-blog/foreign-policy/444291-pacific-defense-pact-renewal-vital-to-the-us-amid-rising/.
Reynolds, Douglas. 1993. *China, 1898–1912: The Xinzheng Revolution and Japan*. Cambridge MA: Council on East Asian Studies, Harvard University.
Rhee, Syngman. 1941. *Japan inside out: The Challenge of Today*. 1st ed. New York: Revell.
Rhee, Syngman. 1945. "Voice of the People: Justice for Korea." *Chicago Daily Tribune*, May 11.
RNZ Pacific. 2023. "Palau to Receive Double What US Originally Promised in New Compact." May 1. www.rnz.co.nz/international/pacific-news/489038/palau-to-receive-double-what-us-originally-promised-in-new-compact.

Robinson, Ronald, and John Gallagher. 1953. "The Imperialism of Free Trade." *Economic History Review.*

ROC Consulate-general in New York to Ministry of Foreign Affairs, March 2, 1957. Archives of the Ministry of Foreign Affairs, Archives of the Institute of Modern History, Academia Sinica (Taipei), 0045/405.1/3.

ROC Embassy in Washington DC to US Ministry of Foreign Affairs, February 2, 1957. Report. Archives of the Ministry of Foreign Affairs, Archives of the Institute of Modern History, Academia Sinica (Taipei), 0046/405.1/2.

ROC Institute of Psychological Warfare. 1959. "The Communist Psychological Warfare." CTC (June), no. CD6:1525.

ROC Ministry of Foreign Affairs, September 17, 1956. Statement. Archives of the Ministry of Foreign Affairs, Archives of the Institute of Modern History, Academia Sinica (Taipei), 0045/405.1/3.

Roff, Sue Rabbitt. 1991. *Overreaching in Paradise: US Policy in Palau since 1945.* Denali Press.

Roosa, John. 2006. *Pretext for Mass Murder: The September 30th Movement and Suharto's Coup d'Etat in Indonesia.* Madison: University of Wisconsin Press.

Roosevelt, Franklin, Winston Churchill, and Chiang Kai-shek. 1943. "Cairo Communiqué." General statement, December 1, 1943. National Diet Library. www.ndl.go.jp/constitution/e/shiryo/01/002_46/002_46tx.html.

Roosevelt, Theodore. 1914. "The World War: Its Tragedies and Its Lessons." *The New Outlook.*

Rosenblatt, Helena. 2018. *The Lost History of Liberalism: From Ancient Rome to the Twenty-First Century.* Princeton: Princeton University Press.

Rosenthal, Jean-Laurent, and R. Bin Wong. 2011. *Before and Beyond Divergence: The Politics of Economic Change in China and Europe.* Cambridge, MA: Harvard University Press.

Roshwald, Aviel. 2023. *Occupied: European & Asian Responses to Axis Conquest, 1937–1945.* Cambridge: Cambridge University Press.

Rostow, Walt W. 1985. *Eisenhower, Kennedy, and Foreign Aid.* Austin: University of Texas Press.

Rotter, Andrew. 1987. *The Path to Vietnam: Origins of the American Commitment to Southeast Asia.* Ithaca: Cornell University Press.

Rusk, Dean. 1990. *As I Saw It.* New York: W. W. Norton.

Sahlins, Marshall D. 1963. "Poor Man, Rich Man, Big-Man, Chief: Political Types in Melanesia and Polynesia." *Comparative Studies in Society and History* 5 (3): 285–303.

Said, Edward. 1979. *Orientalism.* New York: Pantheon.

San Antonio Express. 1945. "Korean Leader Changes over to Communism." November 22.

Sarkees, Meredith Reid, and Frank Wayman. 2010. *Resort to War, 1816–2007.* Washington, DC: CQ Press.

Sarotte, Mary Elise. 2009. *1989: The Struggle to Create Post-Cold War Europe.* Princeton, NJ: Princeton University Press.

Sattayanurak, Attachak. 1995. *Kan Plienplaeng Khong Lokkatat Khon Chonchan Poonam Thai Tang Tae Ratchakarn Tee 4 – Por Sor 2475 [Changes in Attitudes of*

Thai Ruling Elites from the Fourth Reign to 1932]. Bangkok: Chulalongkorn University Press. Sawasdipakdi: Done.
Schaller, Michael. 1985. *The American Occupation of Japan: The Origins of the Cold War in Asia*. Oxford: Oxford University Press.
Schaller, Michael. 1997. *Altered States: The United States and Japan since the Occupation*. New York: Oxford University Press.
Schell, Jonathan. 1976. *The Time of Illusion*. New York: Alfred A. Knopf.
Schelling, Thomas C. 1960. *The Strategy of Conflict*. Cambridge, MA: Harvard University Press.
Scott, David. 2004. *Conscripts of Modernity: The Tragedy of Colonial Enlightenment*. Durham NC: Duke University Press.
Seizaburō, Shinobu. 1988. *"Taiheiyō Sensō" to "mō hitotsu no Taiheiyō Sensō": Dainiji taisen ni okeru Nihon to Tōnan Ajia*. Tokyo: Keisō Shobō.
Seligmann, Matthew S. 2006. "Germany, the Russo-Japanese War, and the Road to the Great War." In *The Impact of the Russo-Japanese War*, edited by Rotem Kowner, 109–123. New York: Routledge.
Seth, Sanjay ed. 2012. *Postcolonial Theory and International Relations*. London: Routledge.
Shafer, Paul W. 1945. "Korea." *Congressional Record* 79 (1)(June): 6580–6581.
Shan, Patrick Fuliang. 2018. *Yuan Shikai: A Reappraisal*. Vancouver: University of British Columbia Press.
Sharman, J. C. 2019. *Empires of the Weak: The Real Story of European Expansion and the Creation of the New World Order*. Princeton: Princeton University Press.
Shigemitsu, Mamoru. 1952. *Shōwa no dōran*, Vol. 1. Tokyo: Chūō Kōronsha.
Shigematsu, Setsu, and Keith L. Camacho, eds. 2010. *Militarized Currents: Toward a Decolonized Future in Asia and the Pacific*. Minneapolis: University of Minnesota Press.
Shilliam, Robbie. 2006. "What about Marcus Garvey? Race and the Transformation of Sovereignty Debate." *Review of International Studies* 32 (3): 379–400.
Shimazu, Naoko. 1998. *Japan, Race, and Equality: The Racial Equality Proposal of 1919*. New York: Routledge.
Shirane, Seiji. 2022. *Imperial Gateway: Colonial Taiwan and Japan's Expansion in South China and Southeast Asia, 1895–1945*. Ithaca: Cornell University Press.
Silove, Nina. 2018. "Beyond the Buzzword: The Three Meanings of 'Grand Strategy'." *Security Studies* 27 (1): 27–57.
Simpser, Alberto, Dan Slater, and Jason Wittenberg. 2018. "Dead but Not Gone: Contemporary Legacies of Communism, Imperialism and Authoritarianism." *Annual Review of Political Science* 21: 419–439.
Slough, Tara. 2023. "Phantom Counterfactuals." *American Journal of Political Science* 67 (1): 137–153.
Smith, Robert. 2010. "Maritime Delimitation in the South China Sea." *Ocean Development and International Law* 41: 214–236.
Smith, Sheila. 2015. *Intimate Rivals: Japanese Domestic Politics and a Rising China*. New York: Colombia University Press.
Smith, Tony. 1981. *The Pattern of Imperialism*. New York: Cambridge University Press.
Soekarno Sosrodihardjo. 1965. *Sukarno: An Autobiography as Told to Cindy Adam*. Indianapolis: Bobbs-Merrill.

Solomon, Anthony M. 1963. *The Solomon Report: America's Ruthless Blueprint for the Assimilation of Micronesia*. Friends of Micronesia; Micronesian Independent; Tia Belau. https://ia802807.us.archive.org/35/items/TheSolomonReportAmericasRuthlessBlueprintForTheAssimilationOf/micronesia3.pdf.

Soman, Appu K. 2000. *Double-Edged Sword: Nuclear Diplomacy in Unequal Conflicts: The United States and China, 1950–1958*. Westport: Praeger.

Songnui, Peerapol. 2012. "Wikritkarn Ror Sor 112: Suksa Bot Rien Jak Prawatisat [The 1983 Crisis: Learning from the History]." *Academic Journal of Chulachomklao Royal Military Academy*: 40–59.

Spivak, Gayathri Chakravorty. 1988. "Can the Subaltern Speak?" In *Marxism and the Interpretation of Culture*, edited by Cary Nelson, and Lawrence Grossberg, 66–112. Champaign IL: University of Illinois Press.

Spruance, Raymond. 1952. "Spruance to Acheson [8 September 1952]." Box 4323, Decimal File 796.5-MAP/1-1250 – 796.5-MSP/12-2452, RG 59, National Archives and Records Administration.

Spruance, Raymond. 1987. "The Ambassador in the Philippines (Spruance) to the Secretary of State [8 September 1952, Document 312]." In *Foreign Relations of the United States, 1952–1954*, Vol. 12, Pt. 2, edited by Carl N. Raether, and Harriet D. Schwar. Washington, DC: U.S. Government Printing Office. https://history.state.gov/historicaldocuments/frus1952-54v12p2/d312.

Statistics Bureau of Japan. 1987–1988. *Nihon chōki tōkei sōran* [Historical Statistics of Japan]. Tokyo: Nihon Tōkei Kyōkai [Japan Statistical Association].

Statistics Bureau of Japan. Various years. *Nihon tōkei nenkan* [Japan Statistical Yearbook]. Tokyo: Mainichi Shinbunsha.

Steinberg, John W., Bruce Menning, David Wolff, David Schimmelpenninck van der Oye, and Shinji Yokote, eds. 2005. *The Russo-Japanese War in Global Perspective: World War Zero*. Leiden: Brill.

Stephanson, Anders. 1996. *Manifest Destiny: American Expansion and the Empire of Right*. London: Farrar, Straus and Giroux.

Stevenson, David. 1997. "Militarization and Diplomacy in Europe before 1914." *International Security* 22 (1): 125–161.

Stoddard, Lothrop. 1920. *The Rising Tide of Color against White World-Supremacy*. New York: Charles Scribner.

Strating, Rebecca, and Joanne Wallis. 2022. "Maritime Sovereignty and Territorialisation: Comparing the Pacific Islands and South China Sea." *Marine Policy* 141: 105110.

Strauss, Julia C. 2023. "From Colonial India to Semi-Colonial Republican China: Imaginaries and Realities of Civil Service and State-Building in Salt Administration, 1912–45." *South Asia: Journal of South Asian Studies* 46 (4): 806–819. https://doi.org/10.1080/00856401.2023.2239066.

Streets-Salter, Heather. 2017. *World War One in Southeast Asia: Colonialism and Anticolonialism in an Era of Global Conflict*. Cambridge: Cambridge University Press.

Streich, Philip and Jack S. Levy. 2016. "Information, Commitment, and the Russo-Japanese War of 1904–1905." *Foreign Policy Analysis* 12 (4): 489–511.

Stubbs, Richard. 2005. *Rethinking Asia's Economic Miracle: The Political Economy of War, Prosperity, and Crisis*. New York: Palgrave Macmillan.

Stueck, William. 2004. *Rethinking the Korean War: A New Diplomatic and Strategic History*. Princeton, NJ: Princeton University Press.
Sturm, Paul J. 1959. "Semi-Annual Assessment of the Economy of Taiwan [20 May 1959]." Folder 893.00/5-559, Box 5073, 893.00/1-159 – 893.02/9-657, 1955–1959 Central Decimal File, RG 59, National Archives and Records Administration.
Sun, Jessica and Scott Tyson. 2019. "Conflict as an Identification Strategy." SSRN. https://ssrn.com/abstract=3258725.
Suzuki, Shogo. 2009. *Civilization and Empire: China and Japan's Encounter with European International Society*. Oxford: Routledge.
Swenson-Wright, John. 2005. *Unequal Allies? United States Security and Alliance Policy Toward Japan, 1945–1960*. Stanford: Stanford University Press.
Swope, Kenneth M. 2009. *A Dragon's Head and a Serpent's Tail: Ming China and the First Great East Asian War, 1592–1598*. Norman: University of Oklahoma Press.
Swope, Kenneth. 2020. "Ming Grand Strategy during the Great East Asian War, 1592–1598." In *East Asia in the World: Twelve Events Shaped the Modern International Order*, edited by Stephan Haggard, and David C. Kang, 108–128. Cambridge: Cambridge University Press.
Sylvan, David, and Stephen Majeski. 2009. *U.S. Foreign Policy in Perspective: Clients, Enemies and Empire*. London: Routledge.
Szonyi, Michael. 2008. *Cold War Island: Quemoy on the Front Line*. Cambridge: Cambridge University Press.
Tanigawa, Yoshihiko. 1987. "Taiheiyō Sensō to Tōnan Ajia minzoku dokuritsu undo." *Hōsei kenkyū* 53 (3): 361–398.
Tapia, John E. 1997. *Circuit Chautauqua: From Rural Education to Popular Entertainment in Early Twentieth Century America*. Jefferson: McFarland.
Tate, D. J. M. 1972. *The Making of Southeast Asia*. Oxford: Oxford University Press.
Taylor, Brendan. 2018. *The Four Flashpoints: How Asia Goes to War*. Melbourne: La Trobe University Press.
Taylor, Charles C. 2022. *Race: A Philosophical Introduction*. Cambridge: Polity.
Taylor, Jay. 2009. *The Generalissimo: Chiang Kai-shek and the Struggle for Modern China*. Cambridge, MA: The Belknap Press of Harvard University Press.
Taylor, Jay. 2011. *The Generalissimo: Chiang Kai-shek and the Struggle for Modern China, with a New Postscript*. Cambridge: The Belknap Press of Harvard University Press.
Thomas, Martin, and Pierre Asselin. 2022. "French Decolonisation and Civil War: The Dynamics of Violence in the Early Phases of Anti-colonial War in Vietnam and Algeria, 1940–1956." *Journal of Modern European History* 20 (4): 513–535.
Thomas, Nicholas. 1989. *Out of Time: History and Evolution in Anthropological Discourse*. Ann Arbor: University of Michigan Press.
Thompson, Roger R. 1995. *China's Local Councils in the Age of Constitutional Reform, 1898–1911*. Cambridge MA: Harvard University Asia Center, Harvard University.
Time. 1956. "Formosa: An End to Rumors." January 16.
Tobe, Ryōichi. 2017. *Jikai no byōri: Nihon Rikugun no soshiki bunseki*. Tokyo: Nihon Keizai Shinbun Shuppansha.
Tong, Xiaopeng. 1996. *Fengyu Sishinian (Forty years of trials and hardships)*, Vol. 2. Beijing: Zhongyang wenxian chubanshe.

Togo, Kazuhiko. 2010. *Japan's Foreign Policy, 1945–2009: The Quest for a Proactive Policy*. 3rd ed. Leiden: Brill.
Tokyo Asahi Shinbun. 1941. "Dairisō, chokusai ni hyōgen." December 13.
Tooze, Adam. 2014. *The Deluge: The Great War, America, and the Remaking of the Global Order, 1916–1931*. New York: Viking.
Tooze, Adam. 2015. *The Deluge: The Great War, America and the Remaking of the Global Order 1916-1931*. New York: Penguin Books.
Truman, Harry S. 1976. "Statement by the President [27 June 1950, Document 119]." In *Foreign Relations of the United States, 1950*, Vol. 7, edited by John P. Glennon. Washington, DC: U.S. Government Printing Office. https://history.state.gov/histori caldocuments/frus1950v07.
Ts'ai, Shih-shan H. 1976. "Reaction to Exclusion: The Boycott of 1905 and Chinese National Awakening." *The Historian* 39 (1): 95–110.
Tsang, Steve. 2006. *The Cold War's Odd Couple: The Unintended Partnership between the Republic of China and the UK, 1950–1958*. London: I.B. Tauris.
Tucker, Nancy Bernkopf. 2012. *The China Threat: Memories, Myths, and Realities in the 1950x*. New York: Columbia University Press.
Tucker, Robert W. 2004. "Wilson's 'New Diplomacy.'" *World Policy Journal* 21 (2) (Summer): 92–107.
Turley, William. 1986. *The Second Indochina War*. Boulder: Westview Press.
Uchida Jun. 2011. "A Sentimental Journey: Mapping the Interior Frontier of Japanese Settlers in Colonial Korea." *The Journal of Asian Studies* 70 (3): 706–729.
Ugaki, Kazushige. 1968. *Ugaki Kazushige nikki*, Vol. 1: *Meiji 35-nen 9-gatsu—Shōwa 6-nen 6-gatsu*. Tokyo: Misuzu Shobō.
Underwood, Robert. 2006. "Micronesian Political Structures and US Models: Lessons Taught and Lessons Learned." *The Journal of Pacific Studies* 29 (1): 4–24.
United Korean Committee in America. 1942. *Korean Liberty Conference, Washington, DC, February 27, 28, March 1, 1942*. Los Angeles: United Korean Committee in America.
United Nations Department of Political Affairs. 1993. "The Trust Territory of the Pacific Islands (Micronesia) Political and Constitutional Development." *Decolonization* 44 (April): 1–24. www.un.org/dppa/decolonization/sites/www.un.org.dppa.decoloniza tion/files/decon_num_44.pdf.
United Nations Security Council (UNSC). 1947. Resolution 21 (April 2, 1947). UN Doc S/318.
United States Department of State. 1986. *Confidential U.S. State Department Central Files: Formosa, Republic of China 1950–1954*. Frederick: University Publications of America. Microfilm, reel 4, no. 794A.00(W)/11-654.
United States Department of State. 1989. *Records of the Office of Chinese Affairs, 1945– 1955*. Wilmington: Scholarly Resources Inc. Microfilm, reel 37.
United States Economic Survey Mission to the Philippines. 1950. *Report to the President of the United States*. Washington, DC: U.S. Government Printing Office.
United States Government. 1974. "Statement of the United States Government [10 December 1948, Document 696]." In *Foreign Relations of the United States, 1948*, Vol. 5, edited by John G. Reid, and David H. Stauffer. Washington, DC: U.S. Government Printing Office. https://history.state.gov/historicaldocuments/frus1948 v06/d696.

US Army, Historical Division. 1953. *History of the United States Armed Forces in Korea*. The War Memorial of Korea. https://archive.org/details/history-of-the-united-states-armed-forces-in-korea.

US Central Intelligence Agency. 1948. "Korea." CIA Intelligence Report, CIA Electronic FOIA Reading Room, www.cia.gov/readingroom/document/cia-rdp78-0 1617a001400030001-2.

US Central Intelligence Agency. 1958a. CIA Central Intelligence Bulletin, October 27, no. 06232623. CIA Electronic FOIA Reading Room.

US Central Intelligence Agency. 1958b. CIA Central Intelligence Bulletin, October 29, no. 06232625. CIA Electronic FOIA Reading Room.

US Central Intelligence Agency. 1971. "Peking-Taipei Contacts: The Question of a Possible 'Chinese Solution'." CIA Intelligence Report (December), CIA Electronic FOIA Reading Room, www.cia.gov/readingroom/document/cia-rdp85 t00875r001000010045-7.

US Congressional Research Service. 2021. "The Senkakus (Diaoyu/Diaoyutai) Dispute: U.S. Treaty Obligations." CRS Report, March 1. https://sgp.fas.org/crs/row/R42761.pdf.

US Department of State, Memo, August 5, 1960. "Review of Offshore Island Problem and United States Policy Relating Thereto." In *Confidential U.S. State Department Central Files China: 1960-January 1963 Internal Affairs*, edited by US Department of State. Frederick: University Publications of America. Microfilm, reel 11.

US Department of State. 1976. "Department of State Policy Statement [21 April 1950, Document 96]." In *Foreign Relations of the United States, 1950*, Vol. 6, edited by Neal H. Petersen, William Z. Slany, Charles S. Sampson, John P. Glennon, and David W. Mabon. Washington, DC: U.S. Government Printing Office. https://history.state.gov/historicaldocuments/frus1950v06/d96.

US Department of State. 1977. "Department of State Policy Statement for New Zealand [30 July 1951, Document 1]." In *Foreign Relations of the United States, 1951*, Vol. 6, Pt. 2, edited by Paul Claussen, John P. Glennon, David W. Mabon, Neal H. Petersen, and Carl N. Raether. Washington, DC: U.S. Government Printing Office. https://history.state.gov/historicaldocuments/frus1951v06p2/d1.

US Department of State. 1982. *Foreign Relations of the United States (FRUS). 1952–1954*. Vol. 13, *Indochina*. Washington, DC: U.S. Government Printing Office.

US Department of State. 1996a. "Memorandum of Conversation [22 October 1958, Document 203]." In *Foreign Relations of the United States, 1958–1960*, Vol. 19, edited by Harriet Dashiell Schwar. Washington, DC: U.S. Government Printing Office. https://history.state.gov/historicaldocuments/frus1958-60v19/d203.

US Department of State. 1996b. "Joint Communiqué [23 October 1958, Document 209]." In *Foreign Relations of the United States, 1958–1960*, Vol. 19, edited by Harriet Dashiell Schwar. Washington, DC: U.S. Government Printing Office. https://history.state.gov/historicaldocuments/frus1958-60v19/d209.

US Department of State. 1996c. "Memorandum of Conversation [23 October 1958, Document 207]." In *Foreign Relations of the United States, 1958-1960*, Vol. 19, edited by Harriet Dashiell Schwar. Washington, DC: U.S. Government Printing Office. https://history.state.gov/historicaldocuments/frus1958-60v19/d207.

US Department of State. 2001. *Confidential U.S. State Department Central Files China: 1960-January 1963 Internal Affairs*. Frederick: University Publications of America. Microfilm, reels 1, 2, 11.

Bibliography 355

US Department of the Interior. n.d. "Compact Trust Funds." Office of Insular Affairs. www.doi.gov/oia/compact-trust-funds.

US Government Accountability Office. 2022. "Compacts of Free Association: Implications of Planned Ending of Some U.S. Economic Assistance." GAO. February 14. www.gao.gov/products/gao-22-104436.

US Ministry of Foreign Affairs to ROC Embassy in the United States, March 19, 1957. Report. Archives of the Ministry of Foreign Affairs, Archives of the Institute of Modern History, Academia Sinica (Taipei), 0046/405.1/2.

US Office of Reports and Estimates. 1949. "Consequences of US Troop Withdrawal from Korea in Spring, 1949 (ORE 3-49)." Central Intelligence Group (February). www.cia.gov/readingroom/document/0000258388.

US Office of the Historian. 1920. "Inaugural Address of the President Yuan Shih Kai." In *Papers Relating to the Foreign Relations of the United States, with the Address of the President to Congress, December 2, 1913*, edited by Joseph V. Fuller. Washington, DC: U.S. Govt Printing Office. Document 76a, https://history.state.gov/historicaldocuments/frus1913/d76a.

US Office of the Historian. 1950. "The Ambassador in Japan (Grew) to the Secretary of State," April 26, 1934. In *Foreign Relations of the United States Diplomatic Papers, 1934, the Far East*, Vol. 3. Washington, DC: U.S. Government Printing Office.

US Office of the Historian. 1961. *Foreign Relations of the United States: Diplomatic Papers, the Conferences at Cairo and Tehran, 1943*, edited by William N. Franklin, and William Gerber. Washington, DC: Government Printing Office. Document 263, https://history.state.gov/historicaldocuments/frus1943CairoTehran/d263.

US Office of the Historian. 1963. *Foreign Relations of the United States, 1943*, Vol. 3, edited by William N. Franklin, and E. Ralph Perkins. Washington, DC: Government Printing Office. Document 975, https://history.state.gov/historicaldocuments/frus1943v03/d975.

US Office of the Historian. 1969. *Foreign Relations of the United States, 1945, the British Commonwealth, the Far East*, Vol. 6, edited by John P. Glennon, N. O. Sappington, Laurence Evans, et al. Washington, DC: Government Printing Office. Documents 775-81, https://history.state.gov/historicaldocuments/frus1945v06/d780.

US Office of the Historian. 1974. "Statement of the United States Government [10 December 1948, Document 696]." In *Foreign Relations of the United States, 1948*, Vol. 5, edited by John G. Reid, and David H. Stauffer. Washington, DC: U.S. Government Printing Office. https://history.state.gov/historicaldocuments/frus1948v06/d696.

US Office of the Historian. 1976. *Foreign Relations of the United States, 1949, the Far East and Australasia*, Vol. 7, edited by John G. Reid, and John P. Glennon. Washington, DC: Government Printing Office. Document 209, https://history.state.gov/historicaldocuments/frus1949v07p2/d209.

US Office of the Historian. 1985. *Foreign Relations of the United States, 1952–1954, China and Japan*, Vol. 14, part 1, edited by David W. Mabon, and Harriet D. Schwar. Washington, DC: Government Printing Office.

US Office of the Historian. 1996a. *Foreign Relations of the United States, 1958–1960, China*, Vol. 19, edited by Harriet Dashiell Schwar. Washington, DC: Government Printing Office.

US Office of the Historian. 1996b. *Foreign Relations of the United States, 1961–1963, Northeast Asia*, Vol. 22, edited by Edward C. Keefer, David W. Mabon, and Harriet Dashiell Schwar. Washington, DC: Government Printing Office.

Valenti, Jack. 1965. "Meeting on Vietnam, July 21, 1965, Notes." Meeting Notes File, Lyndon Baines Johnson Library, Austin, Texas.

van de Ven, Hans. 2014. *Breaking with the Past: The Maritime Customs Service and the Global Origins of Modernity in China*. New York: Columbia University Press.

van de Ven, Hans J. 1996. "Public Finance and the Rise of Warlordism." *Modern Asian Studies* 30 (4): 829–868.

Veenendaal, Wouter P. 2017. "Analyzing the Foreign Policy of Microstates: The Relevance of the International Patron-Client Model." *Foreign Policy Analysis* 13 (3): 561–577.

Vitalis, Robert. 2015. *White World Order, Black Power Politics: The Birth of American International Relations*. Ithaca NY: Cornell University Press.

Von Glahn, Richard. 2020. "The Political Economy of the East Asian Maritime World in the Sixteenth Century." In *East Asia in the World: Twelve Events Shaped the Modern International Order*, edited by Stephan Haggard, and David C. Kang, 44–64. Cambridge: Cambridge University Press.

von Ranke, Leopold. 2011a. "A Dialogue on Politics." In *The Theory and Practice of History*, edited by Georg G. Iggers, 54–74. New York: Routledge.

von Ranke, Leopold. 2011b. "The Great Powers." In *The Theory and Practice of History*, edited by Georg G. Iggers, 29–53. New York: Routledge.

Wada, Haruki. 2013. *The Korean War: An International History*. Lanham, MA: Rowman & Littlefield.

Wagner, R. Harrison. 2007. *War and the State: The Theory of International Politics*. Ann Arbor: University of Michigan Press.

Walt, Stephen M. 1999. "Rigor or Rigor Mortis: Rational Choice and Security Studies." *International Security* 23 (4): 5–48.

Waltz, Kenneth. 1979. *Theory of International Politics*. Reading: Addison-Wesley.

Wang, Guanhua. 2001. *In Search of Justice: The 1905–1906 Chinese Anti-American Boycott*. Cambridge, MA: Harvard University Asia Center.

Wang, Zheng. 2008. "National Humiliation, History Education, and the Politics of Historical Memory: Patriotic Education Campaign in China." *International Studies Quarterly* 52 (4): 783–806.

Wagner, R. Harrison. 1993. "What Was Bipolarity?" *International Organization* 47 (1): 77–106.

Waqavakatoga, William. 2023. "How the 'Pacific Way' of Diplomacy Shored up the PIF." *East Asia Forum* (March). www.eastasiaforum.org/2023/03/07/how-the-pacific-way-of-diplomacy-shored-up-the-pif/.

Weiss, Jessica Chen. 2014. *Powerful Patriots: Nationalist Protest in China's Foreign Relations*. Oxford: Oxford University Press.

Weiwei, Zhang. 2012. *The China Wave: Rise of a Civilizational State*. Danvers: World Century.

Wendt, Alexander. 1992. "Anarchy Is What States Make of It: The Social Construction of Power Politics." *International Organization* 46 (2): 391–425.

Wendt, Alexander. 1999. *Social Theory of International Politics*. Cambridge: Cambridge University Press.

Westad, Odd Arne. 2005. *The Global Cold War: Third World Interventions and the Making of Our Times*. New York: Cambridge University Press.
White, John Albert. 1964. *Diplomacy of the Russo-Japanese War*. Princeton: Princeton University Press.
White, John Albert. 2015. *Diplomacy of the Russo-Japanese War*. Princeton: Princeton University Press.
William Langdon Memo on the Korean Liberty Conference, March 3, 1942, 895.01/84. In 美國務省韓國關係文書 *[Internal affairs of Korea, 1940–1944]*, Vol. 1. Seoul: Wonju.
Wilson Center Digital Archive. 1972. "Record of the Third Meeting between Prime Minister Tanaka and Premier Zhou Enlai." September 27. http://digitalarchive.wilsoncenter.org/document/121228.
Wilson, Sandra. 2001. *The Manchurian Crisis and Japanese Society, 1931–1933*. New York: Routledge.
Wimmer, Andreas. 2008. "Elementary Strategies of Ethnic Boundary Making." *Ethnic and Racial Studies* 31 (6): 1025–1055.
Winichakul, Thongchai. 2009. *Siam Mapped: A History of the Geo-Body of a Nation*. Honolulu: University of Hawai'i Press.
Wolfers, Edward. 1971. "The Significance of Protectorate Status." Letter to Richard Nolte, Executive Director, Institute of Current World Affairs, February 5, 1971.
Wolford, Scott. 2007. "The Turnover Trap: New Leaders, Reputation, and International Conflict." *American Journal of Political Science* 51 (4): 772–788.
Wolford, Scott. 2017. "The Problem of Shared Victory: War-Winning Coalitions and Postwar Peace." *Journal of Politics* 79 (2): 702–716.
Wolford, Scott. 2019a. "Neutrality Regimes." *Security Studies* 28 (4): 807–832.
Wolford, Scott. 2019b. *The Politics of the First World War: A Course in Game Theory and International Security*. Cambridge: Cambridge University Press.
Wolford, Scott. 2023. "Great Power Intervention and War." *International Studies Quarterly* 67 (1): sqad003.Wolford: Done, see 1 comment.
Wolford, Scott, Dan Reiter, and Clifford J. Carrubba. 2011. "Information, Commitment, and War." *Journal of Conflict Resolution* 55 (4): 556–579.
Wong, Sin-Kiong. 1998. "The Chinese Boycott: A Social Movement in Singapore and Malaya in the Early Twentieth Century." 東南アジア研究 36 (2): 230–253.
Wong, Young-tsu. 1992. "Revisionism Reconsidered: Kang Youwei and the Reform Movement of 1898." *Journal of Asian Studies* 51 (3): 513–544.
World Bank. 2023. "GDP Per Capita (Current US$) – Marshall Islands." Accessed January 31. https://data.worldbank.org/indicator/NY.GDP.PCAP.CD?locations=MH.
Wright, Mary Clabaugh. 1957. *The Last Stand of Chinese Conservatism: The T'ung-Chih Restoration, 1862–1874*. Stanford: Stanford University Press.
Wright, Mary Clabaugh. 1968a. "Introduction." In *China in Revolution: The First Phase, 1900–1913*, edited by Mary Clabaugh Wright, 1–63. New Haven: Yale University Press.
Wright, Mary Clabaugh, ed. 1968b. *China in Revolution: The First Phase, 1900–1913*. New Haven: Yale University Press.
Wu, Cathy X., Amanda N. Licht, and Scott Wolford. 2021. "Same as the Old Boss? Domestic Politics and the Turnover Trap." *International Studies Quarterly* 65 (1): 173–183.

Wyatt, David K. 2003. *Thailand: A Short History.* 2nd ed. New Haven: Yale University Press.
Xu, Guoqi. 2016. "The Japanese Dream of Racial Equality." In his *Asia and the Great War,* 185–210. Oxford: Oxford University Press.
Yamamuro, Shin'ichi. 2006. *Manchuria under Japanese Dominion.* Philadelphia: University of Pennsylvania Press.
Yan, Wang, ed. 1998. *Peng Dehuai Nianpu (Chronology of Peng Dehuai).* Beijing: Renmin chubanshe.
Yan, Xuetong. 2020. "Chinese Values vs. Liberalism: What Ideology Will Shape the International Normative Order?" In *Globalizing IR Theory,* edited by Yaqing Qin, 1–22. London: Routledge.
Yellen, Jeremy A. 2016. "Into the Tiger's Den: Japan and the Tripartite Pact, 1940." *Journal of Contemporary History* 51 (3)(July): 555–576.
Yellen, Jeremy A. 2019a. *The Greater East Asia Co-prosperity Sphere.* Ithaca: Cornell University Press.
Yellen, Jeremy A. 2019b. "Wartime Wilsonianism and the Crisis of Empire, 1941–1943." *Modern Asian Studies* 53 (4): 1278–1311.
Yellen, Jeremy A. 2022. "What Grand Strategy? Japan, 1931–1945." In *From Far East to Asia Pacific: Great Powers and Grand Strategy 1900–1954,* edited by Brian P. Farrell, S. R. Joey Long, and David J. Ulbrich, 221–250. Berlin: De Gruyter.
Yellen, Jeremy A. 2023. "International Relations and Diplomacy." In *The Interwar World,* edited by Andrew Denning, and Heidi J. S. Tworek, 190–196. New York: Routledge.
Ye, Fei. 1988. *Ye Fei Huiyilu (Memoirs of Ye Fe).* Beijing: Jiefangjun chubanshe.
Yeo, Andrew. 2020. "Philippine National Independence, 1898–1904." In *East Asia in the World: Twelve Events Shaped the Modern International Order,* edited by Stephan Haggard, and David C. Kang, 206–223. Cambridge: Cambridge University Press.
Yi, Zheng. 2009. *Guogong Xiangjiang Diezhan (The KMT-CCP spy war in Hong Kong).* Hong Kong: Wenhua Yishu chubanshe.
Yin, Qiming, and Yaguang Cheng. 1997. *Diyiren Guofang Buzhang (The First Minister of Defense).* Guangzhou: Guangdong jiaoyu chubanshe.
Young, Ernest P. 1968. "Yuan Shih-k'ai's Rise to the Presidency." In *China in Revolution: The First Phase, 1900–1913,* edited by Mary Clabaugh Wright, 419–442. New Haven: Yale University Press.
Young, Louise. 1998. *Japan's Total Empire: Manchuria and the Culture of Wartime Imperialism.* Berkeley: University of California Press.
Zachmann, Urs Matthias. 2006. "Imperialism in a Nutshell: Conflict and the 'Concert of Powers' in the Tripartite Intervention, 1895." *Contemporary Japan* 17 (1): 57–82.
Zanasi, Margherita. 2006. *Saving the Nation: Economic Modernity in Republican China.* Chicago: University of Chicago Press.
Zanasi, Margherita. 2020. *Economic Thought in Modern China: Market and Consumption, c. 1500–1937.* Cambridge: Cambridge University Press.
Zarakol, Ayse. 2017. *Hierarchies in World Politics.* New York: Cambridge University Press.
Zeng, Jize 曾紀澤. 1887. "China: The Sleep and the Awakening." *Asiatic Quarterly Review* 3 (1): 1–10.

Zhai, Qiang. 1994. *The Dragon, the Lion, and the Eagle: Chinese-British-American Relations, 1945–1958*. Kent: The Kent State University Press.

Zhai, Xiang. 2015. "Rewriting the Legacy of Chiang Kai-shek on the Diaoyu Islands: China's Ryukyu Policies from the 1930s to the 1970s." *Journal of Contemporary China* 24: 1128–1146.

Zhang, Chunying, ed. 2004. *Haixia Liang'an Guangxishi (A History of Cross-Strait Relations)*, Vol. 3. Fuzhou: Fujian renmin chubanshe.

Zhang, Feng. 2015. *Chinese Hegemony: Grand Strategy and International Institutions in East Asian History*. Stanford: Stanford University Press.

Zhang, Zhen. 2003. *Zhang Zhen Huiyilu (Memoirs of Zhang Zhen)*, Vol. 1. Beijing: Jiefangjun chubanshe.

Zhonghua renmin gongheguo guojia tongji jubian [National Bureau of Statistics of the PRC]. Various years. *Zhongguo Tongji Nianjian* [China Statistical Yearbook]. Beijing: Zhongguo tongji chubanshe.

Zhou, Taomo. 2014. "China and the Thirtieth of September Movement." *Indonesia* 98: 29–58.

Zhou, Taomo. 2015. "Ambivalent Alliance: Chinese Policy toward Indonesia, 1960–1965." *The China Quarterly* 221: 208–228. https://doi.org/10.1017/S0305741014001544.

Zhu, Ping. 2021. "The Chinese Exclusion Act and the Late Qing Chinese Cosmopolitanism." *Comparative Literature Studies* 58 (4): 863–890.

Zielinski, Rosella Capella. 2012. *How States Pay for Wars*. Ithaca: Cornell University Press.

Zong, Tang. 1963. "Report on the Party Affairs at the Ninth KMT National Congress." Contemporary Taiwan Collection, Library of the Institute of Oriental Culture, University of Tokyo, no. CD6:1679: 39–41.

Zvobgo, Kelebogile, and Meredith Loken. 2020a. "Why Is Mainstream International Relations Blind to Racism?" *Foreign Policy*, July 3.

Zvobgo, Kelebogile, and Meredith Loken. 2020b. "Why Race Matters in International Relations." *Foreign Policy*, June 19.

Index

Acheson, Dean, 238–239, 244
Africa and the Victorians (Gallagher and Robinson), 13
Alien Land Law of 1913, US, 110
alliances, treaties and, *see also specific treaties*
  conceptual approach to, 225–226
  state-building and, 226–228
  hub-and-spokes approach, 226, 240–241
  US role in, 226–228
  perceived threats and, 227–228
  Washington Consensus, 228, 232, 241
Amō Statement, 158
Andrade, Tonio, 4
Angell Treaty, 92, 101–102
Anglo-Burmese Wars, 56, 57, 61
anti-Chinese communism, in Malaya, 264–271
  against Malayan Communist Party, 265–267
anti-Chinese racism, in US, 97–98
  Chinese Exclusion Act, US (1882), scientific racism, 91
  gender as factor in, 101
  through politicization of racial resentment, 99–101
Aritomo, Yamagata, 168
Arthur, Chester A., 92, 102
ASEAN. *See* Association of East Asian Nations
Asia. *See also* East Asia; East Asia, new order in; historical East Asia; Transitional East Asia; *specific countries*; *specific topics*
  postwar settlement in, 8
  as "Yellow Peril," 87, 106–107
Asia-Pacific War, 178–179. *See also* World War II
Association of East Asian Nations (ASEAN)
  formation of, 24
  regional institutions for, 245–246
Australia
  Chinese migration to, 96
  Gold Rush in, 96
  on Japanese racial equality proposal, 128–129
  US security pact with, 32
Austria
  July Crisis and, 81–82
  Serbia and, 81–82, 88
autarky, 166–167
authoritarianism
  colonial rule, 16
  republicanism and, 23
Ava Kingdom, in Burma, 56, 57, 72

Baker, Ray Stannard, 127
Balfour, Arthur, 116
Ball, George, 242, 252, 253–254, 258, 259
Battle of Mukden, 79
Battle of the Tsushima Strait, 80
Battle of the Yellow Sea, 79
Bedor, Roman, 289–290
Benninghoff, Merril, 174
Bigler, John, 98–99
Bo Dai, 275
Boecking, Felix, 158–159
Bonesteel, Charles, 187
Borden, Robert, 116
Bourgois, Léon, 123–124
Bowring, John, 58
Bowring Treaty, 65–66
Boxer Protocol, 78
Boxer Rebellion, 15, 313
Boxer War, 135, 142, 143
Boyce, Robert, 182
boycott movement, against Chinese, 104–106
Brazinsky, Gregg, 234
Bretton Woods institutions, 29–30
Britain. *See also* British Empire
  Anglo-Burmese Wars, 56, 57, 61
  Anglo-Japanese alliance, 86
  credibility of, 251
  on Japanese racial equality proposal, 122–123, 125–126
  Siam and
    under Anglo-French Convention, 64
    colonialism and, 14

Index

through shared sovereignty, 61, 64
Treaty of Nanking, 17
Treaty of Tientsin and, 17
British East India Company, Canton system and, 17
British Empire. *See also specific countries*
  Burma in, 55, 56–57
  colonial expansion of, 55–57
  in historical East Asia, 15
Brooks, Sydney, 83–84
Bundy, McGeorge, 243, 251–252, 256, 258
Burlingame Treaty, 92, 101–102
Burma, 182
  Anglo-Burmese Wars, 56, 57, 61
  Ava Kingdom in, 56, 57
  under British rule, 55, 56–57
  under French rule, 56–57
  reparation agreement with Japan, 36–37
  Treaty of Yandabo, 56
Burney, Henry, 61
Bush, George W., 34, 257
Buzan, Barry, 94, 97–98
Búzás, Zoltán, 107–108

Cairo Declaration, 188, 196–198, 200, 206
California Crisis, 118
Cambodia, 49
  under French rule, 55, 62–65
Canton system, 17
Cao Juren, 214, 215, 217, 218–221, 224
Carnegie, Andrew, 84
CCP. *See* Chinese Communist Party
Cecil, Robert, 122–123
CER. *See* Chinese Eastern Railway
Chamberlain, Neville, 251
Chang Jae Baik, 225
Chen Cheng, 215
Chiang Ching-kuo, 214, 215
Chiang Kai-shek, 39–40, 153
  Dulles, J. F., and, 237
  exile to Taiwan, 208–216, 267
  US response to, 208–213
  Japan and, 156
  trade ban with, 158–159
  Mao Zedong and, 207, 215
  Nationalist Party and, 152–153, 156
  New Life Movement and, 156
  Republic of China and, 207
  Sun Yat-sen and, 197
  Taiwan Straits Crises and, 208–216, 217, 218–221
  US intelligence report on, 222
China. *See also* Chinese migration; East Asia, new order in; Opium Wars; People's Republic of China; Republic of China; Taiwan; *specific topics*
  analysis of, 26–28
  Boxer Protocol and, 78
  Boxer Rebellion, 15, 313
  Canton system in, 17
    British East India Company and, 17
  civil war in, 207
  exclusion from San Francisco Treaties, 34
  extraterritoriality in, 19, 134
  Four-Party Treaty, 21
  historical dominance of, 27
  Imjin War, 309–310, 316
  immigration to US, 93
  Ming dynasty, 94–95
  nationalism and, 91
    foreign presence as influence on, 145–146
    Nationalist Party, 138–140
  Nationalist Party, 138–140
    Chiang Kai-shek and, 152–153
  neighborhood diplomacy of, 5
  Nine-Party Treaty, 21
  Qing dynasty, 94–95, 309, 310
    Opium Wars and, 155
  during Russo-Japanese War, 78–79
  Senkaku Islands dispute, 39–40
  Shandong Treaty, 170
  Sino-Japanese War, 5–6, 15, 45, 48–49
  Supplementary Convention of Peking, 17
  Taiping Rebellion, 95, 309, 310–311
  trade networks in
    Canton system, 17
    hong merchants, 17
  Treaty of Peking, 17
  Treaty of Saint Petersburg, 17
  Treaty of Shimonoseki, 17, 39, 134–135, 155
  US Silver Purchase Act and, 158
China, in early twentieth century
  Boxer War, 135, 142, 143
  finance mechanisms in
    Chinese Maritime Customs Service, 144, 155
    international debt and, 143–145
    international presence influence on, 143–145
  Hundred Days Reform, 135–136
  international presence in
    finance mechanisms influenced by, 143–145
    foreign aggression, 141–143
    nationalism influenced by, 145–146
    state failure influenced by, 141–145
    treaty system and, 143
  Manchu elites in, 136, 137
  nationalism in
    foreign presence as influence on, 145–146

362 Index

China, in early twentieth century (cont.)
   Nationalist Party, 138–140
   Neo-Confucianism in, 136
   New Policy reforms (1901–1910), 136–137, 141
   Opium Wars and, 142, 143
   Qing dynasty, 141–143, 147
   Republic of China
      establishment of, 137–141, 147
      international presence as influence on, 141
   revolutionary movements, 136, 137–141
      democratic transition as, 138–139
      Japanese support of, 139
      Nationalist Party, 138–140
      Railway Rights Recovery Movement, 145
   Sino-Japanese War and, 142, 145
   state efficacy in, 141–143
   state failure between 1900–1916, 134–137
      Boxer War and, 135
      early foundations of, 137–141
      international presence as influence on, 141–145
      Treaty of Shimonoseki, 134–135
   during World War I, 139–140, 147
   Wuchang Uprising, 139
China–Japan relationship
   analysis of, 163–165
   during Cold War, 149
   conceptual approach to, 148–151
   economic interests in, 149–150, 154–160
      Amō Statement, 158
      imperialism and, 155–156
      interdependence as element of, 151–154
      Japan as economic model, 156–158, 159–160
      during postwar era, 160–163
      trade relationship, 157, 159
      under Treaty of Shimonoseki, 155
   after establishment of Chinese Communist Party, 160–163
   Manchurian Incident, 148
   occupation of Manchuria and, 148, 152, 304
   after Second Sino-Japanese War, 150
   security interests in, 149–150, 154–160
      during postwar era, 160–163
   trade relationship with (1880–1980), 149
   Twenty-One Demands and, 140, 146, 168
China Market (McCormick), 13
Chinese Communist Party (CCP)
   China–Japan relationship under, 160–163
   US state-building in competition with, 229–232
Chinese Eastern Railway (CER), 78, 79, 82
Chinese exclusion, in US, rise of, 97–104
   anti-Chinese racism, 97–98, 99–101
   gender as factor in, 101
   exclusion laws, 101–104
      Burlingame Treaty, 92, 101–102
      Page Act of 1875, 92, 101, 106
      Scott Act, 102–103
   global racial hierarchies and, 97–98
   from politicization of racial resentment, 98–99
      in California, 98–99
      as "Chinese question,", 99–101, 107–108
   racism as result of, 99–101
Chinese Exclusion Act, US (1882)
   boycott movement and, 104–106
   Chinese nationalism influenced by, 104–106
      through Chinese home associations, 104–105
      Six Companies association, 104–105
   conceptual approach to, 90–92
   expansion of, 103–104
      for Japanese populations, 91
      for other populations, 103
   extension of, 103–104
      through Geary Act, 92, 102–103, 104–105
   foundations of, 90–91
      Chinese as racial threat, 90–91
   Geary Act as extension of, 92, 102–103
   historical legacy of, 106–108
   origins of, 102–103
   repeal of, 92–94
   scientific racism and, 91
   violence against Chinese as result of, 102–103
Chinese Maritime Customs Service, 144, 155
Chinese migration, 94–97
   during Australian Gold Rush, 96
   through labor recruitment, 95–97
      for railroad companies, 97
      for Transcontinental Railroad, 97, 99
      for westward expansion in US, 95–97
   after opening of China, 94–95
   during Ming dynasty, 94–95
   after Opium Wars, 95
   during Qing dynasty, 94–95
   Taiping Rebellion, 95
   during US Gold Rush, 95–97
"Chinese question," 99–101, 107–108
Christianity, in Korean Peninsula, 190–191, 192
Chulalongkorn (King), 59, 61, 66–69, 71–74
Chung, Henry, 191
Churchill, Winston, 248–249
Cixi (Empress Dowager), 134–135
Cleveland, Grover, 102–103
Coble, Parks, 156
Cold War. *See also specific topics*
   China–Japan relationship during, 149
   conceptual approach to, 21
   Rhee during, 200–205

Index

San Francisco Treaties during, 34, 36–37
US-Korea relations during, 200–205
colonialism, colonial rule and, *see also* British Empire; France; North Pacific region; postcolonialism
  authoritarianism and, 16
  Greater East Asia Co-prosperity Sphere and, 180
  imperialism and, 12–13
  nationalism and, 20
  race and, 25–26
  in Siam, 55–57
    analysis of, 74–75
    expansion of, 55–57
    under France, 14
    under Great Britain, 14, 55, 61
  in Southeast Asia, 55–57
  war and, 16
Communist movement, 226
Congress of Vienna, 89
Copeland, Dale, 151, 152–153, 305
Covenant of the League of Nations
  Japanese provisions in, 109–110
  racial equality clause in, 90
credibility, prestige and
  of Britain, 251
  Johnson, L., protection of, 255
  of US hegemony, 243, 244
    First Indochina War, 247–249
    partial hegemony, 249–254
Cullather, Nick, 238
cultural identity. *See* identity
cultural reforms, in Siam, 70–74
Cumings, Bruce, 201

Dane, Richard, 144
decolonization
  First Indochina War and, 256–259
  in North Pacific region, 278–279
  international pressure for, 287
  Vietnam War and, 256–259
democracy, Chinese transition to, 138–139
Democratic Republic of Vietnam (North Vietnam), socialism and, 24
Deng Xiaoping, 27, 40
Develle, Jules, 63
diplomacy of imperialism, 170, 182
direct rule, imperialism and, 6
Dmowski, Roman, 124
Doner, Richard, 228
Donghak Rebellion, 312–313
Dower, John, 32
Doyle, Michael, 10–11
Du Bois, W. E. B., 91, 119
Dulles, Allen, 236

Dulles, John Foster, 32–33, 38, 208–210, 213, 220. *See also* Taiwan Straits Crises
  Chiang Kai-shek and, 237
  Korean War and, 248
  on Taiwan state-building, 236–237

East Asia. *See also* historical East Asia; San Francisco System; Sinitic order; Transitional East Asia; *specific countries*
  conceptual approach to, 3–6, 166–167
  Greater East Asia Co-prosperity Sphere, 283
  imperialism in, 5–6
  indirect rule in, 5
  methodological approach to, 3–10
  modernization in, 300–303
  trade networks in, 4
East Asia, new order in, 177–182
  analysis of, 182–183
  after Asia-Pacific War, 178–179
  autarky and, 166–167
  East Asian Monroe Doctrine, 174
  Greater East Asia Co-prosperity Sphere and, 166–167, 175, 177, 178–179, 183
  division into colonial regimes, 180
  geopolitical legacy of, 182–183
  in North Pacific region, 283
  state-building and, 181–182
  ideological struggle in, 180–181
  interdependence in, 303–306
  Japan in
    as imperial gateway, 167–168
    Manchuria–Mongolia Problem, 173
    revolt of, 172–177
  Kwantung Leasehold and, 167–168
  League of Nations and, 169–170
  legitimation of, 317–320
  liberal internationalism and, 166–167
  Manchurian Incident, 173
  new imperialism in, 179
  in postwar years, 183
  Soviet Union as influence in, 173
  Wanpaoshan Incident, 173
  war and, 303–306
  Washington System and, 170–171, 172, 173, 175
  during World War I, 167–169
  end of dynastic empires after, 168
East Asian Monroe Doctrine, 174
Economic Interdependence and War (Copeland), 151
economic sanctions, scholarship on, 164
EDC. *See* European Defense Community
Eden, Anthony, 249
Eiji, Amō, 158, 174

364　Index

Eisenhower, Dwight, 212–213, 222, 248, 249–250, 253. *See also* Korean War; Taiwan Straits Crises
Elkins, Caroline, 14–15
Empires (Doyle), 10–11
England. *See* Britain
Esherick, Joe, 23
Esper, Mark, 292
ethnic identities. *See* identity
European Defense Community (EDC), 247
extraterritoriality
　in China, 19, 134
　for Siam, 67

Federated States of Micronesia, 279, 289–295
Ferdinand, Franz (Archduke), 87, 88, 153
First Indochina War, 49
　French defeat in, 249
　US hegemony during, 243, 247–249
　as war of decolonization, 256–259
First Opium War, 15
First World War. *See* World War I
Five-Power Treaty, 170
Formosa Expedition, 15
Formosa Resolution, 212–213
Foster, John W., 104–105
Four-Party Treaty, 21
Four-Power Treaty, 170
France
　Burma and, 56–57
　Cambodia and, 55, 62–65
　First Indochina War and, 249
　Laos and, 63
　Luang Prabang under protection of, 63
　Siam and, 63, 64
　　under Anglo-French Convention, 64
　　colonialism and, 14
　　French rejection of shared sovereignty, 62–65
　state-building in South Vietnam, 240
　Thailand and, 14
　Vietnam and, 56–57, 62–65
free association formula, in North Pacific region, 283, 288–291
Fujitani, Takashi, 179
Fulbright, William, 252, 258–259
Fumimaro, Konoe, 171–172, 176

Gallagher, Jack, 13
Garon, Sheldon, 234
Garveyism, 109
Gaulle, Charles de, 252, 253
Gawthorpe, Andrew, 231
Geary Act, US (1892), 92, 102–103, 104–105
Geneva Agreement, 249

geoeconomics, scholarship on, 164
Germany
　Moroccan Crises of 1905/1911, 81–82
　in North Pacific region, 281
　Schlieffen Plan and, 77–78, 87, 88
Gilpin, Robert, 244–245
Goldberg, Jeffrey, 257
Goldstein, Gordon, 251–252
Gourevitch, Peter, 172
Great Leap Forward, 216–217
Great Pyongyang Revival of 1907, 190, 193
Greater East Asia Co-prosperity Sphere, 166–167, 175, 177, 178–179, 183
　division into colonial regimes, 180
　geopolitical legacy of, 182–183
　in North Pacific Region, 283
　state-building and, 181–182
　Transitional East Asia and, 319
Gresham-Yang Treaty, 92–94, 105
Grew, Joseph, 198–200
grievance theory, 230
Guam, 279

Hachirō, Arita, 176
Haglelgam, John, 291
Harding, Warren G., 170
Harriman, Averell, 199–200
Hart, Robert, 144
Hayes, Rutherford B., 101–102
hegemony, in US foreign policy
　alternative approaches to, 254–256
　analysis of, 256–259
　credibility and prestige and, 243, 244
　in First Indochina War, 247–249
　partial hegemony, 249–254
　incompleteness of, 246–247
　international relations approach, 245–246
　patron–client model, 246
　　classification of clients, 246–247
　role of credibility and prestige in, 243, 244
　in Southeast Asia, 276–277
　in Vietnam, 276–277
　Vietnam War and, 242–259
　　methodological approach to, 242–247
　　partial hegemony, 249–254
Heine, Carl, 287
Heine, Dwight, 289
Herring, George, 257–258
Hideyoshi, Toyotomi, 309–310
hierarchy, as concept, in imperialism, 11
Hikomatsu, Kamikawa, 180
historical China. *See* China
historical East Asia, 299. *See also* China; *specific countries*
　British Empire in, 15

Index   365

hierarchical structure of, 3–4
as peaceful era, 4
state formation in, 3–4
trade networks in, 4
tribute system in, 3–4
Ho Chi Minh, 247, 249–250, 265, 275
Hodge, John R., 201–202, 203–204
House, Edward M., 115
Huang Jici, 214
Huang Shao-Ku, 237
Huang Shaogu, 218
hub-and-spokes approach, to alliances, 226, 240–241
Hughes, Billy, 111, 126, 128–129
Hughes, Charles Evans, 170
Huk Rebellion, 231, 237–238
Hundred Days Reform, 135–136

identity, ethnic/cultural identities and, in Siam
identity promotion schemes, 69–70
promotion schemes for, 70
Imjin War, 309–310, 316
immigration, immigration policies, in US *See also* Chinese Exclusion Act; Chinese migration
Alien Land Law of 1913, 110
from China, 93
Angell Treaty, 92, 101–102
Burlingame Treaty, 92, 101–102
Geary Act, 92, 102–103, 104–105
Gresham–Yang Treaty, 92–94, 105
historical overview of, 92–94
Page Act of 1875, 92, 101, 106
Immigration Act, 90, 94
from Japan, 93
historical overview of, 92–94
Tydings–McDuffie Act, 103–104
Immigration Act, US (1924), 90, 94
imperialism, 5
American hegemony and, 11–12
China–Japan relationship and, 155–156
colonialism and, 12–13
conceptual approach to, 10–19
classical theories in, 10–11
history in, 19–22
periodization in, 19–22
time in, 19–22
definition of, 11–12
diplomacy of, 170, 182
direct rule and, 6
domestic political foundations of, 22–25
in East Asia, 5–6
economic factors of, 12–14
Marxism and, 12
neo-Marxism and, 12

hierarchy concept and, 11
ideational factors and, 25–26
indirect rule and, 6
institutional forms of, 16–19
hybrid forms within, 18–19
international relations theory and, 10–11, 19
legal, 18
nekolim, 260, 269
neo-imperialism, 260
new, 179
postcolonialism and, 10–11
race as factor in, 25–26
repression under, 14–16
strategic factors of, 12–14
treaty port model and, 17
violence and, 14–16
war and, 14–16
after World War I, 20
IMTFE. *See* International Military Tribunals for the Far East
indirect rule
in East Asia, 5
imperialism and, 6
Indonesia, 181
anti-Chinese violence in, 273
Indonesian Communist Party, 272–273
Konfrontasi in, 270, 271
pro-US relationship with, 271–275
reparation agreement with Japan, 36–37
Suharto in, 272–273
Indonesian Communist Party (PKI), 272–273
International Military Tribunals for the Far East (IMTFE), 33
international relations (IR). *See also* Paris Peace Conference; *specific topics*
imperialism and, 10–11, 19
race and, 25, 91
racial equality proposal and, 128–129
Russo-Japanese War and, 76–77
San Francisco Treaties and, 34
Transitional East Asia and, 304–305, 318, 319–320
in US hegemony, 245–246
internationalism. *See* liberal internationalism
IR. *See* international relations
Iwane, Matsui, 172

Jaisohn, Philip, 191, 193
Japan, 5. *See also* China–Japan relationship; East Asia, new order in; racial equality proposal; Russo-Japanese War; Second Sino-Japanese War; *specific topics*
Anglo-Japanese alliance, 86
Chiang Kai-shek and, 156
trade ban under 158–159

Japan (cont.)
  Chinese revolutionary movements supported by, 139
  Covenant of the League of Nations and, 109–110
  as economic model for China, 156–158, 159–160
  Formosa Expedition, 15
  immigration to US, 93
  historical overview of, 92–94
  as imperial gateway, 167–168
  Manchuria–Mongolia Problem, 173
  Mudan incident in, 15
  in North Pacific region, 281–283
  at Paris Peace Conference, 111–115
    delegation to, 112–114
    as global power, 111–112
  Perry in, 5–6
  racial equality proposal and, 119
  reparation agreements, 36–37
  revolt of, 172–177
  ROK-Japan Peace Treaty, 39
  in Russo-Japanese War, 78–79
  settlement option offered by, 81
  San Francisco Treaties and, 35, 38
  Senkaku Islands and, 39–40
  Shandong Treaty, 170
  Sino-Japanese War, 5–6, 15, 45, 48–49
  Tokyo war crimes trials and, 20, 33–34
  as "total empire,", 175–176, 179
  Treaty of Mutual Defence and Cooperation, 35
  Treaty of Peace, 32–34, 36
  Treaty of Shimonoseki, 17, 39, 134–135, 155
  Twenty-One Demands, 140, 146, 168
  US-Japan Security Treaty, 32–34, 41
    success of, 34–35
  US-Smoot Hawley Tariff, 152
  war thought in, 168
  Yuan Shikai and, 146
Japan Inside Out (Rhee), 194
Jirō, Minami, 174
Johnson, Chalmers, 232, 239–240
Johnson, Lyndon, 242, 251, 253–254, 258, 277. *See also* Vietnam War
  Americanization of Vietnam War, 260
  protection of credibility and prestige, 255
Johnson, U. Alexis, 217
July Crisis, 81–82, 87
justice reform, in Siam, 69
Jutarō, Komura, 78–79, 84

Kabua, Kitlang, 293
Kahin, George McTurnan, 249
Kang Youwei, 105, 134–136
Kanji, Ishiwara, 173, 175
Kapstein, Ethan, 230
Kayaoglu, Turan, 18
Kazushige, Ugaki, 168–169
Kearney, Denis, 99
Kellogg-Briand Pact, 170
Kennan, George, 206, 259
Kennedy, John F., 222–223, 277
Keohane, Robert, 225
Kijūrō, Shidehara, 174
Kikujiro, Ishii, 116–119
Kim, Taehyun, 225
Kingdom of Lanna, 61
Kinmochi, Marquis Saionji, 112–113, 114
Kirby, William, 134
Kiribati, 279, 289–290
Kissinger, Henry, 244–245
KMT. *See* Kuomintang
Kohli, Atul, 235
Kōki, Hirota, 174
Konfrontasi, in Indonesia, 270, 271
Koo, V. K. Wellington, 124–125
Korean–American Treaty, 192, 193, 196, 198, 199
Korean Peninsula. *See also* Rhee, Syngman; South Korea
  annexation of, 45
  Christianity in, 190–191, 192
  conceptual approach to, 187–188
  division of Korea, 187–188
  Donghak Rebellion in, 312–313
  geopolitical value of, 187
  Korean Provisional Government in, 190–191
  League of Friends of Korea, 191
  March First Movement in, 190–191
  nationalism in, 191
  Russo-Japanese War and, 78–79, 189
  San Francisco Treaties and, 38–39
  state-building in, 229–230
  in South Korea, 234–236
  US-Korea relations
    analysis of, 206
    under Cairo Declaration, 188, 196–198, 200, 206
    during Cold War, 200–205
    from 1882–1919, 188–190
    Hodge role in, 201–202, 203–204
    Korean–American Treaty, 192, 193, 196, 198, 199
    from 1920–1929, 190–194
    Treaty of Amity, Commerce, and Navigation, 58, 188–189
    during US occupation, 203
    under Versailles Treaty, 188, 190–194

Index 367

Washington Naval Conference, 21, 188, 190–194
  during World War II, 194–200
Korean Provisional Government (KPG), 190–191
Korean War, 7–8, 36–37, 39, 162, 225, 226, 248
Kōsai, Uchida (Count), 114
Kōsuke, Kawanishi, 177–178
KPG. *See* Korean Provisional Government
Kramář, Karel, 124
Kuomintang (KMT) (Nationalist Party), 138–140
  Chiang Kai-shek and, 152–153, 156
  Taiwan and, 208–213
Kwantung Army, 173–174
Kwantung Leasehold, 167–168

labor recruitment, Chinese migration through, 95–97
  for railroad companies, 97
  for Transcontinental Railroad, 97, 99
  for westward expansion in US, 95–97
Langer, William L., 169
Lansing, Robert, 192–193
Laos
  France and, 63
  Luang Prabang kingdom, 63
Larnaude, Ferdinand, 124
Lauren, Paul Gordon, 111
Lawson, George, 94, 97–98
League of Friends of Korea, 191
League of Nations. *See also* Covenant of the League of Nations
  East Asia new order and, 169–170
  in North Pacific region, 281–282
  racial equality proposal and, 117
  Wilson and, 169–170
Lee, James, 24
Lee Kuan Yew, 270–271
legal imperialism, 18
Lenin, Vladimir, 169
Li Hongzhang, 101–102
Li Yuanhong, 140
Liancourt Rocks, territorial conflict over, 38–39
liberal internationalism
  East Asia new order and, 166–167
  under Lenin, 169
  under Wilson, 169–170
Ling Qichao, 135–136
London Naval Treaty, 170, 172
Luang Prabang, French protection of, 63

Ma Yinchu, 160, 161
Macao
  as Portuguese colony, 5
  Treaty of Peking, 17

MacArthur, Douglas, 161, 201
Majeski, Stephen, 246–247
The Making of Modern Southeast Asia (Tate), 14
Malaya, Federation of, 179, 260–261
  anti-Chinese communism in, 264–271
    against Malayan Communist Party, 265–267
  British neo-colonialism in, 263–271
    anti-MCP propaganda and, 265–267
    conceptual approach to, 264
    Malayan Chinese Association and, 267–269
    Sukarno and, 264
  independence for, 269–270
  pro-US relationship with, 271–275
  United Malays National Organization, 268–269
Malayan Communist Party (MCP), 265–267
Malaysia, 260–261
Mamoru, Shigemitsu, 38, 177
Manchu elites, in China, 136, 137
Manchuria–Mongolia Problem, 173
Manchuria region. *See also* Second Sino-Japanese War
  occupation of, 148, 152, 304
Manchurian Incident, 148, 173
Mandate system, 129
Manela, Erez, 20, 90, 190
Mansfield, Mike, 252
Mao Zedong, 207, 208–209. *See also* Chinese Communist Party
  Chiang Kai-shek and, 207, 215
  communism expansion under, 250
  Great Leap Forward, 216–217
  Taiwan Straits Crises and, 211–212, 215–216, 218–221
March First Movement, 190–191
Marco Polo Bridge Incident, 153, 176
Marshall Islands. *See* Republic of Marshall Islands
Marxism, imperialism and, 12
Masatake, Terauchi, 168
Mastanduno, Michael, 243, 245–246
Matray, James, 200
Matsusaka, Yoshihisa Tak, 21
McCarthy, Joseph, 206
McCormick, Thomas, 13
McNamara, Robert, 251, 254
McNaughton, John, 251
MCP. *See* Malayan Communist Party
Mexican–American War, 96
Micronesia. *See* Federated States of Micronesia
Miller, David Hunter, 123, 125
Ming dynasty, 94–95

Mongkut, 66, 68, 71
Moroccan Crises of 1905/1911, 81–82
Morse, Wayne, 199
Mudan incident, in Japan, 15

Nathan, Robert, 235
national security interests. *See also* alliances
  in China–Japan relationship, 149–150,
    154–160
  during postwar era, 160–163
  after Second Sino-Japanese War, 160–163
  for US
    with Australia, 32
    New Zealand and, 32
    US-Japan Security Treaty, 32–35, 41
nationalism, nationalist movements and
  in China, 91
    foreign presence as influence on, 145–146
    Nationalist Party, 138–140
    Chinese Exclusion Act as influence on,
      104–106
    through Chinese home associations,
      104–105
    Six Companies association, 104–105
  colonialism and, 20
  in Korean Peninsula, 191
  in Philippines, 5–6
Nationalist Party. *See* Kuomintang
Nauru, 279
neighborhood diplomacy, of China, 5
nekolim, 260, 269
neo-colonialism, 260
  in Malaya, 263–271
    anti-MCP propaganda and, 265–267
    conceptual approach to, 264
    Malayan Chinese Association and,
      267–269
    Sukarno and, 264
    nekolim, 260, 269
Neo-Confucianism, 136
neo-imperialism, 260
neo-Marxism, imperialism and, 12
new imperialism, 179
New Policy reforms, in China, from 1901–1910,
  136–137, 141
New Zealand, US security pact with, 32
Ng Poon Chew, 105
Ngai, Mae, 90–91, 94
Ngo Dinh Diem, 250
Nguyen van Thieu, 250
Nicholas II (Tsar), 74, 79
Nine-Party Treaty, 21
Nine-Power Treaty, 170
Nixon, Richard, 222–223, 248–249
Nixon Doctrine, 287

Nobuaki, Makino (Baron), 112–113, 115, 119,
  120–122, 125–127. *See also* racial
  equality proposal
North Pacific region
  colonialism in
    by Germany, 281
    history of, 279
    by Japan, 281–283
    League of Nations Covenants and, 281–282
    mandates on, 280–283
    by Spain, 280–281
    transition to sovereignty, 283, 291–295
    under Treaty of Versailles, 281
  conceptual approach to, 278–279
  decolonization in, 278–279
    international pressure for, 287
  free association formula in, 283, 288–291
  geographic boundaries of, 279
  Greater East Asia Co-prosperity Sphere
    and, 283
  migration history for, 280
  Nixon Doctrine and, 287
  South Pacific Nuclear Free Zone Treaty
    in, 286
  strategic trusteeship in, 283–287
  Treaty on the Prohibition of Nuclear
    Weapons, 286
Northern Mariana Islands, 279

Obama, Barack, 40, 257
Ōkita, Saburō, 163
Omi, Michael, 100
Open Door policy, 85, 86, 313
Opium Wars, 5, 19, 65–66, 142, 143
  Britain's defeat in, 155
  First Opium War, 15
  opening of China after, 95
  political economy of, 5–6
  Qing dynasty and, 155
  Second Opium War, 15
  Treaty of Nanking, 17
  Treaty of Tientsin and, 17
Orlando, Vittorio, 123–124
Osachi, Hamaguchi, 172

Page Act of 1875, US, 92, 101, 106
Paik Too Chin, 234
Palau. *See* Republic of Palau
Pan-Asianism, 109, 129, 319
Paracel Islands, territorial conflict over, 41–43
Paris Accord of 1991, 49
Paris Agreement, 49
Paris Peace Conference. *See also* racial equality proposal
  Japan at, 111–115

Index 369

delegation to, 112–114
as global power, 111–112
plenary session of, 112
racial equality proposal at, 109, 111–115
seating chart for, 112
Park Chung Hee, 234–235
patron–client model, 246
The Pattern of Imperialism (Smith, T.), 10–11
Pauley, Edwin, 199–200
People's Liberation Army (PLA), Taiwan Strait Crises and, 209, 210, 211, 216, 217
People's Republic of China (PRC)
foundation of, 5
Republic of China conflict with, 207
San Francisco Treaties and, 36–37
Taiwan and, 41
Perry, Matthew, 5–6, 189
Phibunsongkhram, Plaek (Phibun), 274–275
Philippine Independence Act (1934). *See* Tydings–McDuffie Act
Philippines
Greater East Asia Co-prosperity Sphere and, 183
Huk Rebellion in, 231, 237–238
nationalist movement in, 5–6
reparation agreement with Japan, 36–37
Spanish control of, 5
state-building in, 237–239
PKI. *See* Indonesian Communist Party
PLA. *See* People's Liberation Army
Player, Cyril, 193
political reform, in Siam, 67–70
administrative reforms, 66, 67–69
consolidation of administrative systems, 68–69
Portugal
Macao as colony of, 5
Treaty of Peking, 17
postcolonialism, imperialism and, 10–11
PRC. *See* People's Republic of China
prestige. *See* credibility
Prisdang (Prince), 73
Pyle, Kenneth P., 171

Qing dynasty, 94–95, 309. *See also* China, in early twentieth century
during early twentieth century, 141–143, 147
Opium Wars and, 155

race. *See also* anti-Chinese racism
anti-Chinese racism, 97–98, 99–101
gender as factor in, 101
colonialism and, 25–26
imperialism and, 25–26
international relations and, 25, 91

racial equality, in Covenant of the League of Nations, 90
racial equality proposal, by Japan
analysis of, 127–129
conceptual approach to, 109–111
domestic influences on, 116–119
failure of, 127–129
finalization of, 119–125
international context for, 116–119
in international relations context, 128–129
in Japanese press, 119
language of, 116
League of Nations and, 117
origins of, 110
at Paris Peace Conference, 109, 111–115
presentation of, 115–116
racial legacy of, 111
rejection of, 125–127
by Australia, 128–129
by Great Britain, 122–123, 125–126
by US, 125–126
resistance to, 111, 116, 122–123
support of, 123–125, 127–128
Wilson and, 110, 125–126
Radford, Arthur, 212, 213, 248–249
Rahman, Abdul (Tunku) (Prince), 268–269
Railway Rights Recovery Movement, 145
Ranke, Leopold van, 172
Remeliik, Haruo, 289–290
Remengesau, Tommy, 292–293
Republic of China (ROC)
Chiang Kai-shek and, 207
establishment of, 137–141, 147
international presence as influence on, 141
People's Republic of China conflict with, 207
Taipei Peace Treaty, 41, 42
Republic of Korea. *See* South Korea
Republic of Marshall Islands, 279, 289–291
Republic of Palau, 279, 289–290
republicanism, authoritarianism and, 23
revolutionary movements, in China, 136, 137–141
democratic transition to, 138–139
Japanese support of, 139
Nationalist Party, 138–140
Railway Rights Recovery Movement, 145
Rhee, Syngman, 188, 189, 190–193, 194
as anti-communist, 202–203
during Cold War, 200–205
as first president of ROK, 203
Japan Inside Out, 194
state-building strategies under, 234
Washington Naval Conference and, 192–193
during World War II, 194–200

Ritchie, Bryan, 228
Robertson, Walter, 209–210, 212, 213
Robinson, Ronald, 13
ROC. *See* Republic of China
ROK. *See* South Korea
Roosevelt, Eleanor, 194–195
Roosevelt, Theodore, 80, 86, 189, 190, 192, 193–194
Rotter, Andrew, 227–228
Rusk, Dean, 39, 187, 251
Russia. *See also* Soviet Union
  Boxer Protocol and, 78
  July Crisis and, 81–82
  Treaty of Saint Petersburg and, 17
Russo-Japanese War
  analysis of, 88–89
  Anglo-Japanese alliance after, 86
  Battle of Mukden, 79
  Battle of the Tsushima Strait, 80
  Battle of the Yellow Sea, 79
  Chinese Eastern Railway and, 78, 79, 82
  conceptual approach to, 76–78
  First Sino-Japanese War and, 78
  historical legacy of, 82–83
  in international relations literature, 76–77
  Japan in, 78–79
    settlement option by, 81
  Korean Peninsula and, 78–79, 189
  modern war theories and, 77–78
  mortality rates for, 80
  origins of, 76–77, 81–82
    China role in, 78–79
    Japan role in, 78–79
    Russia role in, 78–80, 81
  outcome of, 80
  overview of, 78–80
  settlement terms, 84–86
    before war, 81
  termination of, 82–86
    commitment to, 83–84
  Treaty of Portsmouth and, 77–78, 80, 84–85, 89
  US Open Door policy and, 85, 86
  World War I influenced by, 86–89

Saeyoung Park, 5–6, 18
Sakuzō, Yoshino, 174
San Francisco System, in East Asian order
  analysis of, 50–52
  conceptual approach to, 29–31
  evolution of, 44–50
    transitions of political order, 47–50
    transitions of power, 44–47
  myth of, 30–31, 37–44
  in postwar era, 29–30

regional conflicts as result of, 30, 37–44
Treaty of Taipei, 30, 33–34, 35–36
San Francisco Treaties, 29–30, 32–37
  China excluded from, 34
  during Cold War, 34, 36–37
  in international relations literature, 34
  Korean Peninsula and, 38–39
  People's Republic of China and, 36–37
  restoration of Japanese sovereignty as goal of, 35, 38
  South Korea excluded from, 34
  territorial conflicts as result of, 30, 37–44
    for Liancourt Rocks, 38–39
    for Paracel Islands, 41–43
    for Senkaku Islands, 39–40
    for Spratley Islands, 41–43
    for Taiwan, 40–41
  Treaty of Mutual Defence and Cooperation, 35
  Treaty of Peace, 32–34, 36
  Treaty of Taipei, 30, 33–34, 35–36
  U.S-Japan Security Treaty, 32–34, 41
  success of, 34–35
Sawasdipakdi, Pongkwan, 14
Schaller, Michael, 227–228
Schlieffen, Alfred von, 87
Schlieffen Plan, 77–78, 87, 88
scientific racism, 91
Scott Act, US (1888), 102–103
SEATO. *See* Southeast Asia Treaty Organization
Second Indochina War. *See* Vietnam War
Second Opium War, 15
Second Sino-Japanese War, 33
  China–Japan relationship after, 150
  economic interdependence between China and Japan and, 151–154
  Marco Polo Bridge Incident and, 153, 176
  mortality rates for, 151
  occupation of Manchuria and, 148, 152, 304
  origins of, 152–153
  postwar conceptions of economics and security after, 160–163
security. *See* national security interests
Seibold, Louis, 192–193
Seishirō, Itagaki, 173
Senjūro, Hayashi, 173
Senkaku Islands, territorial conflict over, 39–40
Seo-Hyun Park, 104
Serbia
  Austria and, 81–82, 88
  July Crisis and, 81–82
Seward, William H., 96
Shandong Treaty, 170
Sharman, J. P., 4

Index

Shigeru, Yoshida, 32–33
Shiraki, Tachibana, 174
Shufeldt, William, 189
Siam (Thailand), 5
  Ava Kingdom and, 72
  Chulalongkorn and, 59, 61, 66–69, 71–74
  colonialism in, 55–57
    analysis of, 74–75
    expansion of, 55–57
    under France, 14
    under Great Britain, 14, 55, 61
  cultural reforms in, 70–74
  economic reforms in, 65–67
    Bowring Treaty and, 65–66
  extraterritorial rights of, 67
  France and, 63, 64
    under Anglo-French Convention, 64
    colonialism and, 14
    rejection of shared sovereignty, 62–65
  Great Britain and
    under Anglo-French Convention, 64
    colonialism and, 14
    through shared sovereignty, 61, 64
  identity promotion schemes, 69–70
    categorization of ethnicities, 70
  justice reforms in, 69
  Kingdom of Lanna and, 61
  Mongkut and, 66, 68, 71
  political reforms in, 67–70
    administrative reforms, 66, 67–69
    consolidation of administrative systems, 68–69
  Prisdang and, 73
  sovereignty for, 58–65
    under Anglo-French Convention, 64
    through borders and boundaries, 59–61
    France and, 62–65
    Great Britain and, 61, 64
    hierarchy of, 58–59
    shared, 58, 59–65
  trade and
    under economic reforms, 65–67
    Treaty of Amity, Commerce, and Navigation for, 58
    with Western world, 58
  Western world and, 58–65
    trade negotiations with, 58
  Westernization of, 70–74
Silver Purchase Act, US (1934), 158
Singapore, 270–271
  Sook Ching incident in, 15
Sinitic order. *See also* East Asia, new order in
  in East Asia, 3–6
  methodological approach to, 3–10
  tribute system and, 4

Sino-Japanese War, 5–6, 15, 45, 48–49. *See also* Second Sino-Japanese War
  early twentieth-century China influenced by, 142, 145
  Russo-Japanese War and, 78
Six Companies association, 104–105
Six Powers, as global financial group, 144–145.
  See also Britain; France; Germany; Japan; Russia; United States
Slater, Dan, 228
Smith, Bedell, 250
Smith, Tony, 10–11
Smuts, Jan, 122–123
Social Darwinism, 25–26, 99, 100, 106, 135, 145
socialism, North Vietnam and, 24
Song Jiaoren, 138–139
Song Ziwen, 158
Sook Ching incident, in Singapore, 15
South Korea (Republic of Korea) (ROK)
  exclusion from San Francisco Treaties, 34
  Rhee as first president, 203
  ROK-Japan Peace Treaty, 39
  state-building in, 234–236
South Pacific Nuclear Free Zone Treaty, 286
South Vietnam
  Paris Accord of 1991, 49
  state-building in, 231, 239–240
    French colonialism and, 240
    US involvement in, 239–240
Southeast Asia. *See also specific countries*
  Cold War alignments in (1940–1969), 264–265
  colonial expansion in, 55–57
  leftwing movements in (1945–1965), 262–263
  neo-colonialism in, 261–264
  US hegemony in, 276–277
Southeast Asia Treaty Organization (SEATO), 209
sovereignty
  in North Pacific region, 283, 291–295
  for Siam, 58–65
    under Anglo-French Convention, 64
    through borders and boundaries, 59–61
    France and, 62–65
    Great Britain and, 61, 64
    hierarchy of sovereignty, 58–59
    shared approaches to, 58, 59–65
  transition from colonialism, 283, 291–295
Soviet Union, East Asia new order influenced by, 173
Spain
  "First Encounter" with Indigenous peoples in Americas, 94

Spain (cont.)
  in North Pacific region, 280–281
  Philippines as colony of, 5
Spratley Islands, territorial conflict over, 41–43
Spruance, Raymond, 238–239
Stalin, Joseph, 198
Stanford, Leland, 97
state-building, and state formation in Asia
  alliances and, 226–228
  alliances and, US hub-and-spokes approach, 226, 240–241
  analysis of, 240–241
  conceptual approach to, 225–226
  Greater East Asia Co-prosperity Sphere and, 181–182
  in historical East Asia, 3–4
  in Korean Peninsula, 229–230
  in South Korea, 234–236
  in South Vietnam, 231
    French colonialism and, 240
    US involvement in, 239–240
  US role in, 228
    competition with Chinese Communist Party, 229–232
    through economic development, 230, 232–240
    in Philippines, 237–239
    in South Korea, 234–236
    in South Vietnam, 239–240
    in Taiwan, 236–237
statecraft, scholarship on, 164
Stimson, Henry, 199–200
strategic trusteeship, in North Pacific region, 283–287
Stubbs, Richard, 228
Suharto, 272–273
Sukarno, 181, 256, 260–261, 269–270
  anti-Chinese legislation under, 273
  on *nekolim*, 260, 269
Sumatra, 179
Sun Yat-sen, 136, 137, 138, 220–221, 237
  Chiang Kai-shek and, 197
  relationship with European banks, 144
Supplementary Convention of Peking, 17
Suriyawong, Sri, 66–67, 68, 71
Sutemi, Chinda (Count), 115, 123, 125–127
Sylvan, David, 246–247

Taipei Peace Treaty, 41, 42
Taiping Rebellion, 95, 309, 310–311
Taiwan
  Chiang Kai-shek in exile in, 208–216, 267
    US response to, 208–213
  Dulles, J. F., and, 236–237
  Kuomintang regime on, 208–213
  People's Republic of China and, 41
  under San Francisco Treaties, 40–41
  state-building in, 236–237
  Taipei Peace Treaty, 41, 42
  territorial conflicts over, 40–41
  Treaty of Shimonoseki, 17, 39, 134–135, 155
Taiwan Straits Crises
  Cao Juren and, 214, 215, 217, 218–221
  Chiang Kai-shek and, 208–216, 217, 218–221
  foundation of, 207
  geopolitical legacy of, 221–224
  Mao Zedong and, 211–212, 215–216, 218–221
  offshore crisis of 1958, 216–221
  People's Liberation Army and, 209, 210, 211, 216, 217
  US involvement in, 214–216, 219–224
    Formosa Resolution, 212–213
  Zhou Enlai and, 40, 214, 215, 217, 218–221
Takao, Saitō, 176
Takashi, Hara, 113–114
Tan Cheng Lock, 267–269
Tarō, Katsura, 78–79, 80
Tate, D. J. M., 14
Tatsunosuke, Takasaki, 163
Taylor, Jay, 218–219
Thailand. *See also* Siam
  Phibunsongkhram and, 274–275
  pro-US relationship with, 271–275
Third Indochina War, 49
Thomas, Charles S., 192–193
Tokyo war crimes trials, 20, 33–34
Tomoyuki, Yamashita, 179
trade networks, trade relationships and, *see also specific countries; specific topics*
  Canton system, 17
  in East Asia, 4
  in historical East Asia, 4
Transcontinental Railroad, 97, 99
Transitional East Asia, 299
  de jure hierarchy in, 312
  Greater East-Asia Co-prosperity Sphere and, 319
  hierarchies in, 315–317
    de jure hierarchy, 312
    rival coalitions and, 316–317
  instability in, 306–312
  international relations theory and, 304–305, 318, 319–320
  legitimation of, 317–320
  Pan-Asianism and, 319
  power competition in, 312–314
  tributary system in, 317–318, 319–320
Treaty of Amity, Commerce, and Navigation, 58, 188–189

Index

Treaty of Mutual Defence and Cooperation, 35
Treaty of Nanjing, 155
Treaty of Peace, 32–34, 36
Treaty of Peking, 17
Treaty of Portsmouth, 77–78, 80, 84–85, 89
Treaty of Saint Petersburg and, 17
Treaty of Shimonoseki, 17, 39, 134–135, 155
Treaty of Taipei, 30, 33–34, 35–36
Treaty of Versailles, 281
Treaty of Yandabo, 56
Treaty on the Prohibition of Nuclear Weapons, 286
treaty port model, imperialism and, 17
tribute system
  in historical East Asia, 3–4
  Sinitic order and, 4
  in Transitional East Asia, 317–318, 319–320
Truman, Harry S, 198–200
Twenty-One Demands, by Japan, 140, 146, 168
Tydings–McDuffie Act (Philippine Independence Act), US (1934), 103–104

UMNO. *See* United Malays National Organization
UN. *See* United Nations
United Kingdom. *See* Britain
United Malays National Organization (UMNO), 268–269
United Nations (UN), 29–30
  Security Council, 270
United States (US). *See also* Chinese Exclusion Act; immigration; Korean Peninsula; San Francisco System; Vietnam War; *specific topics*
  Alien Land Law of 1913, 110
  alliance-building by, 226–228
    perceived security threats and, 227–228
    Washington Consensus, 228, 232, 241
  Australia security pact with, 32
  Cairo Declaration, 188, 196–198, 200, 206
  California Crisis in, 118
  Geary Act, 92, 102–103, 104–105
  Gold Rush era, 95–97
  hegemony of, 11–12
  on Japanese racial equality proposal, 125–126
  Korean–American Treaty, 192, 193, 196, 198, 199
  Mexican–American War, 96
  national security interests for, 32–35, 41
  New Zealand security pact with, 32
  occupation of Korean Peninsula, 203
  Open Door policy, 313
    Russo-Japanese War and, 85, 86
  Page Act of 1875, 92, 101, 106

373

Scott Act, 102–103
Silver Purchase Act, 158
state-building by, 228
  competition with Chinese Communist Party, 229–232
  through economic development, 230, 232–240
  in Philippines, 237–239
  in South Korea, 234–236
  in South Vietnam, 239–240
  in Taiwan, 236–237
Taiwan Straits Crises and, 214–216, 219–224
  Formosa Resolution, 212–213
Transcontinental Railroad in, 97, 99
Treaty of Mutual Defence and Cooperation, 35
Treaty of Peace, 32–34, 36
Tydings–McDuffie Act, 103–104
US-Japan Security Treaty, 32–34, 41
  success of, 34–35
US-Smoot Hawley Tariff, 152
Washington System, 170–171, 172, 173, 175
US-Japan Security Treaty, 32–35, 41
US-Smoot Hawley Tariff, 152

Vahaleva, Faina Epatcheva, 214
Venizelos, Eleftherios, 124
Versailles Treaty, 188, 190–194
Vietnam. *See also* South Vietnam
  First Indochina War and, 49
  French rule in, 56–57, 62–65
  postcolonial, 49
  Second Indochina War and, 49
  Third Indochina War and, 49
  US hegemony in, 276–277
Vietnam War (Second Indochina War)
  Americanization of, 260
  Paris Agreement and, 49
  US hegemony and, 242–259
    methodological approach to, 242–247
  as war of decolonization, 256–259
violence, imperialism and, 14–16
Vu Quoc Thuc, 239

Wang Jingwei, 158–159, 176, 181
Wanpaoshan Incident, 173
war. *See also* Cold War; *specific wars*
  colonial rule and, 16
  imperialism and, 14–16
war theory, Russo-Japanese War and, 77–78
war thought, in Japan, 168
warlordism, 7, 23, 313, 314
Washington, George, 59
Washington Consensus, 228, 232, 241

Washington Naval Conference, 21, 188, 190–194
Washington Naval Treaty of 1922, 7
Washington System, 170–171, 172, 173, 175
Wells, H. G., 192–193
Wen-qing Ngoei, 255
Wendt, Alexander, 94
the West, Western world and, Siam and, 58–65
    trade negotiations between, 58
    Westernization of, 70–74
Whipps, Surangel, Jr., 292–293
Wichaichan, 66, 68
Wilhelm II (Kaiser), 87
Wilson, Woodrow, 190
    League of Nations and, 169–170
    liberal internationalism under, 169–170
    racial equality proposal and, 110
    rejection of Japanese racial equality proposal, 110, 125–126
Winant, Howard, 100
Witte, Sergei, 85
Wood, Tyler, 234
World War I. *See also specific countries; specific topics*
    assassination of Ferdinand and, 87
    early twentieth-century China during, 139–140, 147
    East Asia new order during, 167–169
    end of dynastic empires after, 168
    imperialism after, 20
    international relations after, 169
    July Crisis and, 87
    Russo-Japanese War as influence on, 86–89

Schlieffen Plan, 77–78, 87, 88
"Yellow Peril" and, 87, 106–107
World War II
    Asia-Pacific War, 178–179
    East Asia new order after, 178–179
    Rhee during, 194–200
    US-Korea relations during, 194–200
Wuchang Uprising, 139

Xu Guoqi, 112

Yeh, George, 210–211
"Yellow Peril," 87, 106–107
Yeo, Andrew, 15
"Yoshida Letter," 32–33
Yōsuke, Matsuoka, 177
Young, Louise, 175–176
Yu Dawei, 218
Yuan Shikai, 133, 134, 137–141. *See also China, in early twentieth century*
    as Emperor, 140
    foreign powers and, 146
    Japan demands on, 146
    Six Powers loan and, 144–145
Yun, Joseph, 292–293

Zanasi, Margherita, 156–157
Zhang Shijao, 220–221
Zhang Xueliang, 152
Zhang Xun, 140
Zhang Zhidong, 137
Zhou Enlai, 40, 214, 215, 217, 218–221, 222

For EU product safety concerns, contact us at Calle de José Abascal, 56–1°, 28003 Madrid, Spain or eugpsr@cambridge.org.

www.ingramcontent.com/pod-product-compliance
Ingram Content Group UK Ltd.
Pitfield, Milton Keynes, MK11 3LW, UK
UKHW021031201225
466244UK00020B/485